Experiences of War

The Third Reich

JAMES LUCAS

Experiences of War

The Third Reich

JAMES LUCAS

ARMS AND
ARMOUR

First published
in Great Britain in 1990
by Arms and Armour Press, Villiers House,
41–47 Strand, London WC2N 5JE.

Distributed in the USA
by Sterling Publishing Co. Inc., 387 Park
Avenue South, New York, NY 10016-8810.

Distributed in Australia
by Capricorn Link (Australia) Pty. Ltd,
P.O. Box 665, Lane Cove, New South Wales
2066, Australia.

Jacket illustrations
photograph by Michael Dyer Associates Ltd,
London.

Designed and edited by DAG Publications Ltd.
Designed by David Gibbons; edited by Michael
Boxall.

Quality Printing and Binding by:
Berryville Graphics
P.O. Box 272
Berryville, VA 22611 U.S.A.

Contents

6   CONTENTS

Acknowledgements

It is with thanks that I acknowledge the help received in the production of this book.

My principal thanks must go to the men and women whose names are listed on page 189 and whose personal experiences form so much of the narrative. In many cases the stories they told awoke sad memories for them and recalled times of privation and suffering. I have listed those contributors alphabetically but have not given their ranks and titles, for these, together with the units in which they served, are given in the text.

The second group to whom my thanks are due are the several institutions and publishers, both in Germany and in this country, whose help was invaluable and who have given permission to quote from documents and published books. In this respect I wish to thank, particularly, the Munin Verlag, the Kriegsgraeberfursorge as well as the archives of the Fallschirmjaeger organization, the Bundesarchiv in Freiburg and that of the Gebirgsjaeger organization. In the United Kingdom the Departments of Documents and Printed Books of the Imperial War Museum as well as the Maritime Museum in Greenwich were, as usual, of special help.

The third group are those individuals who helped in the research as well as in the production of the book. These are Claire and Victoria Shaw, Rod Dymott, David Gibbons, Tony Evans and Chris Westhorp. It is, however, to my dear wife Traude, that my warmest thanks go for her constant support and unfailing encouragement.

James Lucas, 1990

Preface

On Friday, 1 September 1939 the Germans invaded Poland and the fighting spread to become, first a European conflict and eventually a world-wide struggle. In Europe the Second World War came to an end on 9 May 1945.

It was a conflict which opened with armies using weapons of types that would have been familiar to soldiers of the Great War. It ended, in Europe, having seen the employment of giant, long-range rockets and of fleets of bomber aircraft whose raids killed thousands upon thousands of civilians. This war touched every German family in some way. The men, seventeen million in all, served in the armed forces. At the war's end the civilians in Germany's eastern and southern provinces, who had been spared much of the terror of aerial bombing, suffered rape, pillage and worse at the hands of the Red Army and of Tito's partisan forces. Every German was affected by the war; millions of them were killed.

The purpose of this book was to obtain and record the stories of ordinary Germans who served in the armed forces. The first avenue of approach was, of course, correspondence with friends in Germany and Austria. The second was through the editors of several ex-service journals who published my letters asking for material. Personal interview was a third source of stories as were the reminiscences of those who attended old comrades' reunions in Germany. In addition to those anecdotes which were written for this book, there were some that had been received too late for publication in books that I had written previously: *The Last Days of the Reich*, *The War Through German Eyes* and *Kommando*.

Then, too, there were certain battles for which no direct personal contributions came in and to cover those another source was sought. During the War German servicemen were encouraged to write for divisional or corps journals. Some of these stories were then reproduced in books published by the Reichs Propaganda Ministry. Men who claimed to have no story of their own service to report sent me photostats of many such official articles in the hope that these might be interesting enough to be included in these pages. Finally, there are a few letters or anecdotes which have been taken, with permission, from post-war military histories.

Inevitably, despite the several avenues of approach, there were some battles for which no stories or accounts were received. In Germany many felt themselves to be too old to write an accurate account, and death has taken many who might have contributed. Nothing at all came in from the Russian-occupied zone of Germany, but sufficient material has been gathered to produce a view of service in the German forces written by the men who experienced it. In addition to the stories from the armed forces I have included a few civilian accounts which serve either as a supplement to the military events or as a counter-point to them.

To all those who have contributed to this work I send my most grateful thanks, as well as to the editors of German service and ex-service journals, magazines and publications through whose columns I gained many contacts.

What are written here are stories which could have been duplicated in the armed forces of any great nation that fought in the war, for service is the same in all of them. The difference is that these are German accounts; the stories of our principal opponents. These are anecdotes of victory and of defeat, of bravery, of boredom, of service life in barracks and of battle. They are the story of Everyman in uniform.

Introduction

The German armed forces were organized as a single body well before the outbreak of the Second World War. The three original branches (the fourth the Waffen SS, was not yet included) were controlled by the Oberkommando der Wehrmacht – OKW. The Head of State was also the Supreme Commander of OKW and orders from him were passed by his chief of staff to the commanders of the fighting services. The Army High Command (Oberkommando des Heeres – OKH) controlled the planning and operations of the ground forces just as Naval High Command (Oberkommando der Marine – OKM) and Air Force High Command (Oberkommando der Luftwaffe – OKL) controlled the planning and operations of their respective branches of service.

The Army was *primus inter pares* and this was reflected both in the hierarchy of the OKW which was dominated by the military and also by the operational demands of the army which were paramount. Both the navy and the air force were considered appendages to the principal combat effort – the ground fighting. Because its role was so well known, the handbook *Der Dienstunterricht im Heere – 1941* does not describe the army's tasks as it does those of the other services, but it does explain the duties of its constituent parts. The following extracts are from that handbook.

'In collaboration with the other arms [of Service] the Infantry gains the decision in a battle, captures enemy positions and holds them. It conducts close combat actions so as to destroy the enemy . . . The high mobility of the Cavalry makes its principal task one of reconnaissance. It is able, in collaboration with other troops, to act against the flanks and rear of enemy [forces] . . . The fire of the artillery supports the infantry both in attack and in defence and it can also engage targets which are behind cover . . . Engineers prepare the way forward for our own troops, repair roads, bridges, etc., remove obstructions and by erecting barricades impede the enemy . . .'

It is interesting to note that Panzer troops were not given much prominence in the 1941 regulations and that neither Paratroops nor SS units were included.

The army had always been the senior service and its commanders had been allowed a great deal of latitude in their approach to service matters. The assumption by Hitler of the role of Supreme Commander of the armed forces on 4 February 1938, began to change the relationship between the

Führer and his military commanders. The oath of allegiance which the army swore, in common with the other services, was of loyalty to him in person and thus bound every officer and man. They had to be loyal because they had pledged their word. There would, therefore, never be a revolt against any move which Hitler, as Supreme Commander, might make. The pre-war opposition to him from certain army circles was against his political and social policies, not his military ones. Not until July 1944, was there a plot to kill him, again, not because of his military mistakes, but because the removal of the Führer was seen as the only obstacle to Germany's obtaining concessions from the Allies.

Through his assumption of the role of Supreme War Lord, the Head of OKW, Hitler became the first soldier of the Reich, but for the first campaigns was content to let the field commanders work in the usual German Army fashion, that is with considerable operational latitude. He began to interfere more and more during the opening stages of the war against Russia and when, in the first disastrous winter on the Eastern Front, his strategy brought the army its first reverses, he seized the opportunity to replace many of its traditional leaders. Hitler retired them and named himself as Supreme Commander of the Army. In that capacity he directed operations on the Eastern Front only, but as Head of OKW, he controlled all the other fronts as well. Thus, in theory, as Head of OKW he issued orders to himself as Head of OKH. This ludicrous situation did not end there and his inter-ference in military affairs grew during the war to the point where von Rundstedt complained that he could not even change the sentries on his HQ without advising the Führer.

The commanders' traditional independence of action no longer existed. Within the space of a few years Hitler had destroyed the General Staff system which had been created during the Napoleonic era. Thereby the brain of the German Army was effectively killed. Although, at intermediate levels of command, General Staff training and methods prevailed and kept the whole machine operating, the Army's Supreme Commander was a man who refused to admit the strategic limitations of time and space.

The structure of the army, like that of the Kriegsmarine or the Luftwaffe, was conventional, but the one thing that set the German Army apart from those of its opponents was its astounding flexibility in action. Nowhere was this demonstrated better than in the creation of battle groups, or Kampfgruppen. Whether in defence or attack a German commander could create a battle group out of the most diverse elements and commit it to the fight, confident that its men would fight as well in this *ad hoc* grouping as they would in a regular conventional formation. Much of the success of this flexible organization can be traced to the peculiar comradeship that bound the men; and this comradeship transcended rank to embrace superiors and subordinates. Officers messed with their men, although there were separate messes in base areas. There was little or no class distinction; it was not unusual to find noblemen serving in the ranks and for senior commanders to have come from *petit bourgeois* or even working-class background.

One very sensible attitude which the army had was in its treatment of military criminals. These were not put into detention barracks where they would serve out their sentences in safety, but were grouped into punishment battalions. In such units a man had the opportunity to redeem the military honour he had forfeited by his sentence and was employed on such tasks as mine-laying, mine-lifting or spearheading 'death or glory' attacks. In the final stages of the war in Africa, the 999th Penal Division was sent to Tunisia. An NCO of the 962nd Regiment of that formation wrote a report on the fighting in those last weeks.

'American troops . . . began their attack on 25th April. They went to ground under fire but, covered by a well co-ordinated barrage, had soon worked their way forward to within hand-grenade range. My Platoon (in No 5 Company) covered the withdrawal of our battalion . . . We had heavy losses because my men had no recent experience of battle. One 42-year-old man who had been convicted of treason and who had helped to beat back the American assaults, said to me, "Sergeant, I don't care what happens now. I have won back my honour," and another man stood up in his slit trench firing a machine-gun and driving back the advancing Americans until he was wounded.'

The officers of the Penal Division were no less proud of the fighting ability of their military criminals, and one commander sought and obtained for some of them the award of the Iron Cross, Second Class.

The view held in the West was that the German serviceman was a robot-like creature, incapable or unwilling to act on his own initiative, drilled into submissive dumbness, unthinking and unimaginative. Those of us who fought the German soldiers, sailors and airmen soon realized that such descriptions of them were those of propagandists who had never met them in battle. We found that the rank and file were not robots but skilled soldiers and we learned that their officers were not the heel-clicking subserviants of Hollywood films, but men who, in the words of von Senger, the defender of Cassino, had a duty because, '. . . the man in authority should devote himself to the protection of the weak [i.e., the men under his authority].' That precept was followed almost as a commandment up to very senior levels of command.

Officers were quick to defend their men against any unjustified criticism. There is on record the angry exchange of words between Helmut Wick, one of the Luftwaffe's top fighter aces and a senior commander in the Luftwaffe. This confrontation took place at the height of the battle of Britain, when the General visited Wick's front-line squadron and complained at not being saluted and pointed out that the men needed haircuts. Wick snapped out, 'We are fighting an implacable enemy and are flying three or more missions every day. My ground staff are working 15 to 18 hours daily. Is not the winning of a battle more important than haircuts or salutes?' It was another Luftwaffe ace, Galland, who defended his pilots against Goering's charge of cowardice. Before the Reichsmarschall left the airfield, he made an effort to placate the angry airman and asked Galland if he needed anything. 'Yes,' came the reply. 'Give me a squadron of Spitfires.'

Hitler actually feared one army commander; the monocled Field Marshal Model. At one conference in which the Führer was deploying armies and giving instructions on how they were to be used, Model fixed his monocle firmly in his eye and asked, 'Who commands the Ninth Army, my Führer. You or I?' At more senior level von Rundstedt's reply to the OKW question, 'What shall we do now?', when the Allies broke through in France was, 'Make peace, you fools!', and the action of SS General Hausser in withdrawing his SS Divisions from Kharkov in defiance of Hitler's direct and unequivocal order saved them from destruction. When it was pointed out to him that to disobey the *Führerbefehl* was to risk his life he retorted, 'My old head does not matter. The lives of my young lads do matter.' Hausser's action was directly responsible for the Red Army's thrust towards Kharkov in the spring of 1943. Stalin knew of Hitler's order that the SS were to stand and to hold Kharkov and was convinced that they would obey those orders. When they did he would be able to destroy them inside the city. He had not reckoned with the Prussian officer's code of protecting the men under his command; a need applied at most levels of the military hierarchy. Paulus, in Stalingrad, and both Keitel and Jodl, at Führer HQ, were guilty of moral cowardice, but their actions prove the rule that a subordinate is not necessarily a rubber stamp. At the lowest military level the 'Spiess', the equivalent of a warrant officer, was concerned not so much with discipline as morale and was expected to represent very strongly to his superiors the views of the rank and file. The Spiess was a military welfare officer, the sort of 'agony aunt', that it has been proposed should be introduced into the British services. Examples will be found in these pages of officers and NCOs acting upon their own initiative to save a situation or to protect their men. Hollywood was never like this. To continue with the 1941 Handbook:

'The Navy.

Consists of the Fleet at Sea as well as shore-based naval artillery and naval infantry contingents. The Fleet Commander in Kiel commands the fleet. The naval land bases are under the control of the Baltic Naval Command (Kiel), or of North Sea Command (Wilhelmshaven.) The tasks of the naval land bases include coastal defence.

'The Air Force consists of flying units, anti-aircraft units, signals and the General Goering Regiment. The flying formations cover both land and sea squadrons . . .'

The relationship of the services to the State were that the army considered itself as having descended in unbroken line from the Napoleonic era. Indirectly it went even farther back; from the time of Frederick Wilhelm of Prussia who had introduced a form of military conscription. His son, Frederick the Great, brought in full conscription and produced a number of revolutionary military ideas such as marching in step and firing by volley. He also started a Staff system which was expanded after the defeat of Napoleon and refined by von Moltke in the 1860s. The army claimed that it had not been defeated in the field, in 1918, and most of the regiments had returned home as disciplined units. It had a tradition of undisputed loyalty.

The Kriegsmarine was a Service burdened with guilt. It was in the Imperial Navy that the Revolution had broken out in 1918, a movement which had overthrown the established order and had forced Germany to accept the terms of the Armistice. That stigma was still deeply felt and the leaders of the navy set themselves the task of being devotedly loyal to the Head of State – Adolf Hitler. Both Admiral Raeder and his successor, Doenitz, were such strong supporters of the regime that it was Doenitz, an admiral, and not an army commander, who was named to succeed to the leadership of the Third Reich after Hitler's suicide.

The Luftwaffe was considered by many, both inside and outside Germany, to be the most National Socialist of all the three services. That belief was based on the fact that Hermann Goering, one of Hitler's closest confidants, was its Supreme Commander. His boast, 'I command everything that flies in Germany,' brought under his control not only the conventional Luftwaffe but also the General Goering Regiment. This had begun as a police detachment but developed into a prototype parachute unit out of which evolved Germany's airborne forces. These, too, formed part of Goering's empire. In contrast to the Kriegsmarine, which was in a lowly position at the outbreak of the war but whose commander-in-chief rose to take supreme political power, the influence of the Luftwaffe, which was high at the outbreak of hostilities, declined because of its leader, Hermann Goering. He fell so much out of favour with Hitler in the last weeks of the war he was lucky not to have been killed by an SS execution squad.

The book *Der Dienstunterricht im Heere*, omits mention of the German paratroop force, just as it ignores the Waffen SS. Yet by 1941, its date of publication, paratroop formations had spearheaded the German Army's assault in the Low Countries and had captured the island of Crete from the British. At the war's end there was an entire Para Army on establishment and ten divisions fighting throughout Europe. By 1941, too, major formations of SS men had seen action in every campaign that the Wehrmacht had fought in continental Europe. It had become the fourth arm of service and by the end of the war thirty-nine divisions had been raised. Paradoxically, for a force which had once proclaimed its faith in Nordic, Aryan superiority, the SS order of battle included not only divisions of Slavic Europeans but some Asian peoples. The Germanic SS created around themselves a legend of total dedication to battle, of élan in attack and of unbelievable tenacity in defence. To read the reports of some of their battle actions is like reading citations for the highest awards for bravery. Hardly unthinking robots and slavish obedience.

Life in the Forces

From the year 1935, service in one of the armed forces was compulsory for every able-bodied German. In order to be accepted a recruit had to be both physically and mentally fit. He had also to be moral, i.e., not to have a criminal record and, of course, he had to be a German citizen. Volunteers were accepted, but conscription was the usual method of obtaining men for the services. The SS, was one of the exceptions to that rule and accepted only volunteers. So did the Fallschirmjaeger, although entry into that arm was more often a sideways transfer from some other arm into the Paras.

SERVING THE FATHERLAND

The German men who were called to service immediately before or during the war would already have undergone a form of pre-military training in the RAD (the Reichsarbeitsdienst or Labour Corps.) In that short period of service they would have learned obedience and by hard work would have had their bodies strengthened and hardened. The following extract from Paul Kamberger shows how eagerly most young Germans looked forward to the opportunity to serve their Fatherland.

'It was in 1943, when I, like so many others, volunteered for our unit [the 12th SS Division]. Even as schoolboys we had served as Luftwaffe auxiliaries and waited impatiently until the orders finally came to report for duty by 15th November to Unna in Westphalia. The train left about midnight from a blacked-out, empty station but imagine our joy when we found in our compartment boys with whom we had served in the Hitler Youth organization. We were all going to the same place and at each station more and more men of our own age entered the compartment each of them carrying the cardboard box or little suitcase – the mark which identified us all. In no time at all we had formed little groups and by the morning, when we reached our destination, there was a first-class feeling in the train.

'The first day and a half were spent in processing us and grouping us formally and then we were off again, this time to an unnamed destination. We were the second contingent for the newly formed 12th SS Panzer Division "Hitler Youth". We crossed the Belgian frontier and reached Turnhout where we detrained and began a march to the billets occupied by the newly created reconnaissance battalion. Soon we were on the parade square waiting for things to happen – and they did. By this time our groups were about battalion size. Each of us joined the group with which he wished to serve, so that the battalions were, at first, of unequal strength. Then a group of about twelve officers began to march along the front of the groups. At our group, where we all wanted to be tank men, the officers halted and began a discussion. Then came the question, "Who is still at school?" Ten to twelve arms were raised. We were called out and lo and behold the motor-cycle DR squadron of the division had been created. Fitters brought up the numbers of our cadre up to strength and we formed the No 1 Group of No 1 Platoon of No 1 Company.

'We started the usual recruit training programme and shortly before Christmas had the task of putting on a show for the rest of the Company. This was such a great success that we were soon "booked" to perform for other Companies. Towards the end of February the actual DR course began and we were posted to a place called Zwanenstrand which was close to divisional headquarters. We climbed on to out Italian Moto-Guzzi machines for our first rides and passed our driving test in a hail storm on the road to Mol. Then we went on to more advanced training, with theoretic instruction followed by practical demonstrations of front-line conditions. This part of our training was often broken by our being called for service at Div HQ. The weeks flashed past and then the division was moved to France and we were equipped with brand-new German motor cycles with side-cars.'

The 12th SS Division 'Hitler Youth' was a unit which had been created and formed in great haste, but it had the advantage that each volunteer had the same background (service in the Hitler Youth Organization) and that each had reached the same level of training. This made it easier for the commanders to post men to the component units of the division without the need for special tests. In the case of other units or branches of service there had been, certainly in the early days of the war, time to give each recruit psychological tests in order to determine the particular branch of service for which he was best suited and to which he would be posted.

THE IMPORTANCE OF SIGNALS

One of the most interesting pieces of information on the organization of the German Army was sent to me by the celebrated author Franz Kurowski. This was, that one in every five soldiers was in Signals.

The Tsarist General Samsonov had sent his wireless messages *en clair* during the battles of August 1914, and an awareness of the disaster which had befallen him as a consequence was responsible for the German Signals Branch emphasis on total secrecy. Confidentiality of information was no less important because the signalman was the first to receive or to decode a message. 'The enemy was always waiting to intercept signals upon which he could act or to which he could react. Particularly in the Signals Branch does the warning apply – The enemy never sleeps.' Kurowski wrote that the Signals detachment which served the German High Command was raised in 1938 as a battalion of Command Signals Regiment No 40, and was renumbered No 601 in August 1940. 'To this unit were seconded the finest signals operators from all three services and they were sent to a barracks at Ohrdruf where they carried out several training mobilization rehearsals. Then, in the second week of August 1939, Command Signals Battalion was called to action and only a few hours later had set out from Ohrdruf with all the wireless trucks and other vehicles. The convoy reached Berlin then left the autobahn and drove to Zossen where the Signals HQ of Army High Command was located. The majority of the battalion was quartered in the barracks at Zossen, but thirty specially selected signalmen were grouped into Wireless Centre "Zeppelin", which was the code-name for Zossen and the general term for the location of OKH and the General Staff of the Army.' One of that special group was Herbert Dammert whose story is recounted in the final chapters of this book.

It is of interest to note that the HQ of OKH remained at Zossen throughout the war – although individual personnel were often sent on detached duty with other major headquarters. It was only in the final weeks of the war that OKH and its ancillary organizations were forced to leave when the Soviets swept westwards. Russian reports state that when the Red Army overran and occupied 'Zeppelin' the telex machines were still chattering as messages continued to come in from distant signallers unaware that OKH had moved to a new location towards Denmark.

CLEAN AND SMART

Recruit training was hard and unremitting and continued until each soldier, sailor or airman handled his weapon or carried out his duties thoroughly and without hesitation. As had been the case in the old Imperial and Weimar armies, each man was trained to do his superior's job and this ideal was striven for throughout the war.

Many barracks were old structures of which only the façades remained. All the internal fittings had been torn out and replaced with modern facilities. H. Werner was one of a number of men who described conditions in barracks, the scale of food and the types of uniform issues.

'All the interiors of the barracks were new and in place of the primitive ablutions which our fathers had described there were excellent shower facilities and huge baths with constant hot water. Great emphasis was laid upon personal hygiene and at every meal the UvD [the Orderly Corporal] would inspect our hands and finger-nails to see that they were clean.

'Meals were basic but both well cooked and plentiful. Of course, I am describing recruit training. Active service was a different matter. There were several scales of active service rations issued generally, when one was out of the combat zone and in reserve. Flying service against the enemy countered towards the best ration scales – the same system applied in the army and navy. Those higher scales included alcohol – even champagne. Cigarettes, cigars or pipe tobacco were issued; many more men smoked pipes in those days than do now. Other desires were catered for – but only outside Germany – in Service-run brothels for which tickets were issued. Without a ticket it was not possible to get into a brothel.

'The pre-war services had a variety of uniforms, but by the time of my call-up [in 1942] the number had been reduced to a twill jacket and trousers for drill, training and fatigues as well as a proper uniform which served as combat dress, parade dress, walking-out dress and so on. The addition of various bits and pieces converted the jacket into Reporting Dress. Medals were worn on every jacket – except the white twill. We had a variety of things to put on to the breast of the jacket – Iron Crosses, sports badges, wound badges, and proficiency badges of all sorts. Nor were the jacket sleeves forgotten. On the left one were worn shields given for taking part in a particular operation such as "Narvik" or "Crimea", for example. On the upper right sleeve there were, later in the war, strips of lace denoting enemy tanks destroyed in close combat actions. On the cuffs there were titles like, "Crete" and "Afrika" which were "battle" commemorations. There were other cuff titles worn as identification by such units as "Grossdeutschland", by the SS divisions and regiments and by certain squadrons of the Luftwaffe. We were, from the point of view of uniform, a good-looking lot.'

In the Kriegsmarine as well as in the Luftwaffe, both of which had fixed bases – either the ship or the airfield – meals were regular and the several types of uniform were on issue throughout the war. The navy put its men into barracks when they were not at sea, to relieve them of the claustrophobic strain of shipboard life. Submariners were treated almost like gods and were sent out on their voyages or welcomed home from them with bands, flowers and guards of honour.

SEX AND DISCIPLINE

In the matter of sex the German nation and its Services were not generally guilt-ridden about carnal feelings. The problem and its solution were approached pragmatically. Servicemen need sexual relief, but they must be protected against venereal diseases. The solution was to set up military brothels where the girls could be controlled and to which soldiers had access. From discussions I have had it would seem that no regulations covering the Services were laid down. Control seems to have been exercised at local command level and some commanders at that level were not keen on their men endangering their health in such a way. One paratroop officer could not forbid his men to use the brothels, but, in the words of one of his former subordinates:

'He made our visits as difficult as possible. Those wanting to obtain a green ticket which would authorize a visit to the nearest brothel, some 8 kilometres distant, had to parade in full kit and personal firearm and was required to march from our camp area to the brothel and back again – in full equipment. During the sexual interlude the kit and equipment might be removed, but once the act had been concluded the Fallschirmjaeger was now faced with an 8-kilometre march back to camp. The system worked quite well in deterring those whose sexual lust was not so powerful and the Company Commander seemed to have been successful in his endeavours until the Christmas concert party troupe displayed its talents. This concert was organized at regimental level and our battalion's main turn remained a closely guarded secret until the opening night. Up went the curtain and across the small stage there parade-marched i.e., goose-stepped, in full equipment, a stage army. The single line of soldiers wearing full equipment marched round and round, each Jaeger waving his green "brothel" slip. The Captain left us not long after this.'

Adolf Strauch recalled an incident involving a military brothel: 'This particular place was open for Other Ranks until lunch time and for officers in the afternoon. Late one afternoon an NCO approached the building and was told by the sentry that it was out of bounds to him at that particular time. The NCO refused to obey the sentry's Dienstliche Befehl to go away whereupon the sentry, very properly, shot him dead.'

The young men of the 'Hitler Youth' Division in Normandy before D-Day, were so young that they were considered ineligible for sexual delights or for the pleasures of smoking. They were issued with boiled sweets in lieu of cigarettes, but I have been unable to find out what the other substitute was. Services which recruit from every strata of society must, inevitably, contain homosexuals in their ranks and the perversions of such people were forbidden and punished under Article 179 of Military Law. Persistent offenders were often transferred to penal detachments after sentencing by a court-martial.

Strauch's description of the sentry at the brothel door mentioned the term 'Dienstliche Befehl'. This was a form of summary justice under which an NCO or an officer – or in this case a sentry – was given great authority. An order that was not obeyed promptly would be repeated twice more and then the person in authority would issue the final warning, 'I am giving you the Dienstliche Befehl [the official order].' Refusal by the offender to comply empowered a superior to shoot him.

Discipline was firm but fair. The 'Spiess' – a combination of warrant officer and shop floor representative – looked after the interests of the men. The SS broke down many barriers between ranks and in the 1st SS Panzer Division Leibstandarte, for example, any private soldier had the right of direct access to the most senior commanders. The use of 'Herr', in the sense of 'Herr Major', 'Herr General', etc., was abolished in the SS – the rank alone being considered a sufficient courtesy when addressing a comrade.

The welfare of the men and their dependants was not only a national but also a unit concern. In December 1939, Sepp Dietrich, commander of the Leibstandarte, set up a small secretariat to deal with just that problem. The committee's terms of reference were to consider:

'1. Welfare of the next of kin of fallen, accidentally killed or missing members of the Leibstandarte.

2. Welfare of wounded or convalescent members.

3. General welfare for those who have left dependants at home while they are in the Field.'

An example of the second term of reference was in the letters which each company commander wrote to his men when they were in hospital and the visits to sick comrades which were arranged at unit level. Goering, as Supreme Commander of the Luftwaffe, had begun such welfare projects even before the war and upon its outbreak ordered that the children of airmen killed in action were to receive cash grants and special help in education. He was determined that the families of those who had fallen for Germany, or who had been severely wounded in her service, should not be penalised financially, for the sacrifices they had made.

VOLUNTEERS FOR ADVENTURE

The term 'comrade' was a term widely used in all the services and among all the arms of service. Most men in the Wehrmacht really did see themselves as comrades taking a personal part in Germany's fight. Thus many who were in non-combatant units volunteered for more adventurous regiments as the following account by Reinhold Hoffmann shows.

'In April 1941 there was an appeal made throughout the Luftwaffe for volunteers to the paratroops. My comrade, Corporal Goldnagel, and I submitted our names and were sent to Paris for inspections, interviews, X-rays and all sorts of medical tests before being released on 15th May, and sent to Quedlinburg. From there we were ordered to report to the Flak Machine Gun battalion, which was in Greece preparing for the Crete operation. Then we learned that more drafts of new recruits were expected and that we were to form something new in the Para organization. We would be No 5 Company and would be equipped with small searchlights. By 20th May, the strength of our detachment had grown to 230 men, many of them young soldiers who had been in operational Luftwaffe squadrons, AA regiments and signals units. Our Company commander, Lieutenant Geyer, a veteran of the campaign in Holland, was not very happy at being left behind to train recruits while his comrades were fighting at Corinth.

'By this time the attack upon Crete had begun and so many men had been lost that we recruits were asked whether we would be prepared to make a para drop even though we had had no jump training. Most of us volunteered but as it turned out we were not needed. We then began a period of infantry and close combat instruction which grew progressively harder with each succeeding week. By the first week of June the Company, now fit for active service, was posted to the Para Training School at Braunschweig–Broitzen. The Company commander and some of the senior NCOs were old hands – the rest of us were all beginners. Nothing was made easy for us in that training school. From Monday to Friday we practised forward and backward rolls as well as all the other Para drills and on Saturday our instructors gave us instruction in infantry combat. It was hard graft but at the end of the fourth week we had our obligatory six jumps behind us and were finally recognized as Fallschirmjaeger. A few men of our group asked to be returned to their parent units after having made just one jump and one other was nearly killed during the training period. This was Sergeant Hammelmann who caught a leg in the canopy lines and started to come down head first. As he fell he had the presence of mind to reach up and grab some of the canopy lines to pull himself upright. He landed safely.

'The war against Russia had already begun and many men believed that the campaign would end before we got into battle. Experiences in the Crete campaign had shown the need for a battalion motor-cycle Company and we were converted to that role during a three-week course at Altengraben. Part of that training [on the course] was carried out with live ammunition and we worked with light tanks in attacking strong points and bunkers. For this we were given Assault Engineer training. In our free time, and to relieve ourselves of the strain of training, we went out with the girls in the local munitions factory, although this was strictly forbidden and could lead to several days' confined to barracks if we were caught. During August we went back to Quedlinburg and met up with the four companies which had served in Crete. As part of a battalion which was considered by Corps to be "ready for action", we new boys were given leave at the same time as the veterans. It was out first leave. When we returned we were posted to the training ground at Grafenwoehr where we practised mass drops and ended that period of training with a route-march through the Main river valley. We had also

been lucky enough to have stage and screen artists to entertain us and were
well treated by the authorities in Wuerzburg.

'By the end of September the battalion, now up to strength, moved to
Radom in Poland. During October No 3 Company was posted to the Neva
river sector of the Eastern Front while the rest of the battalion stayed in
Radom and began to plan for Christmas and New Year. One Saturday, just
before the first group was due to go on leave, we were ordered to parade in
a hut. The doors were shut and after the Senior Sergeant had reported the
Company present and correct, our new commander, Captain Parnitzke, told
us that all leave had been cancelled and that we were to prepare for active
service near St. Petersburg. The other Companies of the Battalion had looked
down upon us as new boys, but now we, too, were going on active service
and this would make us their equals. Some of our group got too enthusiastic
and went out on an illegal shoot in order to practise their sniping abilities.
They were caught by the Military Police and as a punishment were declared
not fit to go with us on active service. They were posted to another Company
which was going back to Germany. We others, were issued with winter
clothing and during the first days of November were loaded into railway
trucks and sent southwards. We were on our way to war.'

One of the phenomena of war was the longing of men on leave to return
as quickly as possible to their units on active service. It was surprising that
men who had been a long time in battle were often unable to adjust to civilian
attitudes in the homeland. The civilian environment had become alien and
Home had become the regiment. It was to the regiment and to his mates in
it that the soldier's thoughts returned once the initial excitement of leave had
worn off and Adolf Strauch's account opens with his hunger to return to the
company of his fellows.

'In March 1943, I rejoined my unit from leave. I had been away a long
time from those mates who had shared so much with me and I looked forward
to seeing them again. On arriving at Moumelon I found that my unit, No 8
Company of 2nd Fallschirmjaeger Regiment, had been sent to Rennes in
Brittany for a para jump exercise. I set out to find them and you can imagine
the high old time we had when I finally caught up with them. But the
pleasure of that reunion was brief. Lieutenant Kirsten, the Company
Commander, told me that the course which I had just completed meant
immediate posting to Battalion Headquarters as Sergeant Armourer. With a
pen stroke I had become a base wallah. I was not overjoyed at the prospect,
not so much because I objected to the change, but rather more because that
posting meant that I could not take part in this series of jumps with my
Company. From earlier experience we had learned that a Jaeger was virtually
unarmed when he touched down and that his search for the weapons
container either took too long or was just not possible under active service
conditions. For that reason our Company was to experiment with making

jumps while carrying weapons. It seemed at first, that I would only be able to watch as my comrades jumped but then I was told permission had been given for me to jump with my detachment because on active service it would be my task to defend HQ Group. My favourite weapon was the MG 42, and soon I stood in front of the old "Auntie", Ju 52, holding my bride, the MG 42, in my arms and linked to her by a drop line.

'First Act. We received the order to board and climbed into the machine. As I would be the first to jump my seat was nearest the door and Sergeant Stark, with whom I had discussed the details of the drop, sat opposite me. It had been decided that before and during the jump I should carry the MG clasped to my chest and that just before touchdown I would release the gun and lower it on a rope so that it would not be damaged on landing. Because I was hindered by the MG in my arms, I could not take up the regulation position in the doorway and would also be unlikely to hear the klaxon sounding when the order came "Prepare to jump". It was arranged that one of my comrades would hit me on the parachute pack as the signal to leave the machine.

'Second Act. It was a lovely day; good vision and no turbulence. The order came "Get ready!" We stood up, clipped our hooks on to the fixed line and waited for the next order "Ready to jump!" I moved to the door and crouched there. Below me there was a wood, then a wide flat area which I took to be the ground around the airfield. I leaned forward into the aircraft's slipsteam and felt a thump on my chute; the sign to jump. I flung myself out of the aircraft.

'Third Act. With the MG pressed to my chest I fell through the air and then felt the welcome thump as the canopy opened. I began to swing and looked around me expecting to see my comrades. But there was no one above or on either side of me and the aircraft was disappearing rapidly into the distance. I was alone – unsupported. What a feeling. Below me I could see nothing but trees and did not dare imagine what would soon happen. I was lucky and my landing was made on soft grass in a small clearing. Although burdened with the machine-gun in my right hand I had landed on my feet and had not needed to make either a forward or backward roll. The canopy collapsed around me. Well that had really been a super drop. Thinking about what had happened brought me to the obvious conclusion that what I had thought to be the blow telling me to jump had been premature. I had made a real dog's dinner of the exercise.

'Final Act. I now had the task of catching up with my comrades. Burdened down with parachute and MG I hurried over ditches and fences. Finally I reached a road. An ambulance and a staff car came towards me. In the latter was Pit, the Commanding Officer. I came to attention and made my report fully expecting the standard three days' punishment. But the "old man" just laughed and said, "Dismiss lad. It was just rotten luck."'

The Years of Peace

The Wehrmacht can be said to have been created in 1935, when Adolf Hitler announced the reintroduction of conscription together with the creation of a new Luftwaffe and a programme of national rearmament.

Conscription for the armed forces was a normal feature of German life and not seen as the grotesque infringement of liberty that many in Britain considered it to be. The condition of the Treaty of Versailles which abolished conscription, was the one most bitterly resented. It struck at the heart of German pride; a national army, for it was no empty boast that the German Army was the German people under arms.

The conditions of the Treaty also restricted the size and power of the German Army and Navy and forbade absolutely a military air force. Senior German soldiers, of whom Hans von Seeckt was the most prominent, together with politicians of the Weimar government sought ways to circumvent those restrictions. Service officers of outstanding ability, whose skills would produce a professional, skilled army and navy, were retained in the Reichswehr. The rank and file for both services would be obtained by voluntary enlistment and, in fact, so many men came forward that only the very best were chosen – those with leadership potential who would become instructors or officers when conscription was reintroduced and the services were expanded.

Under the terms of a secret agreement between Soviet Russia and the Weimar government senior members of the German High Command were allowed to use training grounds beyond the Urals where they could apply in practice their new theories of warfare. The principles of mass employment of armour were developed in the late 1920s and early 1930s in the training grounds of Kazan. In those remote regions of Russia, flying training was carried out with powered aircraft. It is no exaggeration to say that the strategy and tactics of *Blitzkrieg*, that revolutionary form of warfare, were designed and developed during those years of collaboration between Soviet Russia and Weimar Germany.

Adolf Hitler's assumption of power in January 1933, ended the close collaboration between the two countries, but the leaders of the German Army had by this time perfected the techniques they were to use throughout the Second World War, and the Luftwaffe had a pool of trained pilots. In addition there were hundreds of young men who had been trained in the glider schools of the Hitler Youth Organization and who would become pilots when a new Luftwaffe was created. Thus, when Hitler proclaimed the rebirth of the German armed forces in 1935, he knew not only that he had a skilled High Command and a reservoir of potential officers for the three services, but that re-armament would give those soldiers of the Third Reich the best possible weapons. That proclamation of the restoration of national dignity achieved for the Führer two other important objectives. Re-armament meant employment and conscription would take men from the dole queues. Those two things taken in combination would abolish unemployment in Germany.

The Nazi Party reinforced the age-old boast of the German Army being the German people under arms with a new slogan – 'It is an honour to undertake military service on behalf of the German people.' The Party's political charter, drawn up in the 1920s, had mocked the 'mercenary army of Weimar', and had also laid down that only German citizens had the right to bear arms in her defence. The idea of peace-time conscription, of restricting the right to bear arms to native-born citizens and of military service being an honour, were alien to the British people who refused to be alarmed at German re-armament or frightened as that nation's policies gained pace. The British comforted themselves with the fact that Germans were forced to eat *ersatz* foodstuffs and that the German Army was equipped with mock tanks. There were stories of British motorists driving through Germany and encountering soldiers wheeling cardboard or plywood vehicles. The myth was believed that the panzer force was made up of such vehicles.

The reality was different. It was true that the Army did use mock-up tanks and vehicles on manoeuvres – but this was an example of German thrift. On things that mattered expenditure was lavish. Naval gunnery was improved by frequent target practice and by the fitting into ships of the finest optical ranging equipment. German factories produced tanks of standard pattern designed to fit the concepts of *Blitzkrieg* – vehicles which were capable of being improved as the need arose without the need for radical design changes or the creation of new designs. The Luftwaffe, too, received modern aircraft armed with cannon and not machine-guns and had introduced new, deadly combat tactics.

By 1938, the scale of re-armament and the size of her forces through conscription, had brought Germany's forces nearly to a war footing. In March 1938 the Germans annexed Austria and accepting Hitler's pretext that this was a German internal matter, a question of Germans in Austria wishing to be reunited with the Reich, the politicians of Europe did nothing. As a result of the *Anschluss* the strength of the German Army was increased by a number of Austrian, specialist, mountain troops, an armoured division and by conventional infantry formations. In the autumn of 1938, Hitler's pressure upon the government of Czechoslovakia produced a fear of war in

Europe which was only averted by the sacrifice of the Czech Government of an area known as the Sudetenland. Once again the accepted pretext was that the Germans in the Sudetenland only wished to be incorporated into the Reich.

The sacrifice of the Czechs was in vain. In the spring of 1939, Hitler used the threat of massed bombing of the city of Prague to intimidate Hacha, the Czech president into allowing his country to be 'protected' by a German occupying force. Panzer forces struck across the border and units of the newly created airborne forces stood ready for action in the event of any Czech resistance. Hitler arrived in Prague and slept in the Hradschin castle, the palace of the former Kings of Bohemia and the seat of government. But that act of aggression could no longer be justified as the wish of Germans to be united in the Reich; the Czechs were a Slavic people. Slowly the nations of the West realized that Hitler was determined on war. This was not, however, the Führer's last territorial claim in Europe. During March 1939, he forced Lithuania to cede the city of Memel, and Hitler was ready for the next step in his programme. 'Case White'. the plan for a war against Poland was prepared and the most significant sentence in the speech which Hitler made to this senior commanders was, 'We cannot expect a repetition of the Czech affair. We must prepare ourselves for war.'

The German forces were trained and ready when it came. That statement requires qualification – they were prepared and well armed, but for the wrong type of war. Hitler had planned to fight a series of continental land battles. Each brief war would destroy a particular enemy and when each was defeated there would be a short period of retraining and re-equipping before the forces went out to fight the next enemy. The Wehrmacht was armed to fight campaigns for which only tactical weapons would be required. No thought had been given that there might be a need for strategic weapons. The war, as Hitler planned it, would be confined to the European landmass. Aircraft were seen as long-range artillery and thus the Luftwaffe had no squadrons of long-range bombers to match the range and power of the machines which Bomber Command brought into service. In the case of the Kriegsmarine there were too few U-boats, destroyers or cruisers to counter the Allied navies. Neither was there steel in sufficient quantities, nor the factory capacity available to produce the required number of vessels. It came to a clash of priorities; whether raw materials and factory space should be devoted to ship construction, to tank production or to making aircraft. This was a question that was never satisfactorily resolved.

At the opening of the war the equipment was good, the men were well trained and the nation had been directed, however unknowingly, to the prospect of war. By adroit political negotiation a non-aggression pact had been signed between the Third Reich and the USSR. The significance of that pact was that in the coming war Germany would not have to fight on two fronts. Hitler and his Foreign Secretary, von Ribbentrop, had neutralized the danger from the East while the armies of the Anglo-French allies would be held in check by the West Wall, the Siegfried Line. Europe waited to see upon which of his neighbours Hitler's baleful attention would fall. A rising campaign of hate propaganda indicated that it would be Poland.

The Invasion of Poland, 1939

OPERATION 'WHITE'

As a result of her occupation of the rump of Czechoslovakia in March 1939, Germany outflanked Poland to the south just as her East Prussian province outflanked that country to the north. Thus even before war came geography had determined its strategy and OKW needed only to exploit Poland's inferior geographical position.

Hitler's Directive for Operation 'White', was, '. . . the annihilation of the Polish Army . . .' to achieve which OKW planned a double encirclement of the enemy forces. One encirclement would be to the west and the other to the east of Warsaw. In the next phase of the Operation the Polish Army was to be destroyed in the bend of the River Vistula. Then would come the third and final stage; the capture of the Polish capital. The Poles accepted that their army, outflanked and outnumbered, would have to give ground in the west of the country and their strategy was to fall back upon a succession of river lines along which they planned to hold their opponents.

The German operational plan was for Tenth Army of Army Group South to concentrate its motorized and panzer forces and to strike out of Upper Silesia. On either side of Tenth Army's thrust, the Fourteenth Army below it and Eighth Army above it were to 'prevent the enemy in the area between Posen and Kutno from hindering Tenth Army's advance'. Army Group North's Fourth Army, advancing out of East Pomerania and Third Army out of East Prussia, were to advance south-eastwards and southwards along the Vistula and occupy the enemy's defensive positions along that river line before the retreating Poles could occupy them.

In statistical terms the German Army, one and a quarter million men strong, faced 800,000 Poles. The Germans exercised a superiority in infantry of 3.3 to 1; in artillery of 4.3 to 1, and in armour of 8.2 to 1. Against the panzer host the Poles could pit only nine companies of 8-ton tanks and twenty-nine companies of armoured weapons carriers. Supporting the German Army in the field were 1,600 Luftwaffe aircraft. The Poles had only a quarter of that number.

The Operation progressed very much as OKW had planned. The Polish forces in the western part of the country pulled back, not only because they were outflanked but because the speed of the German advance in the south was threatening Warsaw. The Polish army in the west hurried to link up with the garrison in the capital. Army Group South in hard and bitter fighting was able to prevent this. In the bend of the River Bzura the Polish Posnan Army, which had tried and failed to fight its way through to Warsaw, was encircled and destroyed. The campaign closed with a total victory for the Germans and with shocking losses to the Poles. In a letter home one man of the Leibstandarte SS recorded his impressions of the stricken area between Modlin and Warsaw.

'Our advance took us across that part of the battlefield which had been held by the so-called Pomorze Army. The whole area was a scene of death and destruction. The bloated bodies of men and animals blackening under the hot sun, smashed carts, burnt out vehicles and those most tragic victims of war, the wounded horses, waiting for the mercy shot. Everywhere there was evidence of a beaten army covering the ground. Now I understand what the words of the Army song mean, "Man, and horse and wagon – the Lord God struck them down . . ."'

It was not the German Army alone that had struck the Polish Army down. The Soviet invasion on 19 September, trapped it between both its enemies. The campaign had lasted less than three weeks and was the first practical demonstration of the revolutionary theory of *Blitzkrieg*. Although the purists of the *Blitzkrieg* doctrine had not been able to operate armour in the mass in quite the way they had proposed, the successes gained by their fast-moving, wide-ranging thrusts had excited Hitler's imagination. The victory in Poland confirmed his view that the war in Europe would be won in a series of short, land-based campaigns fought with the sort of tactical weapons with which he had equipped his armed forces.

The dynamic of *Blitzkrieg* was movement, fire and surprise. Movement lay in the rapid thrusts of armoured formations. Fire came from the Luftwaffe's bombers used as long-range weapons in support of ground operations. The third element, surprise, was gained by the attack upon a foreign country in advance of a formal declaration of war. *Blitzkrieg* took some time to develop and before the ground units could begin their wide-sweeping operations, it was the task of the Luftwaffe to spring the surprise by carrying out massive air strikes. These were intended to crush the enemy air force on the ground and to overwhelm its remnant in the air. The scenario of the *Blitzkrieg* against Poland set the pattern for succeeding operations.

On 1 September 1939, Hitler announced in a speech to the Reichstag that he had ordered his forces to retaliate against Polish 'aggression'. Even before the Führer had made that declaration the Polish Air Force had been all but destroyed. At 0440 hours, nearly half a day in advance of Hitler's speech, a force of two hundred and nineteen Ju 87s had spearheaded the Luftwaffe's first blow. Their attacks were followed by those of fighter squadrons which machine-gunned aircraft drawn up on airfields across

Poland. Then came medium bombers to destroy the airfield installations with low-level attacks. Finally, the Stukas came back again to smash anything that had survived the first onslaughts.

BLACK HUSSARS OF THE AIR

The heady excitement of those first days was recalled by Franz Heimann, who served with a Stuka squadron during the Polish campaign. 'Returning crews gave us vivid accounts of the missions they had flown. They told of bodies of troops; whole formations of infantry, breaking and running when the "Black Hussars of the Air" as the Stukas were eventually to become known, dropped out of the sky with Jericho sirens howling. Noise; not that of exploding bombs, but nerve-shattering sirens, had become a weapon of war.'

By the time the first army units crossed the frontier the Polish Air Force had been attacked and crushed. Some squadrons did manage to put machines into the air on that first day and for several days thereafter, but these were a forlorn hope fighting an unequal battle. Once the Luftwaffe had gained air supremacy it was free for other tasks – area bombing of Poland's principal cities and low-level attacks against troop concentrations. Precision bombing was carried out by the Stuka pilots who were able to achieve a greater accuracy than the conventional, horizontal bombers, because they aimed the whole machine directly at the target.

On peace-time manoeuvres the Stukas had gained a reputation for accuracy. They demonstrated that ability in Poland. Franz Heimann was proud of belonging to an élite unit.

'One of the first raids which our Geschwader undertook and, certainly one of the most important of the whole campaign, was intended to capture the huge double bridge across the Vistula. At briefing our pilots had been told that there were several firing points in houses near the bridge from which Polish military engineers could explode the charges and destroy it.

'There was no way in which army units could take out those firing points. The bridge was primed for demolition and would be blown up before the army could capture it. But the task of taking out the firing points was a very suitable target for the Luftwaffe. Tactics for the attack were based on the knowledge that single dive-bombers flying at high level would not arouse suspicion among the Poles around the bridge. These tactics were successful. The machines of our Geschwader flew singly to the target and once over it carried out a co-ordinated attack. Before the Poles could react and set off the charges the Stukas had destroyed the firing-point houses.'

There was a sequel to the story. A wounded Polish engineer knitted some cables together and detonated a number of charges but his heroic action was in vain. The explosions only smashed part of the superstructure, causing slight damage to the railway track and to the roadway, both of which were quickly repaired. Within hours, the armoured train which had been waiting to cross, passed over the Vistula, leading the advance of an entire Corps.

In Franz Heimann's narrative the words 'suitable targets' occur and the interpretation of those words was a source of friction between the two Services. The Luftwaffe expressed its policy in the statement, 'The Luftwaffe does not recognize friend or foe, but only suitable targets.' Such an attitude could and did lead to tragic accidents when friendly troops were attacked in error. Hans-Ulrich Schumann of 1st Panzer Division recalled just such an incident.

'As aircraft recognition signals we carried national flags and draped these across the bonnets of cars and over the turrets of panzer. The infantry laid similar flags along their forward line. These signals were intended to let the Luftwaffe know our positions and they were supposed to bomb forward of the flags. But there were many tragic mistakes in which vehicles were bombed, which were not only clearly marked with flags but which were several kilometres behind our lines.

'Of course, one has to accept that in the stress of active service conditions occasional mistakes do occur. My point is that they ought not to have occurred so frequently because Luftwaffe liaison officers had been attached to army formations at divisional level for years before the war began. Those liaison officers had wireless communication with the airborne squadrons so that they could direct the aircraft in accordance with the tactical situation. But even that link could not prevent mistakes. I remember an incident when our advance was stopped dead because of a lack of liaison between the Luftwaffe and ourselves. Our reconnaissance unit was advancing rapidly towards the bridge at Gora Kalvarya. It had fought down Polish resistance on both sides of the river and had radioed back telling the divisional armour that the way ahead was clear. Hardly had that message been passed when Stukas came diving down and blew up the bridge in front of us. It was a bitter joke to ask on whose side the Luftwaffe was fighting.'

FROM PEACE TO WAR

Erich Hoppe, was another correspondent who had served with 1st Panzer Division in Poland. At the outbreak of war he was a junior NCO in a Schuetzen (later Panzergrenadier) regiment.

'It is half a century since the war with Poland began and because I do not recall dates and times with total accuracy, I have consulted the history of our Division to fill those gaps in my narrative which my memory cannot. Rolf Stoves's work confirms my impression that the attack upon Poland was to have begun during the last week of August. We marched, or perhaps I should say we rode, because we Schuetzen were lorried infantry, towards the border with Poland. I do recall that the move was made in bright moonlight. Some distance from the frontier area the lorries halted, we infantry dismounted and began a foot march to the concentration area. When we reached that place there seemed to be a great deal of activity going on among the officers. Nothing happened to us for several hours and then the latrine rumours started. We were not to cross the frontier that night, nor were we to pull back from the area which we had reached. We were, instead, to stay under cover and remain undetected by the Poles until the date for a new D-Day was announced. Later that evening our officers confirmed the rumours.

'All that first day we lay concealed in the woods and at last light were pulled back because it would have been impossible for a large body of men to have remained undetected by the Poles for very long. We marched out of concealment, picked up the transport and returned to our previous camp. Then, late in the afternoon of 31st August, officers were called to a conference and afterwards they briefed us. We were to march back to the concentration area that night. We reached it sometime about 2200hrs. Our divisional history says that it was midnight but I seem to recall it being earlier than this. We were not allowed to light fires, nor to smoke and we were ordered not to move about unnecessarily or to make noise.

'The next morning, just after dawn, there was a lot of noise and much movement as our divisional recce and panzer units moved forward. Then our lorries were brought up. We climbed in and set off. We were at war and yet it all seemed as normal as a peace-time exercise. After about an hour's drive along roads – tracks would have been a better description – our lorried column pulled into a field. We stood about for some considerable time and welcomed the arrival of the field kitchens. We had had our evening meal in Germany in peace-time. Now we were at war and breakfasting in Poland.

'We were at war but there was no sound of conflict, except for a low rumble which could have been thunder but wasn't. It was gunfire, but very distant. There was a great deal of air activity, but otherwise nothing. That first morning of the war was a warm, bright, quiet and peaceful one. I do not remember my feelings about war being declared. As a soldier I had a duty to do and that was that. I don't even remember an Order of the Day being read out to us, although I expect there was one; there usually was. Our transition from peace-time status to war footing did not occur that first morning. Our baptism of fire came next day and after that we knew what warfare meant.'

DESTROYING THE POSNAN ARMY

R. Buchbinder was from a family of professional soldiers. Born in the first year of the Great War, he had enlisted in 1932, and rose quickly from recruit to commissioned rank. His story shows the war from the viewpoint of the trained staff officer.

'To read the stories that have been written of the campaign in Poland in the autumn of 1939, is to gain a false impression of that operation. A lot was written, by contemporary propaganda sources, of the "18-day victory march". It was nothing of the sort. There were times when it seemed that our rapid advance had taken us too far and had placed the outcome of the whole campaign in jeopardy.

'Shortly before the outbreak of war I was seconded from the panzer regiment with which I was serving to take up a junior staff appointment in General Reinhardt's 4th Panzer Division. My pre-war training had been as a staff officer alternating, as was customary, with troop appointments. Now I had been detached from the panzer regiment and been returned to staff duties at divisional level.

'In the Polish campaign, Reinhardt's 4th Panzer Division (still known at that time as Division Reinhardt) together with its sister formation, 1st Panzer Division, formed Hoeppner's 16 Corps, in Army Group South. The advance towards Warsaw had been a brilliant display of our General's ability and within eight days of D-Day, we were at the gates of Warsaw. Our GSO I was concerned that Corps formed a long and narrow salient, running on a general line from east/west. Of more immediate concern to him was that we were not in touch with either 1st Panzer, on our right flank, or with any German formation on the left. We were, in a sense, completely isolated. When we closed up towards Warsaw Reinhardt expressed doubt about the wisdom of committing armour in built-up areas. In a Sitrep to Corps dated 9th September, he wrote, "This morning's attack upon Warsaw was called off because of the severe losses we had suffered. As the city is defended very strongly . . . a single Panzer Division with only four battalions of infantry is too weak to undertake an attack with any prospect of success . . . We shall not renew the attack but shall block off those roads leading to Warsaw from the west which might be used by the retreating Polish army. To carry out that task 4th Panzer needs more infantry as armour by itself cannot hold ground . . ."

'During that day Operations Section was advised that a vast mass of undefeated Polish formations stood at our back. These should have been encircled and destroyed by formations following behind us but this had not happened and now the Poles were behind us, a strong and well-armed force. Our reconnaissance units reported each new enemy sighting and this was marked on the map. Soon an ugly rash of enemy circles far outnumbered our friendly ones. It was not known at that time that those enemy markings represented the huge masses of men, guns, horses and vehicles of General Kutrzeba's Posnan Army. Nor that the General had expressed his determination to fight his way past us so as to bring the Posnan army into Warsaw. By last light on the 9th his force was centred around Sochaczev, clearly regrouping before the grand assault.

'The isolated 4th Panzer Division stood in the path of Kutrzeba's army and was not deployed to meet his blow. Consider the situation – on the 8th we had been advancing eastwards towards the Polish capital. Now, only a day later, we had to meet an attack from the west. Reinhardt was faced with a difficult decision. If he turned the whole of 4th Panzer to face the Posnan Army this would invite attack by the strong enemy forces inside Warsaw. His solution was to place certain divisional formations back to back. Unit commanders were told of the serious situation and warned that hard fighting lay ahead. We alone, he told them, had to stop Kutrzeba. The only reinforcement which Corps could give was a battle group composed of the Leibstandarte SS Adolf Hitler and a battalion of the 103rd Artillery Regiment. That force was rushed forward to plug a gap in our line which had been created when our 7th Reconnaissance Battalion was overrun and almost totally destroyed. That small group of SS and artillery took up position facing westwards – confronting the Posnan army. A mixed group of 4th Panzer Division infantry, artillery and anti-tank guns faced eastwards, i.e., towards Warsaw. Between those two outward-facing groups lay the bulk of 4th Division's 12th Schuetzen Regiment and the division's two panzer regiments, forming a fire brigade reserve which could be switched from one danger point to another as the situation demanded.

'There were in that area of Poland, in those days, very few hard surface roads and these, such as they were, connected the provincial capitals with Warsaw. All other roads were unsurfaced, being little more than cart tracks. Such surfaces were suitable for light units, infantry and cavalry, but heavy equipment needed hard surfaces. Kutrzeba was determined to take his heavy weapons into Warsaw. It was the wrong decision to make and it cost the Poles the Posnan Army.

'Reinhardt was not a defensively minded commander. He was a panzer leader who believed in aggressive action. The SS on the western flank were ordered to attack and while Kutrzeba's attention was drawn to that sector Reinhardt flung our panzer regiments northwards to cut the Modlin–Warsaw road. It was fascinating to watch the development of the battle from maps and to have these moves explained by the GSO at evening briefings. The General was correct in his appreciation of how the Poles would react. The Warsaw garrison and the Posnan army were not so able. They did not see our attacks as the desperate struggles of an outnumbered force, but thought they were evidence that we had been massively reinforced. Acting upon that misappreciation they saw it as essential to break through before even more German forces could arrive. All these things we learned later from prisoner interrogation.

'Of course, our division's attacks were not made without loss and by 11th September, half of our panzers were non-operational. Some of these non-runners were the result of a lack of spares, fuel and ammunition because no supplies were coming forward. A desperate crisis built up as markings on the operational map showed where the Poles were concentrated most strongly and where their attacks was fiercest. At Mokotov a battalion of their tanks charged and furious assaults on the SS sector gained some ground. If that terrible pressure was maintained there was the fear that our forces would drain away. By heroic endeavours our men held the enemy and the Polish attacks weakened in intensity and reduced in number. No sooner had the enemy assaults weakened than Reinhardt was ready with his riposte and flung in our last remaining panzers with the SS riding on their outsides. The enemy began to crumble and give way and our attack showed promise of brilliant success. But before we could consolidate our victory Corps ordered us to break off the operation and to prepare for a mission in the Bzura sector. In the battle which developed the Posnan army was destroyed, but it was an operation in which I had no part. Orders had recalled me to Berlin to take up a new appointment. To conclude, I think it can be claimed with justification that 4th Panzer played the major part in the destruction of the Posnan Army which led, in turn, to the defeat of the Polish forces in the autumn campaign of 1939.'

BITTER RESISTANCE

As the *Blitzkrieg* unrolled the thrusting panzer spearheads spread across the country, leaving behind groups of enemy troops who had been bypassed and were undefeated. Some of these were stragglers hoping to escape detection and captivity in order that they could return home and take up their former life. Other groups varied in size from battalions to brigades. As these fragments of the Polish Army made their way to places which they believed to be still in native hands, they encountered German rear units and when they did the fighting was always bitter and often hand-to-hand. There was no time for mercy or compassion. The Poles had no facilities to deal with prisoners and the Germans considered these men debouching suddenly from dense forest to be not soldiers but partisans who, if caught, were given summary punishment.

In view of the confusion that existed and the danger that was present behind the German front, it is surprising to learn that officer couriers drove about without escort. Such men may have considered that the risk was acceptable; they may not have seen that they were taking a risk or, perhaps considered the German uniform they wore to be a sufficient protection, even in 'bandit'-infested areas. One officer who had been a courier was Max Hildenbrandt who, from the tone of his letter, was one of those who had not appreciated the dangers of driving about without an escort. That part of the narrative he wrote is glossed over almost as if it had not needed to be considered.

'The following account of the first patrol I led, is based upon the post-action report which I wrote at the time. It was standard practice in the German services that after each mission, from a patrol upwards, a report had to be written and submitted to the next highest military authority. These reports had to follow a certain pattern and had to be as detailed as a textbook on tactics. I have abbreviated the official version and taken out much that would not be interesting to your readers.

'The action opens in September 1939, about a week after hostilities had begun in Poland. It had been part of my duties from the first day of operations, to act as an officer courier carrying messages that could not be entrusted to the field telephone. In the role of courier I had driven between our battalion HQ and Division or even Corps, sometimes several times each day.

"One of the unpleasant features of the Polish campaign was the very high officer casualty rate which was suffered as a result of the activities of *franc tireurs*. These snipers were dressed in civilian clothes and were therefore in a good position to pick out officer targets. As a result of the high casualty rate I was ordered to rejoin the battalion which was in action at Przansnysz. I was at Divisional HQ when the message came ordering my return to battalion. I was aware from the operational maps of the huge gaps there were between many of our units and that, as a consequence, I would be unlikely to find food or fuel en route. Forewarned is forearmed and I loaded my Kubelwagen with extra drums of petrol, oil and rations and set out.

'The road to Mlava bore the marks of bitter and prolonged fighting. Houses, farms and outbuildings had been either severely damaged or else burned out. The road surface, which even in peace time must have been poor, was now pitted with so many holes that my car lurched from side to side. I was quite concerned whether the suspension would hold up under such treatment. A blown bridge forced me to divert off the road, a decision I soon regretted because the car was soon stuck in deep sand. It took hours to get it out and going again and as I did not wish to continue the journey in the dark I stayed overnight in a requisitioned flat. The next morning saw me on the road bright and early but it took me a long time to find battalion TAC HQ. By the time I reached it it was too late to set out for the Company positions. My sleep that night was less comfortable than the flat of the night before. This time I was bedded down in a barn with TAC HQ below me in a cellar and a great many rats to share the accommodation in the barn.

'No I Company which I reached late in the following morning was in position west of Modlin with its right flank resting on the Vistula. From the high bank we had good observation along the length of the river. We ate well – mostly chicken – flocks of which were in every abandoned farm. I spent one day becoming accustomed to active service conditions and late in the afternoon of the second day an O Group was called. The CO briefed us that night. Our Company was to send out a fighting patrol which I was to lead. Shortly before 2000 hrs our guns opened a softening-up barrage and soon the whole village was alight. In the fading light and with the whole area obscured by smoke it was difficult to determine the Polish positions. Then it began to rain and we sat, waiting to begin the patrol, huddled in our slit trenches.

'A report from the Intelligence officer was that a deserter had come across and had said the morale of the Poles opposite us was low. Our artillery fire was very accurate and had unnerved a great many of the deserter's comrades. At 2200 hrs the CO gave us final orders. The main patrol was split up into four smaller groups. The intention was to fight our way to the other side of the village and then to return. Our artillery which was already firing a barrage would cease fire between 0430 and 0600 hrs – the time when we were expected to be fighting in the village. The duration of the patrol was 90 minutes.

'I went round the Company positions talking to my men and climbed back into my own trench convinced that the cold and the noise would stop me sleeping. How wrong I was. At 0355 hrs an NCO woke me and we moved to where the men were already waiting. The whole patrol made its way through the outpost line and then split up. Each group carried a light machine-gun. One group member was the scout and another was the getaway man in the rear. Once in the open we jog-trotted across the ground but in the dawn light the Poles saw us and opened fire. So much for the barrage softening up the enemy. We grouped in a fold of dead ground and then charged through the village firing as we ran. It is strange what the mind absorbs at such times. I remember seeing to our right the Vistula shining in the growing daylight. To the left was a narrow cutting with a white house on one side of it. The cutting led to a village which I could not see. The walls of the cutting were about 8 or 9 metres high and were very steep. The patrol moved forward hugging one side of the cutting wall and when bursts of machine-gun fire tore into the sand wall we leapt across to the other side and flung ourselves down. There was a sudden explosion just in front of us and somebody cried out. I needed to regroup the patrol and pulled back my little group to the protection of the white house. I had a look at the wounded man

who had been hit in the chest by hand-grenade fragments. Another man had
had his cheek cut by a splinter.

'An NCO and two men who had been sent to climb the cutting wall met
opposition and then the sound of firing was heard on the right flank. One of
the three men came back and reported that a trench on top of the cutting
was filled with Polish soldiers. I gave orders for the other two men to pull
back. The first man reached us safely but the other collapsed suddenly. An
NCO took one look and reported that the dead man had been shot through
the head. We dragged the body into cover and sent the wounded man back
alone. There was no one whom we could spare to accompany him.

'We then came under direct fire from the house and I gave orders that
we were to pull back. As we withdrew one of the men cried out and reached
out a hand to me. It was wet with blood. Then the man on my right was
shot through the calf, fell down and tried to drag himself through the sand
on his stomach. Two of us went to help him and one of the NCOs carried
him in the fireman's lift the whole time under fire. We finally reached cover
where we lay down to gain our breath. After a short pause we moved back
to the outpost line where our comrades came out to help carry the wounded.
It was by now 0600 hrs.

'While I was in the outpost line three men were spotted bringing in a
fourth, dragging him slowly up the steep bank and all the time under fire.
These were the survivors of the fourth group of the fighting patrol. The
group leader had been killed and his body was hanging on the Polish wire.
Two other group members had been wounded. One of them, the man who
had been dragged up the river bank, had been shot in the stomach while the
other had been wounded in the upper arm as he flung hand-grenades into
the enemy trenches.

'The battalion commander arrived at Company HQ at about noon. From
post-action reports it was clear that the village was held in strength and that
the Poles were not demoralized, as the deserter had said, but had shown
themselves determined to resist and had fought well. In the evening, as I was
writing the post-action report, two NCOs came to see me and told me that
they intended to bring in the body of their comrade which was hanging on
the wire. The dead man was only 30 metres from the Polish trenches and
although it was a risky business they succeeded and in the course of their
action shot up the enemy trenches and showered the Poles with hand-
grenades. The campaign in Poland was made up of such incidents and had
been, so I thought, filled with violent action. From experiences in later
campaigns I was to learn that this had been an easy patrol.'

BATTLESHIP *SCHLESWIG HOLSTEIN*

The Kriegsmarine had only a very minor role to play in the campaign against Poland although, of course, U-boats and commerce raiders, notably *Graf Spee*, were already at war station in the oceans of the world before war broke out. The Kriegsmarine's small role was due to the fact that Poland's outlet to the Baltic Sea was only a narrow strip of land; the Polish Corridor. It was the task of the German Navy to shell that narrow strip of land and then to disembark troops who would go on to occupy it.

The battleship *Schleswig Holstein*, a veteran of Jutland in the First World War, was the major naval unit that carried out the bombardments. She went into action very soon after the opening of the Polish campaign, shelling various targets, chiefly, the Westerplatte, in the estuary of the Vistula. Danzig, the chief city in the region, fell on 8 September, leaving *Schleswig Holstein* and her escorts free to move up to Gdingen, the Polish naval base. That city was not so easily taken and did not surrender until 20 September by which time the land campaign had all but ended.

Only the first paragraphs of Albert Richter's account of his life as a sailor described the Polish campaign and those paragraphs dealt with the bombardment of Westerplatte.

'Our ship, the *Schleswig Holstein*, was an old ship of the line, and carried 28cm guns as main armament and 15cm guns as secondary armament. We reached the mouth of the Vistula and took up position opposite the Westerplatte. Our main armament had a range of more than 10km, but we were anchored little more than a kilometre from our target; the Polish fortress on the Westerplatte.

'Our ship opened fire just after dawn. It was an unusual feeling to fire ur guns in a war situation. When the 28s opened up the whole ship shook and she rolled a bit. We were firing at such a close range and at such a large target that each of our shells was a direct hit. I was below decks on a fire control point and could see nothing of the effects of our gunfire, but at intervals an officer gave us details. He told us of vast explosions as our shells exploded, of debris flying about and of the destruction that was being caused. After a ten-minute barrage it was time for the infantry assault company to carry out their landing. We wished them luck as they passed us, burdened down with flame-throwers and weapons. Their first assault was driven back by determined resistance and it was clear that the Poles were not yet "softened up". We opened fire again but still the Poles would not surrender and Stukas had to be brought in. They had as little success as our ship's artillery had had. The infantry company suffered so many casualties that a detachment of assault engineers had to be brought in to fill the ranks. At last, on 8th September, the Poles gave up the fight.'

VICTORY

Although the major land battles were over by 19 September, Polish resistance at Gdingen lasted a day longer. Within a week the remnant of the Polish Army were being rounded up and marched to prisoner-of-war compounds – both German and Russian, after which the German Army held a Victory Parade through Warsaw, through streets which held no people as R. Holder recalled. 'It may well have been the Poles had no wish to view our triumph but it could also have been that they were ordered to keep away. It was an eerie sensation to march through streets that are empty and which should be filled with people.'

With Poland smashed in a matter of weeks, Hitler had no worry about his eastern flank. The pact with Russia had cleared his back. Now he could concentrate on winning the war in the west. He would open a new land campaign and bring the overwhelming mass of the Luftwaffe and the army against the Franco-British enemies. He had intended to open the new war during the autumn of 1939, but his demand was turned down by OKW, whose leaders pointed out that the dry weather needed for a successful campaign was nearly at an end and would give way to winter, during which no major military operation could be begun and completed. The Führer was forced to postpone his strike in the west until spring, but before he could open Operation 'Yellow', a crisis on Germany's northern flank could only be resolved by a new campaign against Denmark and Norway: Operations 'Weser' and 'Weser North'.

The War in Western Europe, 1940

DESTINATION SCANDINAVIA

There were two overriding reasons for the German attack upon Norway in the spring of 1940: The first was economic, the second strategic. The economic reason was Germany's dependence upon Swedish iron-ore which was shipped out through the Norwegian port of Narvik. That ore was essential to meet Germany's armaments production; native supplies alone could not meet the demand. Germany depended upon foreign supplies and that flow was jeopardized by the Royal Navy's seizure of ore ships inside Norwegian territorial waters. Hitler demanded measures to counter this British action although he was well aware that the German Navy was too weak to protect the traffic between Narvik and German ports. The only way to ensure that the ore flow was uninterrupted would be for Germany to invade Norway. Thereby she could control both production and shipment. That imperative would have been reason enough, but in addition Hitler feared that Britain and France would pre-empt his own aggression. Such an act by the Western Allies would outflank Germany in the north. Hitler's fear of an Allied strategic move in Scandinavia was the second of the reasons for the German invasion.

The reason for the attack upon Denmark was that her northernmost airfields and her harbours were needed as bases by the German forces which would invade southern Norway. All the strategic objectives in Denmark were to be taken within an hour by two airborne assaults behind which would come conventional forces to occupy the country. The attack upon Norway, being both sea and airborne, would take longer to complete but was planned so that the capture of the principal objectives would be completed within a matter of hours. The OKW plan was for a double operation Exercise 'Weser' (the occupation of Denmark) and its extension Exercise 'Weser North' (the ocupation of Norway). The German High Command plan was based on the fact that the military forces for the two Operations did not need to be vast, for no real military opposition was anticipated from either Scandinavian army. D-Day for both operations was to be 9 April. In order to meet that deadline certain slow-moving tanker and supply ships left German ports in advance of D-Day so as to be in position to refuel the vessels of the attack force as they arrived to carry out the invasion.

When D-Day came the occupation of Denmark was carried out according to plan, but the attack upon Norway suffered certain setbacks which will be described below. To begin with, however, the campaign opened with two successful airborne operations. No 3 Company of 1st Fallschirmjaeger Battalion dropped over the Stavanger/Sala airfield while Captain Walther's battalion HQ and No 2 Company were airlanded on Oslo/Fornehu aerodrome. These assault detachments were followed by other lightly armed paratroops who were brought in by a stream of transport machines. Then the first ship convoy arrived carrying, principally, heavily armed infantry, because the immediate need was to occupy Oslo in force. Tanks, guns and other bulky equipment came in subsequent, follow-up convoys.

German units, airborne and seaborne, invaded other harbour towns of southern Norway; Trondheim, Bergen, Stavanger and Egersund. The Kriegsmarine's all-out effort in 'Weser North' was carried out by eleven groups of ships which was the minimum number required to undertake all the seaborne assaults and escort duties on D-Day. More important than the objectives in the south of Norway was the town of Narvik, in the far north of the country. The need to occupy the ore-shipping port before the anticipated Franco-British assault posed a number of complex problems. North/south road and rail communications in Norway were too poor to allow the speedy movement of large bodies of troops to the battle areas. Nor were there suitable airfields in the Narvik region on to which transport machines could land. The OKW solution was to send a convoy of fast destroyers racing to the port. It is the No 1 Destroyer Group, under the command of Commodore Bonte, sailing northwards toward Narvik, and the subsequent fighting around that place which is of special interest to this book. '. . . To begin with there were fourteen destroyers each of which carried about 200 of us Gebirgsjaeger and our equipment . . . The embarkation port was Wesermünde.' (L. Schumann)

The two destroyer groups, 'Narvik' and 'Trondheim', left their berths at 2300 hrs on the night of 6/7 April and at 0300 hrs on the following morning the ten 'Narvik' ships concentrated around the battleships *Scharnhorst* and *Gneisenau* which were to escort them. The remaining four destroyers were grouped around their escort, the cruiser *Admiral Hipper*. The armada set out at 0510 hrs and had soon passed the narrows between the Norwegian coast and the Shetlands, a sea area patrolled by the Royal Navy. Emil Hammer was a seaman with the 'Narvik' group. He recalled:

'The night of 7/8th April was pitch black. It was raining and the wind force rose from 7 to 8. Thanks to those appalling conditions we passed the Bergen–Shetlands narrows without being intercepted. The seas, whipped up by the wind, forced the convoy to reduce speed to 22 knots. This meant that we were late arriving in the objective area. During the early hours of 8th

April, there was an engagement between HMS *Glowworm* and the *Hipper*, as a result of which the British ship was sunk. Later that night the two German convoys parted. We maintained course for Narvik, led by the *Wilhelm Heidekamp*, the Command ship, while the other flotilla made for Trondheim. During the evening of the 8th the heavy units parted company from us in the destroyer group and took station west of Lofoten. They were to cover our back while we steamed towards Narvik. Any attack by the British Navy would almost certainly come from the south-west and would find our two battleships waiting.'

LANDING AT NARVIK

The men carried in the destroyers were part of General Dietl's 3rd Gebirgs Division. One of these was Franz Puechler, a rifleman in a Jaeger regiment. Among the documents which came to me was the photostat of a letter which Franz had sent to his family in the Austrian Bundesland of Steiermark. Rifleman Puechler fell in action in his native province during the last days of the war. In the account quoted below and written after the campaign in Norway had ended, Puechler recalled the voyage to Narvik and the first day of battle.

'Let me now give you my impressions of the first part of the Norwegian campaign. We, that is the army units, left northern Germany by ship. Before we boarded our vessel, a destroyer, our CO gave us a short talk letting us know what tasks lay ahead of us. Then we climbed up the steep gangway, took off our kit and went below deck. Because there is so little space on board a warship we left it to the sailors to stow away our kit for they knew where to stack it. We washed, were given a meal and then afterwards chatted for a long time about the new campaign.

'The ship's crew treated us well and we landlubbers had complete trust in them. At about midnight we turned in, tired after the long day's journey. At reveille, the naval equivalent of the orderly sergeant (I do not know what he is called in naval terms) woke us. Although the ship was fitted with ventilators the close conditions had given most of us headaches. When we went up on deck we found that we were already on the high seas. It was a splendid sight to see a long line of twelve ships positioned on one side of us driving through a calm, bright, sunlit sea. But we were not to enjoy the pleasure of a calm sea for very long. A wind blew up and soon high waves rocked our ship. Together with several of my mates I lay down on the deck so that I would be less affected by seasickness. A number of other men joined us and then a sailor told us that the best method was to sleep if we could. Soldiers can sleep anywhere, but soon we were wakened by the sound of our anti-aircraft guns in action against ten British bombers flying high overhead.

The aircraft dropped a few eggs but did not hit anything. Their attack lasted only a few minutes.

'By now it was getting dark. The sea was so rough that our quarters were in a terrible mess. Everything that was not nailed or screwed down had been flung about. At reveille next morning we were not as bright as we had been on the previous day. Our stomachs were still churning and heaving. Suddenly a British destroyer steamed over the horizon. Our ship's captain ordered "Action stations" and within a short time everybody was at their post. But then the destroyer could no longer be seen. Our heavy ships had opened fire and had sunk her. Only a handful of survivors could be rescued from the stormy waves. Our quarters were in an indescribable mess. Sleep was really out of the question but we managed to doze fitfully now and then. In time our ship's pitching and tossing lessened and a sailor told us we had left the high seas and had entered coastal waters.

'By the grey light of dawn we saw we were sailing along a fiord. The enemy was firing at us and our ships were returning that fire. Some distance from shore the ship halted and dropped anchor. We Gebirgsjaeger paraded on the upper deck, put on our equipment and climbed down into small craft which carried us towards the shore. It was a marvellous feeling to have firm ground under our feet again. Once we had disembarked we went immediately into action, fighting in a blinding snowstorm. There was a lot of gunfire from the shore which was answered by our ships and the noise of the explosions echoed around the fiord. We made our way over every type of obstacle, natural as well as artificial and by midday had worked our way close to the coastal guns which were our objective. One of my mates said to me "Do you see that barracks: We'll be in there tonight." He was right. After hours of fighting we could report to Berlin that our mission had been accomplished.'

BATTLES IN THE FIORD

By 0810 hrs on 9 April, the German Admiralty communiqué could report that Dietl and his men were in control of Narvik town and the light railway along which the iron-ore was freighted. That communiqué was technically correct, but neither the area nor the railway line were firmly in German hands. There were to be hard and wasteful land and sea battles fought in the Narvik area. The naval engagements were over within a matter of days, but on land the Gebirgsjaeger and sailors fought for months, because terrain conditions dictated that this campaign could not be a *Blitzkrieg*.

On D-Day morning, so far as Bonte and his flotilla were concerned, their part in Operation 'Weser North' had been successfully completed. They had brought the Gebirgsjaeger to Narvik. The Kriegsmarine plan called for the group to be refuelled and then to return at top speed to Germany. A

ALLSCHIRMJÄGER

OUNGEN BEI ALLEN WEHRBEZIRKSKOMMAND

Left: On 7 March 1936, the German Army received a warm welcome when it re-entered the Rhineland, which had been demilitarized under the terms of the Treaty of Versailles.

Left: This photograph was taken during army manoeuvres in 1937, on the occasion of a visit by Mussolini to Germany. Goering and Mussolini are in the foreground with Hitler and Ciano in the background.

Left: German infantry marching through Wenceslas Square, Prague, and German tanks, Panzer IIs, at a parade after the occupation of Czechoslovakia in March 1939.

Right: German soldiers remove the Polish eagle marking the border between the two countries, 1 September 1939.

Right: The German battleship Schleswig Holstein *bombarding the Westerplatte during the Polish campaign in 1939.*

Right: German civilians listen to the public radio announcement on 1 September 1939 telling them that their country is at war.

Left: When the commandant of the Polish forces in Lemberg was forced to capitulate he insisted that a German Gebirgsjäger formation take the surrender.

Left: Hitler visiting servicemen who had been wounded during the Polish campaign.

Left: Hitler and General Busch watching German soldiers cross a river in Poland.

speedy refuelling was out of the question. Although two fleet tankers had left German ports ahead of the destroyers, so as to be in position when those ships needed to refuel, only one, the *Jan Weddlem*, made the rendezvous. The other, *Kattegat*, had been sunk. Its loss meant that now only two destroyers and not four, could be refuelled simultaneously and refuelling took seven hours to complete. Because the German Admiralty timetable could not be kept the destroyer group was still in the Narvik area when the ships of the Royal Navy came on the scene. A former officer of the Kriegsmarine wrote the following account of the first naval battles which were fought out in Narvik Fiord.

'The Gebirgsjaeger whom we had brought to Narvik were disembarked and we in the destroyer flotilla awaited orders to return to Germany. We were never to make that journey home in the ships which we had brought to Narvik. In the early hours of the morning of 10th April, a British destroyer flotilla of five vessels, entered the fiord and under cover of a snowstorm reached the entrance to Narvik harbour without being detected. They opened fire with guns and torpedoes upon shipping in the harbour, but they did not know that part of our destroyer group was anchored in nearby fiords to the north and south of the town. Those ships came immediately to our aid and the British were caught between two fires. Very soon three enemy destroyers had been sunk and another badly damaged. The fifth vessel made off westward at high speed. The enemy flotilla commander, flying his flag in HMS *Hardy*, was killed in this action.

'We, too, had suffered losses. Not long after the alarm bells called us to action stations, our flotilla leader was torpedoed. We lost a great many comrades, including Commodore Bonte, whose vessel was sunk. Then our ship was struck by a torpedo but we managed to lay her alongside a Swedish vessel and this stopped her from sinking.'

That action was the first of a series of destroyer engagements fought out over the following four days in and around Narvik Fiord. When these battles ended the German flotilla had been totally destroyed, a disastrous blow because, as a result, the destroyer strength of the German Navy was halved. In addition, in southern Norway, the cruiser *Blücher* had been sunk and other major units had been badly damaged. The German Navy's losses were to have their effect upon the course of future operations; in particular the plan to invade Great Britain. The narrative continued.

'From an inspection of the ship made after the battle, it was clear that the damage we had suffered could not be repaired locally. We could not leave Narvik and so we removed material which could be used in the defence of the town. We sailors now had no ships but we could play a part as gunners, or if it came to it, as infantrymen. A couple of hours after laying alongside the Swedish vessel we had removed hand weapons and ammunition as well as light flak and a 3.7cm flak gun from our ship. This material was stored in bombproof shelters by some crewmen while others worked on the defences in that area around the harbour which we had been allotted. The ground was covered with snow over a metre deep and we used this to camouflage our positions. We produced camouflage clothing from table cloths, bed sheets and other linen, and concealed machine-gun posts with the parachutes which had been fitted to air-dropped supplies.

'We spent three days in those positions standing-to each time the British ships returned, determined to fling back any attempts which they might make to land troops in Narvik. The enemy undertook no landing operation. We were joined in our defensive positions by the crews of other German destroyers who had fought to the last round and who had then blown up their ships. All the naval detachments were grouped and given tasks, such as defending the railway line, driving trucks or storing the supplies taken off ships in the area. It was clear that the Narvik garrison was isolated, that it could expect neither reinforcement nor supplies and that we had to make do with what we had. Our naval engineers soon had the railway working again, but Norwegian forces still held the last section of the line before it reached the Swedish border. Our engineers fitted steel plates as a form of primitive armour to the locomotive and that "armoured train" went into action with the Gebirgsjaeger. The last section of the line was captured from the Norwegians. Part of the naval infantry group not only fought in the mountains but went on patrol wearing skis. Some crews patrolled in small vessels to maintain contact with isolated outposts to the north and south of the town.

'During the following weeks British ships came up the fiord and bombarded us and we could make no reply to that aggression. We did have our victories, however, and extended the bridgehead perimeter. In time the general situation deteriorated and became very serious indeed. We were a long way from home and totally isolated. There was no airfield on to which supply transports could land and we were beyond the flying range of most of the Luftwaffe's machines so that an air drop was out of the question. Only when Trondheim and its airfield passed into German hands could we be supplied by air on a regular basis.

'It will be appreciated that there was no shelter for our men fighting in the mountains and that they lay out on the bare slopes without protection from the bitter wintry conditions. We sailors shared those privations with our army comrades. At the end of April, French and British pressure on the Gebirgsjaeger sector of the bridgehead drove it in and to thicken the line the naval infantry detachment was ordered forward. The memory of the terrible approach march to the forward positions will always remain with us. It had to be undertaken at night, firstly for reasons of concealment from the enemy and, secondly because the night temperature froze the knee-deep snow and made marching less tiring. The misery of the days and nights spent out in

Right: It was during the presidency of Paul von Hindenburg that Adolf Hitler became Chancellor of Germany. (M. Klein)

Right and below: Under the conditions imposed by Versailles, the German Army was forbidden armoured fighting vehicles. To overcome that restriction the future commanders of the Panzer force learned how to control armour en masse by using plywood or canvas substitutes, on military manoeuvres.

Left: A member of the Hitler Youth receiving flight training in a glider. Such measures produced a pool of pilots for the Luftwaffe, as described by Georg Cordts in his account of jet fighter training.

Below: Taking the oath of allegiance was the climax of a recruit's life and the focus of much tradition. This is Brunswick in January 1936.

Bottom: The new German Army's Standards are paraded in Berlin in the days of power and glory before the Second World War.

Right: A poster recruiting men for the paratroop arm of service.

Far right: A formal parade by a Luftwaffe unit in pre-war days.

Bottom right: Senior military commanders attending a pre-war parade; from left to right, Generals Milch (Luftwaffe), Keitel (OKW), von Brauchitsch (OKH), and Raeder (OKM).

ALLSCHIRMJÄGEI

DUNGEN BEI ALLEN WEHRBEZIRKSKOMMAND

Left: On 7 March 1936, the German Army received a warm welcome when it re-entered the Rhineland, which had been demilitarized under the terms of the Treaty of Versailles.

Left: This photograph was taken during army manoeuvres in 1937, on the occasion of a visit by Mussolini to Germany. Goering and Mussolini are in the foreground with Hitler and Ciano in the background.

Left: German infantry marching through Wenceslas Square, Prague, and German tanks, Panzer IIs, at a parade after the occupation of Czechoslovakia in March 1939.

Right: German soldiers remove the Polish eagle marking the border between the two countries, 1 September 1939.

Right: The German battleship Schleswig Holstein *bombarding the Westerplatte during the Polish campaign in 1939.*

Right: German civilians listen to the public radio announcement on 1 September 1939 telling them that their country is at war.

Left: When the commandant of the Polish forces in Lemberg was forced to capitulate he insisted that a German Gebirgsjäger formation take the surrender.

Left: Hitler visiting servicemen who had been wounded during the Polish campaign.

Left: Hitler and General Busch watching German soldiers cross a river in Poland.

Right: German soldiers guard Polish prisoners of war at a water point. The Poles fought hard but they could not stem the German Blitzkrieg.

Right: HMS Glowworm *laying smoke as she attempts to ram the German cruiser* Admiral Hipper *during operations off Norway in 1940.*

Right: German Alpine troops disembarking in a Norwegian port, April 1940.

Left: German Alpine troops prepare for the battle ahead.

Left: German military units disembark from their improvised landing craft in Norway.

Left: German infantry massed behind a ruined Norwegian building take cover while preparing to continue with their advance.

Right: Narvik harbour, April 1940. The German destroyers are moored; the ships in the background are either sinking or burning.

Below: Kapitän zur See Bonte, who led the ten destroyers of Naval Battle Group 1 at Narvik. He was killed in action on 10 April 1940.

Below right: Fregatten-Kapitän Berger, who commanded the 1st Destroyer Flotilla of Naval Battle Group 1 at Narvik.

Above: Fregatten-Kapitän Schulz-Hinrichs, commander of the destroyer Erich Koellner, which was sunk by the Royal Navy on 13 April 1940. Note the 'Narvik Schild' he is wearing on his sleeve, a distinction awarded to all ranks of the services who fought in the Narvik battles.

Above and below: Korvetten-Kapitän Wolff, captain of Georg Thiele, which was sunk in Narvik Fiord.

Above: *The front page of issue no 6 of the newspaper published for the German forces serving at Narvik. It was the product of the Naval Propaganda Company, whose editorial offices were in Room 21 of the Grand Hotel in Narvik.*

Above: *General Dietl, commander of the German military forces at Narvik, with two naval officers from ships sunk during the battle.*

Below: *Dietl with men of the Gebirgs regiments that captured Narvik.*

Left: The Ju 87 dive-bomber, one of the two principal components of Blitzkrieg. Although nearly obsolete at the outbreak of war, the Stuka went on to serve effectively for several more years.

Left: The first German vehicles move into Roermond, Holland, in May 1940.

Left: Campaigning in Holland, May 1940. Reconnaissance units of the SS Panzer Division Leibstandarte Adolf Hitler drive past Ju 52s which had made unsuccessful attempts to air-land Fallschirm-jäger on Dutch airfields.

Above: A motorized half-track column passing marching infantry during the German advance towards Dunkirk in late May 1940. (H. Schmidt)

Right: German assault troops crossing the River Maas during the opening stages of the French Flanders campaign in May 1940.

Right: SS General 'Sepp' Dietrich shaking hands with Wilhelm Monke, who was accused of shooting British prisoners of war at Wormhoudt, Belgium.

Above: 'Das Ganze –
Halt', the traditional
German army bugle-
call; in this photograph
it has brought the
campaign in France to
an end.

Left: At the end of the
campaign in the West,
Hitler made a visit to
France, during which
he returned to those
areas of the Western
Front where he had
fought in the First
World War and made a
pilgrimage to military
cemeteries. He then
went on to inspect
fortifications in the
Maginot Line.

Right: German troops inspecting a causeway of army lorries on the Dunkirk beaches that the British used as embarkation piers.

Right: An exercise along the Atlantic coast by units training for the invasion of Britain.

Below: A vehicle of Rommel's 7th Panzer Division on the Channel coast at the St. Valéry area, where he received the surrender of a combined Anglo-French force in 1940.

Below right: A river barge converted to an assault craft in preparation for Operation 'Sealion', the invasion of Britain.

[Anlage]
L I L   F.H.Q., den 25.6.40

<u>Betr</u>: Luftwaffenseitige Grundlagen für eine Landung in England.

1)   Voraussetzung ist <u>Luftüberlegenheit</u>.

      Diese kann errungen werden im Zuge der Belagerung Englands durch Angriffe gegen die Luftfahrtindustrie, gegen mögliche Zufuhren von Übersee und durch den Materialverschleess des Gegners bei der Abwehr unserer Angriffe.

      Wann diese Überlegenheit erkämpft ist, kann gegenwärtig noch nicht angegeben werden, z.Zt. ist sie noch nicht vorhanden.

2)   Die Unterstützung des Übergangs kann aus den derzeitigen Aufmarschräumen erfolgen. Hierbei ist es bei der gegenwärtigen Stärke der Fliegerverbände noch gleichgültig, ob an einer oder mehreren Stellen übergegangen wird. Jedoch kann auf Grund eintretender Verluste eine Zusammenfassung der restlichen Kräfte zum Schutz <u>nur einer</u> Übergangsstelle notwendig werden.

3)   Die Luftwaffe kann den Übergang ferner durch Einsatz der 7.Flieger- (Fallschirm-) Div. vorbereiten. Die Division ist in etwa 4 Wochen (?) voll verwendungsfähig. Es stehen zu diesem Zeitpunkt jedoch nur etwa 7 Transportgruppen zur Verfügung, so dass die gesamte Division in einem Anflug <u>nicht</u> abgesetzt werden kann.

      Hieraus folgt, dass die Fallschirmkräfte für den ersten Überfall verhältnismässig gering sind, was eine Zusammenfassung nur an <u>einer</u> Übergangsstelle zur Folge hat. Die Wahl der Absetzstelle bedarf noch einer gründlichen Erkundung.

4)   Da der Übergang des Heeres sich nur sehr langsam vollziehen wird, ist eine rasche und laufende Verstärkung der zunächst eingesetzten Teile der Fallschirm-Div. notwendig. Hierfür stehen in erster Linie die restlichen Kräfte der 7. Flieger-Div. zur Verfügung.

      Ferner kann jedoch eine Unterstützung durch <u>Luftlandung</u> notwendig sein. Hierzu ist es erforderlich, geeignete Luftlande-Einheiten beschleunigt aufzustellen und für diese Zwecke auszubilden. Eine Anordnung für baldige Umwandlung der 22.I.D. zur Luftlande-Div. ist deswegen notwendig.

                      [gez.] Frhr. v.F.

Above: A Luftwaffe memorandum setting out the conditions required for a successful invasion of the United Kingdom.

the open, under constant fire, with no warm food and little sleep can only be truly appreciated by those who have had experience of such conditions. We lost more men from sickness than we did from the actual fighting, but we held out, beating off many enemy infantry assaults. On 26th May, under severe enemy pressure from three sides, we were forced to evacuate Narvik, but we did not let the enemy enter the town.

'It was the news from France that robbed our opponents of their élan and they became less aggressive. At last the Luftwaffe was able to airdrop supplies and Gebirgsjaeger and paratroops were dropped as reinforcements to fill the gaps in the ranks. By the beginning of June the enemy realized that he could not take Narvik and his forces withdrew back to England. The strategically important iron-ore town of Narvik had been held by us – the navy and by Dietl's Gebirgsjaeger. It was our victory.'

THE SEIZURE OF TRONDHEIM

Another success was gained when a naval group seized Trondheim. This account of the voyage and action was written by two former Naval officers, Oberleutnant Grosser and Leutnant Schmokel.

'"The ship is to be ready for sea by 0900 hrs tomorrow." At last the order which we had been anticipating. Something was obviously afoot and next morning when we paraded on the after deck the Captain warned us, in his address, that hard fighting was to be expected. As soon as he had finished speaking we began to prepare. The ward room was cleared and space made to accommodate the soldiers whom we were to carry. Three train loads of them arrived and boarded the ships of our flotilla. After dark there was a communal dinner and then we sailed out heading northwards.

'Next morning a wind force of between 7 and 8, brought heavy seas crashing over the bridge of our ship. Water flooded everywhere. For the soldiers it must have been a miserable experience. The bad weather also made for poor visibility but had the advantage that we were not spotted by British sea or air reconnaissance. We travelled at top speed and it seemed at first that our journey would be completed without incident. Then the bells rang for action stations. Six or seven heavy explosions shook the ship, probably aircraft bombs set to explode on impact. We were lucky, not one of them hit us.

'The protective cover of darkness fell quickly. We were thankful because although we were keen to fight the British we were in no situation to do this loaded up as we were with troops and equipment. The whole of that night and half the following day we sailed without interference from the British, but late the following afternoon as we were nearing Trondheim, our objective, the flotilla leader wirelessed that he was in action against a British

destroyer. We were ordered forward in support. "Clear the decks for action!", was not an easy task with our extra burden of men, but soon they were safely below the armoured deck while we sailors prepared for battle. The soldiers were able to follow its course by the commentary relayed over the Tannoy, as well as by the sound of our guns firing and noise of the enemy shells exploding in the sea. When the British saw our ship it was obvious they thought us to be one of their own cruisers. We soon put them right and salvo after salvo struck them. The enemy was not beaten easily and fired a number of torpedoes forcing us to take such strong evasive action that our ship heeled hard over for a time. But soon it was the British vessel which was lying on its side with its weapons silent. Our guns ceased firing and we set about rescuing the enemy sailors of whom about forty were taken from the freezing waters.

'It had been a good day for us so far but we still had ahead of us the passage up the Trondheim Fiord and the landing of the troops we carried. We knew that the entrance to the fiord was only a few hundred metres wide and that it was protected by heavy gun batteries. We would have to run the gauntlet in the dark but we were determined, if fired upon, to give the Norwegians as good as we got. In the dark night of 9th April, we took up formation with our destroyers in line astern of us. Our group moved slowly and silently, completely blacked out through pitch darkness towards the guns. Then the order came "Full speed ahead!" and simultaneously the challenge from a Norwegian patrol vessel. "What is your name?" There was a long silence before we slowly sent the word "Mustard". What we had to do was to gain time; twenty minutes at least. The Norwegians, as we had hoped, did not understand our signal and asked us to repeat it.

'By the time we had sent off the false name a second time we had rounded the dangerous point only to be caught in the beams of land-based searchlights. We shone our own searchlights at the enemy blinding them completely. Then the enemy guns opened up but the ship's armament dominated them and we passed without being hit. We had done it; we had passed through. A little way past the batteries some of our destroyers disembarked soldiers whose task it was to capture the guns to use against the British when they try to land.

'Soon we had arrived in Trondheim harbour and dropped anchor. The army units began to disembark. The town looked peaceful in the early morning light. Very soon we received word that our soldiers had occupied the town's strategic points. The mission had been successfully concluded; Trondheim had been reached and taken.'

THE SINKING OF *BLUCHER*

On that first morning of Operation 'Weser North', the Kriegsmarine suffered a grievous blow. The OKW communiqué dated 10 April, admitted that the cruiser *Blücher*, had been sunk on the previous day and told how she had replied to the fire of Norwegian coastal batteries. The communiqué continued, '. . . our ship's armament silenced the enemy battery but *Blücher* had been hit several times and badly damaged. The ship then steamed into a minefield and was lost . . .'

One of the soldiers aboard *Blücher* wrote an account which was published, first by his unit and, subsequently, in an armed forces yearbook. A photostat of the article was enclosed in a covering letter sent by E. Hauber, who wrote, '. . . As a young boy during the war, I read the accounts of what our men were doing, with pride and pleasure. The enclosed story was a particular favourite of mine.'

'The fight and end of the cruiser *Blücher*, by one who was there.

'Although the night is pitch-black, we soldiers shipped on the cruiser *Blücher* knew we had passed the Kattegat and were somewhere near Oslo Fiord. The crew is at action stations but like most of my army comrades I find it impossible to sleep. Standing on deck as *Blücher* enters the fiord we can just make out to the left and right of us sparse forested, snow-covered mountains . . . As our eyes become accustomed to the darkness we can see how narrow the fiord is and how close is the land on both sides of the ship. Slowly and completely blacked out, *Blücher* sails into the fiord. It is about midnight. Action stations is sounded. We soldiers are ordered below decks where we can do nothing but wait.'

Seamen who are trained to fight sea battles can submerge their natural fears by concentrating upon the duties for which they have been trained. Consider, however, the feelings of soldiers en route to fight and who are confined in the cramped and unfamiliar interior of a warship, particularly when that ship has to fight a sea battle. Unaware of what is happening, interpreting or often misinterpreting, every noise and each detonation, soldiers have no task upon which they can fasten their mind. No duty upon which they can turn their full concentration. They must wait until the sailors have won the battle or until the order comes that allows them to leave the dank and echoing vessel in which they have been transported.

Such were the experiences shared by many soldiers who fought in the Norwegian campaign. The opening stages of that operation afforded one of the rare opportunities for the German Army to be shipped overseas to fight, because the German soldier's usual theatre of operations was the continental land mass. For Operation 'Weser North' the German soldiers brought to battle by sea, were not carried in troopships, but in warships, vessels neither built to carry large bodies of troops nor designed for comfort. That was the situation which faced the soldiers sailing in *Blücher* and the story continues:

'Presently a sailor comes down and tells us that shore searchlights have caught *Blücher* in their beams. From what he says it seems we shall not be able to slink past the Norwegian defences undetected. There is a terrible crash and the whole vessel shakes. "That's it," said our officer. "Move to a lower deck, lads." He has hardly spoken when another frightful crash comes from the rear part of the ship and the steel plates on which we are standing vibrate alarmingly. "It must be our guns in action," says someone. We feel that *Blücher* must be returning the fire from the coastal battery. There is a fresh detonation, then another; the first one weaker, the second much louder. *Blücher* shudders alarmingly. The distant noises die away. Perhaps the enemy battery has ceased firing.

'But it is clear that *Blücher* has been hit. A mine, perhaps, or a torpedo. We do not know which. The ship slowly heels over and more slowly rights herself. Sailors bring down wounded men and lay them on scrambling nets. There is a constant metallic rolling and rumbling. Near us ammunition hoists are working so *Blücher* must still be action. The sailors moving the ammunition are sweating hard. "What's happening?" I ask one of them, but he is too busy to give me an answer. Once again *Blücher* heels over, but this time does not come upright again. Suddenly I am aware that the pulse of the ship has stopped. There is no gentle vibration of engines. I have the feeling that *Blücher* fought until the last heart beat.

'The group I am with is made up of fifty soldiers. We are unafraid although none of us has ever been in this situation, standing deep down in the bowels of a warship during a battle. A voice cries, "Fire!" and a sailor rushes toward the cry carrying an extinguisher in his hand. The fire must be aft of us because it is some time before smoke reaches our araa. "Everybody on deck!" comes the order. Things must be serious, but there is no panic. Daylight floods through a hole in the side of the ship. It comes as a shock to realize that it is daytime; just before six in the morning. We breathe in the fresh morning air. Land seems to be near, just beyond our fingertips. We clamber along the sloping deck and see that *Blücher* has heeled so far over that her port side is only about two metres above the sea's surface. Men come out of the forward part of the ship and group themselves along the starboard railings. The rear of the ship is burning fiercely. Thick clouds of smoke rise vertically into the air and spread over the fiord.

'We are not left long without orders. There is a group of small islands not far from us and our officer tells us that boats and liferafts will take us off the ship to one of the islands. There is an alarming, sharp whishing sound. Torpedoes are being fired off, so that they will not explode when the fire reaches them. Because of the angle of the ship the tubes lie almost vertical and as the torpedoes are fired they fly through the air before falling back into the water of the fiord, then surface and run to explode harmlessly two hundred metres away against the rocks of the fiord. We are told to undo our belts and to take off our overcoats and boots. A violet signal lamp on the top mast flickers and some way away down the fiord comes an answering signal. "The boats are coming to rescue us," someone says. We slide slowly down the deck to the port side of the ship and find sailors launching rubber boats and rafts. Everybody lends a hand and the task runs as smoothly as if we are on manoeuvres.

'The rubber boats fill with men. I lose my footing as I try to get into the craft and fall into the icy cold waters of the fiord. Although it is only a short row to the shore I am soon frozen through and my whole body shakes with the cold. As we paddle I turn round and see *Blücher*, now nothing more than a burning wreck. We land on one of the little islands, find a small summer house and soon the two rooms are filled with soldiers. I take off my wet clothes and massage warmth into my body. Some time later I leave the hut and go down to the shore where I witness the tragic spectacle of *Blücher* going down. The colossus which had been lying still in the water suddenly turns. Her bows dip, her stern rises sheer out of the water, turns slightly and then *Blücher* disappears into the deep.

'A chain of boats sets out to rescue the men in the water and to bring them back to our little island. Nobody says much. The loss of our lovely ship has affected us all but our officers soon have us organized. A fire is lit to dry wet clothing and the morning passes. In the afternoon the Luftwaffe comes. First one plane, and then a squadron and then still more. The islands on which the Norwegian guns are situated are bombed from the air. The fort begins to burn. We wave cloths, pants, handkerchiefs, anything to let the flyers know where we are marooned.

'During the afternoon a Norwegian coastguard vessel approaches the island. One of our officers gives us permission to board the enemy vessel and be taken as prisoners of war to Oslo, if we wish, but no one takes advantage of that offer. Help from our own side cannot be far off. On the shore a great fire has been lit around which men are cooking the fish which were killed by the explosion of the torpedoes that morning. On the roof of the little house a sailor has written in white paint the one word "Food", to let the airmen who fly at low level above us know what we need most. Another sailor has painted a red swastika on a white shirt. Anything to attract attention.

'Then the first German rescue ships arrive. We are saved. A motor boat ferries the groups from the shore to the waiting ships. On board we are given warm soup, eggs and grog after which we go to sleep. Well, we may have suffered a heavy loss in the sinking of the *Blücher*, but Oslo has been taken and when we wake from our sleep we learn that the most important places in Norway are in German hands. We have gained a splendid victory.'

ARMY ENGINEERS

The impression given to the German public at large and cultivated by the media, that the campaign in Norway had been fought and won largely as a result of the navy's self-sacrifice and by the heroism of Dietl and his men, annoyed many others who had served in the campaign. This selective emphasis by the Propaganda Ministry was used very often during the Second World War and each time it caused bitterness and resentment among those servicemen who were not named in the newspapers or on the wireless. It seemed to them that their efforts, their skill and their heroism were ignored in favour of a preferred minority.

Emil Grohl was in the engineers and saw action in an infantry division. He wrote in, not to describe an incident during the campaigns in which he had fought, but to suggest that the role of the army engineers in Exercise 'Weser North', had not been fully appreciated.

'The Engineers had a particularly difficult time during the Scandinavian campaign and the High Command must have been aware of the need for a higher than normal ratio of engineering troops in the campaign, because the War Establishment included not only field but also mountain and railway engineering companies. The speed of the campaign and the nature of the terrain meant that there was little mine laying or clearing, but there was a great amount of bridge building, constructing ones which were able to bear heavy vehicles. We also laid corduroy roads across swamps and muddy areas and carried out demolitions. Field companies were used principally on road works, improving surfaces to make them suitable for wheeled and tracked vehicles. Or, more usually, making roads where none had existed before, because in northern Norway roads were often little more than tracks. Those tracks had been adequate for peace-time civilian use, but for the movement of military vehicles, proper roads were required.'

It was the traditional role of German Army engineers to spearhead infantry attacks with explosive charges or close-quarter weapons such as flame-throwers. Emil Grohl remarked that there was little need for such specialized engineer activity in the Norwegian campaign. 'The terrain did not allow the use of major military formations. Most operations were carried out at regimental or even battalion level. For such missions there was enough infantry strength so that we engineers were not often called upon to act as assault infantry in the campaign.'

AFTERMATH

To conclude the accounts of Operation 'Weser–North', the final paragraphs of Franz Puechler's letter describes events after the fighting had ended.

'The countryside around here is very much like home. On both sides of the fiord the mountains, covered with ice and snow, rise sheer out of the water. We are so far north that the nights here are never completely black and the darkest part of the night lasts only an hour or two. Now that the campaign is over we have a lot of free time in which we go sailing. Mail is coming through quite regularly and we have a radio set. We get on well with the local population and there is plenty in the shops to buy, so we are quite content.

'A few days ago our company commander read out an Order of the Day that the Führer had awarded us a special decoration for the Narvik operation. This is to be in the shape of a shield bearing the name "Narvik", an edelweiss, an anchor and a propeller, with the date "1940". This decoration will be worn on the left upper arm. It is rumoured that our commander, General Dietl, will make the presentations himself, but I cannot believe that he will hand the shield out to every man in the division. I think he will make personal presentations to just representatives from each company or battalion of the division.'

It was mentioned in the destroyer officer's account that the British and French efforts to take Narvik lessened as a result of the campaign in France. This new war had opened in the second week of May and within days the *Blitzkrieg* had had disastrous effects upon the armies of the Western Allies. The military forces of Holland, Belgium and France were all subjugated in a series of swift operations and the British Expeditionary Force was forced to withdraw from the mainland of Europe. By the end of June 1940, Hitler was master of Europe.

OPERATION 'YELLOW'

As we have seen from the preceding section it had been Hitler's intention to open the war in the west immediately after the conclusion of the campaign in Poland. The differences in opinion between the Supreme Commander and Army High Command on the future conduct of the war, can be seen as early as 17 September 1939, when von Brauchitsch issued orders for the forces in the west to go over to a defensive posture.

The OKH rejection of Hitler's demand for quick action against the powerful Western Allies, was a logical decision. The Polish campaign, although brief, had disclosed certain tactical weaknesses and faults in equipment. These would have to be corrected before the Wehrmacht could with confidence launch a new campaign. Nor was it possible to carry out a change of fronts with the speed which Hitler demanded. He had no idea of the difficulties and complexities of such a major operation. OKH not only over-estimated French and British strength but was firmly against an escalation of a continental war into a world-wide conflict.

On 9 October, less than three weeks after the OKH memorandum, Hitler laid out his plans for the 'Conduct of the War in the West'. In this document, addressed to the Supreme Commanders of the fighting services, he stressed the successes which had been achieved by the Luftwaffe and the panzer arm which, as assault weapons had '. . . reached a level not attained by any other State . . .' He followed this memorandum with Directive No 6 which included the sentence, 'Thus I am resolved . . . to be active and aggressive . . .' Despite this intention the army chiefs knew that campaigning weather would not return until the end of April, by which time the relocation of formations, improvements in tactics and troop retraining would have begun and been completed. In his determination to control events Hitler ordered and cancelled the date of D-Day for the opening of the war in the west no fewer than twenty-nine times; moves which the Allies considered were part of a war of nerves.

A serious decision faced the planning staffs at both OKW and OKH. This was whether the strike in the west should be made along the traditional northern route or whether it should come via some other east/west thrust line. In the case of the first the German right-wing armies would advance across Holland and Belgium before changing direction and wheeling southwards to confront the Anglo-French armies. The German senior military commanders were all veterans of the Great War, as indeed was Hitler himself. Like him they had endured the years of stalemate produced by trench warfare and the efforts to break the military deadlock through large-scale and bloody offensives. They sought to avoid a war of attrition, aware as they were that Germany's manpower and material resources were insufficient to sustain a long and wasteful conflict. In that they were in accord with Hitler who intended to prosecute the whole war as a series of swift, decisive and victorious campaigns after each of which his forces could be re-equipped, reinforced and trained to fight a new enemy and to gain the next success on the road to total victory.

In view of Hitler's demands, a northern strike would not gain the quick victory over France which was required. A new route would have to be found through which France could be struck down swiftly – but where was such a route to be found? It was clear, even in the early planning stages, that Hitler rejected outright a re-run of the Schlieffen Plan, that is to say the northern route through Holland, Belgium and northern France. As early as the beginning of November the Führer was insisting upon a reinforcement of the mobile formations which would thrust towards Sedan. By the end of that month he was convinced that '. . . the planned attack in the west would be the greatest victory in the history of the world . . .' From the middle of January planning was concentrated upon a military decision being reached as the result of a break-through in southern Belgium. The choice of that region was due to the fact that the alternatives to a northward attack were westward thrusts, either out of the Mosel valley or else through the Belfort Gap. But France had constructed along her eastern frontier a modern system of fortifications, the Maginot Line. The Great War had demonstrated the strength of even simply constructed field fortification and how costly in casualties it was to take trenches in the face of a determined defence. The OKH planners, aware of the strength and depth of the concreted defences of the Maginot Line, must have felt that the German Army would bleed to death if it attempted to force that line. Those permanent defences, which ran from Switzerland to the French Ardennes, thus ruled out any attack against central or southern France.

There was, however, one gap along her eastern frontier through which France could be invaded. The Maginot Line ended in the French Ardennes and there were no strong defensive positions in the Belgian Ardennes. Contemporary military opinion considered that the region, one of high wooded hills and lacking an adequate road or rail network, was unsuitable for the passage of a modern army. It was that Allied miscalculation which was exploited by the German High Command.

Hitler as Supreme Commander was able to force through his ideas on the battle plan and OKH issued an order in November 1939, that the concentration of mobile formations, '. . . at or to the south-east of Sedan [were] to gain the west bank of the Maas so as to create favourable conditions for the continuation of the operation . . .' Concurrent with Hitler's own intention was the thinking of von Manstein, Chief of Staff of the Army, which agreed in broad outline with the Führer's proposals. '. . . the mobile formations . . . must pass to the south of Liège [and drive] towards Arras and Boulogne. Thereby [those forces] which the enemy puts into Belgium will not be attacked frontally . . . but will be cut off from the Somme. The southern wing must also be strong enough to fend off any French counter-attack against its left flank, so that the thrust to the coast can be completed . . .'

OKH remained unconvinced of the potential of von Manstein's plan. Then, on 17 March, he was ordered to report to Hitler and when asked by the Führer for his assessment of the situation described his idea in detail. At the end of the briefing Hitler had decided on von Manstein's plan, the most important part of which was the creation of an armoured fist; von Kleist's Panzer Group. This would provide the impetus for the thrust to the Channel ports as well as providing the flank guard against French attacks coming from south of the Somme. The Panzergruppe was composed of Reinhardt's 41 Panzer Corps on the right and Guderian's 19 Panzer Corps on the left with von Wietersheim's 14 Motorized Corps, the follow-up troops, ready to reinforce a successful thrust by either wing. To protect the northern, i.e., right, flank of the Panzer Group, was Hoth's 15th Panzer Corps, while farther north was Hoepner's 16 Panzer Corps and on its right wing, 9th Panzer Division serving with Eighteenth Army in Holland.

Von Manstein anticipated that the Allied reaction to a German attack through Holland and Belgium would be to advance their first line armies into the Low Countries. When that happened their back would be protected only by second-rate French troops against whom von Kleist's panzer fist must prevail. When the French broke and the panzer mass extended across northern France the Allied armies would be split and could be destroyed in detail. Those in Belgium and in northern France would be crushed first. Then would come the strike across the Somme to drive back the French armies positioned there on to the guns of Army Group 'C'.

Long before D-Day for the operation, 10 May 1940, the armies that were to carry out the assault were positioned and ready. Thanks to Germany's excellent rail and road network the whole force was echeloned in depth, a situation which not only hid the build-up from the Allies but also helped to confuse them as to where the German point of maximum effort would be. Those excellent road and rail systems did not exist in the steep, wooded hills of the Belgian Ardennes. That region was poorly served and it was expected that there would be difficulties in passing formations through the areas as well as maintaining supplies and follow-up troops. Lieutenant-Colonel Graber of the Supply Service wrote: 'To facilitate movement three roads were given the status of "*Rollbahn*" or highway and these were reserved for the use, either exclusively or as required, of the panzer formations. Once the panzer columns were clear of the obstructive terrain of the Ardennes, they could use the first-class network of roads in northern France and in Belgium. That road system was so extensive that there was no need to operate a *Rollbahn* system west of the River Maas.'

It was a campaign which contained several innovative features: the use of gliders to capture strategic targets in Belgium; of paratroops and air-landed formations and, more importantly, the employment of tanks in the mass. No military plan, so it has been written, should extend beyond the initial clash of arms and, certainly, Operation 'Yellow', for all the planning and the daring innovations, could have failed. That it did not was due to the determination of junior leaders. The leadership at regimental level together with the freedom of action enjoyed by the senior commanders enabled the German Army to fight and to win the campaign. OKH left the control of operations in the field to the commanders on the spot, aware that only they could judge the situation as it existed at the time and not as it appeared to be when viewed from a distant headquarters hours later. Guderian recalled: 'I receive no further orders as to what I was to do once we had secured bridgeheads across the Maas. All my decisions [from that point on] until I reached the Atlantic seaboard at Abbeville were taken by me and by me alone...'

Taking Guderian's panzer corps as a mark, his men had captured Bouillon by D-Day plus 2 and had gone on by last light of that day (12 May) to reach the eastern bank of the Maas. During the 13th the river was crossed and a barrier which the French had hoped to hold for a week went in a single day. *Blitzkrieg* was proving itself. It was helped in its early stages by the Nazi Party's deployment of its uniformed organizations. In Germany at that time there was not so strict an enforcement of the black out regulations as in the United Kingdom, and to aid the movement of troop convoys towards the frontier areas in preparation for D-Day, they were considerably relaxed as Rolf Steiner's letter shows:

'I had fought in the Great War and in 1940 was a member of the NSKK, the Nazi Party's Motorized Corps. It was in the first week of May that preliminary orders were issued from HQ in Bitburg to our unit. We were to parade on 9 May, and to bring with us rations for two days, our waterproof clothing, a torch and a map. Before we mobilized our officers had carried out a reconnaissance of the roads in our area. In the afternoon of the 9th, we paraded and were given a briefing. Small groups of us were to stand at each crossroads or road junction. We were given signs bearing large white letters and an arrow. Field telephone links were set up between each group and its local headquarters with more sophisticated links between local and higher HQs. We were told that what we were doing was a troop movement exercise which would last all night and probably well into the next day. Our most important task was to ensure that the motorized columns kept moving. Any vehicle that broke down was to be pushed to one side and kept there until a maintenance unit had been called for by telephone and got it running again.

'It was about 9 in the evening when the first column came along and I was surprised to see that they were driving on full headlights. The black out masks which were normally fitted had been removed and the headlights were blazing. The column – it was light armoured cars – drove past us at high speed. Then there was a telephone message telling us that there would not be another column for about an hour. We were to use the time as a meal break. At about 11.30 the telephone rang again ordering us back on duty – this time for lorried convoys which rushed past us non-stop until about 2 in the morning. We had no idea of where the convoys were going but thought they were doing a road test of driving skills. From 2.30 to 4 we had another break and it was already light when we left the inn where we had been eating our food. There was now no need for the vehicles to carry headlights, but we were still kept on duty to hold the lettered placards. Being old soldiers we soon worked out a roster, whereby some were on duty with the boards while the others slept. It must have been about 8 in the morning when one of the group turned on the radio. After a fanfare of trumpets there was the announcement that the army had begun operations in Holland and Belgium. Our first thought was that we had been taking part in a deception plan with vehicles driving on full headlights to make the enemy believe that the attack was being made on our sector. Imagine our delight when we eventually realized that our actions had not been part of a deception plan but the actual assault.'

Steiner's unit had been only one of many in action during the night of 9/10 May. To the north lads of the Hitler Youth had helped to build bonfires which laid a pathway of fire across Westphalia to mark out the route for the glider-towing aircraft and the transports filled with Fallschirmjaeger heading westwards to objectives in Belgium and in Holland. The Ju 52 'mother' aircraft, towing the gliders filled with airborne men who were to take out Eben Emael and the bridges in the area, cast off their 'daughters' at a height of 3,000 metres and then turned for home so that the noise of their engines would not alarm the Belgians. The DFS gliders had more than 25 kilometres to cover to the target areas and descended slowly out of the night sky to touch down as planned and on time. The German Army's operations plan had been dependent upon the glider landings around Eben Emael. Now these had been accomplished and the divisions, corps and armies that had been waiting moved into action. The time was just before 0530 and Operation 'Yellow' had opened.

The great mass of Army Group 'A' debouched out of the Ardennes and headed towards its first main objective – the Maas. Earlier paragraphs have shown that Guderian's panzer corps virtually 'bounced' that river barrier and had begun its drive to the Channel. His 19 Corps [2nd, 1st and 10th Panzer Divisions] advanced with its left flank resting on first the Aisne and then the Somme. Von Kleist's panzer group separated the Allied armies as von Manstein had intended and although the Anglo-French force in the north was strong it could not defeat the panzer mass. The dynamic leadership from the front, which was a characteristic of *Blitzkrieg*, was superior to battle by consensus which was the Allied method. The Anglo-French forces in Belgium were either destroyed or were constricted into a perimeter around Dunkirk.

OPERATION 'RED'

On 24 May, just as it seemed that the German armour was about to deliver the *coup de grâce* to the forces within the perimeter, Hitler ordered his armies to halt. Halder's caustic comment on Hitler's leadership throughout the battle is contained in the diary entries: '. . . . The Führer is terribly nervous.

Frightened by his own success he is afraid . . . unaccountably [he] keeps worrying about the southern flank . . .' Not all the units investing the Dunkirk perimeter obeyed the Führer's 'Halt' order. The Leibstandarte SS Adolf Hitler did not and 'Sepp' Dietrich, its commander, was taken to task for this disobedience.

The British Expeditionary Force was taken off the Dunkirk beaches by the Royal Navy and the rearguard, mainly French in composition, fought on until it was overwhelmed. The Allied hosts in the north had been destroyed or scattered. Holland and Belgium had capitulated. The German Army, no longer with an enemy at its back, could regroup for the second part of the war in the west. This operation, code-named 'Red', also known as the 'Battle of France', opened on 5 June.

The divisions of the panzer group attacked along the whole line with various degrees of success, but then OKH set two panzer groups, von Kleist's and Guderian's, side by side and sent them striking southwards on each side of Reims. This massive blow smashed through the enemy resistance and when the first German motorized units reached the Swiss frontier on 17 June, the French Army overwhelmed in a fast battle of pursuit, just fragmented. An armistice, asked for on 18 June, was in operation by the 25th. What the might of Imperial Germany with decades of preparation, planning and husbanding of resources had not achieved in four years, the Wehrmacht of the Third Reich, with only six years of preparation, had accomplished in less than two months.

BARRAGE ON THE WEYGAND LINE

One of the contributors to this book, Richard Stahlmann, who helped me with my book Last Days of the Reich, served as an anti-tank gunner in an infantry division and first saw action during the 1940 campaign in France. He wrote:

'It would seem that you favour an easy breaking in [of the soldier] to the privations of ground warfare. I do not think that is the right way. My own initiation was as easy as your own but it left me unprepared for the terrifying experience of Russia. The first part of the war in northern France had been concluded so quickly that my division did not enter the fighting. We marched a great deal and each night dug slit trenches and prepared our anti-tank gun ready for instant action, although none came. Until the first week of June our campaign experience had been limited to marching, digging in and mounting guard. We passed through villages that seemed deserted, as if all the inhabitants had fled. We knew they had not because here and there one saw civilian figures moving about.

'It was at the beginning of June when we marched into the area of the Somme and carried out a relief of another division. We were now in the combat zone but still there was no sight or sound of warfare, at least not from the enemy side. There was no shelling, no machine-gun fire and only the occasional aeroplane, which was soon chased off by our Messerschmitts. It was different on our side of the river. Things were very lively. Each night a stream of vehicles, guns and tanks moved into the combat area. On 4th June our anti-tank gun platoon was ordered down to the river bank to give direct support fire when the battle opened.

'We moved our guns into position that night and camouflaged them. Our orders were that there was to be no talking, smoking or fires. We were to lie in our slit trenches all night and all next day until the barrage opened. Then we could come out of cover, but even then we were not to move far as we might be called to action at any time. It was during that day that the French opened up with their big guns and although their shells did not fall among us but in our artillery belt they caused damage. It could not be otherwise considering the men, guns, horses and vehicles that were packed into the assault area.

'There was an Order of the Day read out, but we anti-tank gunners did not hear it until the following day. We were all lying in our slits pretending not to be there – in accordance with orders. The French called the defences on this sector the "Weygand Line" and these defences consisted chiefly of field fortifications. There were a few strong-points, but these were very old and dated from the war of 1870. Our division's orders were to cross the river and to build a bridgehead. The panzer units would break out from that bridgehead. A quarter of an hour before the barrage opened wireless silence was lifted and we in the forward positions were given final details over the radio of what was about to happen. Not far from us bridge-building units had brought up their material by night and assault engineers had carried their boats to the edge of the river. Everything was now ready.

'The barrage when it opened was an incredible sight. It was the first real bombardment most of us had seen. It began with a rumble of explosions behind us and then whistling sounds as the shells passed overhead to burst with splashes of bright light on the enemy across the river. Soon the whole of the area on the other side of the Somme was shrouded in smoke so that we could not see the shells exploding but only a fiery red where some house or farm had begun to burn. By now we were standing on the river bank watching a spectacle we had not seen before, fascinated by what we were seeing. Figures ran past us carrying rubber assault craft. The infantry were going into action. Ahead of them the Assault Engineers had already crossed the river and had disappeared into the clouds of smoke on the far side of the Somme. From the French positions there must have been a machine gun in action for a steam of tracer flew slowly overhead. The machine gunners must have been firing blind because they were not aiming at anything but were firing for effect.

'We heard later on that the French in their positions had survived the shelling and come out as our infantry closed in. The assault battalion of our regiment suffered very heavy losses but had taken the trenches from a Senegalese regiment which held them. The blacks had resisted heroically and there had been hand-to-hand combat in some places. Then, quite suddenly, the Senegalese had broken and just stopped fighting although their snipers were very active all day and had to be winkled out one by one. The other infantry regiment of our division crossed the river under quite heavy fire and lost a lot of men although, again, because of the smoke and the morning mist we did not see any fall. All we saw were figures climbing up the river bank and disappearing into the reeds and bushes along the bank.

'At 0700 hrs we were called to take post. The French were making a counter-attack with armour. We waited for several hours but apart from hearing shell and machine-gun fire we took no part in the fighting. The other Senegalese units of the Colonial Division facing us began to crumble under the pressure of the infantry and panzers which had crossed into the bridgehead. The black division just ran away. Strangely enough the soldiers took their boots off so that they could run more quickly.

'Our division rolled over the field defences of the Weygand Line and into the Champagne region of France. Two days later we anti-tank gunners received the order to move forward and cross the river. The smell of burned-out houses was very strong but there were no dead bodies to be seen. Our military police had organized the Senegalese into burial details and had had to be very firm because at first they had refused to do this type of work.

'My introduction into the soldier's trade had been a very easy one. I saw a battle, but took no part in it, saw no dead bodies and not even wounded men although our division suffered quite heavy losses in this, its first action. The only sights of war were the burned-out houses and the only sounds the shellfire and the machine-gun fire which passed over and caused us in the anti-tank gun platoon no casualties. As I said this easy battle had not prepared me for the horrors I encountered during my first battle in Russia.'

OPERATION 'SEALION'

After the signing of an armistice with France there was no nation on the mainland of western Europe to challenge Germany. Those countries that she had not subjugated by force of arms were anxiously neutral and hopeful of remaining so. The United Kingdom remained, as yet, unassailed. The Republic of Ireland was neutral but had, if not a pro-German then at least an anti-British, bias.

'A group of islands remained as yet unassailed.' Therein lay the problem which faced the Führer. Should he attack Britain or not? His first inclinations were to hope that the British Government, aware of the country's hopeless military position, would accept his offer of peace and bring the war to an end. Working along the line of reasoning that conciliation might influence the population of Great Britain, he ordered a reduction in the scale of air operations in the UK area and forbade the bombing of the British mainland. If Hitler at that time was uncertain of what he should do this was because events had moved so suddenly. Hermann Goetzel was a Captain and a company commander of Fallschirmjaeger. Recalling those days he wrote:

'During the planning of the campaign against France in 1940, neither Hitler nor the German General Staff reckoned with the need to attack the British Isles at the end of the campaign. We were not prepared mentally for such an enterprise. Hitler had evidently drawn the wrong conclusions from British political attitudes and intentions . . . When at last plans were issued for Operation "Sealion" much valuable time had been lost. Lacking any sort of planned preparation one had to depend upon improvisation . . . Whether Hitler had any serious intention of carrying out "Sealion" is doubtful. He had a reluctance to undertake operations overseas. The pre-history of the Crete operation and the abandoning of the planned attack upon Malta would seem to confirm this.'

Luftwaffe General Deichmann, at the time Chief of Staff of 2nd Flieger Corps, believed that there had never been a real intention to invade Britain. He bases this on the fact that when Admiral Raeder spoke about a landing in Britain, Hitler rejected it as 'impossible to carry out'. The wording of Hitler's Directive of 16 July, contained, in Deichmann's words the unusual sentence, 'I have decided to prepare a landing operation and, if necessary, to carry this out . . .' The General's opinion is that the measures taken for 'Sealion' were political pressure applied to the British to force them to make peace. As he sees it, 'There is no other explanation why an operation which he had described as impossible should become possible within the space of three months.' To develop his theme Deichmann cites the introduction to the OKW Directive of 7 August, which contains the phrase 'Whether and if we land in England . . .' One does not, in Deichmann's opinion, '. . . use such words if one is resolved upon a course of action . . . I can remember', he continued, 'that the impression which I received from this order was that we would not undertake a landing. One must also bear in mind that this Directive was issued before the air war expanded . . . The only connection between the expansion of the air war against Britain, a purely political aim, and of "Sealion" is that Directive No 17 contained the order that the Luftwaffe was to remain fit for action. That goes to prove my belief that the expansion of the Air War and "Sealion" were two independent tasks . . . As Chief of Staff of 2nd Flieger Corps, which served at the main point of the Battle of Britain and who controlled the Fighter mass during the first phase of the operation, I see "Sealion" and the Battle of Britain as two completely separate projects.'

It would seem, however, that some people were thinking about an assault upon the United Kingdom. Late in 1939 OKH, perhaps to exercise its own mind and that of its sister services, asked for comments on 'Study Northwest – a proposed invasion of Great Britain', which it had produced. The Luftwaffe High Command reply was brief and negative. 'The planned air landings would be made at the point where the enemy's air defences are strongest. Even allowing for the fighter strength which would be available [to us] in the summer of 1940, we should still not have sufficient to succeed. The planned operation can only be considered within a framework of absolute air superiority and even then only when surprise can be guaranteed.' The conclusion to this brusque rejection reads, '. . . a combined operation whose objective is a landing in Great Britain must, therefore, be rejected. It should only be made as the final act of an already successful war against England, for otherwise the pre-conditions for the success of a combined operation do not obtain.'

Lord Halifax's laconic rejection of Germany's offer of peace was taken by Hitler as a deliberate insult and the Führer decided upon 'Sealion'. He knew with what speed his Command staffs could produce a battle plan and his Directive No 16, ordered that active planning be undertaken. What he did not anticipate was being dragged into a dispute between OKH and OKL. The army demanded the widest possible assault area because a narrow one, in Halder's view, would be tantamount to 'putting the troops through a mincing machine'. The navy pointed out that it lacked escort vessels for the width of front demanded by OKH and asked the Führer for a decision. On one thing all parties were agreed; there could be no successful invasion without superiority in the air over Britain. The senior commanders of the Luftwaffe had no doubt they could achieve this with little difficulty although they accepted that the RAF would not be caught on the ground and there destroyed as had been the case in Poland. It would, therefore, be necessary to crush Fighter Command in aerial battle. 'Thereafter', in the words of a Luftwaffe memorandum, 'the bombers will be able to attack the centres of British industry, to operate against shipping bringing in supplies to British ports and to support the army in its field operations to the north of London.'

Hermann Goetzel described a War Game organized by Colonel General Busch, commanding Sixteenth Army, which had as its base line the situation as it would be on D-Day plus 4. The premise was that air superiority would have been gained by that time. Things did not, in fact, develop as the two hundred participating commanders had anticipated. The air superiority which each service had insisted upon as a sine qua non for a successful invasion never materialized.

During the time that the Battle of Britain was being fought Hitler had already decided to attack the Soviet Union, but, in an obvious attempt at a war of nerves, allowed the planning of 'Sealion' to continue. Among the units committed to practising the now pointless invasion exercises was 1st Gebirgs Division. Alfred Spies's unit was stationed just behind the Channel coast. He wrote:

'We had been trained in Alpine warfare and the task we would face when we landed in Hastings would have been very easy for us. We were to disembark, cross the shingle beach and scale the cliffs which are behind the promenade. Part of our training had been to drive British Army lorries – captured during the campaign in France and from the Dunkirk beaches. In that way we would be able to use British vehicles once we had broken out of the bridgehead. After we had carried out the first landing on the beach at Hastings we were to move inland.'

Orders issued by 7 Corps confirm this. Paragraph 6 of those instructions, dated 10 September, that is to say when Hitler had already turned his mind eastwards, includes the sentence, '. . . The first rule for all leaders and men is that immediately upon landing on the English coast, efforts must be made to reach a line at least 2 kilometres from the beach . . .'

PREPARING FOR OCCUPATION

As if it were not farcical enough that men and machines were being trained for an invasion that would not take place, consider the SD Detachment Wolff, which was formed in order to act as a provisional government in England. The recruiting methods were bizarre. More emphasis was laid upon adherence to Party doctrine than to any other likely essential qualification. For example, candidates enlisting into this highly secret body were required to have a knowledge of English, of England and of the way of life in these islands. Included among those who were accepted as meeting this qualification was a man whose knowledge of England was limited to a weekend spent in Yorkshire, made several years before the war. Another man spoke English which was heavily accented with Boer overtones for he had spent a long time in South Africa. Another's command of English was limited to conventional expressions, halting and fragmentary. To begin with the unit was incorporated into a Waffen SS battalion. 'We asked who these people were,' recalled one former member of the unit, 'because they were obviously not part of our organization. We were told to mind our own business. Then, one day they were gone.' They had been posted to a quieter place where lessons in Nazi political dogma were the principal tuition, followed by lectures on Trades Unionism, Freemasonry and the British political system. There were practical lessons on using small arms, and many instructions, such as the one which directed that upon arrival in England the SD members were to obtain civilian clothes from British tailors. The group's billets were to include the Strand Palace Hotel and a club in St James's and they would avail themselves of the archives and facilities of Scotland Yard to combat any resistance movements.

In connection with the SD group obtaining civilian suits before they arrived in London, it is interesting to note from Appendix No 4 to Corps orders that: '[In order] to avoid a strain on the supply services from the mainland of Europe, troops are to live off the land. The need of the troops takes priority over those of the civil population. Receipts in the German language will be given for all materials taken for the prosecution of the war (food, fuel, etc.,) as well as payment for any services performed by the civil population. The removal of any object for private purposes without payment will be considered as looting and will be punished accordingly.'

'The question which must have been uppermost in the mind of those who were Fallschirmjaeger at the time [of "Sealion"] and who would have had to fly the mission, must have been, for how long they would have to hold out without support? Lightly armed para and glider troops may be able to drop and seize an objective using combat aggression and surprise. It is another thing to hold the objective against every type of heavy weapon that the enemy can bring up. Experience in Holland in 1940 had shown that it had taken three days for the army to link up with the Paras and that the Jaeger had been found to be physically exhausted. The question must have been, how long would it take the panzers and heavy weapons to be brought across the Channel? Every soldier knows he has to take risks in battle. None, however, is keen to go into a fight from which there will be no survivors. A Himmelfahrtskommando [a suicide mission] is not something one enters into in cold blood.' (R. Hoffmann)

Among the units created for the first phase of the 'Sealion' assault were flame-throwing tanks 'These were of two types – standard and submersible. I served on the standard version and our training was connected mainly with embarking and debarking from the ferries. These were very unstable craft which dipped when we boarded and which wallowed in even a light sea. They frightened me. I was afraid that they would capsize and that we crew would be trapped and drowned. I had heard that some standard tanks were sealed around the turret to prevent seepage in the event of a wet landing. The tanks in our Troop were not sealed in that way. We expected to roll off the ferry and on to the beach near St Leonards.'

As the days of inaction turned into weeks OKM warned that favourable weather and tide conditions were limited to a handful of days. Unless an invasion took place before October the chance would be lost until the following spring. This ultimatum forced Hitler to make a decision. He confirmed that no invasion attempt would be made in 1940, because the preconditions for a successful undertaking had not been gained. Instead he would launch a quick war against Russia and once that had been won would come back to deal with the stubborn British.

As the wind-down continued without word that the operation had been cancelled, the SD group members were reduced to writing internal memoranda on the type of piping and braid that would be carried on uniform shoulder-straps. Alfred Spies's division marched away from the Channel coast leaving a battle group to train for an attack on the rock of Gibraltar – another aborted mission – and the mass of the army moved east to prepare for the new war with Russia. Then a new crisis arose. Italy, whose troops had invaded Greece, suffered a defeat at the hands of the outnumbered Greeks, to whose aid Britain then sent an expeditionary force. The British were back on the mainland of Europe and this alarmed Hitler. In the middle of the preparations to invade Russia he now had, thanks to Mussolini's incompetence, to intervene in the Balkans.

There remains as an epitaph of Operation 'Sealion', Hitler's bitter comment in 1944, to Engineer General Jacob, 'If I had only listened to my Engineers and not to the Navy, the invasion of Britain would have succeeded and the war would have been ended long ago.'

Lebensraum in the East, 1941

OPERATION 'MARITA'

For a period of almost a year after the surrender of France the German Army was not involved in active military operations. During that period of time the Luftwaffe fought the Battle of Britain and the Kriegsmarine continued to send out its U-boats and commerce raiders. In one famous surface action the German Navy gained a victory when *Bismarck* sank the British battleship HMS *Hood*, but suffered a crippling loss when *Bismarck* herself was destroyed. But the army, except for planning a number of missions which were then aborted, remained inactive until General Rommel took his divisions into a new continent – Africa.

Although the army was not involved in ground fighting in Europe, OKH was planning new campaigns. The one which was due to open in April 1941, Operation 'Marita' was planned to counter the British re-entry into the continent of Europe. A new BEF, drawn from units of Wavell's desert army, had entered Greece to support that ally in her fight against the Italian invaders. Hitler and OKW understood well the British strategy behind this move. The RAF component of the BEF now had bases on the European mainland from which to bomb the oil wells of Ploesti. The British had to be expelled from the Balkans if the oil supplies, essential to fuel the German war machine for the imminent campaign in Russia, were to be assured.

Only days before Operation 'Marita' was to be launched a crisis arose which expanded the parameters of the Greek operation. In the last week of March 1941, Paul, Prince Regent of Yugoslavia was overthrown and the young King Peter renounced the Treaty which Paul had so recently signed in Berlin. In Hitler's eyes this was base betrayal and he ordered that the attack upon Yugoslavia was to '. . . smash her as quickly as possible . . .' Within two days the Army High Command had produced a battle plan. Forces positioned in Austria, in Hungary and in Bulgaria were to strike from four directions to capture the capital Belgrade and to prevent a link up between the easternmost formations of the Royal Yugoslav Army and the Anglo/Greek forces.

The speed with which High Command planned and opened the campaign against Yugoslavia provides an excellent example of staff work. German Second Army, stationed in southern Austria, received sudden and totally unexpected orders to take part in the forthcoming operation. High upon the list of army's imperatives was the capture intact of the bridge across the Mur at Radkersburg and orders descended swiftly through the echelons of command to the battalion selected for the task. Battalion organized a fighting patrol to carry out a surprise attack, the success of which would open the way for Second Army to flood into Croatia and head toward the capital.

ADVANCE ON BELGRADE

'An Oberfeldwebel from our battalion carried out the assault and for it he was awarded the Knight's Cross . . . An account of his action was printed in the divisional newspaper and this read that the NCO had inspected the objective through binoculars and had realized how strongly protected it was. There was a large garrison of soldiers and armed officials occupying a Customs post on the far side of the bridge and on a low ridge, behind the customs post, there was a bunker with a field of fire which dominated the approaches to the iron bridge as well as the bridge itself.

'The Oberfeldwebel's plan was to take his patrol by assault boat across the fast-flowing Mur, entering the water some distance below the bridge. He would then take out the enemy positions from the flank. At dawn on 6th April his group launched their craft and began to paddle. Before they were half way across the river an alert Yugoslav sentry saw them and opened fire. There could now be no question of a surprise attack. Now it would be a matter of speed and determination. Half swimming and half wading the patrol reached the enemy bank and almost immediately came across a sentry near the customs post. The Yugoslav soldier was paralysed with fear. He was shot down and then the Oberfeldwebel rushed past the dead body and flung hand-grenades in at the windows. The men inside the building surrendered.

'By this time the soldiers in the bunker had opened fire and our battalion's engineers could not cross the bridge to take out the explosive charges. One of the battle patrol spotted the detonating cable and cut it with the blade of his entrenching tool. The sergeant fired a Very light to signal that the patrol was going into the last stage of the operation – the capture of the bunker. The patrol members gave the NCO covering fire as he charged forward and flung explosive charges into the slits in the walls of the bunker. When the smoke cleared there was no longer any fire coming from the defenders. The shock which the Yugoslav soldiers in the bunker had suffered did not last long, but in that short time the engineers took out the fuzes and an infantry company stormed across the bridge to reinforce the battle patrol. The bunker was taken. The road forward was clear for Second Army.' (Alois Redl. Oberjaeger)

BREAKING THE METAXAS LINE

The resistance of that first morning at Radkersburg was not repeated all the way along the battle nor was it met during the succeeding days of the campaign. There were, in fact, many units of Second Army which did not fire a shot in the eleven-day war against Yugoslavia which opened on the 6th and ended on 17 April. Operation 'Marita', the war against Greece, had begun on the same day but had not, however, been so swiftly concluded nor had the German Army trapped the Anglo-Greek formations in northern Greece as had been planned. The Allies fought a series of delaying actions, battles which although often brief of duration were bitter in intensity.

One of the longest and certainly the most bitter battle of the Greek campaign was the offensive by 18 Gebirgs Corps (5th and 6th Gebirgs Divisions), to break the Metaxas Line, a system of permanent fortifications, built to bar a Bulgarian invasion into the heartland of Greece.

'For several days we had been waiting in the mountains which separate Bulgaria from Greece and during the night of 5/6 April, moved forward to assault positions just below the crest. The night was bright, clear and bitterly cold and we lay out on the open slopes for the better part of six hours. At 0520 hrs the war began and we moved forward into the attack. Ahead of us our artillery was shelling the Greek main positions which we had been told were concrete bunkers, well sited and mutually supporting. Our officers had warned us not to under-estimate the Greeks. They were good warriors, holding first class positions. None of us realized at the time that it would take four whole days to break the enemy. Our infantry attacks, artillery barrages, even air bombardments by Stuka squadrons, had little effect upon the Greek defenders.

'During one attack our assault engineers, armed with flame-throwers and explosive charges, had taken out one bunker. The strain of the battle had its effect and having driven out the Greek defenders we sat down on the ground totally exhausted. My life nearly ended at that point. From out of nowhere, or so it seemed, a company of Greek infantry came charging at us with bayonets fixed. It was an absolutely frightening experience as the enemy charged down the slope towards us. I had not seen enemy soldiers close up before, but now they were frighteningly close. Then one of our machine-gun groups went into action and, almost as if being awakened from a dream, the rest of us opened fire. We killed all the enemy soldiers before they could reach us with their bayonets and fight us hand to hand.'

The heroism of the Greek units holding the Metaxas Line delayed Twelfth Army, but in other parts of Greece German advances reached the point where the Line was outflanked and its usefulness was at an end. The German offensive then pushed on, obstructed but not halted by the Greek, British and Imperial forces who fought one delaying battle after another as they were pushed southwards towards Athens and Corinth. Harry Keilhaus, who served in the operations section of an infantry division, wrote: 'It must be admitted that the British campaign to slow down our advance was, by and large, very successful. As they withdrew, in leap-frogging moves, they left rearguards which then held our division's advance. As soon as we had regrouped to renew our attack the British units which had held us would slip away at night and behind them there would be another rearguard holding another important height. So it went on day after day. At Themopylae the British rearguard held the German advance for five whole days.

'At Thermopylae the gap between the sea and the mountains was a first class defensive position and a skilful commander like Wilson, in charge of resolute soldiers, the cream of Britain's Imperial army, exploited to the full the strength of that position. We received reports that ships in Piraeus harbour were loading with British units and it was vital that our forces overhaul and capture those fleeing Tommies before they could embark and escape. The rearguard at Thermopylae held us until a great many units had pulled across the Corinth Canal and into the Peloponnese. To stop the remainder escaping, OKW mounted a para/glider drop to capture the Corinth bridge. The attack upon the bridge was successful but those British who had already crossed the canal escaped to Egypt and to Crete.'

The following post-battle report by No 3 Company of Leibstandarte SS 'Adolf Hitler' was written by a former member of the Regiment (as it then was) and appears in the Leibstandarte history published by Munin Verlag. The advance of the SS Standarte had been held at several places by the determined resistance of Imperial units and in particular in the area of the Klidi Pass.

'At 1800 hrs Witt's battlegroup, reported that No 3 Company which had gone forward to reach Ptolemais had reached the entry to the [Klidi] Pass. It had encountered strong enemy opposition coming from field fortifications set up on the high ground on both sides of the road. The road forked. The left arm rose towards the village of Vevi, the right fork twisted towards the Klidi Pass. No 3 Company had the task of thrusting through the pass. Before it reached the level ground at the end of the pass, [it was] to halt and to take up positions against possible enemy attacks. Our battle patrol was led by Ustuf. Witt, a brother of the battalion's commanding officer.

'A motor-cycle combination headed the group. Then followed the patrol leader's car, then a 3.7 flak on a self-propelled gun carriage and a half-track carrying a platoon group and, finally, the first vehicles of the platoon. The motor-cycle combination dropped out with a puncture less than a kilometre from the objective and the AFV moved past it. Suddenly there was an explosion in front of us and enemy machine-guns opened up. We flung ourselves out of the vehicle and dived into wet ditches [on either side of the road]. The vehicle drivers could not turn the trucks on the road. We kept our heads well down until the "gentlemen from the other side of No-Man's Land" quietened down a little. The first aid men came puffing up to us and told us that the three people in the car, Witt, Koch and Branhoff, the driver, were dead. Witt had been still alive when the stretcher bearers reached him . . . The CO's vehicle had run over a mine. That detonation must have unnerved the crew of the SP because they abandoned the vehicle leaving the driver to defend it with a pistol. Then, he removed the breech-block of the gun and took it with him as he, too, left the area . . .

'At 2200 hrs No 3 Coy disengaged from the enemy and dug in . . . At 2230 No 2 Platoon of 1st Company met strong enemy opposition near Vevi . . . 0200 on 11th April. No 1 Company is fired on. Enemy fire comes from along the whole length of the heights between Vevi and Keli and the main defence was based on 15 machine-guns backed by mortars. Later that night medium artillery reinforced the enemy defenders . . .'

OPERATION 'MERCURY'

However tenacious the British and Imperial rearguard actions were, the German advance could not be halted and the campaign in Greece ended on 29 April. There was no rest for the German soldiers. Reinhold Hoffmann recalled a new song being sung: 'We have swept the Tommies from the Continent.' He continues:

'Europe, so the Party papers said, was once again under German control and in Africa, too, there had been dramatic developments. Erwin Rommel and the Afrika Korps had flung back General Wavell's desert army and was racing for the Suez Canal. If we Fallschirmjaeger could land at Suez and link up with Rommel, the war in Africa would be won. The difficulty was that Germany had no staging post in the eastern Mediterranean from which an assault [upon Suez] could be launched. Nor were our aeroplanes capable of flying non-stop from Greece to Egypt and back. Finally, we did not have a vast number of transport machines. The pre-condition to any assault upon the Suez Canal was the capture of an island between Athens and Egypt. The most obvious one was Crete. The orders were that we of 7th Flieger Division were to seize the island by para drop and glider landing.

'As I wrote earlier in this letter, the Luftwaffe did not have sufficient transport aircraft and could not, therefore, carry the whole assault wave in a single drop. As a consequence, the plan was for two waves of Jaeger; the first going in at dawn and the second later in the morning. This second assault was subsequently postponed until the afternoon. We were supported by a back-up division, not 22nd Airlanding, our sister division in Corps, but by 5th Gebirgs. Because of the shortage of aircraft it was anticipated that the first elements of 5th Gebirgs Division would not be flown in until D plus 1, at the earliest.

'Our officers made it clear that it was the Fallschirmjaeger task to capture the island and we accepted this. We said in jest that our follow-up division would arrive in time to take part in the ceremonial parade to mark the end of the campaign. In those days we were very lightly armed with none of the recoilless artillery and rocket-propelled weapons of later years. We could not take our heavy weapons – artillery and anti-tank guns – in the aircraft with us. The Ju 52 could not carry such loads. The heavy weapons would have to come by sea, but again our mood was so optimistic that we thought we Fallschirmjaeger by ourselves would be enough to bring the British and Greek defenders of Crete to their knees.'

REINFORCED BY SEA

The island was invaded by airborne forces but the paratroops were at first only able to establish small bridgeheads. In order to defeat the defenders and to capture the island a fast back-up force, equipped with heavy weapons was needed. To General Student's dismay the 22nd Airlanding Division, which had been the back-up formation during the 1940 campaign, could not be made available and 5th Gebirgs Division was substituted. This formation had gained an excellent reputation in the Greek campaign and in view of terrain conditions on Crete, was the logical choice for OKW to make. It was intended to airlift the 5th's Gebirgsjaeger regiments to the island once the Fallschirmjaeger had established firm bridgeheads. Oswald Jahnke writes:

'Much of what I now know of Operation "Mercury", I have only learned since the end of the war. At the time of the operation we, the ordinary Gebirgsjaeger, knew nothing of the planning involved or why we had been chosen for the task. All those things we were to learn in later years and as a result of that post-war reading it is clear that when our division was selected for the Crete mission our General was given less than three weeks to organize its part in the operation. Planning the ground operations was the last link in the chain. We had first to reach the island before we could fight on it. We know now that the Luftwaffe had too few transport aircraft to carry both 7th Flieger Division and ourselves. The paras were to drop and to capture airfields. Then we Gebirgsjaeger would be brought in by air and the artillery and other heavy weapons would be brought by sea.

'Although General Ringel had full authority to requisition the vessels which he needed, he received little help from the navy in the choice of craft. The convoy in which I sailed was made up of caiques – sailing vessels fitted with an auxiliary engine. The Greek crews had to be pressed into service. Some deserted before we sailed and to make good the losses we were given Italian naval personnel.'

Because of the low speed of the caiques and so that the support weapons would be immediately available to the paras when they dropped, the sailing component left the Greek ports two days before D-Day.

'We boarded our caique in Piraeus harbour. It was a small, smelly vessel harbouring a wide variety of tenacious insect life. Most of us decided to sleep on deck rather than go down into the vermin-ridden hold. We set sail after dark and hugged the coast. The sea was slight but the ship rolled alarmingly, probably due to the artillery pieces on the deck, which had altered the centre of gravity. Once we reached the open sea it became calmer and our caique rolled less. There was a lot of creaking and other noises as the ship chugged slowly along. We were forbidden to smoke on the deck and as there was nothing to see but waves, most of us lay down, wrapped our greatcoats around us and tried to sleep.

'Suddenly and without warning the sky was filled with brilliant white parachute flares which lit up whole areas of the sea. That blinding light lasted for about three minutes and when it died the night seemed to be darker than before. Then searchlights swept across the water and fixed on the ship ahead and to our port side. We saw several flashes from behind one of the beams and soon realized that these must be from enemy guns because soon shells began to explode on that caique. Soon she was alight and we could see our boys jumping into the sea. Our ship was illuminated by the fire and the lieutenant told us to put on our life-jackets and to remove our heavy, nailed boots. Barely had we done this when we too were caught by the searchlights and shells began to hit our ship. Some of our group took away the wooden partitions [bulwarks] and we formed two ranks. Our officer called "Good luck boys!" and ordered the first rank to jump into the sea. I was in the second rank and we had to wait until the first rank was clear of the ship's side. While we were waiting we were ordered to cut the lines on the life-rafts and to fling the rafts overboard. When we had done that we in the second rank formed up and jumped into the sea which was only two metres below us.

'All this happened in less than five minutes from the first ship being held by the searchlight to our jumping into the sea, but just as when one has a car accident, everything seemed to slow down so that it seemed as if hours had passed. The water was very cold and the shock of it took my breath away. Not far from me my section corporal was calling us to rally to him. The other NCOs were doing the same. Some men joined their groups towing behind them large pieces of wood and our lieutenant ordered that the wounded and the non-swimmers were to be put on to them. Those of us in the water joined hands so that we would not be swept away and also to give us mutual comfort. All round us there were burning ships: a terrifying sight. Few of us had ever been on board ship in our lives and we could not imagine that we would be rescued. We just hoped and prayed that we would.

'It was a very long, cold night. The cold started at the toes and then worked up the legs, into the stomach and chest. The whole body seemed to be turning into a block of ice. During the night some of the wounded died and we lost men from the circle as well. At dawn the officer said that soon the sun would warm us and that the Luftwaffe would sent out aircraft to look for us. It must have been about 8 in the morning when we saw the first seaplanes. They swooped over us and one of them fired off a signal flare. Not long after that a plane landed some distance from us. We were hauled aboard and given hot tea with rum. On the plane some of us became sea sick. We had not felt sick while we were in the sea, but the plane's motion upset us. After a thirty-minute flight back to Greece we were taken to a field hospital for examination.

'Two days later I landed on Crete – this time by Ju 52. It was there I fired English 25pdrs in action. We had been trained to use enemy weapons for just such an eventuality. These guns had been captured in the first days of the campaign and as our own had been lost when the convoy was sunk, we used the enemy's weapons against him.'

R. Pichler, another Gebirgsjaeger, wrote of his experiences during that sea journey.

'The High Command communiqué gave details of the action in which we were involved and this read, in part, "The first attempt, on 21st May, to bring reinforcements to Crete using motorized sailing vessels, was thwarted by the intervention of British light naval forces. In this operation British propaganda claimed to have killed thousands [of German troops]. In fact it was less than 200."

'We sailed out of Piraeus in the evening of 19th May, reached Milos during the evening of the second day's sailing and took course southwards to Crete. The convoy of twenty-one caiques was escorted by an Italian torpedo-boat . . . An alarm, false as it later turned out, forced us to return to Milos and later in the day the convoy changed course again, once more heading for Crete. As a result of these contradictory orders we did not reach Crete in daylight, as we could have done. Had we done so we would have arrived under the protection of the Luftwaffe, but instead we were still heading for the island when night fell. We were to learn that the enemy navy operated with safety in the hours of darkness.

'Shortly before last light a strong south-westerly wind whipped up the sea, which had been until then relatively calm and there was a heavy swell. Towards 2230 hrs, there was the sound of explosions which woke those of us sleeping on deck. Then we saw a huge shadow on our starboard side. That large vessel was obviously a warship. A searchlight beam from the port side caught us. Then the searchlights went out and the night was lit only by one blazing caique. The enemy ships opened fire and it was soon clear that we were caught in a sea battle between our Italian escort vessel on the western side and the Royal Navy ships to the east.

'Things happened very quickly. We tried to escape by taking a south-easterly course but we seemed to be heading towards another naval battle. There seemed to be fighting going on all round us. We could see to the north-east of us, caique after caique hit and burning and lighting up the night sky. Quite suddenly the firing ceased and as the caiques sank there was darkness again.

'Course was changed to the south-west, our original course, and then the engine stopped. We had broken down but our Italian engineer soon had us moving again and with the motor running we breathed more easily. During the 20 minutes or so that we had no power we drifted helplessly and were nearly run down by a large ship which loomed out of the darkness. We sailed on with our nerves on edge. Most of us had fitted on two life-jackets, the wounded had all been provided for and we had taken off our heavy mountaineering boots. We were ready, if need be, to abandon ship taking our wounded with us. Two men equipped with knives stood by the ship's railings ready to cut the ropes holding in position one large and four small life-rafts.

'We altered course northwards and passed behind a large ship which suddenly blew up. It was clear she must have been loaded with ammunition. Then we turned eastwards leaving the blazing wreck behind us. To the south there was suddenly a violent explosion and three searchlights came on. Luckily their beams were directed westwards where a group of vessels from our convoy were illuminated and fired on. Our ship's motor stopped again. This time for a longer period. We turned our boat with its dead engine back on a northern tack and drifted with the waves. Suddenly our engine started up again and we steamed off changing direction several times. Behind us British searchlights swept backwards and forwards across the sea. The moon rose at 0300 hrs and we were afraid that we might be sighted. We prayed for daylight so that the Luftwaffe could attack the enemy ships. At about 0400 hrs we saw a German aeroplane, probably on reconnaissance, and felt that the Luftwaffe had saved us. The waves had gone down and so we sailed across a millpond sea to Milos. It was a glorious morning.'

A short time after the end of the campaign Leutnant Andreas Steiner of the Fallschirm Pioniere wrote an account of the action to a friend. This extract from his letter describes the voyage to Crete on board a caique carrying the heavy weapons of the Assault Pioniere:

'The belief expressed by our senior officers that the airborne assault would be sufficient [to capture Crete] proved false. We were ordered to board the caiques. Experiences gained from the Norwegian campaign showed it was best to load one platoon on each ship. I was with No 2 Platoon and Company Headquarters Troop on the fastest ship which made 6 knots, maximum. Our departure was scheduled for the evening of D-Day minus 2 [D-Day was 20 May]. That was then cancelled, which meant that we would arrive in Crete 32 hours after the initial airborne landings had been made. According to rumour the delay was because the entire British Mediterranean fleet had sailed from Alexandria and was heading for Crete.

'The evening of 19th May saw us at sea escorted by an Italian torpedo-boat – the *Lupa*. During the morning of 20th, waves of Jus flew overhead en route to Crete. During the morning of 21st while between Crete and Milos, we changed course and sailed in the opposite direction for a couple of hours before returning to our former course. That night when we were about 20 sea miles from Crete the British fleet caught us . . . I was below deck when we were intercepted, having turned in about 2130 hrs. Another officer and I had been discussing how unpleasant it would be if a torpedo were to smash into the ship. I had just gone off to sleep when noises on the deck awakened me. I took a life-jacket and on the deck soldiers were pointing and shouting, "There's one burning!" Between 500 metres and a kilometre distant from us a ship was alight. Lieutenant Goette, officer i/c the 3.7 flak which was being carried on deck, shouted out, "The Greeks are getting panicky. Quick, put a guard behind each of them!" It was too late for, by that time, the Greek skipper had jumped overboard. Then suddenly two giant steaming lights came alongside us. I shouted out, "Alarm! Clear away the life-rafts!", but already machine-gun fire and anti-aircraft shells flying over the bows had struck our port side. A searchlight opened up and then on the port side there was a huge ship heading straight for us. I was just able to say "There . . ." when we were hit and our caique's stern was torn off.

'I shouted out, "Keep calm. Abandon ship!" when a shell from a second British ship hit us. I felt something strike my head and when I stood up, for I had been flung into a corner like a football by the force of the explosion, there was another explosion. I was suddenly conscious of being alone and in the water and swam about almost deaf and blind. Then I heard voices calling and swam towards them. They were some of my men who were gingerly sitting on a few pieces of the wooden platform that had supported the AA gun. On that wooden support, no bigger than a table top, we spent the night. I have never been so cold in my life, for I was dressed in just a short-sleeved sports shirt, trousers and socks. We sat in the water up to our waists and were often soaked as waves broke over us. The wind force was between 7 and 8. We continued calling out and attracted three other men, one of whom was a badly burned gunner. His hair had been burned off and his hands and face were terribly burnt. The British continued their bombardment and soon three ships were in flames. A destroyer turned towards us suddenly and its searchlight swung in our direction. We all took cover and, thank God, we were not seen. That destroyer followed by six others raced past us, only a few hundred yards away. Quite near us they shot a vessel to pieces. There were sounds of battle, some close at hand but others some distance away. Searchlights swept the sea and star shells lit up the sky.

'The night was unendingly long. During the course of the following morning we found a small life-raft into which we placed the wounded. Then seven Gebirgsjaeger came along in another life-raft and gave us two paddles. We already had one and with them tried to reach Crete which was between 10 and 15 kms away. Some of us sat on the raft and paddled while the others swam. There were frequent changes between rowers and swimmers. After a few hours we saw a sailing vessel and paddled like mad to reach her. It turned out later that the vessel had been abandoned because the engine had stopped and the wind was too light for the sails. During the day a few sea-planes flew about but we could not attract their attention. We all expected to have to spend another night at sea but then a Dornier 18 landed about a kilometre from us . . . There were 27 men on board that sea-plane, including eight men from my ship. At Phaeteron I met four men of my company who had been rescued earlier that morning. My men were taken to the military hospital. One of the doctors found me quarters in the officers' mess of a Flak regiment.'

A Paratrooper Remembers

A great friend, Adolf Strauch, who contributed to *Storming Eagles*, my book on the German airborne forces, has supplied, for this work, an account which he has entitled 'A paratrooper remembers'.

'I was recently on holiday in Crete. Lying in the sea, not too far from the beach, to the west of Heraklion are a number of large stone discs. These hundreds of metres of stone form a long wall. It is not clear whether they are man-made or a natural phenomenon. One morning while paddling slowly through the water on my lilo I passed over the discs and noticed in the crystal clear water, half concealed by algae and seaweed, a round object. I dived in and soon had a German steel helmet in my hands.

'In the shade of the beach umbrella the sand was cool. In the distance cruise liners were sailing into Heraklion laden with holidaymakers impatient to enjoy a country whose ancient culture is the product of waves of ship-borne conquerors. The helmet in the sand reminds me of the 9,000 soldiers who, in May 1941, flew over the sea to capture the island. For the first time in the history of warfare the invaders came out of the sky. On the veranda of our bungalow hotel I sat talking with my wife with the helmet, the product of my snorkelling, near me. My mind recalled things. Here in this peaceful area runs the old road to Rtheymnon. We fought in the nearby vineyards and olive groves and saw our first comrades die. I can still see it all in my mind's eye. They were late in jumping from the transport machines and fell in the sea. The weight of their equipment dragged them down. That was nearly forty years ago and the helmet is lying here by my side.

'A new morning. I crossed the old road and went through the vineyards to Tsalikaki. Here we had set up our field dressing station. Friendly young girls direct me to the little chapel where I light a candle and then eating bread and honey sit on a wall at the edge of the village and look westwards across the vineyards and olive groves. I am moved. Thoughts come and go. The vineyard in front of me was where I landed. It was 1600 hrs on 20 May. The shroud lines of my factory-packed 'chute – my old one had been left behind in Corinth – were entangled. I landed like a crashing helicopter near a weapons container. The searing heat took my breath away.

'The early summer was particularly hot with temperatures of 40 degrees in the shade, or more. Throughout the following days we suffered from a shortage of water and from terrible thirst. The sun blazed down upon our steel helmets. Distributed around our bodies – we had no tropical uniform – and in the pockets of our jump suit (known as a bone bag) we carried about 40kg of weapons, ammunition, rations and special equipment. Then we were given additional arms and ammunition from the container. Burdened down with that monstrous load we soldiers had to attack and fight.

'We, 7th and 8th Companies of 2nd Fallschirmjaeger Regiment, commanded by Captain Schirmer, had the tasks of covering the attack of our 1st Regiment upon Heraklion and holding a defence line facing to the west. Contrary to the battle plan we landed before 1st Regiment arrived over the target area. Enemy resistance was slight. We had soon found all our weapons containers, had grouped and had reached our start-line. At this point 1st Regiment flew in. I shall never forget it. The Ju 52s, without fighter escort, flying at an altitude of about 100 metres and with engines throttled back were met by a curtain of enemy flak and machine-gun fire. We saw burning and crashing transport aircraft; men leaping from the burning machines with their 'chutes on fire . . . and knew that we had lost a great many comrades.

'The earth these days is warm and open. In the vineyard busy hands are breaking up the soil. An old man spoke to me about his son in Germany. I look at the olive groves behind the vineyards. It was there that the enemy attacked us in battalion strength. They suffered heavy losses and I can still see the dead lying under the trees in front of us. The old man whose son is in Germany walked ahead of me through the field. It was from there that armed Cretans attacked us. We had not expected to fight against civilians and this upset us. After the Corinth Canal operation we, the first German soldiers in the Peloponnese and Argos, had been greeted by the civil population with oranges. But here the civilians had attacked us with weapons taken from our own containers; some of the Cretans were dressed in

camouflaged jackets taken from our own dead comrades and to deceive us they carried swastika flags. They were protected by neither the Hague nor the Geneva Conventions. We called them snipers. They had been told that we were not only airborne invaders of their island but also the sweepings of German gaols who would rape, plunder and destroy.

'In front of our positions a white cloth was waved. A sign for us to cease firing. We could see only the cloth. Was this an ambush? Some new trick by the insurgents? A volunteer was needed to find out. I volunteered and together with a Greek soldier who was to talk to the enemy, I walked forward and had soon found a badly wounded partisan (both the word and its meaning were unknown to us at that time). A burst of machine-gun bullets had smashed his leg. A German carbine lay only a few metres from him. We carried him back to our dressing station where he was treated by the Medical Officer.

'My wife and I made a pilgrimage to the German military cemetery at Maleme. I spoke to our courier about the Crete operation and he told me about his friend Manolis. On 20 May 1941, the 12-year-old Manolis was fishing near the harbour when we dropped from our aircraft. He was caught between the British and ourselves. A German paratrooper took him under cover, quietened him and gave him some chocolate from his rations. In an attempt to get the child to safety the paratrooper was killed.

'The walls of Heraklion are the mightiest in the whole Mediterranean area. Not far from the grave of the Cretan writer "Nikos Kazanzakis" (Alexis Sorbas) one can enjoy a magnificent view over the town and the sea. Below this place, at the west gate and the harbour we had our heaviest fighting. Here my school chum was killed. En route to Knossos I asked our German-speaking taxi driver to stop near the aerodrome. There was a ridge that I remembered. During the night of 25th/26th May, we had moved out of our positions to the west of the town to support Brauer's Group. The objective was a ridge, Point 296, which dominated the aerodrome. During the night we managed to get round the enemy's outpost line and to reach the high ground. For days we had been without sufficient water or food and were at the end of our strength. We lay down to rest on the ground. At about 0900 hrs we were attacked by a British unit. At first we could not have cared less – we were all so exhausted. But then, collecting out last reserves of energy, we stormed forward in a counter-attack and drove the enemy back.

'In this attack Peter fell and near me Hans-Christoph was wounded. We bandaged Hans-Christoph's knee as best we could and laid him under an olive tree near one of our comrades who had been blinded by a head wound. Convinced that our stretcher-bearers would find the wounded and bring them in, we carried on with the attack to capture the strategically important north side of the heights. By the afternoon we had reached the objective. There we heard of a brilliant piece of flying skill. A Ju 52 had landed on the southern side on a plateau and flown off loaded up with wounded. We thought that our wounded comrades would be with that flight. Some years after the war I met Hans-Christoph in Munich and he told me his story. A story which cannot describe in a few short sentences what he suffered; of a man wounded and left behind in an attack. Badly wounded, not found and not rescued. The man lying near him soon died. In that heat the corpse began to decompose very quickly. Flies and the smell of decay sickened him. He collapsed into unconsciousness. When Heraklion was captured a miracle happened. Retreating British troops found Hans-Christoph and carried him to the south side of the island where he was given medical treatment and left to be picked up by our side. He was flown to Athens where his leg was amputated and for weeks his life hung in the balance. The doctors gave him no chance but he survived.

'On the ridge which we had taken there was neither water nor cover from the blazing sun. Thirst was our constant companion. The wounded suffered terribly and to ease their sufferings we negotiated with our opponents. They took our wounded and looked after them, a humane action that has never been forgotten. As a result, when the fighting for Crete ended there was no tension, feeling of hate or problems with the blokes from the other side of No-Man's Land (the soldiers' term for our opponents). I look at the view from the summit of the ridge. We left it on 29th May, coming down to attack the town and the aerodrome. It was Whitsun and a miracle had happened; the enemy had pulled out. The fighting for Heraklion was over.

'Before we fly home to Germany I go down to the beach once again. The helmet has fallen to pieces and has been cleared away by the beach sweepers. Our aircraft climbs steeply through the clouds and into the sunlight.'

OPERATION 'BARBAROSSA'

In the autumn of 1940, Adolf Hitler, unwilling and unable to attack Great Britain, turned his attention eastwards and determined to open a war against the Soviet Union. For a number of political and military reasons he considered that this would be a short campaign and that, in a matter of months, a ramshackle Communist Russia, defended by a Red Army which had shown itself as incompetent during the war against Finland, would be destroyed. Once the Soviet Union had been overthrown there would be a short period to re-equip and to re-arm the Forces after which Germany would turn westwards again and defeat the United Kingdom.

With the benefit of hindsight one can see that the planning and conduct of the new war were dangerously faulty. One of the principal reasons for the attack upon Russia, according to notes taken by the senior officers who

attended the Führer's briefing, was patently absurd. This was the need to capture so much territory that the cities of the Reich could not be bombed by the Red Air Force. This was a nonsense. Hitler was determined on war for political as well as economic reasons and to conduct it created three huge army groups. Von Leeb's Army Group North was to attack out of East Prussia in the general direction of Leningrad. Von Bock's Army Group Centre, the main striking force, was to advance out of Poland and smash through at Smolensk. Those two Army Groups would then combine to destroy the enemy in the Baltic areas. Von Rundstedt's Army Group South was to strike out of southern Poland and aim for the bend of the lower Dnieper. The plan was that the Army Groups would destroy the Red Army in western Russia and not allow it to escape into the vastness of the Soviet Union. All planning was predicated upon the fact that the Red Army must fight to hold the territory west of the Dnieper. The Germans saw this as strategically unavoidable for the Russians. General Marcks, one of the principal planning officers advanced the premise that, '. . . the Russians cannot avoid a decision as they did in 1812. Modern armed forces of one hundred divisions cannot abandon their sources of supply. It is anticipated that the Russian Army will stand to do battle in a defensive position protecting Great Russia and the eastern Ukraine . . .' That the Red Army would stand and fight was seen by the German planners as a military imperative and when they did the three Army Groups would destroy them.

To bring about this great victory Hitler had laid down that '. . . at most one hundred divisions would be fielded . . .' Such confidence is bewildering. The Führer, knowing his army to be numerically inferior to its new enemy, intended to deploy only marginally more divisions than had been put into the second stage of the campaign against France. Yet, France has an area of 50,000 square miles while the expanse of the Soviet Union in which the three Army Groups were to fight extends across about a million square miles. There was one vast area, the Pripet Marsh, which divided Army Groups North and Centre, but Hitler chose to ignore the danger of that terrain factor. He did not want the army to be bogged down in the Pripet but to strike eastwards in wide-ranging, destructive blows. Not that he had laid down a point of main effort, a firm objective which was to be attained. Rather, he intended his direction of the war to be flexible and chose, seemingly almost at random, objectives that he considered to be important.

Thus, the German Army, inferior in number to its enemy, was to advance into a country deficient in road and rail communications, was to fight along a battle front which ran for nearly two thousand miles and without any firm idea of what its true objectives were. There were no accurate maps of the country and many of those which were available carried misleading details. Overestimating the ability of their own forces while underestimating those of the Red Army, ignorant of Russia's weapons production, ignoring terrain and communications difficulties, OKW, its subordinate commands of army, navy and airforce, as well as its supreme commander waited for the new D-Day. This was Sunday, 22 June 1941, and H-Hour was to be 0330.

Precise to the second, German artillery opened the first barrages and Luftwaffe aircraft, which had taken off well before H-Hour, struck at Red Air Force airfields. Behind that curtain of fire German infantry and panzer troops moved forward. The war which Josef Goebbels had claimed would make the world hold its breath had begun. Three million German soldiers, 600,000 vehicles, 3,580 panzers, 7,184 guns and 1,830 aircraft were put into the fight. So great a concentration of military might, backed by victories in three campaigns, must surely prevail. The new war would be over very soon and so confident were those in command that even the notoriously cautious Halder, wrote in his diary on 3 July 1941, on the 12th day of operations in the East: 'On the whole one can already claim that the orders we had been given, to smash the Russian Army in front of the Duna and Dnieper rivers have been carried out. I am in agreement with the statement made by a captured Russian General officer that, east of the Duna and Dnieper we shall have only remnants to defeat. It is not too much to say that the campaign in the East has been won within fourteen days.'

THE LUFTWAFFE WAR

The role of the Luftwaffe in Operation 'Barbarossa', was the same as that which it had played in earlier campaigns. It was to destroy the Red Air Force on the ground and when this initial task had been accomplished the squadrons were then to support the army in the role of flying artillery. Several correspondents described the build-up of the Luftwaffe before the opening of 'Barbarossa' and the actions of that Service in the first weeks of the new war. I am indebted, chiefly, to Odilo Kumme and to J. Meyer, both of whom served in the early days of the war with Russia and from whose accounts, as well as from others, the following picture of the scene in the summer of 1941, has been compiled:

'The Luftwaffe was subordinated to the strategic aims of the army and was organized accordingly. For some reason the destruction of the Red Air Force both on the ground and in the air was not seen as a strategic but as a tactical operation which was to be completed quickly. After that the Luftwaffe would go on to what was considered the more important duty; to support the army's ground operations.

'Each of the three Army Groups had an attached Air Fleet and to cover any gaps in the battle line, special Commands were set up, each under the command of a Fliegerführer. For example Fliegerführer Baltic commanded the area between Luftflotte 1, attached to Army Group North and Luftflotte

5, the Norway Command. The Fliegerführer Baltic was given the task of ensuring air cover at the junction of those two Air Fleets. There was a similar grouping on the southern flank, and this was known as the Luftwaffe Mission to Roumania. It had two chief tasks: to cover the extreme right wing of Army Group South and to protect the oil fields at Ploesti. Luftflotte 4 was attached to Army Group South and Army Group Centre controlled Luftflotte 2.

'Thanks to high-altitude flights which had been carried out by special units from the end of December 1940, the Luftwaffe had a very good idea of the location of the principal airfields and of other targets in the western regions of the Soviet Union. Luftwaffe aircraft had, in fact, been flying over Russian air space well before the outbreak of war, and on the first day of "Barbarossa" its bombers had to take off before the declaration of war so as to be over Soviet airfields at H-Hour. Certain squadrons, selected to take part in the initial raids, were given intensive training in night flying. On D-Day they took off before H-Hour, flew high over the frontier region and then came down to bombing level by 0315 hrs, just as the first shells of the German artillery barrage were being fired. In those first missions no fewer than 637 bombers or Stukas and 231 fighters took part. Only two German aircraft failed to return.

'According to unit war diaries on each and every Russian airfield which was attacked the enemy aeroplanes were drawn up in rows as if on parade. Surprise was everywhere total. Most bombers carried 2kg fragmentation bombs, which caused great damage to the parked aircraft. When the captured Red Air Force commanders were interrogated they revealed that they had known of our pre-war, high-altitude reconnaissance flights and that they had been warned of our air strike, but on orders from Stalin, Russian units had been forbidden to act provocatively and even normal air patrols had been reduced or stood down altogether. There were a few sectors where Russian fighters did take off during our first raids and engaged our aircraft in battle. In one of these a Soviet pilot who had used up his ammunition deliberately rammed one of our fighters and both pilots were killed. It was an early demonstration of how hard the battle in the skies would be fought. From the first to the last day the Red Air Force airmen fought, if not always with skill, then certainly with overwhelming and undisputed courage.

'The first Russian aircraft to be destroyed in action was a Rata fighter at 0340 hrs and on other sectors more victories were being gained. During the first weeks of "Barbarossa" the initiative lay with the Luftwaffe and few Russian machines penetrated German air space, although towns in the German-occupied areas of Poland were bombed. When the first claims of Russian aircraft destroyed on the ground and in the air reached Luftwaffe headquarters they were disbelieved. Goering could not accept that 4,017 enemy aircraft had been destroyed in eight days and for a loss of only 15 German aircraft. Halder was no less sceptical and for a very good reason.

From estimates supplied by experts at OKW and OKL, the Red Air Force was thought to have on establishment about 6,000 aircraft. If the claims put in by squadrons were to be believed, this meant that the Russian Air Force had been reduced to just 2,000 machines. But that figure was obviously incorrect given the numbers of Russian aircraft which were being reported as intercepting German raids and carrying out bombing raids. A thorough sifting of post-battle reports made it clear that the Soviet Air Force operational strength was still considerably more than 2,000 aircraft. On the evidence available Red air strength at the opening of "Barbarossa" was not the 6,000 machines which had been estimated but was more likely to be in excess of 8,000 machines in western Russia alone. If that figure were the true one, the Red Air Force, even after the terrible losses it had suffered in the opening week of "Barbarossa", was still twice as strong as the Luftwaffe. It was a daunting prospect and thus, the intention to destroy the Soviet Air Force ". . . on the ground and in the air . . ." had not been realized despite the claim from OKL, that ". . . the timing of the air attacks against Russian airfields on the first day of operations was a total success".'

Buoyed up by the euphoria that the Red Air Force had been destroyed on the ground and in the air, OKL switched the squadrons on to the second task; that of giving support to the army in the field. That change of emphasis gave the Red Air Force time to recover as well as the opportunity to regroup and to be resupplied with new aircraft and fresh pilots. Although the Soviet air arm was to be paralysed for several months the Germans had failed to destroy it totally and it rose again to become a potent force in the years of fighting which lay ahead.

The Kriegsmarine had no operational role to play in a war that would be fought on the Russian land mass, except to ensure that the Baltic remained a German sea. It was in the Atlantic that the German Navy was fighting its principal battles, both in submarine and in surface actions.

SS DIVISION 'DAS REICH' ON THE BERESINA

On 4 July 1941, the OKW communiqué reported that the Beresina had been crossed. Among the formations which had passed over that historic river was the SS Division 'Das Reich', forming part of Guderian's Panzer Group Centre. The division's orders were to cross the Beresina and to cut off the Russians who according to reports were said to be fleeing in disorder. There were, by contrast, other reports which did not mention that the enemy was fleeing but spoke instead of bitter fighting against his repeated attacks. Impressions of the confused actions of those early battles were recorded by Oberscharführer Roman Geiger of the division's artillery regiment:

'Ushakova, lying on a long ridge, was a typical small Russian village running on a general line west to south-east. Some 200 metres outside the village there was a single, large tree visible from a very long way away. This was, if I remember correctly, known as Point 306.

'Our No 8 battery of the division's 2nd Artillery Regiment, took up position some 2 to 3 kms to the south-west of Ushakova, in support of infantry from our own division as well as from army units. The OP was manned by Untersturmführer Kindl, a signaller and a telephonist. It was the second day [in that position] and the Russians had been attacking without pause. Shellfire regularly cut the telephone line and over the radio Kindl asked for protection for the OP. Untersturmführer Schuelke ordered me, "Geiger, take a machine-gun and go forward to protect the OP and the infantry in Oshakova."

'My No 1 on the gun, Hasenkopf, took two boxes of ammunition and I carried the gun and we followed the telephone line. Although I did know from map coordinates where the OP was located, following the wire would bring us to the spot more quickly. We moved through the village which was under Russian artillery fire and infantry fire. The OP had been set up some 50 metres to the right of the large tree. Kindl waved to us and pointed out the position we were to take up in a ditch about 30 metres to his right. The "Black Sow", an 18cm Russian gun, began firing at the big tree on the ridge. Far away we could hear the soft thump as the gun fired, then 15 to 20 seconds later there would be a rushing sound and then a frightful explosion. The rate of fire was about one round every three or four minutes. The next shot landed about 10 metres from us. Then the Russian infantry began an attack. With the sun at my back I had good observation in an easterly direction and fired short bursts at them. But there was a small area of dead ground which I could not cover and the Russians worked their way forward through this until they were about 50 metres away. I could see their brown helmets shining in the sunlight. They got no farther forward than that. Kindl left the OP together with the wireless operator as it was impossible to give clear fire orders over the radio. He shouted out to me, "Do a good job, Geiger", as I flung the first egg grenades. By this time the fire of the "Black Sow", was being laid on the village itself and shells had begun to explode in the first houses. Once again that whistling sound was followed by a crashing explosion. Then there would be a pillar of smoke and when that had cleared away, there was nothing to be seen. Some houses were burning like tinder boxes. Untersturmführer Kindl was hit during the bombardment and lost a leg. He died on the way to the RAP. The signaller was killed immediately. I kept the Russians back with short bursts of fire and by throwing grenades. Our right flank was covered by marshy ground, so we had nothing to fear from that sector.

'Ushakova was now completely alight. There was the sound of rifle and machine-gun fire and shouts of "Ooooorah!" as the Russians stormed the village. It was time for me and my No 1 to get out. To our right and to our rear there was a piece of swampy, meadow land. We made our way back through this firing bursts of fire from the machine-gun and throwing grenades. Just as we were nearing the battery area we saw the last prime mover drive off towing its gun and disappearing in a cloud of dust. The battery had had to move because its position had become too dangerous. As we two made our way back to our unit we realized that there were wounded men lying in the side-cars of motor cycles.

'As a result of the furious Russian assaults our front line had collapsed. Then I saw an armoured car flying the "Reich" pennant. In the vehicle was our divisional commander, Obergruppenführer Hausser. I reported to him and he looked through his binoculars in the direction of Ushakova. It did not look all that good. Over the radio he ordered up the Stukas. That was comforting. An hour later, by which time Hasenkopf and I had reached the battery positions, the Stukas were on their way. Seven of them swung round in a great curve and gathered over the signal flares that were being fired to indicate targets. Less than a kilometre in front of our positions dive-bombers screamed down out of the sky with their sirens howling and plastered the enemy with bombs. It was frightening to think of that rain of fire. We supported the Stukas with all the shells we could fire off. For the rest of the day we were stood down but on the following day we went in with panzer and SPs and recaptured Ushakova.'

THE DEFENCE OF SVERDLIKOVO VILLAGE

There were certain factors which set the Eastern Front apart from the campaigns which had preceded it. To begin with there was the vast length of the battle line and the numbers employed in the fighting. A second factor, developing from the first, were the encirclement battles, particularly those of the autumn of 1941. The tempo of the advance of the Panzer Groups, in this case that of von Rundstedt's Army Group South, broke through the Russian lines, outflanked the defenders and had soon surrounded whole Russian armies. The thin line of German panzer and motorized infantry – not yet known as Panzer Grenadiers – fought against the Red Army's frantic attempts to escape. Where the situation on the ground became very desperate and a Red breakthrough threatened, the Luftwaffe was called upon to carry out its support role. The following account by a war reporter with the SS Regiment 'Westland' describes the defence of a Russian village of Sverdlikovo by a handful of men of the Regiment and of a flak unit.

'During the great battles of annihilation fought around Uman the Soviets sought to break out of our encirclement. Between Uman and Slatopol, in and around Sverdlikovo there were only weak German forces. During the night of 1st/2nd August, the Bolsheviks carried out a major assault which lasted 14 hours. The defeat of that breakout attempt by a German force which was outnumbered 80 to 1, played a significant part in winning the battle of Uman.

'The night was too dark for the lieutenant in charge of the flak guns to see clearly. A recce patrol was his last hope. He realized how desperate would be the position of his unit if the enemy were to attack in strength. But he also knew that he had to fight to the last shell. He was isolated here with three light flak guns and a handful of infantry, and SS men dug in on the outskirts of the village. His orders were to hold out until the mass of the German infantry could reach and relieve him. It was a shocking night whose darkness was accentuated by driving rain. Everything was soaked through and wet uniforms clung to wet bodies. The ground was being turned to clinging mud in the downpour.

'Suddenly there were bursts of machine-gun fire and rifle shots from close at hand. Bullets struck the sides of the armoured vehicles and between the curses, cries and shouts came the call "Lieutenant!, lieutenant!" It was the leader of the recce patrol who reported that the Reds had already occupied the south-west edge of Sverdlikovo and were moving deep into the village under the protection of armour. The officer made a quick decision. "Bring back the guns to the centre of the village and group round the little bridge across the stream. We shall hold out there for as long as the ammunition lasts." Barely had the half-track vehicles begun to move when a storm of artillery fire crashed down upon the village and enemy hand-grenades began to explode close by. "Its high time, men," called the young officer. "Back to the bridge and we'll stop them there." From the edge of Sverdlikovo, where they had been standing only a few minutes earlier, there was a thunder of shellfire, machine-gun bursts, mortar bomb explosions and the animal cries of "Hooooray!, hooray!", as the Red infantry attacked some German unit isolated there. And above all that confusion signal flares rise into the night sky; white, red, yellow and green. The approach of a Russian tank was the signal for a general assault upon the group. Every Red Army weapon in the village seemed to be turned against the gunners and the SS men. Streams of yellow, green, white and red tracer whizzed all around them, pattering against the steel sides of the vehicles like a rain storm. Three and a half hours that storm of steel lasted and for all that time the gunners could only reply with rifle shots fired into the darkness. The guns could not be brought into action. Slowly the enemy closed in on the bridge but at last the light of dawn allowed the lieutenant to identify the shapes of enemy soldiers setting up anti-tank guns and mortar positions. Now his little command could take effective counter-action. The officer took up the post of aimer on one of the guns and selected a target. "Magazine!" he calls. "In place!" comes the reply from the second gun and then both open up on the Soviets advancing toward the bridge. The other men of the flak unit open up with rifles and pistols on the enemy now only a bare 150 metres away. Under the fire of the two light flak guns the first line of Soviet soldiers was swept away. But new waves of them, earth brown, screaming figures stormed across the little stream and made for the bridge. At first in company strength and then by battalions they storm forward with fanatical determination to take the bridge. The living climb over the bodies of their dead comrades in their eagerness to attack the Germans.

'It is soon clear to the lieutenant that however good his aim is there are so many enemy soldiers advancing that it will be only a matter of time before the position is lost. Rifle fire coming from a number of directions also shows that his unit is surrounded. Well, he will do his duty to the last and gives orders that the vehicles are to be driven right on to the bridge. There the last stand will be made. Then, as if by a miracle, the enemy fire from the rear dies away and German helmets can be seen on the hills behind the flak unit. A Company of "Westland" has broken through to reinforce the little group. With this reinforcement, small though it is, the lieutenant decides to recapture the village. Led by the flak vehicles the infantry storm forward. The guns fire at demonic speed and pump shells into the huts of the village. Enemy counter-fire strikes at the little groups storming their way through Sverdlikovo. At places there is bitter hand-to-hand fighting and the Red Army men fight with fanatical bravery.

'Suddenly the houses on both sides of the narrow street begin to burn. Four hours the fighting lasted before the centre of the village was cleared of the enemy. But the situation for the German soldiers is as hopeless as before. Masses of Russian troops have been brought forward and have now completely surrounded Sverdlikovo. Then the German infantry report that they are running out of ammunition. An enemy mortar has taken up position in the bed of the stream and begins to range in on the crossroads where the lieutenant's gun is in action. "Quickly!; fire on the hill over there!", but not a shot is fired. Everybody is astonished at the sight of hundreds of Red Army men charging down a hill only 250 metres distant, running, stumbling and falling. They are firing from the hip and seem to be totally disorganized. Can it be that their commissars are driving them into the fight? The moment of surprise passes and the guns open up again. The attack collapses. The shortage of ammunition is now critical and the half-tracks are driven so as to form a circle. Orders are given to fire only when the enemy is so close that every shot will strike a target. One of the prisoners, a Roumanian who speaks German, says that on the hills and in the bed of the stream there are hundreds of Russian dead. In reply to the question of how strong the Red Army units are around the village, the prisoner gives the answer, "Five regiments".

'At last, when all ammunition has been used and the flak guns have only a magazine or two left, the German troops outside the village break through and Sverdlikovo is systematically cleared, an operation that takes so long that it seems almost as if the village will never be free of the enemy. By midday it is finally and firmly in German hands. Later that day the Soviets mount another series of attacks but these are broken up by infantry fire and then totally destroyed by Stuka attack.'

The bitterness with which the Red Army fought and the efforts it made to defend or capture some obscure village, worried the German commanders and men alike. The 20th Panzer Division's report included the bitter comment, "Experience shows that to capture a village costs us 60 men"; and western Russia was covered with little villages. The drain upon German infantry strength was alarming and yet, as 4th Panzer Division reported, "Panzer without infantry protection cannot be used to clear wooded areas." It was a problem which was to grow more difficult to resolve as the war continued and losses mounted.

STUKA UNIT 'HUNTING AT WILL'

Following upon the successful destruction of the Uman pocket, Army Group South roared on a hundred miles past the flanks of South West Front and on to Konotop. At that point it was planned that Panzer Group 2 would drive southwards to meet the rising thrust of Panzer Group 1. Within those jaws would be trapped no fewer than five Red Armies. The length of front that was being covered, as has already been explained, created difficulties for the ground forces which were too few in numbers to hold back the Red Army's break-out attempts at every point. When that pressure grew too great Luftwaffe units were called in to support the army. The following account is of a Stuka unit serving with Army Group South:

'Our task was to fly missions to destroy the enemy's tanks, lorried columns, fortified defences and artillery positions. The enemy was making a wild attempt to bring his troops across the Dnieper in an effort to avoid encirclement and yet, at the same time, was sending reinforcements into the area in an attempt to hold back that encirclement.

'Our Stuka squadron was put in to substitute for the panzer formations which were fighting against the Red Army's giant machines on another sector. We in the squadron were aware of our responsibility. In continual missions from dawn to last light we opened the way forward for our own troops and smashed breaches in the wall of Red armour. Our squadron had

hardly returned from a mission east of Boguslav when we were tanked up
and loaded with bombs. We were to join with the other seven squadrons of
our Wing in carrying out fresh operations. There was no time to discuss
tactics. There was not much point because it was the same sort of mission
we had been flying over the past days. "Hunting at will in the area of
Boguslav–Jachny." In other words we can attack any target we choose – and
we know there will be plenty to choose from. We line up for the take-off.
The engine roars and the pressure of take-off forces me forward. To the right
and left the other comrades of the squadron have already left the ground.
The sky is filled with Ju 87s. As one squadron leaves on a mission another
is landing after carrying out its task and we know that another will be over
the target area.

'There is a quarter of an hour's flying time to the target area and then
through the earphones comes a message from one of the returning squadron.
"Achtung! Strong concentrations of armour about 3kms east of Jachny." The
message is repeated. Now we know our objective and the squadron turns
towards the new target area. We identify it while still some way away. Fires
are everywhere – burning villages and vehicles. As yet we are too far away
to identify tanks. Then, we are over the target area, a landscape of gently
rolling hills and valleys. On the footpaths which criss-cross it there are
Russian tanks, hard to detect because they are cleverly camouflaged. Our
own troops lining the railway embankment fire off Very lights to show their
positions. It is clear that the Russians intend to drive towards the
embankment and to overrun our men.

'Like hawks we circle over the target area and then we detect the enemy
armour. There are not just twenty or thirty tanks but nearly a hundred of
the 52-ton monsters. Some are camouflaged with sheaves of corn or bushes.
Between their rows are gun lines and then trenches in which Red infantry
are waiting to attack. To the rear of the Russian assault group are fuel and
ammunition lorries. We have excellent targets. The Squadron Leader gives
the signal to attack and immediately the pilot puts our plane into a steep
dive. We dive and dive, towards the enemy. As the pilot makes last-minute
adjustments I look out and see our target, a group of five tanks moving away
at high speed. The pilot corrects the direction by a fraction and then there
is a slight jump as the first bombs are released. We pull out of the dive and
I feel the G-force pulling at my face and body for just a fraction of a second.
Then everything is normal again. I open fire with my machine-gun upon the
enemy on the ground below as we climb and gain height. Our comrades are
diving towards their targets so that every few seconds a bomb explodes
among the enemy concentration. I look to see the effect of our attack. One
tank has suffered a direct hit, but what has happened to the other four
machines? Two are close to the dead tank, probably suffering from the effects

of blast or shrapnel upon the tracks or suspension, but the remaining two are still moving. We dive again, annoyed that our bombs do not score a direct hit each time. But one of the tanks is smothered in smoke. It is burning. The fifth gets away. Then we bomb the soft-skin vehicles.

'It must be hell down there. Burning tanks and lorries cover the ground, and flames from the burning villages threaten the tanks concealed nearby. We have no more bombs to drop but fly over the enemy at low level firing our machine-guns. It is surprising how much material the Russians have ready to put into action. Tanks and lorries and thousands of soldiers ready to take the places of those whom our attacks have destroyed. It is frightening to realize just what masses of men and material the enemy has at his disposal.

'On our flight home we meet three squadrons which are directed on to the target we have just left. And so it goes on – a succession of attacks until nightfall. It was worth it. Our squadron alone has destroyed 62 tanks and over 200 trucks. Our attacks have smashed the enemy's break-out attempts. And so it goes on day in day out from 9th to 16th August, until the battle ends and our ground forces finally capture Kanev.'

THE RENEWED POWER OF CAVALRY

Other unique factors of the Eastern Front were the terrain and climatic conditions which Second Panzer Army, in a report dated 18 November, described as, 'being outside our previous experience'. Another contrast between 'Barbarossa' and the campaigns which preceded it was that western Europe had extensive and sophisticated road and rail systems. Russia lacked both. So dependent did German units fighting in Russia become upon the rail link that 3rd Panzer Division in a commentary on the fighting reported that '. . . troops are bound to the railway and have to be within horse and cart or horse and sledge distance of it'.

There were several reasons for this. One was that vast distances and the lack of roads meant a reliance upon horses because the German Army had insufficient trucks to maintain lorried movement. Another reason was that any German supply column was liable to be intercepted and destroyed by detachments of Russian cavalry which infiltrated through the loose, German defensive zones and which then harassed the rear areas. The dependence upon horses was another feature of the Russian front, a dependence which was great in the summer months but which was crucial to movement of supplies during the winter period. By comparison with Britain, whose military transport was motorized and whose guns were towed by portee, the German Army depended to a great deal upon cattle to move its guns and carts. The image of armoured columns carrying out deep penetrating thrusts is a familiar one, but does not show that those panzer spearheads were often many miles ahead of their own forces and that frequently they were isolated and unsupported even by their own lorried infantry.

One Panzer Division officer wrote in an analysis of operations: '. . . infantry regiments of panzer divisions are lorry-mounted but, given the road conditions in the Soviet Union, it is often impossible for them to keep pace [with the armour]. The establishment of motor vehicles in panzer divisions is too low and thus [in encirclement battles] it is necessary to call upon infantry divisions for support. These have to footmarch to the objectives and their transport is, in the main, horse-drawn.'

It may well be that Hitler, who hated with equal passion horses and the horse-riding aristocracy, was determined to make the German Army a completely motorized one. Certainly he reduced the cavalry establishment of the army to a single brigade whose two regiments served with distinction in the 1940 campaign in France. But it was on the Eastern Front that the German Army first came to realize that it was absolutely dependent upon the horsed regiments which it no longer had on establishment. The brigade that had fought in France went on to achieve a number of successes in the Pripet Marsh and as a consequence was expanded to achieve divisional status. This was followed by a fresh order to break up the division. Its major formations were stood down but the smaller units which had been serving away from the division at the time of the order did not disband. Instead, as the importance of cavalry was appreciated, these became the cadres around which new detachments were created. Then more and more cavalry units were raised. The German Army became so dependent upon horses that two and a half million animals were on its establishment in Russia. Another statistic was that, on the Eastern Front, a thousand horses died each day. The greatest number of these were killed by shellfire or by bullets, but a great many died of disease or of heart failure. The Eastern Front was a murderous place for cattle as well as for the soldiers. Although armoured operations are the accepted image of the Russian front, there were many areas in which horses were used *en masse*, particularly by the Red Army. A number of former soldiers described how their units had been attacked by Russian cavalry. These stories were so similar in content that I have amalgamated them to form a single narrative.

'As early as the encirclement battles in the autumn of 1941, we became aware of several frightening elements; the Red Army's manpower reserves, the rigidity of thought of its commanders and men and the stoicism of the rank and file. There can have been few units of the German Army which served on the Russian Front, that did not have experience of clashes with Cossack cavalry. Often these were patrols of four or five riders who charged out of woods or maize fields. Or else they were company-strength detachments, which struck quickly and disastrously at units that had grown careless. It was during the autumn battles of 1941, that massed Red Army cavalry tried to smash a hole in our lines so that Russian armies which we had trapped could break out of our encircling ring.

'One day, either the 15th or 16th September 1941, we had seen cavalry, small groups to begin with but whose numbers grew as the morning wore on. Early in the morning there had been a mist hanging low over the fields and in the vast woodland area to our front. We were waiting for another infantry division to pass through us and go on to clear the Ivans from the woods. With that mist hanging about it would not be an easy task. We had had the order to stand down even though visibility was poor and despite the fact there was the noise of tanks moving about in the mist in front of our trenches. We in the rifle companies were on open ground with battalion headquarters and the Heavy Weapons Company in a village behind us. It would have been about a couple of hours later, say about 10 a.m., when the sun dispersed the mist and produced a fine, warm morning. Nothing much seemed to be going on when suddenly we were called to arms. An artillery observer on the roof of a hut in the village had seen about seventy horsemen trotting out of the forest towards us. The FOO had also alarmed his battery and a troop of guns opened fire. The riders raced back through the shellfire into the shelter of the trees. Then a group of T-34s rolled towards the village and came under fire. Two were knocked out and the others drove away. The joy we felt at that little victory was premature because it soon became clear that the Reds had only been feeling out our strength and fire discipline.

'For about another hour there was no movement or sound and it was hard to believe that there was a war going on and that we were part of a cordon flung round a huge mass of Soviet divisions. The pocket was a huge one – 150 kilometres long and about 70 deep, and for the past days we had had to face probes by Red Army infantry, and on this morning only the cavalry and tank probing assaults. Nothing of consequence, really. It would have been nearly midday when more cavalry were seen threading their way through the trees. We had excellent vision of the ground over which they were advancing and a good field of fire. Other horsemen were seen coming out of the small ravines [a feature of the terrain]. There was no shot fired by the battery which was supporting us and we wondered why the FOO was not firing at this splendid target. Then we saw that whole squadrons had come out of the woods and were forming up. The squadrons became battalions and the battalions, regiments. The Russian cavalry deployed and began to trot towards our trenches.

'We made ready to open fire and as the line of horses broke into a gallop, the shells of our artillery crashed around them. I was an NCO observer on a medium machine-gun and saw clearly behind the first line of horsemen, that there was a second and then a third line. The intervals between the lines was wide and it was not a matter of a single charge which we would have to meet, but three separate charges. We infantry opened up and in a little time the first line of cavalry had been almost wiped out. Over the bodies of their comrades and across the thrashing limbs of the wounded horses the second line came on. They reached no farther than about 200 metres past the first line when they, too, were destroyed. The third line gained a little more ground but was crushed by our artillery and machine-guns.

'I can never forget the sight of horses and riders being blown into the air by shellfire and seeing blood pouring from wounded animals, mad with fear as they galloped across our positions. Cease fire was ordered and we went out to attend to the wounded Russians and to put down the horses. It was a miserable afternoon. According to the Intelligence Officer the prisoners we took told him that the attack had been made by an entire Red Army cavalry division and should have been supported by a regiment of tanks. The armour had not made the rendezvous by H-Hour and the divisional commander had decided to postpone the attack until the tank regiment did arrive. His decision was overruled by the commissar who believed us to be too weak to withstand a cavalry charge and who had insisted that it take place. The purpose of the attack had been to carve a way through so that the trapped units facing us would escape and link up with other Red Army units fighting on the outside of the pocket. As it was the Reds had lost the best part of an entire division but had gained nothing. The men in the squadrons had seen their comrades killed but had still charged with determination and courage. Our battalion had four men wounded.'

In the area of Army Group South, according to Curzio Malaparte, an Italian war correspondent, a Hungarian hussar regiment mounted a cavalry charge against a Red Army infantry unit which was holding out and refusing to surrender. German infantry attacks against the entrenched Russians had been bloodily repulsed. Panzer assaults had been flung back with loss. Even the terrifying Stukas could not shake the determined Red Army men. The colonel of the Honved Hussar Regiment, seeing that the attacks were halted, asked the reason, was given details and promptly offered help. This was accepted. He formed his regiment into two lines and with himself at the centre of the first line swept down upon the Red Army defenders. Those men, who had resisted the most modern weapons of war, broke and ran when faced with the infantryman's oldest enemy, the horsed soldier. As the Hussar colonel said, 'I have trained for twenty years for this moment. It was the opportunity of a lifetime and one not to be missed.'

Above: *Reichsmarschall Hermann Goering, Commander-in-Chief of the Luftwaffe.*

Top right: *Goering and senior commanders of the Luftwaffe on the Channel coast discussing plans for the air offensive against Britain.*

Right: *Werner Mölders, one of the Luftwaffe's fighter aces during the Battle of Britain.*

Above: *The first elements of Rommel's Afrika Korps marching through Tripoli, North Africa, in February 1941.*

Left: *General Wilhelm List, who commanded Twelfth Army during the campaign in Yugoslavia and Greece.*

Below: *Men of a Gebirgsjäger regiment shelter from the bitter weather while waiting to attack the Metaxas Line during the opening of the Greek campaign in 1941.*

Right: A bunker on the Metaxas Line after its capture by men of 5th Gebirgs (Mountain) Division.

Right: Gebirgsjäger pursuing the retreating Anglo-Greek armies, seen here passing through the pass of Thermopylae, scene of the epic stand by Leonidas and his Spartans.

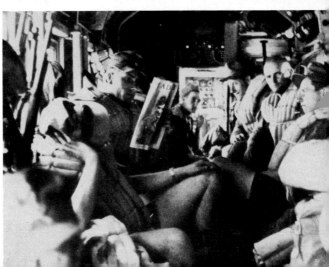

Right: Alpine troops of 5th Gebirgs Division wait on a Greek airfield to be airlifted to Crete.

Above left: *Ringel, General of Mountain Troops, who commanded the 5th Mountain Division during the Crete campaign in May 1941.*

Above: *Men of the Para Assault Regiment move into Maleme after capturing Point 107, the hill dominating the airfield on Crete.*

Left: *German paratroops killed during the fighting for Heraklion, Crete, in May 1941. The positions held by the Fallschirmjäger were in the line of trees in the background; note the parachutes in the olive tree.*

Below: *A German paratrooper moving through the ruins of Heraklion.*

Top right: *Jubilant German paratroopers move into Heraklion.*

Bottom right: *In August 1941 a parade was held in Berlin to celebrate the victory in Crete. This picture shows Adolf Strauch (marked with a cross) and his comrades in the Hermann Goering barracks forming up for the parade.*

Left: *Ringel, General Officer Commanding 5th Gebirgs Division, presenting decorations and awards to men of his division at the end of the Crete campaign.*

Right: *The Reichs War Flag is hoisted over the Acropolis in Athens following the city's capture.*

Far right: *A German paratrooper's grave outside the field hospital at Tsalikaki, Crete.*

Left: *Adolf Strauch, qualified paratrooper and holder of the Iron Cross, Second Class. He fought in Greece, Crete, Russia, and north-west Europe.*

Right: *German paratroops using a captured British lorry in Heraklion.*

Left: Ringel, General Officer Commanding 5th Gebirgs Division, presenting decorations and awards to men of his division at the end of the Crete campaign.

Right: The Reichs War Flag is hoisted over the Acropolis in Athens following the city's capture.

Far right: A German paratrooper's grave outside the field hospital at Tsalikaki, Crete.

Left: Adolf Strauch, qualified paratrooper and holder of the Iron Cross, Second Class. He fought in Greece, Crete, Russia, and north-west Europe.

Right: German paratroops using a captured British lorry in Heraklion.

Far left, top: Lütjens who led the Bismarck break-out attempt. He went down with his ship in May 1941.

Top left: Friedrich August Freiherr von der Heydte, battalion commander in the Fallschirmjäger, leading his men through Braunschweig in July 1941.

Bottom left: Look-outs keep watch from the conning tower of a U-boat in the Atlantic while a

British tanker burns in the background.

Above: A U-boat running on the surface in the Atlantic, 1941.

Below left: Grossadmiral Karl Doenitz who succeeded Raeder as Supreme Commander of the German Navy.

Below: A propaganda photograph of a U-boat commandant and his coxswain on the voyage home after a long patrol at sea.

Left: The first day of Operation 'Barbarossa' 22 June 1941. German troops cross the bridge in Poland over the river boundary with the Soviet Union.

Left: German soldiers near the Soviet frontier in 1941.

Left: A German infantry advance during the early days of the Russian campaign. Owing to the absence of railways and a shortage of trucks, the mass of the invading force followed the Panzer divisions on foot.

Right: General Guderian, commanding a Panzer Group, with his subordinates at a battlefield conference.

Right: Men of SS Panzer Division Das Reich crossing a Russian river in summer 1941.

Right: Men of No.12 Company, Deutschland Regiment of SS Division Das Reich, in house-to-house fighting during the autumn advances in Russia.

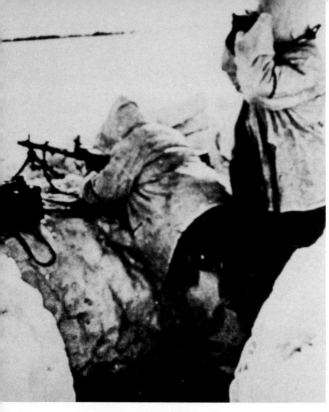

Above: The losses suffered by the Red Army in desperate attacks against the Germans were frighteningly high, but their sacrifices gained time for Stavka to organize a proper defence and bring up reinforcements.

Right: Men of Deutschland Regiment holding the line at Sytshevka in the winter of 1942.

Above: *These men of Meindl's divisional headquarters defence company were regrouped to form the divisional reserve to be used in counter-attacks and spearheading assaults upon Russian defensive positions.*

Left: *An SS soldier dressed for winter weather talking to the driver of a locomotive in Russia.*

Above: Dead German paratroopers near Ivanovka, along the River Mius.

Right: The battle line occupied by Meindl's men in northern Russia had several dangerous salients. These he straightened out in a number of short, sharp shock operations. Here he briefs a battle group before it leaves on such an operation in February 1942.

Right: SS General 'Sepp' Dietrich with Reichsführer Heinrich Himmler on the Eastern Front in 1942.

Above: *The failure of the Allied landing at Dieppe was a propaganda coup for the Germans, who produced posters and placards detailing the extent of the defeat and circulated them throughout Europe.*

Left: *Girls of the Luftwaffe Signal Corps on a sight-seeing tour of the Acropolis in 1942. Girls such as these were later seconded to anti-aircraft batteries.*

TICHWIN: THE KEY TO LENINGRAD

One area in which horses could have been used to advantage in the opening phases of the war with Russia was the flat and swampy ground into which Army Group North was advancing. That Army Group had the Leningrad region as its objective, but it was not to take the city – Hitler had no intention of wasting good men on house-to-house fighting. He intended, instead, to cut off the city and starve the beleaguered inhabitants to death. Artillery and air raids would destroy the buildings so that those Russians who did not starve would freeze to death in the ruins.

One of the units of Army Group North was 12th Panzer Division. On 19 October, this formation was given the task of capturing the town of Tichwin. The Soviet Union's poor railway system made Tichwin strategically important for whichever side held it controlled the railway line to Lake Ladoga, the shipping to Leningrad and thus the rations for the people of that city. The terrain was swampy and to bring the armour forward special corduroy roads had had to be constructed in many areas. It was ideal terrain for horsed operations, but one for which panzers were useless. As 12th Panzer crossed its start-line snow began to fall – several weeks early. It was a bad omen. It was more than just bad – it was frightening for those who realized the implications. The German Army was not prepared for winter conditions. No warm clothing had been issued nor were the weapons and vehicles prepared for the difficulties to come. The Division's experiences were described by Alexander Stahlberg:

'Somehow or the other we reached Tichwin. From the archives I have established that it must have been on 8 November 1941. In the town there had been little resistance. Why should there have been? Once inside Tichwin, we were rats caught in a trap. The little town had been evacuated. There was not a soul to be seen. In a dead silence the troops began to prepare the defence. A deadly quiet lay over the little market square which was now deep in snow. The infantry dug in quickly, our guns vanished into cover. The tanks hid themselves in barns and cow stalls. Holes were made in the walls through which their guns would fire. Tichwin had now become a "fortress" and the 12th Panzer Division, which had been trained for mobile warfare, was now entrenched. Who was responsible for such an order?

'We had captured Tichwin, as we had been told to do and we had cut the railway line. But only a few days later we found out from reconnaissance patrols that the Russians, by employing thousands of soldiers and civilians, had built a new road to the north of Tichwin and that that road was beyond the range of our guns . . . In the meantime the Russians, as was to be expected, had surrounded Tichwin . . . and used us as target practice. Worse yet was the effort of trying to maintain our line of communication to the Volkov. Supplies had to be either escorted by armed units or rescued by them from Russian attack. Taking back the wounded was the worst. The Russians did not respect the huge red crosses painted on our ambulances.

'One day I saw one of the Baltic aristocrats who was serving with us. His head was covered with a huge fur hat and in place of regulation leather jackboots he was wearing felt boots. In reply to the Colonel's question, "Where did you get that stuff?", he replied, "In the town, and in my cart I have more." The Baltic aristocrat with experience of Russian winters had organized a collection of winter clothing. He knew that without furs and felt boots one could not last out in a winter in northern Russia.

'Of course, all of us, officers and men, were still wearing the clothing and equipment with which we had crossed the frontier on 22nd June. We had not received one item of winter clothing. Sentries on duty had to be relieved at short intervals, by day as well as by night. The thermometer was already showing 20 degrees below and our Balt told us that it would get still colder. Whatever clothing was found in Tichwin was immediately confiscated . . . The winter did, indeed, become colder . . . To camouflage our vehicles we buried them in the snow. The lorries could not be used in their proper role and thus became instead a form of heating apparatus. Their motors were kept running the whole time – day and night. Eventually, fuel supplies began to run out, so we had to cut down on our "heating". But once an engine had not been used for some time it was difficult to get it going again. To save the batteries the engines were warmed before being started up. To do this we filled tin cans with diesel oil, lit them and placed them under the vehicle. But every driver kept enough fuel in reserve for the time when we might have to retreat. There were more cases of frostbite every day. Feet, hands, ears, noses. What caused us most concern was looking after the wounded. If frost got into an open wound the man was unlikely to be saved. It was better to be dead than to be wounded. In all of us, from the simplest private to the commander, doubts began to nag, but we comforted ourselves with the thought that "those up there" would have taken note of the mistakes that had been made and would avoid them in future. There was nothing else we could do but grit our teeth and not give up hope . . .

'We did not think that the order to withdraw would ever come because the German Army had not retreated at all in this war. Would Tichwin be the end of us? Then, at last came the order to pull back – late but at least before the Russians would have a chance to attack us . . . I can remember little of that retreat. I was conscious for only a few moments at a time. Suddenly I had a high fever, but did not know then, nor have I found out since, what the illness was. I was wrapped in blankets and placed on a tracked prime mover . . . I can remember sounds of battle, of orders being given, but had no interest in anything any more. At one time, and this I recall with terrible clarity, I took a blanket away from my face and saw around me piles of bodies. Wounded comrades. They sat, lay, or slumped huddled all around me while on the tailboard of our prime mover lay the dead. No! they did not lie there, they were stacked there and tied on with rope. Our soldiers would not leave one dead comrade behind in the snow. For as long as it was possible they loaded them on to the vehicle. The mound behind us grew daily higher and higher. It may well be that that mound of dead saved my life, because some of those who had fallen must have been hit by the bullets which might otherwise have struck me. I came to my senses again in about the last days of the year. The unit had crossed the Volkov and the doctor told me I had pulled through and that I was in a village to the south-west of Leningrad. I had missed Christmas and while I had been unconscious Hitler had dismissed the Supreme Commander of the Army and had taken the job himself. Another surprise was to learn that Hitler had told a cheering audience in the Sportspalast in Berlin that he had declared war on America. It was clear that we were in the hands of a madman.'

THE SIEGE OF MOSCOW

The SS Division, 'Das Reich', on the establishment of Army Group Centre, had been in the thick of the fighting for Moscow. The division had been fighting without relief or pause since it crossed the Beresina at the beginning of July. Five months later the division was buoyed up with the firm belief that one final offensive would capture the Russian capital. The loss of Moscow might not bring the war immediately to an end, but it would help to bring about the end of the Soviet regime. Heid Ruehl, serving with the 'Deutschland' Regiment of 'Das Reich' Division wrote of the fighting in the weeks before Christmas 1941.

'On 30 November, after hard fighting, the 3rd Battalion [of Deutschland Regiment] managed to capture the station and the factory in the north of Stalino. On the previous day the regiment's 2nd and 3rd Battalions, supported by the assault guns, "Blücher", "Lützow" and "Derfflinger", had captured Kryokovo after bitter fighting against a determined enemy. Losses to the battalions had been heavy. During the fighting the CO of 3rd Battalion, Hauptsturmführer Kroger was shot and killed by a bullet in the head fired at close range. While "Deutschland" was consolidating on its objectives, heavy losses of the past weeks made it imperative for 3rd Battalion to be broken up in order to raise the strength of the other two battalions. The survivors of 3rd Battalion were thereupon incorporated into the 1st and 2nd Battalions.

'On 2 December, the advanced guard of "Deutschland" regiment was directly facing Lenino. After forming up on either side of the Rochdestven-Lenino road the battalions moved off into the attack. In the woods to the west of the town, both battalions had their way obstructed by strong Russian trench systems and were soon involved in heavy fighting. At the same time heavy barrages of mortar fire came in and the bombs exploding in the tree tops inflicted heavy casualties among which were a great many officers including the regimental commander, Schulz, and the COs of both battalions. The regimental commander and the CO of 2nd Battalion both refused to leave the field and led their units until nightfall. Fighting for Lenino went on until late in the night. To begin with only certain areas could be taken but at 2300 hrs the 2nd Battalion received orders to attack Lenino from the west and to take it regardless of cost. The SPs went in with No 6 Company but found the enemy had fled. He had pulled out during the night. Lenino was taken and secured. By gaining that place we had reached an outer suburb of Moscow – only 17 kms from the city centre. Lenino was a terminus of the Moscow bus line. In clear weather it would be possible to see the towers of the Kremlin. My God, how close we were to this historic objective. Then on 3rd December, Panzer Group 4, reported to Army Group Centre that it no longer had the strength to maintain the offensive. The troops were physically and mentally exhausted . . . Fourth Army pulled back its divisions to their jumping-off points behind the Neva. The frontal attacks by both Fourth Army and Fourth Panzer Army were brought to a close . . . On the 5th December, the Red Army's counter-offensive opened.'

Although other writers than Ruehl had reported that the German Army changed from attack to defence and wrote that the Red Army had gone over to the offensive on 5 December, according to OKW the attacks which came in on that as well as on subsequent days were purely local. It was not until 10 December that the STAVKA of the Red Army issued a communiqué which read, in part, 'The Soviet armed forces have opened an offensive along the whole front from the White Sea to the Black Sea.' It was two weeks before Christmas.

CHRISTMAS IN RUSSIA

The first Christmas of the war in Russia was described by a member of No 1 Company of the Para Engineer Battalion:

'We had been looking forward to a comfortable Christmas in the dug-outs we had built for ourselves, but then on 22nd December, came the order to move to a new location about 18 km away. The march was exhausting and for every five steps we moved forward we slid back two on the snowy and icy paths. It took hours to reach the new area and we were given a filthy room in a stone-built house. There were twenty-four of us in that lousy hole, all of us dreaming of the lovely dug-outs we had left behind and wondering who would be celebrating Christmas in them.

'On the next day we started building new dug-outs to drive out the misery of not having a proper Christmas. We had no mail, but consoled ourselves that we would get a whole bundle in the New Year. We had made a tree and had decorated it with silver paper taken from cigarette packets and cheese wrappers. We had also got hold of some cotton wool from the first aid men. We had also been practising carols so that we would be prepared for the holy days. We were determined not to let anything depress us and to find humour where we could. There was one man, for example, who was very busily delousing himself while we were singing "Silent Night" . . . We knew of course, this coming Christmas would stand no comparison with the past ones but we would be happy with some proper food and perhaps a couple of packets of sweets, a few cigarettes, or a drop of Schnapps . . . The nicest thing would be a letter from home – but that was out of the question.

'On Christmas Eve we worked until midday, had lunch and were ordered to parade at 1500 hrs by which time we all had to have proper haircuts, were to be washed and shaved and have cleaned up our uniforms. It was a real carnival as 24 men tried to wash, shave, clean their teeth, polish their boots and brush their uniforms all in one little room. The barber came and gave us all a quick run over. At the appointed time we were all ready.

'We paraded in a deep gully as deep as a house and filled with snow. An open space had been shovelled out and in the centre of the area was an undecorated Christmas tree. I must say that I went on parade without any sort of feeling, but when the parade was dismissed after half an hour I had tears in my eyes – and I wasn't the only one. Captain Foelsche, a veteran of the Great War and a man who had spent several Christmasses in the front-line trenches, took the parade. We started to sing "Silent Night" and at the first notes I felt choked and tears came into my eyes. Our elderly, grey-haired commander made a little speech. Imagine it! In Russia, 15 degrees below zero, on parade in an open space surrounded by walls of snow, there were 150 German soldiers celebrating the event. Our thoughts flew homewards to our parents, children, wives and fiancés. Very unwillingly we came back to the brutal reality of where we were.

'When we got back into our room we lit the candles on our own tree. There was no mail so we had to make do with what the Company had organized. As I said before, we had not reckoned on getting much and were pleasantly surprised. We each received a Christmas cake, 250 grammes of biscuits, a kilo of peppermints, six tubes of sweets, 50 cigarettes and tobacco. We also had an issue of real bean coffee. We ate our Christmas cake with the coffee, then the biscuits and finally the peppermints. Then a good cigar and the atmosphere got quite pleasant. We sang carols and soldiers' songs and there was talk of the old days and even jokes. Suddenly Sergeant

Unversagt came in with two big parcels which had been packed and sent to us unknown soldiers by some young girls in Pomerania. If they could only have known the pleasure that we got from their kind action.

'I split the contents of the parcels into twenty-four separate groups. The main things in them were a harmonica, a pipe, 25 cigarettes, 10 cigars, note-paper, writing blocks, toothpaste, chocolate and other things. There was great excitement when we drew lots. Of course, everybody wanted the pipe. One of our comrades had arranged with his wife that at 2100 hrs he would go out into the night and look up at the Great Bear constellation. She would do the same. He left our room at 2100 hrs, all of us went with him and began to sing. After a time we all struck up with "The stars of our homeland", and faced westwards to where, more than 2,000 kms away our loved ones were sitting around their Christmas trees at home.'

It had been apparent to OKH as early as August, that the war in the east could not be won during 1941, and they made representations about the need for cold weather clothing. Their proposals were turned down and as a result the German Army, as we have seen from the narratives in this chapter, froze, fought and died in the winter battles of that first year in Russia. One of those who fought was Rudolf Lanz, a gunner in the flak artillery.

'The winter of 1941/42, was one of the coldest on record. It was hard and bitter and we were unprepared for it. The terrible snowstorms halted our march upon Moscow, but worse was to come. As a result of the Russian attacks we were forced to retreat. This was the first time in the war that this had happened.

'As a mark of distinction for what we had suffered on the Eastern Front during those bitter months, the Führer ordered that a commemorative medal be struck. This was in one grade only. There was no Second or First Class, just one medal for us all, Generals as well as ordinary soldiers. The medal fitted into the same button-hole as that for the Second Class Iron Cross and, like the EK II, displayed only the ribbon. That ribbon was predominantly red in colour with a narrow central stripe of white and black.

'Although the winter campaign medal was an award, nearly equal to the EK II in status, the ordinary soldiers in their usual cynical fashion, had soon given it other names. The two usual ones were "The Order of the Frozen Meat", or the "Mincemeat Medal". Those names reminded us of the agonies we had suffered from the terrible cold and that we had lost many comrades, not only as battle casualties but as the result of the shocking living conditions. There was nothing subversive in giving the medal those particular names – these were soldiers' descriptions.'

Confident of Victory, 1942

WINTER, THE NEW ENEMY

The Red Army's counter-offensive forced back the formations of Army Group Centre from the approaches to Moscow and the retreat of the German divisions began amid scenes of confusion. To bring order out of this chaos Hitler's directive of 18 December 1941 ordered that 'Major retrograde movements are not to be carried out. They lead to complete loss of heavy weapons and equipment . . . Troops are to be ordered to offer fanatical resistance to enemy units which have broken into their positions and are not to worry about the enemy who has broken through on the flanks or in the rear . . . The objective is to gain time . . .'

He admitted, in a speech on 30 January 1942, to commemorate the anniversary of the assumption of power in 1933, that 'It was not easy to change the direction of the war in the East from one in which we had always advanced to one in which we were on the defensive. It was not the Russians who had forced this change, rather it was the cold; 38, 40, 41 and sometimes 45 degrees below zero. Soldiers unaccustomed to such depths of cold cannot fight . . . As soon as the time came when we had to go over to the defensive, I saw it as my duty to take the responsibility for such an action upon my own shoulders . . . I want to tell my soldiers, here and now, wherever they may be listening to me in their frozen trenches – I know what you are going through, but I also know that the worst is behind us . . . Winter was the great hope of the eastern enemy . . . In four months we had reached almost to Moscow and Leningrad. Four winter months in the north have passed. The enemy advanced a few kilometres in a number of places and it cost him dear in blood and corpses. That may not concern him, but in a few weeks' time, in the south, the winter will break and spring will arrive . . . Then will come the time when the ice in the north will melt, when the ground will harden and when the German musketeer with his equipment can go into action again . . . I can tell you this, the German soldier at the Front knows he has not lost his infinite superiority over the Russian . . .'

That confidence was expressed by R. Stahlschmidt, of a field artillery regiment, who was certain that 1942 would be the year of victory. 'We knew that man for man we were better soldiers than the Russians. They had excellent weapons, vast amounts of material and overwhelming numbers of men. But we who had survived the winter and the Red Army's massive attacks, were confident that we had their measure. It was in that optimistic spirit that we waited for the summer campaign to open.'

As early as February 1942, Army Group Centre had set up a defensive front sufficiently strong to hold the assaults of the Red Army, which was itself now tired from the strain of battle. The exhausted soldiers of both sides welcomed the bitter winter which brought a halt to major operations. Both sides now had to wait until the ground had hardened. Only then could new and far-ranging offensives be undertaken. Hitler, who in his speech claimed that Germany had 'the strongest army in the world and the strongest air force in the world', went on to claim that 1942, would be, 'once again a year of great victories'. He had already planned an offensive for the summer. It was code-named Operation 'Blue'.

ALLIED DEFEAT AT DIEPPE

It was not only on the Eastern Front that the German Army was embattled. It was also fighting in Africa where it seemed, in the early summer of 1942, to be riding on the crest of a wave to victory. By the end of the year, however, it was in full retreat and heading for total defeat. In another theatre of operations, in France, the German forces did gain a positive victory, this one against a Canadian/British landing operation at Dieppe. Of this, Heinrich Kiss wrote:

'I was in an infantry unit in a division stationed near Dieppe. There was no warning that a British landing was expected although an increase in activity by enemy aircraft should have warned us. Late in the night of 19th August, I was relieved from guard duty and turned in to sleep. I remember it as being a bright, warm night and from the top of the cliffs in our area I can also recall that when I looked out to sea there was nothing suspicious to report. We were woken very early. An alarm call had come in from regimental HQ and we stood to arms. It would have been about 6 in the morning when a furious barrage opened. This came from the ships of the British navy and while their shells were falling all round us the RAF came in and bombed us.

'From our trenches on the top of the cliffs we saw emerging through a smoke-screen which the English had laid, lots of small craft racing through the sea towards us. Very quickly the British ships had grounded, the infantry had landed and were charging up the wide beach. Then our artillery opened up and shells began to land among the little boats. We opened fire upon the infantry with out machine-guns and mortars. Then more and more waves of boats came through the heavy defensive fire to land their men and there was talk of tanks coming down a sort of ramp on the ships. One of our battalion

officers was killed while attacking a tank with a flame-thrower and some of our men on top of the cliffs dropped hand-grenades on the heads of the Tommies sheltering at the base of the cliffs.

'The RAF had been flying about without any opposition, but, several hours later, our Luftwaffe fighters came into action attacking the landing ships and the larger vessels out at sea. This was something we only learned about later because at the time we could see nothing because of the smoke-screens which the British were still laying. I was wounded shortly after this and taken away to the RAP. According to my comrades not long after I was evacuated the first groups of British troops began to wave white flags and to surrender. The whole enterprise finished late in the afternoon. We had stopped the Tommies' invasion of Europe in 1942, or so we thought. They came back in 1944, and that time their invasion was successful.'

OPERATION 'BLUE'

It is to the Eastern Front that we return, to that theatre of operations where the principal burden of the war was being carried and in which the next major offensive, Operation 'Blue' would open. For this the military formations of the army and the Luftwaffe belonging to Army Group South were to strike eastwards. The confidence to launch 'Blue' lay in the false conclusions which Hitler drew from the German Army's opening attacks in the late spring of 1942. To Halder's observation that the Red Army was withdrawing according to plan, Hitler retorted that the Russians were fleeing in disorder; that the army's blows had finally destroyed the enemy. Unshake-ably convinced that his appreciation was correct, the Führer drew up his plans. He divided Army Group South into two Army Groups, 'A' under Field Marshal List and 'B' commanded by Freiherr von Weichs. Army Group 'A' was to strike for the Caucasus and oil supplies of Georgia. Army Group 'B' was to drive eastwards to the Volga and capture the sprawling city of Stalingrad.

Hitler's confidence was not altogether shared by those in command. Many Generals realized that the vast salient which that eastern advance would create, so enormous a length of front, could not be held entirely by the formations of the German Army. These were now too few in number to permit this. Germany would be compelled to rely upon the forces of the less well armed and less experienced satellite nations, Roumania, Hungary and Italy. While Paulus's Sixth German Army, part of Weich's Army Group 'B', fought to take the city, the foreign units, positioned to the north and to the south of Stalingrad, would hold the shoulders of the attack.

In November the Red Army's carefully prepared, major counter-offensive opened. Its blows struck and dispersed the satellite hosts. Through the gaps which had been created the Soviet forces poured and encircled German Sixth Army. The permission which Paulus sought from Hitler to withdraw the trapped forces, was refused. Instead Hitler planned that a fresh German battle group, Army Group 'Don', created from armoured units outside the pocket should break through. This new grouping was to smash a passage and reach Paulus's Sixth Army, but not to bring it out. Rather the task was to create a channel through which reinforcements would pour in such strength that they would eventually defeat the Red Army, keep a German grip on the Volga and, thereby, fulfil the principal objective of the summer campaign.

Despite heroic efforts the relief operation failed. Still the Führer refused to countenance Sixth Army's withdrawal. Instead, he ordered that Stalingrad was to be supplied by air. Goering had assured him that the Luftwaffe could do this. Goering was lying. Such an operation was beyond the capabilities of the German air force. There soon came time when Sixth Army was starving in the ruins of the dead city. At one point in the siege one of Paulus's staff officers was flown out of the pocket so that he could tell Hitler the true and terrible situation in which the troops were placed. The Führer refused to accept the facts which were presented to him; that the dead were unburied, that wounded lay untended in the roofless ruins of factories, in cellars and in sewers. That the army was freezing, starving and suffering in misery. That Generals whose divisions had been destroyed had taken up rifles or machine-pistols and had fought as ordinary soldiers until they too fell in unequal battle – as their soldiers had.

LETTERS FROM STALINGRAD

By the middle of January 1943, the Soviets had compressed Sixth Army's pocket and had split it in two. Both German enclaves fought on but the end was never in doubt. Shortly before it came the soldiers were told that each could write home. These letters were then flown out of the pocket. In the Reich the mail was read in order that the Nazi leaders could establish the mood of the army which they had condemned to death. Most letters were subsequently delivered but some were not and several sacks of undelivered mail were found by the Allies at the end of the war. Those letters make poignant reading and extracts from a few are reproduced here by permission of the German War Graves Commission. They express every sort of emotion: rejection of God, professional acceptance of the situation and loving, tender farewells.

'In Stalingrad one rejects any idea of a God. I must say this, dear father, and it saddens me for two reasons. You raised me because there was no mother and you kept always before my eyes the picture of God and of an immortal soul. I regret my words for a second reason, because these will be the last which you will receive from me and I shall never be able to tell you why in explanation . . . I looked for God in every crater, in each ruined house, on every corner, with each comrade; when I lay alone in my slit trench . . . God did not show himself although I cried out to him with all my heart . . . No, father, there is no God. I write this and know how terrible it is that I cannot make a reconciliation. And if there is a God then he is in your hymn books and prayers: in the pious words of priests and pastors, with people who have the sound of bells and the perfume of incense. He is not here in Stalingrad.'

'Dear Father! The division has been selected for the big battle but this will not take place. You may wonder why it is to you that I write and also to your official address. But what I have to say in this my last letter can only be said between men. You will find ways to tell Mother what has happened. Today we are being allowed to write. That means, for anybody who has an idea of the real situation, that this is the last time.

'You are a Colonel on the General Staff, Father, and you know what is happening. Thus I do not need to write things which might sound sentimental. This is the end. I think it may last another eight days and then it will be the finish. I do not seek explanations for our present situation here. These are now unimportant and serve no purpose. But if there is anything I want to say it is this: do not seek the explanations for our present situation from us, but from those around you and from those who are responsible. Keep your chin up, Father, you and those who share your opinions. Be careful to ensure that nothing worse happens to our Fatherland. Let the hell here on the Volga be a warning to you. I beg you, do not throw away this knowledge.

'And now to present things. Of the whole division only 69 men are still fit for duty. Bleyer is still alive and so is Hartlieb. Little Degen has lost both arms and will almost certainly be back in Germany now. It is the end for him, too. Ask him for any details which you may need to know. D . . . has lost all hope. I should love to know what he thinks of our situation and its consequences. We have two machine-guns and 400 rounds of ammunition, one mortar and ten rounds. Other than that only tiredness. Berg . . . broke out with 20 men, in defiance of orders. Perhaps it is better to know in three days what will happen than to wait three weeks.

'Finally, to the personal. You may be certain that we shall make a good end although at 30 it is a bit premature. No sentimentality. Give Lydia and Helen each a handshake from me and greetings to one and all. With my hand at the rim of my helmet in salute, Father, your son, Lieutenant . . . takes leave of you.'

'I have been looking for some time at your photograph. In my mind is the memory of that lovely summer evening of the last year of peace as we

walked through a valley of blossom towards our house. Life was such a rich
carpet spread before us . . . Now there is no valley of blossom; you are not
with me and in place of the carpet of colour there is an unending field of
white in which there is no summer but only winter. And there is no future
any more . . . at least not for me . . . If you receive this letter, read it well
and you may hear my voice . . . They told us that we are fighting for Germany
but they are very few here who believe that our pointless sacrifice can serve
any purpose at all to our Fatherland.'

CAPTIVITY AND THE STRUGGLE FOR SURVIVAL

When the battle of Stalingrad ended on 2 February 1943, the Russians
claimed to have taken more than 190,000 German soldiers prisoner. That
figure was reduced within weeks to the more realistic figure of 100,000, but
was lowered still further several times during the war to an absurd total of
35,000. Of all the German soldiers who were taken captive at Stalingrad less
than 5,000 came back home. Those whom summary execution and untreated
wounds did not take away immediately, died within weeks from the bitter
cold. For this was the depth of winter with temperatures often 25 degrees
below zero and the first overnight halts on the march into captivity were
made on the open steppe. In the following months others died of typhus and
dysentery. Those who survived were put to work in the mines of Siberia and
died from the sicknesses associated with mining for lead, copper and other
dangerous minerals. So it is not surprising that I have met only one man who
survived the horrors of Stalingrad. Johann Radl served as a gunner in an
infantry division. He set out to return to his native Austria even before the
war ended. He was released from a camp east of the Volga in the first weeks
of 1945.

'The situation [in Stalingrad] when the order came to surrender
[February 1943] can only be described as inhuman. Towards the end the
Red Army infantry seldom bothered to attack our positions. We – Sixth
Army – were more or less already dead men and there was no sense in the
Russians losing good soldiers in unnecessary assaults. They could afford to
wait until the end came and to bring about that end used only shelling and
bombings.

'I do not need to describe the misery of the first days as a prisoner. Let
me just say that there were thousands of us and that the Soviet Army had
more important considerations than feeding and sheltering this mass of
enemy soldiers. This does not forgive, but does explain why so many died
in the first weeks. We were too big a problem for the local authorities.
Eventually the unwieldly column was broken up into manageable groups and
mine was quartered in a Kholkoz somewhere to the north of Stalingrad – not

too far from the Volga. We were each interrogated and when I told them that my father had been in the illegal Communist Party of Austria, they did some checking up. About a week after my interrogation I was called to go to the camp commandant's office and was interrogated by a civilian who spoke Austrian/German. He mentioned several things connected with past events in Austria and then asked why I had not told my first interrogators that my father had been given an 18-month sentence in a concentration camp. The Soviets were so well informed about conditions in Austria that they knew my father had been sentenced for listening to a foreign radio station.

'My work norm was reduced because my principal duty was to re-educate my fellow prisoners in right thinking – as a political activist. At the end of January 1945, after nearly two years as a prisoner, I was called up to the Kommandantura and given my discharge papers together with a pass which authorized me to be fed by Red Army units. A special pass was needed to travel by train, and I was not issued with one of these so I walked most of the way home. I found the going easier once I had crossed out of the Soviet Union and was in Roumania and then Hungary. I always made for the Communist Party HQ in a town and flourished my free meal pass. It never failed and even if the food was not lavish it was marvellous to eat proper food again after prison diet. The most difficult part of my journey was in the Russian-occupied Zone of Austria. The Party Officials all had a Red Army officer in their offices most of whom were not very pleased to be helping a former enemy, despite my family's pro-Russian attitudes. I reached home during August 1945.'

Radl was lucky that his servitude finished quickly and did not end in death. Another man who came back from Stalingrad was the unknown author of a report published in the German War Graves Commission book, *Kriegsgraeber in Europa*.

'After our last bits and pieces had been plundered, haversacks and blankets stolen, medals and badges ripped from our coats with curses and imprecations, the thousands of those who had been assembled were driven out on the march by an enemy who knew no mercy . . . Towards evening we reached the ruins of a place named Yersevko and stayed overnight there encamped on the snow. In the morning we headed for Dubovka. We left behind in Yersevko thousands of our comrades; German soldiers who had died on a steppe where there was neither food nor shelter.

'Our second march day took the column of misery and dying to Dubovka on the Volga. En route we were attacked and robbed by civilians who stole anything we still had with us. Boots were taken from the soldiers' feet so that they had to march bare-footed through the snow. Thousands died that day. They sank, helpless, to the ground right and left of the road and died in the snow which soon covered them. During the evening of 4th February 1943, we reached Dubovka. There was no POW camp there, only a simple, guarded, Collecting Point. There were no shelters, cookhouses, sanitary arrangements or anything else. Outside the town there were the ruins of a monastery, a large sheep pen and, in another place, a former Red Army troop camp consisting of earthen huts. There was no heating material. The only drinking water was a frozen puddle near a blown-up water pump. The Red Army left us to our own devices. Some supplies of raw salt fish and dry bread were issued. In the camp there was spotted typhus. Soon everybody was infected. In the camp there was starvation, cholera, dysentery, paratyphus and hunger delusions. Soon there were more dead than living. We never saw any Russian personnel. After twelve days we survivors were driven away from the heaps of dead to the gates of the monastery; first of all the rank and file and then, a day later, the officers. Two columns left this place of the dead. We left behind 17,000 dead comrades. The survivors, perhaps two to three thousand in number, marched southwards for two days, driven through the ruins of the city of Stalingrad. Whoever was too weak to go any farther was shot by the guards at the rear of the column, supervised by Soviet officers.

'After 120 kilometres we reached Beketovka. A large living area had been cleared of civilians and surrounded by barbed wire. This was to be our prison camp. Those just arriving had a shock. The two-storey houses and the open places – in short the whole area surrounded by barbed wire – was packed with the dead bodies of those who had been taken captive in the Stalingrad South pocket and who had died here of disease. The number of dead was thought to be about 42,000 . . .'

AIR SUPPLY

It is usual when considering the battle of Stalingrad to think particularly of the ground fighting and the loss of the soldiers of Sixth Army. The role of the Luftwaffe is seldom considered and when it is, the view is often a critical one; of a Service which failed its army comrades. It is an unjust accusation for the Luftwaffe lost nearly 500 transport planes in its attempt to carry supplies by air to the encircled troops.

Goering's boast that his air force could fly-in sufficient supplies caused Hitler to order Sixth Army to hold its position on the Volga. Responsible Luftwaffe officers in charge of operational units knew that Goering's claim was not possible. Lieutenant General Fiebig, commanding 8 Flieger Korps, was astonished when he discussed the situation with Schmidt, Paulus's chief of staff, to be told that the army would have to be supplied by air. To this demand Fiebig retorted, 'It is absolutely impossible. Our transport aircraft are needed in Africa and on other Fronts. I must warn against any exaggerated hopes,' and in a later conversation emphasized, 'I must warn against placing too much confidence upon being supplied by air . . . I have thought deeply about this and come back to the conclusion that Sixth Army cannot be supplied in this fashion. It is just not possible to calculate the effects of the Russian winter or enemy action upon the conduct of the operation.'

Fiebig was correct in his assessment of the situation. The minimum daily requirement of Sixth Army was 480 tons of fuel, ammunition and food. The maximum load which a Ju 52 could carry was 2 tons. Therefore each day the air bridge would need no fewer than 240 machines to make the round trip. Even under normal conditions the effects of enemy action, crashes upon take-off or landing and mechanical failures of all sorts would reduce the number of operational aircraft. It had also to be considered that, as a general rule, only one in three aircraft would be operational at any one time. Accepting that equation as correct, then a minimum of 720 Ju 52s was needed, and the Luftwaffe had only 750, some of which were in Africa or serving in other theatres of operation. It was, of course, possible to use other aircraft types, but these had shorter ranges and lower pay loads. Thus more of those types would have to be taken away from other important, operational duties – and, of course, there was the ever-present precarious fuel situation. The question of air supply to Stalingrad was an insoluble problem.

But Goering had assured Hitler that it could be done and General Schmidt, who had come to Sixth Army direct from Hitler's headquarters, was also convinced that it was possible. It was not – and unit war diaries record the attempts made by Luftwaffe crews to supply their comrades on the ground. The following report has been supplied by Franz Kurowski, author of the book, *Luftbrücke Stalingrad*, and shows the conditions under which crews of the Luftwaffe's transport aircraft carried out their missions.

'An icy wind, the biting cold of Russia, thrusts chilling fingers into our faces. Crammed into flying-suits we lean so that our backs rest against the warm sides of the starting-up lorry. For more than half an hour now hot air has been thawing out the engines of our aeroplane. Along the runway Ju 52s stand in a long line. We shall be off soon on a night operation, a supply drop to our army comrades who have been encircled for months past.

'There are gashes and holes in our aircraft's wings and tail; the scars of yesterday's mission. Today we shall be the first machine to take-off. It is already late in a bright, clear, winter afternoon. The engines roar as they are revved to full power. Ready for take-off. The machine lumbers through frozen snow up to the starting-point where a figure, muffled to the eyes, raises the white flag with green diagonal stripes. There is a cloud of powdered snow as our aeroplane roars down the strip, takes off, circles the airfield and then sets course for Stalingrad. As we get near to the city we remove the aircraft door and icy air howls through the machine. It gets dark very quickly. Below and in front of us we can see a great many points of light;

down below there are houses and whole villages lit up. We are over enemy territory and the first flak salvoes come up but burst harmlessly behind us. Half an hour later and the altimeter indicates we have descended to 4,000 metres. The numbing cold penetrates our flying-suits. I sit on a parachute attached to a box of ammunition which has been pushed near to the door.

'Searchlights sweep the sky and then on our starboard side and behind us there are AA bursts. The fire from the enemy flak stops abruptly and one lot of searchlights goes out only to be replaced by others whose beams criss-cross the sky. We are nearing the target area. Searchlight beams catch us and for as long as we are held there we are blinded by the intense light. Once out of them and below we can see long columns of vehicles driving with headlights blazing. These are Russian supply columns. Their blazing headlights are evidence that we do not have air superiority. Our pilot throttles back and we begin to descend in a series of tight curves. The altimeter shows that we are now just a few hundred metres above the ground and it is time for the run in to the 'pocket'. We expect that any second now the enemy will open fire, but there is no firing. What has happened? Not one single shell; no tracer? The pilot presses the horn; we are over the target. As we throw out the first box we are caught in the blinding light of a cone of searchlights, but apart from that there is no other reaction from the enemy. Has the ground fighting ended?

'We are flying at a height of 150 metres. The heavy ammunition boxes are dragged across the floor of the aircraft to the door and are then flung out. The observer sees, with a sense of shock, a black shadow racing towards us. There is a sudden deafening crash. An enemy plane has rammed us. Our machine rears up, seems to stand still and then the nose dips and we drop like a lift. I had been flung against the opposite wall by the force of the collision, but with a single leap reach the aircraft door again. I think of baling out but my parachute is in the tail of the aircraft. I grip the door handles tightly. The earth rushes up to meet us. There is a bright flickering light behind us; an enemy aircraft is on our tail firing at us and then comes another heavy thud. He has rammed us again.

'Slowly the pilot gains control of the machine. Then there is another crash. We have struck the ground and our Ju rolls, with flaps raised and only on one wheel between bomb and shell craters. Frightening thoughts race through my mind. Shall we be left here in the "pocket"? To get maximum power the pilot overrides the "governor" and opens the throttle as far as he can. The roar of the engines rises to a scream. The tailwheel still drags along the ground, but the Ju 52, shuddering under the strain, begins at last to climb. Two minutes later the AA guns fire at us and although we are hit again in the tail and wing we gain a little height and then begin to climb quickly. The right wing has a wide gash, a metre deep. The flap end is torn off, one-third of the elevator is missing. Another piece, almost a metre long stands vertically in the air. Thank Heaven, it tears off in the slipstream and the steering difficulties it has caused go with it. We have more than 300 kilometres to cover to reach our aerodrome and the most important question is, will the plane hold out? It did and we landed safely but shakily on our own airfield.'

TANK-TO-TANK COMBAT

As we have seen Army Group Don was given the task of creating a passage through to Sixth Army and one of the formations which bore the burden of the assault was 6th Panzer Division. Its task was to force a crossing of the River Aksai and then to advance north-eastwards along the railway line to reach Stalingrad. R. Pohl remembers.

'D-Day for the operation was 12th December, and by the third day our advance was slowing down. Ivan put in everything he had to halt us, using massed formations of tanks. On the 15th I was wounded near a miserable hell-hole called Verky Kumsky. Very early in the morning of that day great numbers of T-34s had attacked us and had split our regiments forcing them for a time to fight individual battles. Then, later in the morning, hundreds of Ivan's tanks came into sight. By this time we were outnumbered probably by 3 or 4 to 1. Those reinforcement tanks were backed by whole regiments of anti-tank guns. We had been ordered to make an attack to capture towards Verky Kumsky and as soon as we moved into the opening stages of our assault the Russian mass which had been thundering towards us suddenly halted. This was a good tactical move on their part because in those days it was not usual to fire the main armament of a tank while on the move. To do so forfeited accuracy. To achieve accuracy one needed a stable platform i.e., a stationary tank. That is why the Russian tanks had halted. Even now, fifty years after the event, I remember that day well and particularly the sight of that fleet of tanks whose wide front overlapped ours and which was echeloned in great depth. It was a huge block of tanks – line after line of white-painted machines whose vehicle numbers, painted in black, stood out against the white-painted turrets.

'Our panzer companies rolled forward tactically disposed and as commandant of our Pz IV, I had a good view of what we were facing. It seemed that every gun in that mass of Ivans was pointing at my vehicle. I suppose that the Red gun tactic was to concentrate the fire of a group of tank and anti-tank guns upon a single panzer and thus to knock us out one by one. We had one advantage; mobility. They were like a herd of buffalo which does not have the freedom of movement enjoyed by the leopards which prowl round the flanks of the herd – and we were the leopards. We manoeuvred and picked them off because they were immobile whereas we were moving

and therefore harder to hit. Being stationary had its disadvantages as well as
its advantages. Practically every shot we fired was a good hit. Of course, we
lost machines but our vehicle repair workshops were up with us and changed
damaged parts under fire. Some of the knocked out panzers which could not
be repaired were cannibalized to get parts, fuel and ammunition.

'Two of our Companies were in Verky Kumsky but they were
surrounded and in danger of being overrun. To rescue them our Colonel
grouped the last reserves, five companies of tanks, and ordered a head-on
charge at the Russian mass in front of us. This was a desperate move because
some of our panzers had fired off all their main ammunition and had no time
to load up again. The unexpected bold move succeeded. The panzers that
had no shells fired their machine-guns to keep the enemy anti-tank guns and
infantry down while those panzers that still had shells shot their way through
the weakest part of the Russian mass. We charged into the village and
engaged the twenty or so T-34s which were milling about inside it, rescued
our trapped comrades and took them back to the main body. Then we tanked
up, loaded fresh ammunition and went back to the battle. During the early
afternoon my panzer was hit three times in quick succession by anti-tank
shells. There was a battery of guns, so well concealed that I never saw them
until it was too late. Two of their shots hit and passed through our body but
did no great damage. The third penetrated our right-hand side but did not
exit and continued to whirl around inside the vehicle. We were lucky to
escape with only two casualties; the driver killed and me wounded. The other
crew members were unhurt. Shell fragments wounded me very badly in the
calves and feet. The radio was undamaged and we called up a couple of
vehicles from our Company. One of them fired air bursts over the Reds to
keep them down while the other moved to a flank and ran over the guns and
crews. That gave us a breathing space until the recovery panzer came up and
towed us to where the workshops carried out emergency repairs and ordered
up a new crew to replace mine.

'I was taken to a base hospital and when the Red Army's winter offensive
threatened the whole of Army Group South was taken into Poland. I
convalesced in Germany before being returned to unit in March 1943, just in
time for the preparation for the Battle of Kursk.'

The Turning-Point, 1943

REST AND RECREATION

Heid Ruehl, serving at that time with the artillery regiment, recalled the late spring and early summer of 1943, when 'Das Reich' Division, part of Army Group South, was in reserve.

'The heavy fighting in which the SS Panzer Corps had been involved around Kharkov, during the spring of 1943, had finally come to an end. One recalls those months as being the end of a hard-fought, but exciting campaign; one of continual movement, of marches which lasted for weeks on end and of having to make frequent changes of position.

'Today, decades later, one can lose oneself remembering how we stood up on the gun carriages as we raced after the Russians who were trying to escape on their panje-sledges. And smile as we recall how we loaded our trucks with sacks of flour and sugar, with barrels of melting butter, tins of every sort of food – all things which had been looted from German stores during the Russians' westward advance. Now they [the enemy] were going in the other direction and were trying to escape by throwing out the ballast of looted food and thus lightening their sledges. They threw everything away except weapons and these we only found with the dead when the battle was over.

'We did not want for food in those days, nor for some time afterwards. But for weeks we were not able to take our uniforms from off our bodies and we seldom slept under cover. But that did not matter very much. Our winter clothing was excellent, quite different from that of the previous year and, in any case, the cold was not so intense. We could survive it!

'We well deserved the rest that was given us after capturing Kharkov. First we occupied the barracks at Ossnova airfield and then went on to quarters in the village of Polevoya. There was a minimum of parades and we were bivouacked in a romantic region of hazelnut bushes. To begin with we were captivated by the song of the nightingales but after a few days we wished that they would go somewhere else and sing.

'In my ears I can still hear the marvellous singing of the Ukrainians who had volunteered to serve with us. There was a whole platoon of them, intelligent men who were ready to fight against the Soviets. We trained them so well on our weapons that they could have served as gun numbers in our battery. Yet one morning they had all vanished and had all taken their rifles with them. Only one man did not desert and he told us why the others had gone. One of the officers had hit a Ukrainian with a riding whip because he had not saluted properly. It is very probable that most of us would have reacted in the same way to such arrogance.

'I can still see the battalion administration officer standing on the huge scales in the Kolkhoz, the collective farm which housed our Orderly Room, cookhouse and living-quarters. The Admin Officer threatened the entire battery with heaven and hell and the most terrible punishments because one of our men had, supposedly, been seen "requisitioning" a beast. Unfortunately the miscreant had not been caught in the act, but he [the QM] knew very well that the animal in question was hidden somewhere in the Company area . . . He looked round the ring of puzzled faces. When he asked the CO, the platoon and the gun commanders they all agreed that something should be done. Meanwhile a couple of the men in the crowd had to slip away to hide the laughter which would have told the Admin Officer that his suspicions had been correct. He could not know that the spot on which he was making his flaming speech of accusation against the thieves was directly above the place where the cut up beef was buried. As soon as he had gone it was dug up. A couple of days later he was the guest of our battery commander and enjoyed a marvellous goulash with the customary noodles which he ate without making one single reference to stolen cattle.

'At about this time our CO, whom we named "Fieseler Storch" from his peculiar way of walking, took up the suggestion which some of the men had made, to hold an open air summer feast. Not too far away from our billeting area were a number of ladies belonging to the Signals branch. It was not difficult to get them to come to our feast but among the preparations that needed to be made was that of constructing a dance floor. This task was given to me as a sort of 'occupation therapy'. I was helped in my task by the Russian mayor, the Starost, to whom I went for advice and help. He started off with a string of excuses; "No wood, no saw mill, so no boards." Very logical. But he was up against a very stubborn German NCO and once he had agreed I was astonished at the way in which the Russians improvised . . . Within two days a tree-felling commando had brought in some tree trunks and the Russians began to erect a platform in the village square and to cover this with well-cut planks – all done within a couple of hours. We were all very impressed with this performance and filled with admiration at the capability of the Russians. As a reward – money was not asked for – we promised the Starost that he could use the wood for his own people after our unit had moved out. That promise may well have been the impetus for the speed with which they worked. In an open space in our bivouac area we had soon created a sort of Bavarian festival site and the dance floor was almost ready . . .

'Rumours grew that we were to be re-equipped. Out battalion was to be made more mobile, as befitted a panzer unit, by being issued with SP guns, the "Wespe", a 10.5cm howitzer and the "Hummel" a 15cm howitzer. As soon as we had been issued with these new weapons our rest period ended and we began to train hard for the forthcoming summer offensive.'

HOLDING THE LINE AT VOLKHOV

In the northern sector of the Eastern Front fighting was still going on around Leningrad. One of the units engaged was 100th Gebirgs Regiment whose commanding officer, Helmut Herrman, wrote an account of the defensive fighting in the Volkhov area during the summer of 1943. From 1941, Army Group North's attempts to cut off the city of Leningrad had been countered by the Red Army's efforts to raise the siege. The River Volkhov, some 60 kilometres to the south-east of Leningrad, had been since the earliest days of the war the scene of furious, long-drawn-out battles which had gained for it a reputation as terrible as that of Verdun in the Great War, or the more recent Stalingrad.

'At the end of June 1943, I was commanding the battalion during the temporary absence of our CO, Major Wecker. For some weeks past we had been involved in changing our positions, which meant in the vast majority of cases, leaving well-constructed fortifications to take over less strongly built places.

'The front line on such sectors was often that at which a Russian penetration had been sealed off or where a German attack had been brought to a standstill. We finally took over a section of the line upon which, only a few weeks later, the full force of the enemy's long-expected offensive was to fall. The area was marshy and dotted with pieces of sandy ground none of which was more than 5 metres high in our sector. On the enemy side the ground climbed slightly. There was dense forest and a few clumps of birch trees. Movement in the marshy areas was only possible along corduroy roads, but there was firm going on the sandy areas.

'The battalion's positions were set up so that we had an area of high ground on each flank. No 1 Company was on the right wing, No 2 on the left and No 3 Company was in reserve. Our right-flank neighbour was the regiment's 3rd Battalion and on the left we had a battalion of the 85th Gebirgs Regiment. From certain places between the battalions as well as between the individual companies the enemy had observation into our lines.

'On my first tour of inspection through the positions into which we had just moved – a place we were to call "Rawhide Height", a squadron of low-flying, slow-flying Russian Il 2s came over. These machines were so well armoured that rifle and machine-gun fire had little effect upon them. It was clear that on this occasion their targets were much farther back so that for the moment I was not too afraid. But the thought stayed with me that if they had bombed our positions they would have destroyed our trenches and dug-outs. It was further clear to me that such air raids would be a feature of the opening phase of the Russian offensive. The question worried me; How could we protect ourselves against this threat?

'I knew that during the First World War dug-outs had been constructed using tree trunks driven into the earth. This is what we would have to do. I turned to Regiment and was able to convince them. Regiment went to Division and work was begun on cutting down trees and sawing these in lengths which were brought by night into our positions. Where the ground allowed it we began the construction of deep bunkers which would be proof against heavy artillery fire.

'The positions held by No 2 Company were the ones in the greatest danger. On the enemy side the ground rose slightly and the Russians had also run out saps and trenches dangerously close to our positions. The only track to the Company was across the swampy sector completely under enemy observation. At that time of the year the nights did not get completely dark so that movement could be seen even during what were normally the hours of darkness. In addition, the Russians sent out battle patrols each night looking for weak spots in our defence. These were always beaten off by using one of the guns of our infantry gun platoon which fired from a flank into the ground immediately in front of No 2 Company's positions . . . It was used in the following fashion: once No 2 Company had established that an enemy attack was under way a flare was fired over the threatened area. Immediately the gun fired. The secret was that the gun was manned day and night and the gun number sat waiting for the warning flare. Before it had died away the first shells were falling.

'It was immediately clear to me that No 2 Company would be a forlorn hope when the Russian attack came in. It struck me as absurd that a natural obstacle, like the marsh, should be behind us and not in front of us. A thorough reconnaissance produced the solution to the problem. If the left sector of the battalion could be withdrawn to the firm ground behind the swamp, work could begin on building good positions and the track leading up to the Company positions would be out of sight of the enemy. My decision was quickly reached. No 3 Company, which was occupying the area into which No 2 Company would move, was ordered to begin work on a system of defence in depth, in what would be the new front line.

'Meanwhile, No 2 Company was suffering from Russian battle patrols as well as from artillery and mortar barrages. As the movement which I proposed meant pulling back the front line for a distance of only 400 metres, I expected that Regiment would authorize this automatically. Major Wecker, our former CO, and now acting as regimental commander, came forward to

see the problem for himself. I showed him the exposed positions of No 2 Company. He agreed to my plan but told me that he would have to get agreement from Division because any withdrawal would affect the neighbouring units. Colonel Glasl, who was acting as divisional commander, came into our battalion area to judge the situation. When I showed him No 2 Company's positions he was shaken . . . He promised that he would immediately contact Corps because a withdrawal of the battle line was not a decision that he could make. There was a Führer Order which forbade the slightest withdrawal of the front line without Hitler's permission. Corps reacted and sent the chief of staff, a colonel. I dragged him through the swamp and across the area over which the Russians had observation. The colonel, who was to be killed in action during the offensive, understood the situation but regretted, because of the Führer Order, etc., that he would have to obtain permission from Army. In the meantime losses to the 2nd Company continued to rise and so did my blood pressure.

'Army could make no decision but sent a lieutenant-colonel from the Staff who was to make a report. I put him through the same routine as the other officers had suffered and explained the measures which I intended to take. He declared himself completely satisfied and promised me that his report would be favourably written. He himself could not make a decision . . . To cut the thing short, Army asked Army Group and received the necessary authority but with the remark that according to the Führer Order, etc., a withdrawal was not permitted, but in view of the need for the action . . . .

'Army Group's agreement was passed down through the channels. This unnecessary toing and froing had cost three weeks, three weeks of daily losses, mostly to No 2 Company. It was unbelievable but a fact that the Eastern Front was seen as "The OKH Theatre of Operations" and Hitler had taken over as Supreme Commander of OKH. Italy, on the other hand was considered as a "Wehrmacht Theatre of Operations" and came under OKW. This allowed the commanders on the ground more freedom.

'During those three weeks the battalion did not remain inactive. No 3 Company helped by No 4 Company built dug-outs and positions which would form the future front line and sited those positions to give mutual support. The positions were built in such a fashion that they could not be attacked frontally. The Pioneer Platoon laid a row of T mines along a 300-metre length of swamp, each mine placed a metre apart and detonated the whole 300 in one huge blast. This created a small earthquake, a wall of mud rose into the earth and when it had settled a swampy, impassable water-filled ditch some 100 metres wide protected the front line. Barbed wire strengthened the defences. We learned later from a Russian deserter that the explosion of our mines had been taken by the enemy to be the detonation of a salvo from the "Stalin organ". No 1 Company was also employed in building bunkers, a very important task as the withdrawal from the old front line made their area that much more sensitive.

'The withdrawal was made just in time and the enemy did not discover it immediately. The Russian offensive opened with hours of drum fire upon our positions. A deserter had told us the date and time of the offensive. It was 22nd July 1943. The Company Commander of No 1 Company had been out looking for his supply column and was just able to return to his positions when the barrage opened. What we had expected happened. The area which No 2 Company had held before being moved back was smothered with shells of medium and heavy calibre. The ground was ploughed up. No one could have survived such a bombardment. Then the Red Army infantry came in in battalion strength, convinced that the shellfire had destroyed everything. They carried on their assault intending to widen the breach which they thought had been created. They advanced straight into our enfilade fire and into the obstructions in the marsh.

'For more than two weeks three Soviet regiments attacked the positions which 1st Battalion held, with the main effort coming in against No 1 Company. The attacks followed heavy barrages and were made usually at dawn. Some of the assaulting troops were caught in their own artillery fire so furious were their assaults. Our men could only survive the shellfire by staying in the deep dug-outs and this meant that the Russians always got into our trenches and had to be driven out by immediate counter-attack. We, the defenders, had the advantage of knowing the layout of our defensive system. During the second week the Red Air Force attacked the whole battlefield as far back as the artillery positions with carpets of bombs. Their raids were made at night and it was then that we experienced, for the first time, the "Christmas Trees", the flares which were the target markers. Each night the Company portering-parties, together with the men of the pioneer platoon, brought up bombs and grenades, repaired damaged trenches and brought back the wounded and the dead. The mortar platoon often had to dig their mortars out of the swampy ground and the signallers went out during the pauses in the barrages to repair broken lines and to repair communications. The stretcher-bearers were always in action.

'During the course of the offensive No 2 Company was badly hit. The Company Commander, Lieutenant Schneider, was killed by shrapnel as he came out of his Tac HQ to get an idea of the situation. The enemy's barrage on that first day destroyed the forest and left only tree stumps standing. By the third day even they had been torn away. The whole landscape was a massive field of craters. One had a longer field of vision, but nothing was recognizable any more. When the battalion, reduced to a handful of men, was finally pulled out we could proudly say that the front line was still intact. For this action the battalion received fifty Iron Crosses (First Class) which I distributed immediately.'

FIRESTORM IN HAMBURG

Whereas at the beginning of 1942, Germany had stood in the position of undisputed power in Europe, the end of that year saw her facing military reverses in two theatres of war, Russia and Africa. Then, in 1943, the first hammer blows of the concerted Allied air offensive struck her cities, reinforcing the unco-ordinated attacks that the RAF and the USAF had been making for years. The first major, terrifying demonstration of Allied air power was made against Hamburg between 24 July and 3 August. The climax of that series of raids was reached during the night of 27/28 July, when the release of hundreds of thousands of incendiary bombs produced a sea of flames – a fire-storm. This raid had been an experiment to see whether such a storm could be created. Its success at Hamburg was followed by attacks upon other German cities and did not end until Dresden was destroyed in February 1945.

The Department of Printed Books of the Imperial War Museum has in its archives the official report by the Police Chief of Hamburg on the result of that series of raids. Its pages describe how a fire-storm was created. 'It is easy to explain its physical development. The simultaneous explosion of a great number of incendiary bombs creates a large number of fires which eventually build up to create one huge conflagration. The hot air rising from that blaze produces a suction effect producing winds greater in power than conventional wind forces . . . There are vast differences in temperature . . . Whereas . . . temperatures of 20 to 30 degrees Celsius can be measured, in fire-storms the differences lie between, 600, 800 and even 1000 degrees . . . The terrifying power of fire-storms cannot be measured by normal meteorological standards . . .'

The violence of such fire-storms were beyond the capabilities of the fire brigades to control let alone extinguish. There were reports that some fire crews were sucked into the holocaust and other stories that furniture and even motor cars were seen flying through the air towards the flames. There was also a story that some survivors had been splashed with napalm. To extinguish the flames they had submerged themselves in the rivers and canals of the city only to begin burning again as soon as they emerged from the water. A development of that story was that after a time the SS went round and shot them, to put them out of their misery. It is a story that was refuted by Martin Middlebrook who found no evidence to support it. But the raids themselves had been terrifying in the scale of destruction and in the way in which the victims had died. Hans Schumann wrote:

'My brother lived in Hamburg and when news of the raids was released was granted home leave. He was stationed at that time on the Channel coast working as a storeman in a naval depot. The change in him when he came to our parent's home was terrible. For days he would say nothing, but then it all came out in a burst of words. His wife and children, together with their neighbours, had all taken shelter in the air raid cellar of their house. He and another man opened the iron door which formed the entrance to the shelter. It was still warm and yet this was five days after the last raid had ended. As the door opened there was a sickening smell of burned and decaying flesh. By the light of their torches the men looked inside at the bodies. All those in the cellar were sitting like statues – statues made of leather. Inside the door was a pile of ashes and bones. Those nearest the door had been crumbled into dust by the heat of the fire. My brother kept saying that he hoped those in the cellar had been overcome by smoke and died in that fashion. He could not bear to think that they had been roasted alive. I think that what he had seen must have in some way mentally unbalanced him because he left his safe job in a stores and volunteered for every suicide mission that the Navy launched and was drowned on a training exercise with a Linse explosive motor-boat.'

WOMEN AT WAR: THE FLAKHELFERINNEN

With the deterioration in her military position which had become evident in 1943, it might have been expected that German women would have been called up for national service, as they had been in Britain and in the USSR. This was not the case and voluntary enlistment was the normal method of entry for the German woman eager to serve her country. Traute Kren's experience was not a normal one. In the coffee house of the airport departure lounge in Vienna, Traute, one of my dearest friends, suddenly started to talk of her experiences in the war. I had known her for more than forty years and in all that time she had said nothing of her service. Aware that I was working on this book she began to describe her experiences, beginning with service in the BDM (the League of German Maidens) and then in the RAD, finishing up with her work as a Flakhelferin in the anti-aircraft defence system.

'Although the main part of my service began late in 1944, I had been serving for two years before that. My first duties were carried out with the League of German Maidens and I worked for a local family. During my eight-month-long term of service I mucked out the cattle stables, cleaned out the pigs and did housework. I thought that that completed my service but only a few months later I was called up again and this time for service with the Reichsarbeitsdienst. My group was taken to Czestochau in Poland and, again, I went to work on one of the farms in the area. The Poles who had formerly owned them had been dispossessed and replaced by Volksdeutsch farmers. We worked for them. There were also Polish families working on the farms as hired labour and their living conditions were appalling. Many of them had to make their homes in haystacks and they were very badly fed. They hated us and showed it. For young girls like us those bitter men were quite frightening and we had an example of how dangerous they were when our commander was murdered. Feeling herself in danger at night she kept a loaded pistol on the table by her bed. A Pole got into her room and shot her. It was not all sadness and work. When on duty we wore a sort of blue denim dress but in the evening our walking-out uniform was a smart, two-piece, brown costume.

'One day the whole of our group was given marching orders. We were posted to Schweinfurt where we were to be trained on the 88mm anti-aircraft guns. From being farm girls we had become artillerymen. Our arrival in Schweinfurt was a shock. The air raid damage was terrible. Coming from eastern Austria we had suffered little from air raids and the damage to Schweinfurt depressed us for it showed how badly the war was going for Germany. Outside the station we were ordered to pick up our suitcases and march – there was no transport. We passed through what can only be described as a desert of brick ruins which had once been houses. There were very few undamaged houses standing. Most had been reduced to walls only a metre or two high.

'Our conversion from farm-hands to gunners was soon completed. My first job was to take the three shells from a wicker container, fuze them and replace them. It got me used to the weight and feel of the 88mm shells. The RAD detachment was made up of both sexes. They boys fired the guns while we girls operated the searchlights or worked on the telephone link between the command post and the firing points. The barracks in which we lived had been dug into the ground as a sort of protection and only the roof projected above the ground. The men were in one barrack block and we girls were in another. A river separated the two sets of barracks. The raids came in by day and night and there seemed to be an air raid every day. We became very tired from lack of sleep, but the concentration upon our tasks kept us from thinking too much about the bombs that were falling. The daytime raids bombed whole areas – so called, carpet bombing. The night time ones aimed at specific targets. The carpet ones were the more frightening of the two. The experience of thousands of bombs exploding at the same time was a really frightening experience, even seen from a distance. Another hazard was that at this time [late 1944] American fighter aircraft escorted the bombers and fired their machine-guns at anything that moved on the roads or fields.

'About the middle of March 1945, we learned that the American Army was approaching Schweinfurt and we all wondered what would happen. Would we be put into action as anti-tank gunners with the 88s? Some time later, it must have been April by this time, we were paraded and told by our CO that he was disbanding the unit. We could all go home. We had no discharge paper or pay – nothing, and those of us from southern Austria were hundreds of miles from our home. My friend, Traute Ott, and I stood by the side of the road with our rucksacks on our backs, trying to hitch a lift. But no lorry would stop for us. We were RAD/Flakhelferinnen and the soldiers thought of us as "officers' mattresses". They would not stop for the likes of us. It was a wounded man who got us a lift. We saw him and bandaged his wounds. A lorry stopped to pick him up and we clambered aboard. Somewhere past Schweinfurt we caught a train and, alternatively riding on local trains and by walking, reached my home village of Gnas in eastern Austria. Almost immediately I left again. The Russians were close and stories were spreading of their terrible brutality and mistreatment of women. Most people in the village decided to leave and buried their valuables in their back gardens before trekking off to Graz.

'A friend from the village, Traude Schranz, and I went on past Graz, firstly to the little town of Koeflach and reached the village of Maria Lankowitz where we worked in the kitchens of the gasthaus in which we were living. It was there that we saw our first British soldiers and ate British Army rations. On 8th May Traude and I were nearly killed. The final cease-fire came into force at midnight and German units which had not reached the Allied zones of Austria were to be handed over to the Red Army. During the afternoon of the 8th there was a sudden thundering noise and a whole mass of riders came galloping through Maria Lankowitz heading for the demarcation line some miles away. These men were, so far as I recall, Galican SS, who would receive no pity from the Russians. They charged through the narrow streets of the village knocking down anyone who was not quick enough to escape them. Traude and I had to squeeze ourselves against the walls of the houses in order to avoid being trampled on.

'With the end of the war things settled down enough for us to return to Graz, firstly to see Traude's invalid mother and then to go on to our home village. We did not reach it because at Feldbach, some 10 miles away, the attitude of the Red Army men was menacing. A group of them followed us into the woods and their intention was clear. We were quite frightened of being raped and returned to Feldbach where we took the train back to Graz. It was not until July when the Red Army pulled out and the British Eighth Army occupied the county of Styria that we felt it safe enough to return home to eastern Styria. There we found that much of what had been buried had been dug up and stolen, but at least we were alive and the war was at an end. I had been on active service for years and yet I was not even 23 years old. What I had been through was enough for two lifetimes.'

CRISIS IN THE LUFTWAFFE

From 1943, to the end of the war the burden of carrying the nation's effort fell more and more upon the army. Both the Luftwaffe and the Kriegsmarine were, in a strategic sense, on the defensive. Although both continued to mount offensive operations, with only limited and declining resources they had only a tactical role to play in the prosecution of the war.

In place of raids using masses of aircraft, which had been the feature of Luftwaffe activity during 1940 and 1941, most attacks upon the British Isles in 1944 were made by pilotless, rocket-propelled machines, the V 1, and then by long-range rockets, the V 2. German bomber strength faded away almost totally and Luftwaffe emphasis then concentrated upon building fighter aircraft to challenge the RAF and the USAF bombing offensive.

The introduction of the first jet engine in aviation history should have given the Germans an advantage in air-to-air combat, but Hitler, obsessed with the need for bomber aircraft, insisted that the Me 262 be adapted to carry a bomb load. That decision cost the Luftwaffe the advantage which that fast jet aircraft had over Allied machines. Late in the war the young and active leaders of the Luftwaffe – Goering was by that time only a cipher – began to build up a reserve of fighter machines and fuel. Their plan was to put a thousand fighters into the air in one mission to strike at and to destroy a whole division or 'box' of American heavy bombers. Galland and his subordinates were of the opinion that the frightful losses which such a mission would inflict upon the Americans would cause them to abandon their daylight raids. Hitler, learning of this fighter plane reserve, squandered it on one useless ground-support mission on New Year's Day 1945. The remnant were regrouped and deployed in an operation on 7 April 1945, but with so little effect that 8th Air Force did not even realize that this had been a major effort by the Luftwaffe.

Thereafter, with no fuel supplies for training purposes, new means had to be found to train pilots to fly against the Allied air invaders. Georg Cordts, one of Germany's principal aviation authors, was one of those who was trained in the last weeks of the war. Modestly, he wrote that his war service was so brief that nothing of interest happened. The reader may judge for himself the trueth of Georg Cordt's disclaimer.

'The 'National Socialist Flying Corps' (NSFK), raised by a Führer decree of 17th April 1937, was placed directly under the control of the Minister of Aviation. Many pilots of the Second World War came to the Luftwaffe through the NSFK where they had received a thorough pre-Service training in flying gliders.

'Germany lost air superiority above the Reich late in 1943 and never recovered it. Discussions were held at senior Luftwaffe level on the question of fighter pilot replacement. One proposal discussed was whether sufficient fighter pilot replacements could be obtained from glider schools. A scheme entitled "Fighter pilot replacement for special purposes" was proposed. Under this, intensive glider training would be given to selected candidates and this would enable them to pass directly from flying gliders to piloting the jet and rocket-propelled machines which were coming into service. Another question under discussion, whether pilots should be asked to fly what were in effect suicide missions, decided that pilots must be given some chance of survival. The "Natter" was also discussed. This was a rocket-propelled missile which the pilot aimed directly at the target before he ejected and parachuted to safety. The concept of a pilot lying horizontal while steering the plane towards its target, which was the method proposed for the Natter, was not a new one but had been found so difficult that it was not pursued.

'In the rocket-driven Me 163 – the Komet – the NSFK leaders thought they had found the plane type they had been seeking. They were convinced that the Me 163 could be flown by trained glider pilots who had not necessarily flown motor-driven or jet-propelled aircraft. Experienced pilots disagreed, considering that training on powered aircraft must follow glider training. The commanders of the Luftwaffe's Fighter Arm, of whom Galland was one, accepted that the Komet aircraft landed like a glider, but argued that its take-off speed, in excess of 300kms/hr, demanded that if a pilot were to fly it successfully he must have had more than just glider training.

'Despite this professional objection special courses to obtain "Fighter pilot replacements for special purposes" were organized and the selection of volunteers was carried out in all the 17 Groups of the NSFK. The Hitler Youth Flying units were a reservoir of volunteers each of whom had certificates of proficiency at A, B and C levels, and who had ambitions to become fighter pilots. This flying élite, perhaps no more than a few hundred men, went on courses in Brunn–Medlan, Lauch and finally in Trebbin. These prospective Komet pilots underwent extensive glider courses and the first lesson which had to be mastered was the ability to land their machines at a specified aerodrome. Training which had been carried out on a standard glider was completed on a 'Habicht' machine whose wing span had been reduced to 8 metres in order to increase its landing speed approximately to that of the Me 163. The prospective pilots then went on to familiarization flights in a towed Me 163A or 163B. Despite this intensive training there was no case known where the pilots, having completed this special course, went immediately on operations with the Luftwaffe. The 163 had flown a number of successful missions during 1945 and had proved its ability, but fuel shortage required that the available machines be piloted by the best Luftwaffe airmen. Production of the aircraft was halted during February.

'A call came for pilots to fly the 'Volksjaeger'; the He 162. This machine, which was powered by a single unit, went into production although it was inferior in performance to the twin-powered Me 262. Saur, the senior Civil Servant in the Armaments Ministry's main department, envisaged the Volksjaeger rolling off the assembly lines in large numbers. Under his influence Keller, the Corps Commander of the NSKF, promised all the men and workshops of the Corps to support the new project. It was proposed to take one specific Hitler Youth age group, to train the volunteers on gliders and then, without intermediate training on powered aircraft, to put them into action in the available He 162. Training in marksmanship would be given on the ground.

'The fighter pilot ace, Baumbach, was able to convince Axmann, leader of the Hitler Youth, that Saur's intention was absolute madness. To fly the Volksjaeger required fighter pilot training. As if to emphasize Baumbach's argument for such training, Galland and Keller were witnesses to a furious air battle being fought out above an airfield which they were visiting. Suddenly an Me 262 dropped vertically and crashed. Its pilot was Nowotny, an ace with 250 "kills". The question did not need to be asked; if so experienced a pilot could be shot down, what chance would the totally untrained boys of the Hitler Youth have? Nevertheless, the intention to man the Volksjaeger with "Fighter pilot replacement for Special purposes" continued, this being in the words of Ernst Heinkel, the aircraft designer, ". . . a demonstration of the misguided fanaticism of those years".

'The first He 162 was ready for action on 6th December 1944. For the purposes of pilot familarization a few machines were built without propulsion units and were towed like gliders. I put the question to General Galland whether the development of the Me 163 and Me 262 could have changed the course of the war. Galland admitted that they might have prolonged it, but could not have affected the end result.

'The confusion which existed in Nazi Germany towards the end of the war was responsible for the fact that the training of "Fighter pilot replacements for special purposes", continued, one might almost say until Russian tanks rolled on to Trebbin airfield. The final course in Brunn ran until 19th March, and those in Laucha and Trebbin until 20th April. When Brunn was no longer operational the trainee-pilots went to Laucha and then on to Trebbin. The pilot courses were finally halted and training given in fire-arms, hand weapons and panzerfausts. On 20th April, the group was sent to fight in Berlin. Some trainees met tragic ends. They flew low-level missions in old fashioned Buecker aircraft fitted with four panzerfausts. Their targets were the Soviet tank columns. All were shot down and of the four, whose aircraft crashed in flames, one made his way back to the unit. Some trainees reached north-western Germany and stayed there until the end of the war. Others, of whom I was one, were posted to "Jahn" Division which was surrounded near Potsdam. The division was rescued by Wenck's Twelfth Army. It then went into action again, this time to hold the last remaining bridgehead on the Elbe, so as to cover the rear of Busse's Ninth Army and hold open an escape route for refugees from eastern Germany. Thus ended the "Fighter Pilot replacements for special purposes".'

SELF-SACRIFICE OF THE KRIEGSMARINE

In 1943, the Kriegsmarine was a spent force. Its surface fleet, although made up of new ships, had never been able to operate cohesively. From the loss of *Graf Spee* in 1939 and then *Bismarck* in 1941, the major units had had bad luck. Some capital ships remained and were put into action. *Scharnhorst*, together with *Tirpitz* and ten destroyers, attacked Allied installations at Spitzbergen during September 1943, but *Tirpitz* was herself attacked by midget submarines only a week or two later and was badly damaged. *Scharnhorst* came out of Altenfiord on Christmas Eve, with the intention of attacking Allied convoys sailing to Murmansk. Two days later she was intercepted and sunk off the North Cape. Her loss removed the last major surface threat to Allied convoys on the North Russia route.

With its capital ships sunk, crippled or bottled up in harbour, the Kriegsmarine was reduced to producing small craft in order to take the war to the British enemy. Basing their ideas on Italian and British types, the German Navy introduced, as a first weapon, manned torpedoes which had the disadvantage that they asphyxiated their crewman. These dangerous craft were succeeded by motor-boats which exploded among enemy ships and then by one-man submarines. In every case successes were few and losses were high.

The main emphasis of Kriegsmarine activities remained, as it had from the beginning of the war, with the U-boat fleet. Submarines operating either individually or in packs had sunk millions of tons of Allied shipping. But the Allied navies had not been passive. Improved tactics, long-range aircraft and new inventions had helped them to meet and then to master the U-boat menace and their success is acknowledged in an entry of the War Diary of the Commander of U-Boats dated 6 May 1943:

'The enemy's sound detection equipment [the Germans still thought in terms of acoustic weapons] both in aircraft and on surface vessels, does not merely limit the operations of a single ship [U-boat]. More seriously it enables the enemy to discover the preparations made by and the dispositions of U-boat [packs] and how to avoid them. It is thus possible for them to nullify the U-boat's most important advantage, its undetectability. The enemy air force is also now able to cover almost the entire area of the North Atlantic to protect the convoys.'

Allied counter-measures so reduced the scale of U-boat operations that, whereas in the first months of 1943, nearly 120 vessels had been operating in the North Atlantic, by the middle of May that number had been reduced to less than a hundred. Doenitz was forced to break off the battle until he could re-equip with boats with quieter engines and able to stay submerged for longer periods. The measure of Allied success lies in the fact that by the end of the war 739 U-boats had been lost with all hands. Nearly 30,000 of the 40,000 of its men perished; the highest percentage casualty rate in any arm of service.

JOURNEY TO THE BLACK SEA

The last great effort of the Kriegsmarine, the rescue of the civilians and soldiers from the east, is recorded later in this book, but before we reach that chapter of self-sacrifice let us go back in time to 1942, when, as a result of the first successes of Army Group South, the German forces had reached the Black Sea. It was not enough that the army held the ground. The strong Soviet Black Sea Fleet needed to be countered at sea. There was a problem in that German shipbuilding capacity was unable to produce new vessels for such operations and craft had to be taken from existing flotillas. Gerd-Dietrich Schneider, commanding a minesweeper in the Channel, recalled the order and its consequences.

'Towards the end of February 1942, our flotilla was ordered to transfer immediately from the Channel ports and proceed to Cuxhaven. Then came a more astonishing order. Our ultimate destination was to be the Black Sea, a move which would reduce quite seriously the strength of our naval forces in the Channel. At the beginning of April 1942, we arrived in Cuxhaven flying the customary "paying-off" pennant to show that we were returning from overseas service. Our short auxiliary mast was really too low to fly the 20-metres-long pennant correctly, but we did our best.

'To reach the Black Sea would require that part of the journey be made overland with the ships being carried on the autobahn between Dresden and Ingolstadt. The superstructure on each ship was removed to lower the height so that it could pass under the autobahn bridges. This reduction in height also brought down the vessel's gross weight to a more easily transportable 65 tons. The removal of the ship's engines and the propellers brought our weight down still further to a more manageable load, although those removals brought with them the disadvantage that during the "wet" parts of our journey we would be unmanoeuvrable and would have to be towed. One amusing thing was that civilians in Cuxhaven, seeing our ships with their superstructures removed thought they were some sort of aircraft carrier.

'The heavy equipment had been taken out, but an auxiliary diesel engine and a battery were left on board for the comfort and convenience of the group which would accompany the ship during the "dry" parts of its journey. The

first two ships of our flotilla, the *R 166*, Horst Mertineit's vessel and my own
R 35, were towed out on the morning of 31st March by a sea-going tug. At
Hamburg it left us with the news that a river tug would shortly arrive to take
us on the next leg of the journey. That vessel did not arrive until May 2nd,
and when it did it was already towing two stripped-down Luftwaffe security
ships. The manoeuvring required to get four ships ready for towing took
some time, but eventually we were all set and then the tug, with a fine plume
of smoke pouring out of its funnel, took us upstream. By the end of the
second day we had reached Magdeburg. The Luftwaffe authorities had given
their crews ration cards but neither food for the journey nor sufficient
drinking water. The airmen had to rely upon the navy to supply their needs.
After an interesting, not to say picturesque five-day journey, we tied up in
the Albert Docks in Dresden. The steamship company responsible for
organizing the next part of our trip had considerable experience in moving
ships overland but our hopes of being quickly en route were dashed. We
were told that there would be a delay of some three weeks before we could
be dealt with because the ships of No 1 E-boat Flotilla had still not been
loaded and dispatched. Dresden in the early summer of 1942, showed none
of the signs of war as did the ports of northern Germany. There was a naval
quartermaster's store in the town and as we had been in action against
England our crew had totted up enough "Channel service time" to qualify
for three months' special rations. We lived on the highest ration scale and
enjoyed such extras as extra meat, real coffee, chocolate, tobacco and alcohol.
Our travel permits also allowed us to use express trains so that even those
living as far away as East Prussia could get home on leave.

'In order that we did not lose touch with naval routine a ten-man crew
was kept on board and was rotated regularly. But soon the pleasant time in
Dresden was at an end and shortly before Whitsun our sister ship, the *R 166*,
was made ready. We could see from the difficulties she was having what
needed to be done. The problem was that our ships were all wood
construction not steel. They would not be able to stand up to the strain of
an overland journey unless they were given special protection. This was in
the form of elastic suspension; a number of bands about 2 metres wide,
cushioned with timber baulks. These slings were fastened to a low form of
scaffolding called a "Trog" which resembled an upended railway bridge. The
Trog was over 40 metres long and was mounted on a number of heavy lorry
wheel bases each consisting of eight rubber wheels mounted on four axles.
All the wheels were steered by two drivers, one at the front and one at the
back of the Trog. The drivers, were linked by telephone. Two powerful
lorries driving side by side pulled the giant framework carrying the ship and
another two at the back pushed it. There was a third lorry, a sort of
Command vehicle, driving independently at the front.

'We were loaded on to the Trog in Ubigau on the broad and flat right bank of the Elbe and it took all our efforts and those of a Company of military convalescents to winch the vessel the 30 metres from the river to the lorries. On the second day the "corsets", the five, wide, carrying bands were fitted and screwed into position. The ship lay suspended on these, not held rigid but able to swing gently. Some parts of the keel had to be sawn off in order that the ship lay properly in the slings. Once she had been loaded and secured the "Trog" was covered with sheeting to hide the identity of the cargo. The "dry" part of the trip lay ahead and next stop would be Ingolstadt where the remainder of the crew was to rejoin the ship. The journey along the autobahn from the Elbe to the Danube took five days with the speed being restricted to a walking pace. The police closed those parts of the road along which the convoy was driving and at night two of our NCOs guarded the ship.

'One of the chief difficulties encountered was that the height of the bridges across the autobahn was not constant and often clearance was reckoned to be less than 15cms. One of the pieces of equipment which we carried was a high-pressure hydraulic pump because in those days it was possible to raise the bridge height by hydraulic means. One phenomenon of the trip was a vast build-up of static electricity with the result that workers in Ingolstadt who clambered on to the Trog received sharp electric shocks. We "earthed" the construction with a short length of chain. Our organization was so good that we kept to our timetable and those of us returning to the ship from Berlin arrived as the "corsets" were being taken off.

'By the afternoon of our arrival in Ingolstadt our ship, R 35, was afloat once again, but now it was sailing on the fast-running waters of the Danube. During the following morning a motor tug arrived. This was about the size of a naval pinnace. We could not believe that this miniature vessel was strong enough to tow us down stream, but we soon learned differently. Passing under the Danube bridges was an exciting experience because the river at this point is not navigable by large vessels and even though we had no superstructure we still rode high out of the water. As we passed under those bridges the crew members had to lie flat so that they were not swept off the ship and into the water. We reached Weltenburg where we were supposed to tie up for the night, but found there was neither a pier nor anchoring facilities. Our mini-tug pushed us on to a sand bank and two of the crew jumped ashore and tied us to a tree. The beer brewed by the monks of the Benedictine abbey of Weltenburg went down very well. It was here that we learned that a ship of our flotilla had encountered Field Marshal Goering who was surprised to see this unusual construction on the autobahn. The whole route was explained to him and the difficulties of passing under the bridges pointed out. He is said to have remarked, "Well, let's blow up the bridges," and he probably meant it. It was explained to him that these were protected by the Fine Arts Commission and, in any case, the ship had got that far without having to blow anything up.

'Beyond Regensburg the Danube is navigable and we made good time although fog delayed us and was responsible for the unique entry in a naval war diary: "0830 hours, Anchored in the mouth of the River Isar owing to fog." We reached Linz and there the superstructure was refitted and the engine replaced so that, once again, we were a warship. The refit took eight days after which we carried out trials on the Danube. Trying to find a stretch of the river wide enough to turn was one problem. Another was that although the ship had been held in "corsets" during the "dry" stage of the journey there had been some shrinkage. Being of wood construction she was not rigid like a metal ship and, in addition, she had dried out. This meant that when the main engines were fitted and the steering mechanism installed the mounting holes no longer matched up. New ones had to be bored, a necessary task even though the differences were of millimetres only. When we reached the Black Sea the ship's shape had righted itself so that the new borings created difficulties and the speeds that we had formerly reached could no longer be attained. One more day of refitting and then we were ready to sail. Together with *R 166* we set out from Melk to Vienna, spurred on by the flotilla commander's cry, "Sevastapol is waiting!" We were still having to be towed, not because we lacked power, but because of the strict regulations regarding traffic on the Danube. The large upper deck of the towing vessel was used for training and pleasurable pursuits. Less pleasurable was the knowledge that below decks there were 500 tons of bombs, en route to Bulgaria for onward transhipment to Greece.

'Our progress along the Danube was slow and when the flotilla commander asked why he was told that the varying depths of the river bed made high speeds impossible. In Budapest we were not anchored outside the city, as was the custom, but directly opposite the Parliament building. For this singular honour the crew wore their best parade uniforms. Our next port of call was Semlin near Belgrade where we were fitted with twin machine-guns to counter Yugoslav partisan activities. The so-called "cataracts" section of the Danube was the final difficulty, with the river pilot sitting on the roof of the wheelhouse and passing orders to another pilot who then relayed them to our coxswain. For this section we were not towed, but we minesweepers sailed tied together in what were called 'packets'. We passed through the narrow channel filled with roaring water and then entered into tranquil water on a quiet stretch of the river. One last, natural and unexpected phenomenon was the "Kossova" a very strong wind which blew up during the night and which tossed us about on high waves. The gale-force winds and the pouring rain caused us a number of anxious hours when the moorings parted, but we switched on our searchlights and managed to tie up. Our convoy broke up at Ruscuk where the river was in high flood. Although we had maps of the

Danube delta the water had risen over the river banks obscuring landmarks and making it impossible to tell whether we were sailing in the river or on the flood water. The answer to my question on how we were to navigate was, "Just steer round the houses."

'Eleven days after leaving Linz we arrived at the Roumanian port of Galatz. From there we steamed along the central arm of the Danube and reached Constanza, the main port. En route we exchanged signals with a pair of German warships going back up river and then, at last, completed the final stage of our journey and reached the Black Sea where our Flotilla Commander sent the signal "Thalassa!, Thalassa" [the Sea!, the Sea!].'

AFRICAN SIDESHOW

The Germans did not see the campaign in Africa in the same light as we did. Britain fought to maintain an Imperial link, a lifeline to the Far Eastern Empire. To OKW it was never more than a minor operation which became a sideshow once the Russian war opened. It is, perhaps, because of its low military importance that no histories have been produced by any of the German divisions that fought the campaign and yet what they achieved brought credit to the German forces.

German intervention in Africa came at a time when there was no military activity on the European mainland, and this campaign in Mussolini's colonies soon captured the imagination of the German public. They were captivated by the dynamism with which the operations were conducted, by a commander who had personal magnetism, who was a Master of the Field and enjoyed a great measure of good luck. That man was Erwin Rommel.

Hitler's decision to send a military force arose from his fear that Italy would lose her North African Empire and that that loss would take her out of the war as an ally of the Third Reich. General Ritter von Thoma was sent by OKW on a tour of inspection to determine the most effective methods of shipping and deploying German troops in this new theatre of operations. Von Thoma's report concluded, 'In the event of German formations being sent to Africa, then this must be a panzer force no fewer than four divisions strong. It would be pointless to send fewer because a smaller number could not achieve success. Conversely, it would serve no purpose to send more, since it would not be possible to supply more than four divisions in any advance across the desert to the Nile Delta.'

That last sentence contains the essence of military success in the desert. This depended upon supply and reinforcement, which in turn meant possession of the principal ports between Tripolitania and Egypt. Tobruk was the most important harbour in the battle area and the efforts to seize and to hold that place determined the strategy of the entire campaign.

Günther Rolf served in a lorried infantry regiment on the establishment of a panzer Division.

'I reached the desert as a replacement early in March 1942, having made a sea crossing from Sicily to Tripoli and then by lorry up the Via Balbia towards the Front. We did not need to become acclimatized because it was still not too hot during the day.

'Before the offensive opened [May–June 1942] we were briefed on Rommel's intentions. The chief aim was to capture Tobruk which had been surrounded a year earlier but which had not fallen. Our training was geared towards taking out the concrete defences of the fortified town in all-out assault. One part of the defensive system was a deep and wide anti-tank ditch. The Pioneers did a really heroic task in laying bridges across the ditch over which the panzer crossed with us immediately behind them. There was a lot of dust, so much that I thought there was a *Ghibli* blowing. The fog was so thick that our officers worked on compass bearings to locate the objectives we had to take out. Then we went into action. The battle was short but hard.

'When Tobruk fell the British ration stores fell into our hands undamaged. We were all impressed at the quantity and quality of British Army rations. They had marvellous tinned fruit from their colonies, various sorts of jam, corned beef – lots of corned beef – and meat and vegetable stew. We had, by comparison, very poor rations and when our own supplies did not come through we had to rely upon the Italian Army's hard tack; tinned meat embossed with the initials "A.M." (Amministrazione Militare) which we preferred to call *Arme Mussolini* [poor Mussolini] or *Alter Mann* [old man].'

Thomas Schulze wrote:

'I was in the desert with 8th Panzer Regiment and was nearly drowned there. This happened towards the end of November 1941. Almost out of the blue it began to rain. The Italians told us later it had not rained in that area for sixty years. It was as if one was under a very strong shower spout. The rain went on for a long time. I was with a motorized infantry battalion near Halfaya Pass and the wadis there quickly filled with water that poured down the walls of the Pass. I was busy helping to dig our trucks out of the mud which the rain had caused when I slipped and fell into a water-filled wadi and was taken rapidly away by the force of the flood. I cannot say that my past life flashed in front of my eyes. I remember being more annoyed at the fact that I was in such a grotesque position – in a flooded wadi in what was normally a dry desert. My comrades formed a chain and dragged me out.'

Günther Resch was in a Supply battalion, driving a truck in the offensive of May–June 1942.

'During the battle to capture Tobruk I was in the same sector as Flak Regiment 135. Reports came in that a British tank force was coming up out of the desert. I can still see that scene. The Tommies were deployed in line abreast, advancing, then halting to fire and then advancing again. It was like a sea battle because each tank threw up a cloud of dust that looked like smoke from a funnel. There were more British tanks than we had panzer to oppose them and things looked black for us. I do not know whether the British knew it, but TAC HQ of Afrika Korps was only a short distance from where we were positioned. Then I saw a three-gun battery of 88mm anti-aircraft guns line up on the flat surface of the desert and open fire. Within a matter of minutes the British had lost more than twenty of their tanks. The rest turned away. Colonel Wolz of the Flak regiment was awarded the Knight's Cross for what he did that day.

'We who fought in Africa were also very proud of Gefreite [Corporal] Huebner, who served in another flak regiment and was, like Wolz, awarded the Knight's Cross for bravery in action. This happened very early in the campaign during the first advance to Halfaya Pass. A group of 30 British tanks approached the position where Huebner's gun was dug in, but then retreated when the battery opened fire on them. A few hours later seventy tanks began an attack. Huebner alone destroyed eleven of them in a few minutes. A third British tank attack came in during the early afternoon. For this a group of forty machines advanced and then divided so as to split German fire. Huebner opened fire at 800 metres and closed at 8 metres when a Mark II was knocked out almost at the edge of the gun pit. Later that afternoon eighty-five tanks attacked the four 88s of Huebner's group, but the arrival of panzer from our 5th Light Division saved Huebner and his comrades from certain death and destruction.'

The importance of Tobruk to operations in the desert has already been touched upon. Rommel's failure to capture the town in the spring of 1941, led to Operation 'Hercules', a plan designed at the start of 1942, to take out Malta by airborne assault, for it was an unsinkable aircraft carrier in the Mediterranean, lying athwart the Axis line of communications to Africa. Student, the Para Corps commander, was called to Rome where he found one of his subordinates, Ramcke, already waiting to brief him on the proposed plan. Ramcke had raised and trained a division of Italian paratroops, the Folgore Division, and planned to use them in the combined German/Italian air drop. Mussolini was so keen for Malta to be taken that he promised to support the airborne attack by committing the entire Italian Fleet. General Student was ordered to report to Führer Headquarters to brief Hitler and found him in a pessimistic mood. 'The building of a bridgehead on Malta using your airborne forces is guaranteed,' Hitler told him. 'What I also guarantee is the following. As soon as the attack goes in the British Fleets will sail from Alexandria and from Gibraltar. Do you know what the Italians will do? As soon as the first reports come in, they will run back to port, warships and transports alike. And you and your paras will be left sitting on the island alone.' The capture of Tobruk by Rommel in the June 1942 offensive made Operation 'Hercules' redundant, but by this time British military power had been built up for a major offensive and control of operations in the desert had passed to the British. The offensive which Montgomery launched has passed into history as the Battle of El Alamein and its outcome destroyed Rommel's hopes of a victory in Africa.

That battle, fought in October–November 1942, forced the Axis armies to retreat. Shortly after it ended an Anglo-American force invaded French North Africa, nearly 1,500 miles to the north-west. The Allies raced towards Tunis, aware that if they could seize the capital they would have cut off Rommel's Panzer Army which was, at that time, retreating towards southern Tunisia. The Germans were just as aware as the Allies of the importance of Tunisia and sent over a miscellany of units to create and hold a bridgehead in that country. Among the units which were locally raised to increase Axis fighting strength were such unusual ones as local native volunteers and 361st Afrika Regiment, a unit made up of two battalions of former Foreign Legionaires who were German nationals. 'I do not know what you thought of your allies,' continued Günther Resch, 'but ours were useless. A whole Italian division, the 6th, surrendered in the desert with all their arms and vehicles. The men of "Tunisia" Battalion, an Arab unit, deserted to the enemy or just vanished into the hills as did a battalion of Algerians and an Italian machine-gun battalion.'

KILLING ON CHRISTMAS MOUNTAIN

One hastily created German unit was the 334th Division, which was put into the perimeter to the west of Tunis and which occupied a strategically important hill, known to the British as Longstop and to the Germans as the Christmas Mountain. There were three passes which led into the plain of Tunis the most important of which was that which went along the foot of Christmas Mountain. This feature was more than three kilometres long and 300 metres high. Whoever held it dominated operations around Medjez el Bab, which was itself the 'key to the Gate' of Tunis. Christmas Mountain was garrisoned by Battle Group Lang consisting of a battalion each from the 60th and the 754th Infantry Regiments. The German garrison held the mountain until the last weeks of the campaign in Tunisia. Heinrich Stolz:

'My infantry regiment was part of 334th Division which was raised during the autumn of 1942. We left Germany for Naples, then crossed to Sicily and arrived in Bizerta after a terrible sea journey. On 22nd December, as soon as the battalion had grouped, we moved off to take up positions to the west of Tunis, in the area of Medjez el Bab. Our battalion TAC HQ was set up near a great mountain which we knew as the Christmas Mountain.

That mountain was the key to the whole campaign and it was fought for during Christmas week of 1942, hence its name. The slopes were captured by the British, but their advance was held in a mine-field which we had hastily laid and they were then saturated with fire from our machine-guns and mortars. They tried again to take the hill – it was really two peaks, Jebel Ahmera and Jebel el Rhana – but we flung them back. Then bad weather brought the fighting to a halt and gave us the opportunity to improve our dug-outs and trenches. By the end of January 1943, the whole of 334th Division had arrived and was in the line. During February our 2nd Battalion, which had been in position on Christmas Hill, was relieved by a battalion of Gebirgsjaeger.'

My very good friend, Hans Teske, was a paratrooper with 5th Regiment and records one particular memory of the campaign:

'At dawn on 28th February, I was ordered to take some wireless equipment to our forward positions just north of El Aroussa. I drove my motor-cycle combination to some Arab huts and left it with our signallers who had just put up a communications post in one of the adjoining sheds. I strapped the equipment to my back and started to walk, hoping not to be spotted by British positions which were still holding out in some areas. We did not have either the time or the men to mop up what had been until only a day or two earlier, part of the British front line. It was a warm, spring-like day and everything appeared to be peaceful. But it had been like that yesterday, when suddenly all hell had been let loose.

'This day, however, nothing moved, not even a rabbit. The silence was uncanny. I reached the road from Tally Ho Corner to El Aroussa unmolested. A German parachutist of my battalion appeared from behind a haystack urging me to hurry. By a stroke of luck rather than by good map reading I had come upon the very men who needed the equipment. A bullet had put their set out of action. It was even luckier I had not carried on walking for only 200 yards farther on were several British Churchill tanks. A little to the right lay a farm, later to be known as "Steamroller Farm", from where I saw the opening shots of the battle known by that name.

'With my mission completed I returned to the motor cycle as fast as my legs would carry me. When I eventually arrived at the Arab huts and my machine, I was confronted by another problem. A number of German wounded were asking for a lift. One man had had his nose shot off, another was shot through the chest, some had less severe injuries. I had only two seats available, one on the pillion, the other in the side-car. I was trying to work out how to carry as many men as possible when someone pointed out that there was a badly wounded British soldier lying helplessly in a ditch. The sector in which he lay was covered by British machine-gun fire, but the gunners probably could not see their own helpless comrade. Certainly no one from their side was trying to rescue the wounded man. He lay some 60 feet from a wadi which I would be able to reach. But now I was in a dilemma. As a combatant I was not protected by the Red Cross. The man in need was an enemy. Should I ignore him or should I risk my own life to help the wounded enemy? It was a great risk, not made any easier because I had to cross a short stretch which was mined, but that route would be out of sight of the British machine-gunners.

'I took the risk for an enemy just as I would have done for any of my own comrades. It was expected from us to do such a thing. I crossed the mined strip and followed the path of a wadi until I could hear a faint moan. Looking over the edge of the wadi I saw the man. I leaped from the protection of the wadi and sprinted towards him drawing fire from the British machine-gunner. A bullet hit me in the right foot. I got the man up and pulled him into the wadi because he was too heavy to lift. Fortunately, the British machine-gunner realized what I was doing and stopped firing. In the wadi I put the man into a sitting position and gently shook him. After a little while he seemed to recover sufficiently to become sensible. He had been shot through the chest and may well have been out there for the past 24 hours. I asked him to put his arm around my shoulder and we started walking. He had great difficulty in moving his legs but his grip around my shoulders was very tight. We crossed the minefield safely and I put him in the side-car. I took him and six others to the First Aid Post. On a stretch of the main road I came once more under fire.

'At the aid post I asked for permission to pick up more wounded. My request was granted and a VW was made available to join me. The surprised lieutenant behind the steering wheel was temporarily put under my command (I was a lance-corporal) and we were able to bring back all the wounded who were still waiting for transport. Before leaving for that trip I looked at the rescued enemy soldier. He was a member of the London Irish Rifles. Our MO, Dr Scheiffele, ordered his immediate transfer to Tunis and was confident that the man would survive his ordeal. Then, and only then, did the MO attend to my injuries, which fortunately were not serious.

'Of course, as my action had been observed by a great number of men, a recommendation for an award was made. Shortly after that action we were withdrawn from the front. On 16th March, 1943, in front of the assembled battalion, Hauptmann Hans Jungwirt decorated me with the Iron Cross, Second Class. The first officer who came forward to congratulate me was Dr Scheiffele, the surgeon.'

STAR OF AFRICA, A SUPREME FIGHTER ACE

It had been my hope that the memories of the war in Africa would include one of the Luftwaffe ace who was nick-named the 'Star of Africa'. Hauptmann Hans-Joachim Marseille was the most successful Luftwaffe fighter pilot in the North Africa theatre of operation and after his death journal articles were produced by the Propaganda Ministry describing the air battles of 1 September 1942, during which he shot down seventeen Allied aircraft.

It is one of the accepted facts of war that enemy claims are dismissed as crude propaganda exaggerations. That the enemy does not accept tested and proven figures is bad enough, but it is worse when one's own side expresses doubts. There were many examples of this disbelief on the German side during the war, one of which concerns the claims made by Marseille for his victories of that single day's battle. Not only had he made what seemed to be an extravagant claim, but his own squadron had not lost a single aircraft in the fighting. It all seemed so improbable. The need to double check his claims led to the figure for the day being one less than he had stated. The missing 'kill' could not, at first, be accredited for 1 September, but was adjusted later.

The squadron war diary shows that Marseille took-off on three separate occasions, the first at 0700 hrs when the squadron task was to escort a group of Stukas carrying out a bombing raid on Imayid. By 0730 hrs Marseille's unit had picked up the dive-bombers and the whole group flew towards the target area. One account put out by the Propaganda Ministry begins with an account of this particular engagement:

'On approaching the target at an altitude of 3,500 metres the group commander reported ten enemy fighters approaching. At first these were seen only as little points of light but as the two groups of machines closed the Curtiss aircraft became more distinct. When only a couple of kilometres separated them the Stukas made ready to meet the assault. The German pilots saw Marseille's machine make a tight curve and heard his cry "I am attacking!" As he opened fire the group of Curtiss's turned away and his fire hit the last aircraft.

'Marseille's victim seemed suddenly to halt in midair, then shuddered and fell like a stone to crash in a violent explosion. The time was 0820 hrs. Before the first victim had hit the ground Marseille had left banked and had attacked the next machine. This, too, fell burning and struck the ground some 2 kms from the first "kill". It was now 0830 hrs. The Stukas bombed the target and headed for home. A Curtiss dived out of the sky to intercept them but was spotted by Marseille who with his usual accuracy, shot down the gallant intruder. The time was now 0833 hrs.

'As the squadron flew back to base the cry "Spitfires!" was raised. Marseille and his wing man turned to meet the six enemy aircraft which were swooping down upon them. The young commander flew level towards the Spitfire group. He had already selected the enemy at whom he intended to fire but it was still too far away for accurate shooting. Marseille could see clearly the muzzles of the cannon and machine-guns pointing at him but

knew that for as long as he could see these clearly he was safe. Then flames
and light smoke obscured the enemy's guns. The Spitfire pilot had opened
up at 150 metres. At the last moment Marseille swung his aircraft into a left
climbing curve so that he was above the enemy machine. He knew that the
turning radius of his own aircraft was smaller than that of the enemey's and
he was soon on his victim's tail and only 80 metres behind the Spitfire. He
opened fire and saw a plume of black smoke pour out of the fuselage of the
stricken aircraft. Just before 0839 hrs, at a spot east-south-east of Imayid, it
crashed in flames.

'Marseille's squadron touched-down at 0914, to be refuelled and re-
armed. The armament artificers found that as usual the commander's
marksmanship had been so good that for each victim he had used only 20
rounds of cannon shell and 60 rounds of machine-gun ammunition. Two
hours later the "Star of Africa" was airborne again, his squadron acting once
again as escort to a Stuka unit which was en route to bomb Alam Halfa. Some
way short of the rendezvous point Marseille saw two groups of British
bombers heading towards the German lines and noticed that each bomber
group was escorted by between twenty-five to thirty aircraft. Suddenly, a
group of eight British fighters broke away from the main body to attack the
Stukas. As Marseille turned to meet them the Allied machines formed a
defensive circle. This tactic might have worked against an ordinary pilot but
not against one so experienced in aerial combat. Flying straight and level
towards the circle of Curtiss fighters he opened fire at 50 metres. One
machine fell and half a minute later a second followed it. The British
commander lost his nerve and his fighter group began to retreat. Marseille
pursued them, came to within 100 metres and inside two minutes had gained
a third victory. The remaining Allied fighters then closed up and headed first
eastwards before turning north seeking to escape over the sea. It was in vain.
A fourth victim was gained and two minutes later, at 1101 the fifth kill was
registered. The sixth fell at 1102 when Marseille shot down the fighter that
was on his wing man's tail.

'The battle had now drifted eastwards and Marseille, seeing another
group of Curtiss machines heading east, climbed to intercept them. From
their open formation it was clear that none of the Allied pilots had seen the
German planes. Marseille took the enemy squadron in flank and in a short
burst of fire blew the tail off his next victim. Now, with fuel running low,
the young commander headed for home but then saw below him another
enemy aircraft heading eastwards. He dived to the attack and saw the wings
and tail planes of the enemy machine fly off under the impact of his bullets.
Eight enemy aircraft had now fallen to his guns; the equivalent of a whole
squadron destroyed in ten minutes. When his own group touched-down
Field Marshal Kesselring was there to greet them. He had arrived at the
airfield on a tour of inspection and had delayed his departure until the aircraft

had returned. In regulation manner Marseille reported the return of his squadron and the day's total of twelve victories. "And how many are yours?" asked Kesselring. "Twelve, Herr Feldmarschall." The Supreme Commander sat down wordlessly.

'The next take-off was at 1358 hrs but a burst tyre prevented Marseille flying that mission so that it was not until 1700 hrs that he was back in the air for a third time that day. Once again the task was to escort a group of Ju 88s undertaking a bombing raid on Imayid. What then occurred was a repetition of the morning's fighting. Fifteen Curtiss P 46s attempted to attack the Ju 88s. Marseille's squadron split the enemy formation. The battle lasted less than six minutes and in a series of combats at altitudes between 100 and 1,500 metres five more aircraft fell to the guns of Marseille's fighter. The first four went down at intervals between 1745 and 1750 hrs. The fifth three minutes later, at 1753.'

Marseille was credited with only 16 'kills' that day because OKW could not confirm the location of the seventeenth victim until the following afternoon.

ATTACK THE GIBRALTAR CONVOY

The role of the Kriegsmarine in the African campaign was restricted, chiefly because of the Italian Navy's larger presence in the Mediterranean. With the exception of motor torpedo-boats and a few other light craft the German Navy's chief activity was in submarine operations. These reached their climax during the Allied landings along the North African coast during November 1942.

The Kriegsmarine units in the Mediterranean had been ordered into action by a telegram from Hitler, dated 6 November, which read: 'The fate of the army in Africa depends upon the destruction of the Gibraltar convoy. I anticipate a relentless and victorious operation.' All available U-boats in the Mediterranean and operating off the west coast of Africa were ordered to attack the convoys carrying Allied troops. Although the U-boats were able to sink a number of warships their own losses were high and a great many were sunk. The Naval war diary records the operation of *U 515* commanded by Oberleutnant zur See Werner Henke:

'12th November 1942. 1915hrs. Cruising on the surface. Cruiser squadron in sight. Two cruisers, one each of *Birmingham* and *Frobisher* class together with three K class destroyers; heading east. Speed 15 knots. I follow on the surface for a further five hours and am attacked by destroyers on several occasions. At 0015 hrs. we close in and attack the rear cruiser, the *Birmingham* one. From a salvo of four torpedoes two run on the surface or in circles. After running for 70 seconds one torpedo strikes the cruiser

midships in the engine room. The ship stops. Three destroyers patrol the
area. The other cruiser heads eastwards at great speed. Within an hour I have
penetrated the [destroyer] screen. At 0128 hrs and again at 0148 hrs we fire
another salve. The first hit is in the aft of the ship. The cruiser turns on to
her starboard side. I aim at a destroyer of the K class at 0201 hrs and hit her
in the rear. There is a massive detonation . . . At 0206 hrs I gain more hits
on the cruiser but the ship still does not go down .´. . Hunted by destroyers
firing star shells. The ship's rudder is malfunctioning and we have a small
electrical fire . . . Forced to submerge and attacked with depth-charges at
depths between 120 and 160 metres. Reload.

'Surface at 0430 hrs. Move up to where the cruiser, lying on her side, is
being towed by a destroyer . . . Fired on by the guns of a patrolling destroyer
and from the forward turret of the cruiser. Alarm given. Crash dive, a great
many depth-charges and sounds of Asdic. Surface again at 0630 hrs and move
towards the cruiser. Fired at by destroyers. At 0650 hrs a double shot from
Nos 1 and 2 tubes . . . One hit heard. Submerge again. Depth-charged again
. . . Next day heard hundreds of depth-charges and observed aircraft through
the periscope . . .'

It was not, however, a cruiser which Henke's U-boat had attacked, but
a depot ship, the *Hecla*, and he had also damaged the destroyer *Marne*.
Neither was a total loss. In fact, the efforts of the Kriegsmarine to destroy
the Allied convoys can be assessed as having failed, although some sinkings
were achieved.

Defeat Looms, 1944

ITALY INVADED:
GERMAN RESISTANCE IN THE LIRI VALLEY

In May 1943, when the war in Africa ended, the island of Sicily was seen by the Western Allies as the stepping-stone to the mainland. The Axis powers, too, saw Sicily as the gateway to Europe and were determined to hold it against Anglo-American attack. They failed in that endeavour and when the campaign was brought to a close after only a month's fighting, both sides knew that an invasion of Italy proper was only a matter of time.

On 8 September, the government of Marshal Badoglio, which had succeeded the fallen Fascist regime of Benito Mussolini, surrendered to the Allies. The dismay this caused in Germany was reflected in the survey of public opinion carried out by the SD (Security Service). 'Reports from all parts of the Reich confirm the first impression which the Führer's speech and German action in Italy has produced. The peoples' self-confidence . . . has returned. Confidence in the Führer has reached new heights. Statements by the Führer . . . that what has occurred in Italy is impossible in Germany because he can depend upon his Marshals, Admirals and Generals were received with pride . . . German successes announced so far make it appear . . . that no more unpleasant surprises are to be expected from Italy's treachery . . . In conclusion the reports show that morale has been greatly raised by the successes in Italy and by the Führer's speech.'

A succession of assault landings in the heel of Italy and then at Salerno brought the Allied Fifth and Eighth armies on to the shores of Italy whence they began to fight their way up the peninsula against the grain of the country. Skilful German rearguards occupying mountain peaks and contesting river crossings slowed still further the pace of the Allied advance. At several places south of Rome this was stopped completely, albeit temporarily. One of those places was the town of Cassino above which stood the Benedictine abbey. Fearful for the safety of that ancient shrine the Pope, according to an Italian news agency report dated 9 December 1943, '. . . obtained an assurance from the warring powers that the hill [on which the Abbey stands] will not be fortified, nor will it be bombed from the air . . .' General von Senger und Etterlin, the officer charged with the defence of the Cassino sector, wrote in his autobiography, '. . . I had agreed not to fortify the monastery. No one would like to be held responsible for the destruction of such a cultural monument for the sake of tactical advantage . . . [In any case] all German tactical views were that so conspicuous a point is quite unsuitable for an observation post.'

The Allies thought otherwise and the abbey was first bombed from the air and then shattered by gun fire. In the ruins of the town of Cassino both sides lived a sort of troglodyte existence while on the bare slopes of the mountain the soldiers were exposed to all the elements and suffered accordingly. Any thrust by Freyburg's New Zealand Corps, which had replaced the Americans, was met by a German counter-attack. This episode in the fighting on those open slopes was written by a Fallschirmjaeger, Obergefreiter Valentin.

'Our No 3 Company was at first held as the counter-attack Reserve on the rear slopes of Colle San Angelo with No 4 Para Regiment. At the opening of the second battle of Cassino we were placed under the command of Boehmler's battalion and during the night of 18/19 March were told off to spearhead the assault upon Rocca Janula. The track running up to that place was by way of two hairpin bends. No 1 Platoon was to seize those while No 2 Platoon was to infiltrate and to pass through the Gurkhas on Hangman's Hill.

'During the night we reached the forward positions held by our own men. Our Company commander was overjoyed when a whole platoon of us arrived. Our comrades holding the front-line trenches were at the end of their tether and completely exhausted, but our arrival revived their flagging spirits. The commander put us in the picture and then we went into the attack. After a few unsuccessful attempts we seized first the upper and then the lower hairpin bend. The British defended themselves with great tenacity and it was only after we had flung down some large explosive charges upon them and had caused a great deal of confusion that they began to pull back. The area around Rocca Janula was in our hands. Years later, after the war, I learned that on that day and at that hour we had been in battle with the Essex Regiment of 4th Indian Division which had been moving forward towards Hangman's Hill. Less than fifty men of that regiment reached the Gurkhas on Hangman's Hill – too few to carry out the planned attack upon the Abbey.'

Even in the bitterness of the fighting more civilized thoughts were not altogether absent. On Easter Sunday the whole area around Cassino lay quiet, peaceful and bathed in sunshine. There was no sound of aircraft, not even that of the little artillery spotter planes, no crashing thunder of an artillery barrage: nothing to break the calm. Then, in the words of the Para Pioneer history:

'The wind carried to us the barely audible sound of church bells whose gentle tone reminded us that there was something else in the world other

Above: *Hans Teske served with 5th Parachute Regiment in Tunisia, where he saved the life of a British soldier in February 1943.*

Right: *Heinrich Benz (left) who served in No.12 Company of the same regiment as Hans Teske. This photograph was taken at Medjez el Bab in December 1942.*

Top right: *Reinhold Hoffman was taken prisoner in Tunisia and sent to a punishment camp in the desert where he remained until August 1947. (R. Hoffman)*

Hilf siegen
als Luftnachrichtenhelferin
Auskunft erteilt jede Luftwaffendienststelle

Left: Hans-Joachim Marseille, the Luftwaffe ace known as the 'Star of Africa'. He was killed in a flying accident, having gained 158 victories.

Above: Although conscription existed in Germany, the authorities were reluctant to use it to bring women into the services and preferred to rely upon voluntary enlistment. Recruiting posters such as this one invited women to work for victory.

Above: *Towards the end of the war, pressure grew for women to become more involved. Traute Kren, neé Auer, served with a flak unit in Schweinfurt; the photograph shows her in Gnas, Austria, before leaving for her military service.*

Top right: *Traute Auer (left) and Traude Schranz (right) who were nearly knocked down by a fleeing SS cavalry unit on the last day of the war.*

Right: *Luftwaffe Flakhelferinnen operated the searchlights during air raids. Traute Kren worked on just such a site at Schweinfurt.*

Left: *Captain Hans Jungwirth, Hans Teske's commanding officer in Tunisia, 1943.*

Above: Gerd-Dietrich Schneider, here seen in the rank of Oberleutnant zur See, when he was in command of No. 8 Gun Platform Flotilla. He is wearing the Knight's Cross of the Iron Cross, which was awarded to him on 4 October 1944, in recognition of his services in north-west European waters during July, August and September 1944.

Above: Adolf Strauch in Naples, 1943, shortly before a planned operation in North Africa which was later aborted. He is wearing his tunic with the Iron Cross 1st Class, the wounded badge, infantry assault badge, and paratroop qualification badge.

Left: *The stripped-down hulk of the R 35, described by Gerd-Dietrich Schneider, shortly after passing through the Golden narrows in Regensburg; summer 1942.*

Top: *Heavy machine-gun group of No.12 Company of Deutschland Regiment march into positions near Vel Burlook in February 1943.*

Above: *One of the columns of German soldiers of Sixth Army captured when Stalingrad fell in February 1943. Only a small number ever returned from captivity.*

Right: *General, later Field Marshal, Paulus commanding Sixth Army, which was forced to surrender at Stalingrad against Hitler's wishes.*

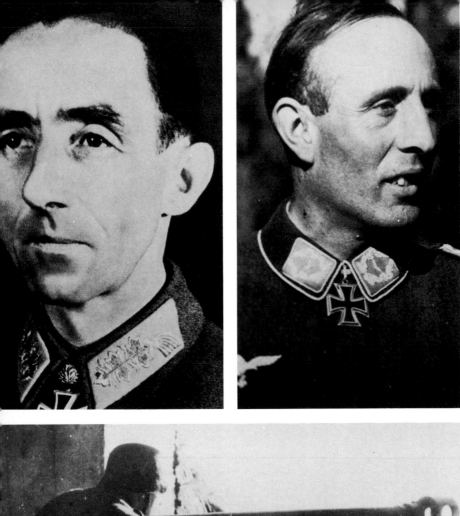

Right: In spring 1944 von Rundstedt (right), Supreme Commander West, visited the Hitler Youth Division, which was being worked up to combat efficiency by officers such as Meyer (left) and Witt (centre).

Opposite page, top left: General Fridolin von Senger und Etterlin who commanded the German troops defending Monte Cassino.

Opposite page, top right: Colonel August Freiherr von der Heydte commanded 6th Fallschirmjäger Regiment in Normandy and led the unit that dropped in the Ardennes during the Battle of the Bulge.

Opposite page, bottom: A German soldier coastwatching from a bunker in the Atlantic Wall, Normandy.

Right: The Allied invasion fleet as seen through the range-finder of a German armoured fighting vehicle on D-Day, 6 June 1944.

Right: Men of Baron von der Heydte's 6th Parachute Regiment and SS Division Goetz von Berlichingen take their wounded to a first-aid post in Normandy.

Above: Michael Wittmann of 101st SS Heavy Tank Battalion was considered to be the finest tank commander in any army during the Second World War.

Above right: Wittmann and Balthasar Woll, a member of his Tiger tank crew. On 13 June 1944 Wittmann and his Tiger were instrumental in halting the advance of the British 22nd Armoured Brigade (7th Armoured Division) by destroying 25 vehicles in half an hour on the road outside Villers Bocage, Normandy.

Below: A heavily camouflaged Tiger tank of 101st Heavy SS Panzer Battalion. Concealment was

essential to avoid the attention of Allied aircraft, which dominated the skies.

Opposite page, top: A Panther tank making its way through the rubble-strewn streets of Caen in July 1944.

Opposite page, bottom left: General of the SS Hausser, GOC Seventh Army, on a visit to the TAC HQ of General Meindl, GOC Parachute Corps. The tall officer is Lieutenant-Colonel Blauensteiner, Meindl's chief of staff.

Opposite page, bottom right: Major Stephani, commanding officer of 9th Parachute Regiment.

Above: *A scene in one of the country roads in the Falaise area, with burning and knocked out German vehicles abounding.*

Left: *One of the weapons with which Hitler tried to win the war was the V-1, a pilotless, rocket-propelled bomb. The first of these fell on the United Kingdom shortly after D-Day.*

Opposite page, top: *Men of the Volkssturm parading in Berlin during the autumn of 1944. Most of them are armed with single-shot Panzerfaust anti-tank rockets.*

Opposite page, bottom left: *Kapitän zur See Reinicke, commander of the cruiser* Prinz Eugen.

Opposite page, bottom right: *In an effort to sustain morale in the latter days of the war, the German Propaganda Ministry mounted live radio concerts using popular artists. This picture shows one of these 'Wunschkonzerte'.*

Left: The after turrets of Prinz Eugen *as she fires on targets on the Sworbe Peninsula in 1944.*

Centre left: American prisoners, taken captive during the Battle of the Bulge, passing by a panzer from Jochen Peiper's battalion.

Bottom left: Josef Goebbels, the Reichs Minister for Propaganda, with a group of newly decorated winners of the Knight's Cross of the Iron Cross. The badges on the arm of the officer in the centre of the picture show that he has knocked out four tanks in close-quarter combat.

Right: *Eva Braun, second from the left, at a party in the Berghof, Bavaria. The SS officer standing next to her is Fegelein, who was shot in Berlin for deserting his post in the Führer's bunker.*

Below: Admiral Scheer *was one of the ships involved in the naval operations in the Baltic at the end of the war intended to hold off the Red Army while German refugees were transported to western Germany.*

Above: German refugees preparing to abandon their farms in the face of the Red Army's advance.

Left: Konter-Admiral Engelhardt, chief of naval transport, who organized the evacuation of German refugees.

Below: Refugees on board Wedel en route from the eastern Baltic to western Germany in spring 1945.

than battle, war, misery and death in an infinite variety of forms. The sound became louder, proclaiming the message, "Peace on earth". Louder and louder still until the sound filled the whole of the Liri valley. The men in their slit trenches heard it. Easter – the celebration of the Resurrection – the victory of life over death. Nowhere was the sound more appropriate than here on a battlefield of the Second World War.

'General Heidrich in his TAC HQ listened to the sound and when the last notes had died away turned to his aide-de-camp and ordered him to find out who was responsible in the middle of a battle for such a moving Easter greeting. It turned out to be six NCOs of the Para Pioneers who had gone down to the church in the valley and who had climbed on to its shattered tower because the bell ropes were missing. In the belfry they had had to swing the bells by hand . . . The little church in Castrolielo, in which for so long no mass had been said, gave to thousands of soldiers from every corner of the world, who had been embattled for weeks, God's consoling message in the early morning of Easter Sunday, 1944.'

DEATH AND DEFEAT ON MONTE GEMMANO

The German defence at Cassino and at Anzio was broken at last, but it had won time for a line to be established across the whole width of the Italian peninsula from south of Rimini on the Adriatic to the Tyrrhenian Sea. This was the last main German defensive position in front of the River Po. It was one which Kesselring had to hold and the offensive to break through those defences has passed into military history as the battle of the Gothic Line. According to Wolf Schirrmacher, in an article he wrote for a German soldiers' magazine during September 1944: 'The Adriatic Sea limits the extent of the battlefield on our left flank. To the right there is the steep Monte Titan which rises like a horn above the little republic of San Marino. In between there is the silhouette of Rimini . . . farther to the right lie one behind the other three long ridges. These are the last pieces of high ground before one reaches the green plain extending seemingly endlessly to the west and to the north.' To the north lay Bologna, an objective of Eighth Army's attack and behind Bologna was the River Po. To the British commanders it was clear that once the German defensive crust had been broken and the ridges captured, the armour could race across the plain towards the Po, overrolling the Germans who would have no opportunity to set up new defensive lines.

To prevent Eighth Army from breaking through and reaching the open plain was Kesselring's intention and the three ridges mentioned by Schirrmacher decided the course of the battle. Longstop Hill in Tunisia, more than a year earlier, had demonstrated the simple truths that he who

held the high ground dominated the battlefield and that mountain tops could be held with small garrisons. One of the élite units holding the ground around Monte Gemmano, the most dominant of the three ridges, was 100th Gebirgsjaeger Regiment which had fought in Crete. Helmut Hermann was the commanding officer of the 1st Battalion which held Gemmano against the successive assaults of a British battalion and then an entire brigade. The feature finally fell to a divisional attack. Helmut Hermann wrote:

'I can give neither exact locations nor timings but it was the middle of September 1944 and we were defending a sector in the area of Montescudo. I was at that time a captain and commanding 1st Battalion of 100th Gebirgsjaeger regiment. It was originally intended that at the beginning of September we would be withdrawn from the eastern Po plain and posted to the high mountains along the French-Italian border where we would have been in our 'element'. Nothing came of that intention. Instead we were put in hastily in the area of Gemmano to meet the major offensive which the British had launched. We spent a great many days under fire from British artillery, from the fire of ships out at sea and from Allied aircraft as well as holding out against infantry and tank attack. We frequently had to change our positions and suffered quite heavy losses.

'Now we had reached the edge of a rather open, high ridge which fell abruptly on its western side. Just below its upper crest there was a small cave in which I set up Battalion TAC HQ. Our anti-tank weapons consisted of "Panzerfaust" for close-combat action and the "Stovepipe" [a rocket-launcher with a range of about 300 metres]. Those weapons were useless against the British tanks which kept out of range of our weapons, but which fired at us from great distances. We realized that a few tanks had broken through on our right flank and were rolling towards regimental TAC HQ. One of the armoured fighting vehicles stopped on the road at a place from which it could have fired into our little cave. We could only hope that we had not been seen and did not dare to leave the cave before nightfall. Those were very anxious hours for us. Our nerves were taut and the time passed so slowly. But at least our telephone lines were intact and we were in radio contact with the rest of the regiment.

'Then came the order to pull back to a new line. Seldom had we longed for nightfall with such intensity. To our relief we were not discovered. Before midnight we had reached the new line and dug in as best we could. En route to the new line I found out that although we were in touch with the units on our left flank, on the right there was a dangerous gap. I took my aide-de-camp, Leutenant Herber Pohlmann, along a path in order to find our right-flank neighbours. The sky was eerily lit by a great number of ship's searchlights which, reflecting from the clouds, produced a diffused light. The British artillery had meanwhile gone over to intermittent fire. During our search we saw a large farm in which there was movement. Hoping that this

Right: The capsized hulk of Admiral Scheer *in Kiel harbour following a raid by the RAF in 1945.*

Right: A column of surrendered Luftwaffe personnel in north Germany, May 1945. (Imperial War Museum)

Right: Field Police were held in groups behind the front lines to collect stragglers and men whose units had been destroyed in battle. Those survivors were formed into battle groups and put back in action. The picture shows a collecting point in Hungary during the spring offensive of 1945.

might be the German unit we were seeking we moved towards a group of men, about a platoon in strength, who were working busily but quietly in the farm courtyard. I was about to approach one man but soon realized that there was something suspicious about the number of soldiers moving about. Then I saw that they were British. It was clear that they had not noticed us. We moved away as quietly as we had approached and found after a further search the lightly held positions of our neighbouring unit. We discussed the situation with them and soon the gap in the line was closed. My aide and I had been walking through No-Man's Land between the enemy's positions and our own.'

THE WEHRMACHT BROKEN

While 100th Regiment was battling to hold Gemmano, other formations and divisions were being forced back on the lower ground along the Roman road which runs from Rimini to Bologna. One of those units was the 278th Division. Rolf Dittmann, of 993rd Grenadier Regiment, wrote of the sacrifice of the German infantry during the Gothic Line offensive. His words are applicable wherever and whenever the infantry bears the brunt of the fighting:

'Our battalion was in position, during the night of 15th/16th September, on the southern slopes of Montescudo . . . Company strengths were about 20 men. I held the vital sector of the battalion line and was told to expect No 3 Company as reinforcement once the 1st Battalion of 993 Regiment reached our area. At about 1 in the morning I went forward with a runner from the relief regiment. The situation in the front line was chaotic and near Marcagnano, some 600 metres behind the front line, we clashed with an enemy patrol. There was a lot of wild firing because it was difficult to determine friend from foe. That episode cost us two wounded . . . We reached the front line where we were to carry out the relief of the survivors of the three companies holding the line. The relief was a noisy one and as the battle lines were only hand-grenade distance apart the Indians soon realized what was happening and made an attack upon No 1 Platoon. The confusion was indescribable. Corporal Marks was able to hold the Indians on his sector but the rest of the group was driven back to TAC HQ. Using those men and the reserve group we launched a counter-attack although we were unfamiliar with the ground. It was a short but fierce engagement but at last we recovered the trenches which had been lost . . . In that counter-attack an NCO and three men were wounded, some had burns from phosphorus grenades . . . At dawn No 3 Company came up at last but once again the relief was made with too much noise and No 3 Company which had just taken over the high ground was driven off it. It was too dangerous to leave the enemy in possession of ground which would dominate us and an immediate counter-attack was launched by No 3 Company (18 to 20 men). We gave them covering fire as they went in. That counter-attack seemed to dispirit the enemy who made no more attacks that day . . . I reported to Battalion TAC HQ in Corianino where replacements had come up. I received eight men to replace those who had been lost in the past days' fighting. I also received an officer replacement, a man who left the Company in January as a lance-corporal and has come from OCTU.'

The sacrifice of the German infantry continued beyond the River Po when, in the spring of 1945, a massive offensive by both Fifth and Eighth Armies broke the German forces and sent them reeling back towards the Alps. But before they could reach the shelter of the high mountains secret negotiations brought the war in Italy to an end. On 2 May 1945, the German Army Group in Italy surrendered, the first in the week of surrenders which brought the war in Europe to an end, and the officers and men of that Army Group passed into captivity.

The German Army had borne the brunt of the fighting in the Italian peninsula and the participation of the sister services was at a lower level of intensity. The Luftwaffe could deploy only a few squadrons in that theatre of operations although nuisance raids by Me 110 fighter-bombers were a feature of life throughout the campaign. One severe raid which gave the Luftwaffe a victory was that carried out on 2 December 1943, by machines of K G 76. Shipping in the harbour at Bari was attacked and more than thirty vessels were sunk. The raid was a complete success achieving total surprise. For its part the Kriegsmarine, with no heavy units in the Mediterranean, was forced to rely upon unconventional means to strike at Allied ships. A 'K' flotilla, a flotilla of 'small' units was formed and equipped with the first of those unconventional weapons – a manned, double torpedo. A 'captain' sat in the upper torpedo which had been hollowed out to take him together with the primitive engine and navigational equipment. Suspended underneath the captain was the armed torpedo which he would fire at enemy vessels. The first mission was against Allied shipping in Anzio harbour and was a failure. The Allied ships had sailed before the 'K' men arrived. That raid did, however, show up a serious fault in this type of 'K' craft. The captain could not remove the clear plastic hood fitted over the cockpit in which he sat and death by suffocation often resulted.

The invasion of north-west Europe on 6 June 1944 then shifted the emphasis of the navy's 'K' units to Normandy and Holland, and naval operations in Italy, which had now become a very minor theatre of war, diminished as a consequence.

DEFENDING THE WESTERN SEABOARD

British plans for an invasion of north-west Europe were laid in 1940, the same year in which the Expeditionary Force had been forced to leave the continent. For certain strategic and political reasons OKW gave no serious thought to the possibility for several years. Then, on 3 November 1943, Adolf Hitler issued Führer Directive No 51. This admitted that the bitter fighting and heavy losses of the past years had had their effect upon the German armed forces and that a new strategy was required. Territorial losses on the Eastern Front, the Directive claimed, would not be disastrous. In the west, however, a successful Allied invasion could bring about the defeat of the Third Reich. The Führer had decided, therefore, to improve the defensive capabilities of the armies in the west. The Directive accepted that the whole area of the western seaboard up to and including Denmark, could not be defended at every point in great strength, but it did order that defences were to be concentrated in the likeliest landing areas.

There were two obvious regions in which an invading force might come ashore: in the Pas-de-Calais or in Normandy. Hitler appreciated that the capture of a major port was vital to the Allied plan of campaign and in the final months before D-Day came more and more to consider that Normandy, with the major ports of Cherbourg and Brest, would be the likelier area. Despite that he still kept an entire army grouped in the Pas-de-Calais region. Having considered where the Allies were likely to land, the next task for OKW was to know the strength of the enemy forces that would fight the campaign. German Intelligence sources deliberately inflated the figure of Allied formations to well over 70, although the actual number which would be eventually, under the command of General Eisenhower, was 37 divisions. Only a small number of these would carry out the initial assault. The greatest number would be brought in after D-Day. Facing the Allied armies were 33 'fixed' divisions in a coast defence role, thirteen mobile infantry divisions, two Fallschirmjaeger divisions and six panzer divisions. There was also an OKW reserve of four panzer/panzergrenadier divisions.

Hitler had ordered, in Directive No 51, that all the divisions in the west were to be fully equipped and up to establishment, but there was a discrepancy between what the Führer ordered and what was possible in practice. Most formations were seriously understrength in men and equipment and their fighting qualities varied. The immobile, 'fixed' divisions, all in the 700 series and made up of middle-aged men, had the task of holding an area near to or on the coast. There they would stay, under fire, until, presumably, they were either relieved or destroyed. But there were in Normandy also the Wehrmacht's élite divisions, Fallschirmjaeger and SS; aggressive and battle-hardened veterans for the most part.

Among the most serious problems facing OKW was that no agreed plan of defence had been worked out. There were differences of opinion in the highest echelons of command in the west on how the invasion should be met. Von Runstedt, the Supreme Commander West, thought it best to let the landing take place and then, before the Allies could consolidate their hold, to attack and to defeat the newly landed divisions in a setpiece battle. Rommel was for an immediate counter-attack while the Allied units were still on the beaches. The failure of the two senior commanders to agree on the strategy to be followed required that Hitler make a decision. He compromised. Mobile units in OKW reserve were to be under his direct control and only he would determine to whom and at what stage of the battle these would be released.

The Allied forces for the coming campaign were known as 21st Army Group and were commanded by General Montgomery. The order of battle of this formation was US First, Canadian First and British Second Armies. Once Patton's Third Army had landed in France and become operational, it and US First Army would combine to form 12th Army Group under Omar Bradley. The Allies landed in the early hours of 6 June and it was against the Anglo-Canadian armies that the bulk of the German panzer divisions were eventually deployed. This was in accord with Montgomery's strategy which foresaw the Anglo-Canadians as forming the hinge on the door – the hinge to which the German armour would be attracted so as to stop the door swinging. This concentration of armour against the British and Canadian beachheads would give the US First Army the chance to break out of its perimeters and swing, in a wide pincer, through Le Mans towards the Seine. Patton's Third Army would strike both into Brittany and also act as a shield along the Loire river to defend the right flank of US First Army. The operations timetable was that by D-Day plus 90, i.e., by the first week of September, the Allied armies should have reached their objectives. They should have reached the Seine and the two great ports of Cherbourg and Brest should have been captured and made operational. A breakout began and an unsuccessful counter-attack by Hitler at Mortain to contain it was responsible for a change in the Allied plan. Patton would not now head for Brittany but would carry out the drive to the Seine in a *Blitzkrieg* operation. As a result of that change of direction Fifth Panzer and Seventh German Armies in Normandy were encircled in a pocket, based on Falaise and during July and August the greatest part of these two major formations were shattered. With their destruction there were insufficient troops to hold the Allies until von Rundstedt, recalled from dismissal, created a loose battle line, chiefly of Fallschirmjaeger units, behind which he established a firm defence. Under Allied pressure and over the course of the next months the German armies in the west were continually pushed back, a German offensive in the Ardennes notwithstanding; the Rhine was crossed and the war in Europe brought to a close.

In the eleven months from June 1944 to May 1945, the German soldiers, sailors and airmen became only too aware of Allied material superiority. From dawn to dusk Allied aircraft ruled the skies, Allied tank armadas swept across the land, and at sea the only response that the Kriegsmarine could make was in the form of small commando-type operations with manned torpedoes and one-man submarines. The Allied soldiers fought in the knowledge of their superiority in numbers and material. The German soldiers fought using their military skill and with a fear that the unconditional surrender demanded by the Allies would reduce their Fatherland to the status of an agrarian, slave State. Reinhold Hoffmann wrote:

'As soldiers we were not told what to do if we became prisoners of war, nor how we should behave as prisoners. We were instructed in our responsibility for the weapons, vehicles and equipment which the German nation had entrusted to us soldiers; the weapons bearers of the nation. To be given a weapon with which to defend our country was an honour and a heavy responsibility. Many units made the issue of weapons a ceremony as solemn as the swearing of the oath of allegiance. The inference was, obviously, that if we used our weapons correctly we should not become prisoners – with hindsight a naïve concept but at that time one which carried conviction.'

The German armies which defended Normandy were no longer the magnificent weapon that had entered France in 1940. By 1944, there were a great many units composed of foreigners and non-Europeans. Large numbers of ethnic groups from the Soviet Union had volunteered to fight against Bolshevism and found themselves battling in the west against their country's Allies. Many of these ethnic peoples belonged to the martial races of the Soviet Union, but were unused to the noise and destructive power of modern warfare. Colonel von der Heydte, commanding 6th Fallschirmjaeger Regiment, recalled: 'Corps [84 Corps] promised me a battalion of Georgians and these, in fact, arrived. They did not stay long, however. They could not withstand air raids. Within three days there was not a Georgian with us.' This was not the only ethnic desertion with which von der Heydte had had to suffer. Just before D-Day all the Alsatian drivers in his unit had deserted. Germany's allies abandoned her as her defeat became more certain and in some cases her former allies changed sides and took up arms against those who had been, until recent days, their brothers in arms.

In the fierce and destructive battles of 1944, German units suffered heavy casualties and the replacements received were neither sufficient in number nor in training. General Meindl, commanding 2 Para Corps, complained to his superior, Student, that the fighting strength of his units was dwindling daily. His last two requests for replacements had been ignored and those few men that had been sent soon became casualties because they had had so little training. Many of them, in Meindl's words, '. . . have never thrown a hand-grenade, fired more than a few rounds with a weapon or have any idea of digging in or of camouflaging their positions . . .' Generally, depleted units were fleshed out, although never completely, with men obtained from disbanded Luftwaffe or naval establishments, thus fulfilling the old slogan, 'A regiment can die ten times over – but it still remains the regiment.' Using all their skill and loyal to their oath the outnumbered remnants of the Wehrmacht fought their way from the bocage country of Normandy, across the polders of the Low Countries, back over the Rhine and into Germany. This was a sacrifice that might not have been demanded of them had more experienced men been directing operations in Normandy. Von Rundstedt's condemnation of Hitler's interference in the strategy of the Western Front, is contained in his conviction, 'If it [the conduct of the Normandy campaign] had been left to me, I would have made the Allies pay a fearful price.' Hitler's meddling extended down to deciding the tactics to be used by sub-units. In his strategic decisions he brooked no contradiction even though these were frequently wrong. He alone controlled the panzer divisions in the OKW reserve, divisions which might have operated against the landings just after these had been made and before the Allied armies had consolidated their hold. But when the Allies landed the Führer was asleep and no one dared wake him. While OKW waited for its Supreme Commander to rise and to make a decision, the Allies poured ashore and established their first perimeters.

The 12th SS 'Hitler Youth' was one of the panzer divisions located in Normandy. It had been raised less than a year earlier but had trained to such effect that by 1 June 1944, that is to say only five days before the Allied landings, the divisional units, with two exceptions, had been classified as 'being in every respect fit for operations'. Those two exceptions were the rocket-projector and the anti-tank battalions, neither of which was up to war establishment in weapons.

HITLER YOUTH DIVISION IN NORMANDY

His experience of the D-Day landings was described by a subaltern of the 'Hitler Youth' Division, Peter Hansmann, commander of the armoured car company of the divisional reconnaissance battalion. Confused details of Allied paratroop landings needed to be clarified. Supreme Command West ordered 12th SS Panzer Division to '. . . carry out reconnaissance, to gain touch with 711th Division, to halt and then to guard its area'. The armoured car company was alerted at about 0230 hrs and the drivers, many of them still in their underwear, rushed to their vehicles. Engines were started and within 15 minutes the Company, ten armoured cars and two groups of motor-cyclists, was ready to march.

'The Sergeant Major reports the unit ready for action. The men gather round me in a half circle and I brief them, speak of the seriousness of the battle that lies ahead and the object of our mission. As recce troops it is our job to be fast but invisible; to see everything but not to be seen and to report the enemy's location back to our commanders. I tell them to watch the road surfaces for mines because partisans may have laid mines and go on to detail the order of march. One group of motor cyclists will form the advance guard, followed by an 8-wheel and a 4-wheel vehicle alternately. Distance between vehicles 50 metres. The second group of motor cyclists will form the rearguard.

'I stand in the turret of the first 8-wheeler and give the order "Panzer marsch!" The night is pleasantly cool and visibility is medium to good – about 50 to 100 metres although the moon is often obscured by cloud or mist. After we have gone a few kilometres I have the feeling that this is just like any of the exercises that we have carried out over the past weeks. The little houses in the villages are unlit. The inhabitants are asleep. There is no sign of the French partisans. Some 15 minutes later and we reach battalion TAC HQ, drive the vehicles under trees in the garden of the château and I report together with my platoon and Section commanders to the CO, Sturmbann-führer Bremer. We are given the latest information about the landings west of the mouth of the Seine near Carentan, but Bremer tells us that accurate details are lacking. It is, therefore, our task to patrol the coastal sector to the north, between the mouth of the Seine and Bayeux. We are to find out whether enemy troops have landed, where they have reached and their intentions.

'I divide the unit into four troops . . . We check the radios and set out at about 0400 hrs. My group is made up of two 8-wheel vehicles whose commanders have experience of the Russian front . . . Visibility is improving and is now more than 100 metres. The front we have to reach is about 80 kms away so I choose the most direct road via Broglie and Lisieux to Caen . . . Within an hour we are in Lisieux and here the first civilians are met. The day is beginning for them, a day like any other day . . . We meet motor cyclists and VW cars on the road. On the bridge across the Touques German soldiers, old enough to be our fathers, report that their unit has been placed on alarm, but that apart from bomber squadrons heading westwards nothing has happened . . . I carry on towards Caen . . . We meet more and more military vehicles on the road, so it must still be open. We approach Caen. On its outskirts there is a great deal of movement. Trucks of all sorts are driving about, platoons of soldiers are taking up position. A lieutenant asks whether we have had a brush with the enemy? . . . An alarm sounds and a report comes in that enemy paras are attacking about 10 km north of the Orne bridges and that heavy fighting is going on. This accounts for the vehicle movement in the streets and explains why the infantry, panzer-grenadiers of 21st Panzer Division, have been turned out. A captain tells me that strong British airborne units have landed on either side of the Orne bridges and that these are probably now in enemy hands. The noise of battle can be heard quite clearly and is probably coming from that area. Fighter-bombers attack indiscriminately. French civilians abandon their homes in a panic and rush out of the town. Back again with my men . . . I send out a patrol with orders to recce to the north. Then I send back my report over the radio . . .

'On the main road to Bayeux I wish that there was cloud or mist. We are a sitting target. There is a lot of traffic on the road so the Tommies cannot reach there yet . . . We enter the town. Civilians running about. The closer we get to the centre of the town the thicker are the crowds. There are troops and vehicles of all sorts and a single platoon of Feldgendarmerie is trying to sort out the chaos. I try unsuccessfully to reach the Town Major's office and hear that artillery has been firing on Bayeux . . . From a Feldgendarmerie sergeant I learn that in Arromanches Bay there has been heavy fighting and that the English are landing along the coast from hundreds of ships. If the sounds of fighting are anything to go by it must really be a hell of a battle because the thunder of heavy artillery is very clear . . . That's it then . . . not only airborne but also seaborne attack. This we must see. I give orders that we are no longer to drive along open roads but under the cover of trees. As we drive up the ridge which lies to the north of the town . . . we look left towards the coast and see fountains of earth and burning buildings. I cannot see the sea at all and drive further forward to gain the crest of the ridge. We park and camouflage the vehicles very carefully under trees and near barns. From the top of the ridge we can see Arromanches Bay . . . What we are seeing is something unimaginable, something totally unbelievable . . . What is that grey mass spread out before us? . . . There to the left is Arromanches. Heavy artillery fire is falling on it. Fountains of earth as tall as houses rise and sink back. To the east there is a seemingly endless grey mass – the sea – endlessly also the horizon but there is, somewhat lighter in colour, something else. I look through binoculars – now I can make out the outlines of individual ships. Close packed and stretching as far as the eye can see, ships, ships, masts and upper works. From the distance I see irregular flashes as the big guns on the ships open up. The sea between the beach and the armada of ships in front of us is dark blue. Across that dark water there are white lines coming from that mass of shipping which extends from Arromanches to the Orne estuary – and they are heading straight toward us.

'These are fast ships with high, white, foaming bow waves. Landing craft which spew out brown balls of soldiers as they touch down on the beach.

Right: *The capsized hulk of* Admiral Scheer *in Kiel harbour following a raid by the RAF in 1945.*

Right: *A column of surrendered Luftwaffe personnel in north Germany, May 1945. (Imperial War Museum)*

Right: *Field Police were held in groups behind the front lines to collect stragglers and men whose units had been destroyed in battle. Those survivors were formed into battle groups and put back in action. The picture shows a collecting point in Hungary during the spring offensive of 1945.*

Left: The scene in the inner courtyard of the Reichskanzlei in Berlin shortly after the city fell to the Russians. (*Imperial War Museum*)

Left: At the end of the war, civil authority broke down in some German cities. These civilians are looting foodstuffs from goods trains. (*Imperial War Museum*)

Left: German civilians standing in front of their ruined houses read the first edition of a newspaper published by the Allied forces to inform them that the struggle is all over. (*Imperial War Museum*)

than battle, war, misery and death in an infinite variety of forms. The sound became louder, proclaiming the message, "Peace on earth". Louder and louder still until the sound filled the whole of the Liri valley. The men in their slit trenches heard it. Easter – the celebration of the Resurrection – the victory of life over death. Nowhere was the sound more appropriate than here on a battlefield of the Second World War.

'General Heidrich in his TAC HQ listened to the sound and when the last notes had died away turned to his aide-de-camp and ordered him to find out who was responsible in the middle of a battle for such a moving Easter greeting. It turned out to be six NCOs of the Para Pioneers who had gone down to the church in the valley and who had climbed on to its shattered tower because the bell ropes were missing. In the belfry they had had to swing the bells by hand . . . The little church in Castrolielo, in which for so long no mass had been said, gave to thousands of soldiers from every corner of the world, who had been embattled for weeks, God's consoling message in the early morning of Easter Sunday, 1944.'

DEATH AND DEFEAT ON MONTE GEMMANO

The German defence at Cassino and at Anzio was broken at last, but it had won time for a line to be established across the whole width of the Italian peninsula from south of Rimini on the Adriatic to the Tyrrhenian Sea. This was the last main German defensive position in front of the River Po. It was one which Kesselring had to hold and the offensive to break through those defences has passed into military history as the battle of the Gothic Line. According to Wolf Schirrmacher, in an article he wrote for a German soldiers' magazine during September 1944: 'The Adriatic Sea limits the extent of the battlefield on our left flank. To the right there is the steep Monte Titan which rises like a horn above the little republic of San Marino. In between there is the silhouette of Rimini . . . farther to the right lie one behind the other three long ridges. These are the last pieces of high ground before one reaches the green plain extending seemingly endlessly to the west and to the north.' To the north lay Bologna, an objective of Eighth Army's attack and behind Bologna was the River Po. To the British commanders it was clear that once the German defensive crust had been broken and the ridges captured, the armour could race across the plain towards the Po, overrolling the Germans who would have no opportunity to set up new defensive lines.

To prevent Eighth Army from breaking through and reaching the open plain was Kesselring's intention and the three ridges mentioned by Schirrmacher decided the course of the battle. Longstop Hill in Tunisia, more than a year earlier, had demonstrated the simple truths that he who held the high ground dominated the battlefield and that mountain tops could be held with small garrisons. One of the élite units holding the ground around Monte Gemmano, the most dominant of the three ridges, was 100th Gebirgsjaeger Regiment which had fought in Crete. Helmut Hermann was the commanding officer of the 1st Battalion which held Gemmano against the successive assaults of a British battalion and then an entire brigade. The feature finally fell to a divisional attack. Helmut Hermann wrote:

'I can give neither exact locations nor timings but it was the middle of September 1944 and we were defending a sector in the area of Montescudo. I was at that time a captain and commanding 1st Battalion of 100th Gebirgsjaeger regiment. It was originally intended that at the beginning of September we would be withdrawn from the eastern Po plain and posted to the high mountains along the French-Italian border where we would have been in our 'element'. Nothing came of that intention. Instead we were put in hastily in the area of Gemmano to meet the major offensive which the British had launched. We spent a great many days under fire from British artillery, from the fire of ships out at sea and from Allied aircraft as well as holding out against infantry and tank attack. We frequently had to change our positions and suffered quite heavy losses.

'Now we had reached the edge of a rather open, high ridge which fell abruptly on its western side. Just below its upper crest there was a small cave in which I set up Battalion TAC HQ. Our anti-tank weapons consisted of "Panzerfaust" for close-combat action and the "Stovepipe" [a rocket-launcher with a range of about 300 metres]. Those weapons were useless against the British tanks which kept out of range of our weapons, but which fired at us from great distances. We realized that a few tanks had broken through on our right flank and were rolling towards regimental TAC HQ. One of the armoured fighting vehicles stopped on the road at a place from which it could have fired into our little cave. We could only hope that we had not been seen and did not dare to leave the cave before nightfall. Those were very anxious hours for us. Our nerves were taut and the time passed so slowly. But at least our telephone lines were intact and we were in radio contact with the rest of the regiment.

'Then came the order to pull back to a new line. Seldom had we longed for nightfall with such intensity. To our relief we were not discovered. Before midnight we had reached the new line and dug in as best we could. En route to the new line I found out that although we were in touch with the units on our left flank, on the right there was a dangerous gap. I took my aide-de-camp, Leutenant Herber Pohlmann, along a path in order to find our right-flank neighbours. The sky was eerily lit by a great number of ship's searchlights which, reflecting from the clouds, produced a diffused light. The British artillery had meanwhile gone over to intermittent fire. During our search we saw a large farm in which there was movement. Hoping that this might be the German unit we were seeking we moved towards a group of men, about a platoon in strength, who were working busily but quietly in the farm courtyard. I was about to approach one man but soon realized that there was something suspicious about the number of soldiers moving about. Then I saw that they were British. It was clear that they had not noticed us. We moved away as quietly as we had approached and found after a further search the lightly held positions of our neighbouring unit. We discussed the situation with them and soon the gap in the line was closed. My aide and I had been walking through No-Man's Land between the enemy's positions and our own.'

THE WEHRMACHT BROKEN

While 100th Regiment was battling to hold Gemmano, other formations and divisions were being forced back on the lower ground along the Roman road which runs from Rimini to Bologna. One of those units was the 278th Division. Rolf Dittmann, of 993rd Grenadier Regiment, wrote of the sacrifice of the German infantry during the Gothic Line offensive. His words are applicable wherever and whenever the infantry bears the brunt of the fighting:

'Our battalion was in position, during the night of 15th/16th September, on the southern slopes of Montescudo . . . Company strengths were about 20 men. I held the vital sector of the battalion line and was told to expect No 3 Company as reinforcement once the 1st Battalion of 993 Regiment reached our area. At about 1 in the morning I went forward with a runner from the relief regiment. The situation in the front line was chaotic and near Marcagnano, some 600 metres behind the front line, we clashed with an enemy patrol. There was a lot of wild firing because it was difficult to determine friend from foe. That episode cost us two wounded . . . We reached the front line where we were to carry out the relief of the survivors of the three companies holding the line. The relief was a noisy one and as the battle lines were only hand-grenade distance apart the Indians soon realized what was happening and made an attack upon No 1 Platoon. The confusion was indescribable. Corporal Marks was able to hold the Indians on his sector but the rest of the group was driven back to TAC HQ. Using those men and the reserve group we launched a counter-attack although we were unfamiliar with the ground. It was a short but fierce engagement but at last we recovered the trenches which had been lost . . . In that counter-attack an NCO and three men were wounded, some had burns from phosphorus grenades . . . At dawn No 3 Company came up at last but once again the relief was made with too much noise and No 3 Company which had just taken over the high ground was driven off it. It was too dangerous to leave the enemy in possession of ground which would dominate us and an immediate counter-attack was launched by No 3 Company (18 to 20 men). We gave them covering fire as they went in. That counter-attack seemed to dispirit the enemy who made no more attacks that day . . . I reported to Battalion TAC HQ in Corianino where replacements had come up. I received eight men to replace those who had been lost in the past days' fighting. I also received an officer replacement, a man who left the Company in January as a lance-corporal and has come from OCTU.'

The sacrifice of the German infantry continued beyond the River Po when, in the spring of 1945, a massive offensive by both Fifth and Eighth Armies broke the German forces and sent them reeling back towards the Alps. But before they could reach the shelter of the high mountains secret negotiations brought the war in Italy to an end. On 2 May 1945, the German Army Group in Italy surrendered, the first in the week of surrenders which brought the war in Europe to an end, and the officers and men of that Army Group passed into captivity.

The German Army had borne the brunt of the fighting in the Italian peninsula and the participation of the sister services was at a lower level of intensity. The Luftwaffe could deploy only a few squadrons in that theatre of operations although nuisance raids by Me 110 fighter-bombers were a feature of life throughout the campaign. One severe raid which gave the Luftwaffe a victory was that carried out on 2 December 1943, by machines of K G 76. Shipping in the harbour at Bari was attacked and more than thirty vessels were sunk. The raid was a complete success achieving total surprise. For its part the Kriegsmarine, with no heavy units in the Mediterranean, was forced to rely upon unconventional means to strike at Allied ships. A 'K' flotilla, a flotilla of 'small' units was formed and equipped with the first of those unconventional weapons – a manned, double torpedo. A 'captain' sat in the upper torpedo which had been hollowed out to take him together with the primitive engine and navigational equipment. Suspended underneath the captain was the armed torpedo which he would fire at enemy vessels. The first mission was against Allied shipping in Anzio harbour and was a failure. The Allied ships had sailed before the 'K' men arrived. That raid did, however, show up a serious fault in this type of 'K' craft. The captain could not remove the clear plastic hood fitted over the cockpit in which he sat and death by suffocation often resulted.

The invasion of north-west Europe on 6 June 1944 then shifted the emphasis of the navy's 'K' units to Normandy and Holland, and naval operations in Italy, which had now become a very minor theatre of war, diminished as a consequence.

DEFENDING THE WESTERN SEABOARD

British plans for an invasion of north-west Europe were laid in 1940, the same year in which the Expeditionary Force had been forced to leave the continent. For certain strategic and political reasons OKW gave no serious thought to the possibility for several years. Then, on 3 November 1943, Adolf Hitler issued Führer Directive No 51. This admitted that the bitter fighting and heavy losses of the past years had had their effect upon the German armed forces and that a new strategy was required. Territorial losses on the Eastern Front, the Directive claimed, would not be disastrous. In the west, however, a successful Allied invasion could bring about the defeat of the Third Reich. The Führer had decided, therefore, to improve the defensive capabilities of the armies in the west. The Directive accepted that the whole area of the western seaboard up to and including Denmark, could not be defended at every point in great strength, but it did order that defences were to be concentrated in the likeliest landing areas.

There were two obvious regions in which an invading force might come ashore: in the Pas-de-Calais or in Normandy. Hitler appreciated that the capture of a major port was vital to the Allied plan of campaign and in the final months before D-Day came more and more to consider that Normandy, with the major ports of Cherbourg and Brest, would be the likelier area. Despite that he still kept an entire army grouped in the Pas-de-Calais region. Having considered where the Allies were likely to land, the next task for OKW was to know the strength of the enemy forces that would fight the campaign. German Intelligence sources deliberately inflated the figure of Allied formations to well over 70, although the actual number which would be eventually, under the command of General Eisenhower, was 37 divisions. Only a small number of these would carry out the initial assault. The greatest number would be brought in after D-Day. Facing the Allied armies were 33 'fixed' divisions in a coast defence role, thirteen mobile infantry divisions, two Fallschirmjaeger divisions and six panzer divisions. There was also an OKW reserve of four panzer/panzergrenadier divisions.

Hitler had ordered, in Directive No 51, that all the divisions in the west were to be fully equipped and up to establishment, but there was a discrepancy between what the Führer ordered and what was possible in practice. Most formations were seriously understrength in men and equipment and their fighting qualities varied. The immobile, 'fixed' divisions, all in the 700 series and made up of middle-aged men, had the task of holding an area near to or on the coast. There they would stay, under fire, until, presumably, they were either relieved or destroyed. But there were in Normandy also the Wehrmacht's élite divisions, Fallschirmjaeger and SS; aggressive and battle-hardened veterans for the most part.

Among the most serious problems facing OKW was that no agreed plan of defence had been worked out. There were differences of opinion in the highest echelons of command in the west on how the invasion should be met. Von Runstedt, the Supreme Commander West, thought it best to let the landing take place and then, before the Allies could consolidate their hold, to attack and to defeat the newly landed divisions in a setpiece battle. Rommel was for an immediate counter-attack while the Allied units were still on the beaches. The failure of the two senior commanders to agree on the strategy to be followed required that Hitler make a decision. He compromised. Mobile units in OKW reserve were to be under his direct control and only he would determine to whom and at what stage of the battle these would be released.

The Allied forces for the coming campaign were known as 21st Army Group and were commanded by General Montgomery. The order of battle of this formation was US First, Canadian First and British Second Armies. Once Patton's Third Army had landed in France and become operational, it and US First Army would combine to form 12th Army Group under Omar Bradley. The Allies landed in the early hours of 6 June and it was against the Anglo-Canadian armies that the bulk of the German panzer divisions were eventually deployed. This was in accord with Montgomery's strategy which foresaw the Anglo-Canadians as forming the hinge on the door – the hinge to which the German armour would be attracted so as to stop the door swinging. This concentration of armour against the British and Canadian beachheads would give the US First Army the chance to break out of its perimeters and swing, in a wide pincer, through Le Mans towards the Seine. Patton's Third Army would strike both into Brittany and also act as a shield along the Loire river to defend the right flank of US First Army. The operations timetable was that by D-Day plus 90, i.e., by the first week of September, the Allied armies should have reached their objectives. They should have reached the Seine and the two great ports of Cherbourg and Brest should have been captured and made operational. A breakout began and an unsuccessful counter-attack by Hitler at Mortain to contain it was responsible for a change in the Allied plan. Patton would not now head for Brittany but would carry out the drive to the Seine in a *Blitzkrieg* operation. As a result of that change of direction Fifth Panzer and Seventh German Armies in Normandy were encircled in a pocket, based on Falaise and during July and August the greatest part of these two major formations were shattered. With their destruction there were insufficient troops to hold the Allies until von Rundstedt, recalled from dismissal, created a loose battle line, chiefly of Fallschirmjaeger units, behind which he established a firm defence. Under Allied pressure and over the course of the next months the German armies in the west were continually pushed back, a German offensive in the Ardennes notwithstanding; the Rhine was crossed and the war in Europe brought to a close.

In the eleven months from June 1944 to May 1945, the German soldiers, sailors and airmen became only too aware of Allied material superiority. From dawn to dusk Allied aircraft ruled the skies, Allied tank armadas swept across the land, and at sea the only response that the Kriegsmarine could make was in the form of small commando-type operations with manned torpedoes and one-man submarines. The Allied soldiers fought in the knowledge of their superiority in numbers and material. The German soldiers fought using their military skill and with a fear that the unconditional surrender demanded by the Allies would reduce their Fatherland to the status of an agrarian, slave State. Reinhold Hoffmann wrote:

'As soldiers we were not told what to do if we became prisoners of war, nor how we should behave as prisoners. We were instructed in our responsibility for the weapons, vehicles and equipment which the German nation had entrusted to us soldiers; the weapons bearers of the nation. To be given a weapon with which to defend our country was an honour and a heavy responsibility. Many units made the issue of weapons a ceremony as solemn as the swearing of the oath of allegiance. The inference was, obviously, that if we used our weapons correctly we should not become prisoners – with hindsight a naïve concept but at that time one which carried conviction.'

The German armies which defended Normandy were no longer the magnificent weapon that had entered France in 1940. By 1944, there were a great many units composed of foreigners and non-Europeans. Large numbers of ethnic groups from the Soviet Union had volunteered to fight against Bolshevism and found themselves battling in the west against their country's Allies. Many of these ethnic peoples belonged to the martial races of the Soviet Union, but were unused to the noise and destructive power of modern warfare. Colonel von der Heydte, commanding 6th Fallschirmjaeger Regiment, recalled: 'Corps [84 Corps] promised me a battalion of Georgians and these, in fact, arrived. They did not stay long, however. They could not withstand air raids. Within three days there was not a Georgian with us.' This was not the only ethnic desertion with which von der Heydte had had to suffer. Just before D-Day all the Alsatian drivers in his unit had deserted. Germany's allies abandoned her as her defeat became more certain and in some cases her former allies changed sides and took up arms against those who had been, until recent days, their brothers in arms.

In the fierce and destructive battles of 1944, German units suffered heavy casualties and the replacements received were neither sufficient in number nor in training. General Meindl, commanding 2 Para Corps, complained to his superior, Student, that the fighting strength of his units was dwindling daily. His last two requests for replacements had been ignored and those few men that had been sent soon became casualties because they had had so little training. Many of them, in Meindl's words, '. . . have never thrown a hand-grenade, fired more than a few rounds with a weapon or have any idea of digging in or of camouflaging their positions . . .' Generally, depleted units were fleshed out, although never completely, with men obtained from disbanded Luftwaffe or naval establishments, thus fulfilling the old slogan, 'A regiment can die ten times over – but it still remains the regiment.' Using all their skill and loyal to their oath the outnumbered remnants of the Wehrmacht fought their way from the bocage country of Normandy, across the polders of the Low Countries, back over the Rhine and into Germany. This was a sacrifice that might not have been demanded of them had more experienced men been directing operations in Normandy. Von Rundstedt's condemnation of Hitler's interference in the strategy of the Western Front, is contained in his conviction, 'If it [the conduct of the Normandy campaign] had been left to me, I would have made the Allies pay a fearful price.' Hitler's meddling extended down to deciding the tactics to be used by sub-units. In his strategic decisions he brooked no contradiction even though these were frequently wrong. He alone controlled the panzer divisions in the OKW reserve, divisions which might have operated against the landings just after these had been made and before the Allied armies had consolidated their hold. But when the Allies landed the Führer was asleep and no one dared wake him. While OKW waited for its Supreme Commander to rise and to make a decision, the Allies poured ashore and established their first perimeters.

The 12th SS 'Hitler Youth' was one of the panzer divisions located in Normandy. It had been raised less than a year earlier but had trained to such effect that by 1 June 1944, that is to say only five days before the Allied landings, the divisional units, with two exceptions, had been classified as 'being in every respect fit for operations'. Those two exceptions were the rocket-projector and the anti-tank battalions, neither of which was up to war establishment in weapons.

HITLER YOUTH DIVISION IN NORMANDY

His experience of the D-Day landings was described by a subaltern of the 'Hitler Youth' Division, Peter Hansmann, commander of the armoured car company of the divisional reconnaissance battalion. Confused details of Allied paratroop landings needed to be clarified. Supreme Command West ordered 12th SS Panzer Division to '. . . carry out reconnaissance, to gain touch with 711th Division, to halt and then to guard its area'. The armoured car company was alerted at about 0230 hrs and the drivers, many of them still in their underwear, rushed to their vehicles. Engines were started and within 15 minutes the Company, ten armoured cars and two groups of motor-cyclists, was ready to march.

'The Sergeant Major reports the unit ready for action. The men gather round me in a half circle and I brief them, speak of the seriousness of the battle that lies ahead and the object of our mission. As recce troops it is our job to be fast but invisible; to see everything but not to be seen and to report the enemy's location back to our commanders. I tell them to watch the road surfaces for mines because partisans may have laid mines and go on to detail the order of march. One group of motor cyclists will form the advance guard, followed by an 8-wheel and a 4-wheel vehicle alternately. Distance between vehicles 50 metres. The second group of motor cyclists will form the rearguard.

'I stand in the turret of the first 8-wheeler and give the order "Panzer marsch!" The night is pleasantly cool and visibility is medium to good – about 50 to 100 metres although the moon is often obscured by cloud or mist. After we have gone a few kilometres I have the feeling that this is just like any of the exercises that we have carried out over the past weeks. The little houses in the villages are unlit. The inhabitants are asleep. There is no sign of the French partisans. Some 15 minutes later and we reach battalion TAC HQ, drive the vehicles under trees in the garden of the château and I report together with my platoon and Section commanders to the CO, Sturmbann-führer Bremer. We are given the latest information about the landings west of the mouth of the Seine near Carentan, but Bremer tells us that accurate details are lacking. It is, therefore, our task to patrol the coastal sector to the north, between the mouth of the Seine and Bayeux. We are to find out whether enemy troops have landed, where they have reached and their intentions.

'I divide the unit into four troops . . . We check the radios and set out at about 0400 hrs. My group is made up of two 8-wheel vehicles whose commanders have experience of the Russian front . . . Visibility is improving and is now more than 100 metres. The front we have to reach is about 80 kms away so I choose the most direct road via Broglie and Lisieux to Caen . . . Within an hour we are in Lisieux and here the first civilians are met. The day is beginning for them, a day like any other day . . . We meet motor cyclists and VW cars on the road. On the bridge across the Touques German soldiers, old enough to be our fathers, report that their unit has been placed on alarm, but that apart from bomber squadrons heading westwards nothing has happened . . . I carry on towards Caen . . . We meet more and more military vehicles on the road, so it must still be open. We approach Caen. On its outskirts there is a great deal of movement. Trucks of all sorts are driving about, platoons of soldiers are taking up position. A lieutenant asks whether we have had a brush with the enemy? . . . An alarm sounds and a

report comes in that enemy paras are attacking about 10 km north of the
Orne bridges and that heavy fighting is going on. This accounts for the
vehicle movement in the streets and explains why the infantry, panzer-
grenadiers of 21st Panzer Division, have been turned out. A captain tells me
that strong British airborne units have landed on either side of the Orne
bridges and that these are probably now in enemy hands. The noise of battle
can be heard quite clearly and is probably coming from that area. Fighter-
bombers attack indiscriminately. French civilians abandon their homes in a
panic and rush out of the town. Back again with my men . . . I send out a
patrol with orders to recce to the north. Then I send back my report over
the radio . . .

'On the main road to Bayeux I wish that there was cloud or mist. We
are a sitting target. There is a lot of traffic on the road so the Tommies cannot
reach there yet . . . We enter the town. Civilians running about. The closer
we get to the centre of the town the thicker are the crowds. There are troops
and vehicles of all sorts and a single platoon of Feldgendarmerie is trying to
sort out the chaos. I try unsuccessfully to reach the Town Major's office and
hear that artillery has been firing on Bayeux . . . From a Feldgendarmerie
sergeant I learn that in Arromanches Bay there has been heavy fighting and
that the English are landing along the coast from hundreds of ships. If the
sounds of fighting are anything to go by it must really be a hell of a battle
because the thunder of heavy artillery is very clear . . . That's it then . . .
not only airborne but also seaborne attack. This we must see. I give orders
that we are no longer to drive along open roads but under the cover of trees.
As we drive up the ridge which lies to the north of the town . . . we look
left towards the coast and see fountains of earth and burning buildings. I
cannot see the sea at all and drive further forward to gain the crest of the
ridge. We park and camouflage the vehicles very carefully under trees and
near barns. From the top of the ridge we can see Arromanches Bay . . . What
we are seeing is something unimaginable, something totally unbelievable
. . . What is that grey mass spread out before us? . . . There to the left is
Arromanches. Heavy artillery fire is falling on it. Fountains of earth as tall
as houses rise and sink back. To the east there is a seemingly endless grey
mass – the sea – endlessly also the horizon but there is, somewhat lighter in
colour, something else. I look through binoculars – now I can make out the
outlines of individual ships. Close packed and stretching as far as the eye can
see, ships, ships, masts and upper works. From the distance I see irregular
flashes as the big guns on the ships open up. The sea between the beach and
the armada of ships in front of us is dark blue. Across that dark water there
are white lines coming from that mass of shipping which extends from
Arromanches to the Orne estuary – and they are heading straight toward us.

'These are fast ships with high, white, foaming bow waves. Landing
craft which spew out brown balls of soldiers as they touch down on the beach.

I see white fountains of water rise. Probably our coastal batteries. Then I hear very clearly the sound of a German MG 42. So our coastal defences have not all been rubbed out. Dahmann points out brown figures, struggling through the sand dunes. They are wearing flat helmets – British soldiers. In groups, platoons, and in whole Companies they move slowly, seemingly without meeting any resistance. They are about 3,000 metres away still and can only be seen through binoculars . . . Then I notice tanks, one, two, three – a whole group of them . . . they come from the Bay, drive along the coast road towards us and then turn eastwards. They make zigzag movements – obviously rubbing out nests of resistance. Then I notice that the tanks are carrying large spoons which they push in front of them. Are they going to build a coast road or are they mine-clearing? Other tanks come swimming out of the sea to the shore. Is such a thing possible? At first only the turret is seen but then the whole vehicle emerges like a monster out of the depths of primeval water. And nothing seems to stop them. Don't we have any 88s? They won't be in action anyway, because fighter-bombers are swooping over the area the whole time . . . But now I must report to Division what is happening here. This is the Invasion . . . Soon there will be more ships than water. But who would believe such a thing if he hadn't seen it for himself.

'Right!, get the facts! Where are we? It is 0745 hrs in the Bay of Arromanches, 3 km south of Magny . . . I estimate the number of ships on one small sector of the sea as being 400 plus and that great mass of ships extends across a stretch of sea more than 30 kilometres long. The British are landing troops all the time and seemingly not meeting resistance. Troops with heavy equipment are being debarked. Eleven heavy tanks identified. Our own coastal defence has been wiped out and overrun. Infantry in battalion strength heading south towards Bayeux. Enemy ship artillery bombarding Bayeux and the roads into the town. Fighter-bombers attacking areas of resistance. I am continuing my reconnaissance in the direction of Creully. Over and Out!'

The Decimation of 6th Para Regiment

The occupied countries of western Europe had once been, for the German forces, a sort of rest camp. Units that had been smashed in the fighting on the Eastern Front came to France, Belgium and Holland to be reinforced and to live well before returning eastwards. The Führer Directive changed the pace of occupation life. The Western Front, he had decided, was temporarily, until the defeat of the Allied invasion attempt, more important than the Eastern Front and first-class units were posted to or raised and trained in the peace, plenty and quiet of the occupied countries. The 12th SS Division was one such unit. The 2 Fallschirmjaeger Corps was another.

One other para formation which was stationed in Normandy when the Allies landed was 6th Regiment, one of the constituent units of 2 Fallschirmjaeger Division.

Oberst Freiherr von der Heydte had been given and had completed the task of reforming the 6th Para Regiment after it had been almost totally destroyed during the fighting in southern Russia. His regiment, in an independent role, was then posted to Normandy where it was involved in the weeks following the invasion, in fighting bitter defensive battles around Carentan. Colonel von der Heydte wrote of his regiment's actions in Normandy:

'On 23rd July, we lay on the heights to the south of Périers, waiting for the Americans who were striking towards us from St-Saveur le Vicomte. Orders came for us to leave our positions and to withdraw further south because St-Lô had fallen. We were told that the Americans were moving quite quickly from St-Lô towards Coutances and Avranches. This news reached us late by which time part of our baggage train had been overrun. It was clear that we, together with other units in the area of Coutances, were surrounded and more or less cut off. We attempted unsuccessfully to break out of the encirclement by riding on the panzers of the SS units which were trapped with us. Then a wireless message ordered my regiment to move to Cerisy-la-Salle and to prepare that place for defence.

'Aware that the ring would soon tighten around us, I decided to disobey orders and to make an attack to reach the woods which lie to the north of Soulles. At that place I would, if there were no other course, set up a defensive position . . . From our positions near Cerisy-la-Salle there was a good view of the main road and one could see columns of American tanks and lorries moving westwards towards Granville. The regiment concentrated during the night of 27/28th July, with orders to reach and to cross the main road. It was unlikely that the Americans knew we were in the area nor could they know our strength. The 2nd Battalion moved rapidly – they could not have been said to have carried out an attack – going via Notre-Dame-de-Cenilly to reach the Soulles forest. Regimental headquarters and the other regimental detachments, together with 1st and 3rd Battalions, were to cross the road during the hours of darkness, by passing through the gaps between the American tank units driving along the main road. The area in which the group was to cross lay between Notre-Dame-de-Cenilly and St-Denis-le-Gast. Once across the road the units were to regroup on another road which runs southwards from Hambye Abbey.

'Nearly a whole day passed before the regiment had grouped ready to undertake the crossing. I gave orders that during the hours of darkness my men were to be carried on the vehicles of Panzer Lehr Division which was making its break-out attempt with us, but that as soon as it was light they were to dismount and conceal themselves in woods on the left of the road.

The commander of my 3rd Battalion, Captain Trebes, was killed at this time. He had sought cover, not in the woods but beneath a panzer which was attacked by a low-flying American aircraft. The Regiment reached the cover of the forest of Soulles; the units had gained touch with each other and had met up with other groups of German soldiers . . . I was taken to see General von Kluge who was busy planning a counter-attack [which did not materialize]. Kluge told me that it was now a case of every man for himself. I set up a regimental aid post in Alençon and it was soon filled with the casualties of the past days. By the beginning of August I had only forty soldiers with me. Some others were missing but the greatest number of men of my regiment had been killed or wounded. Two months earlier I had been the proud commander of 4,600 men.'

ENCIRCLEMENT AND BREAKOUT

Patton's Third Army, which had broken out at the base of the Cotentin Peninsula, found the left flank of Army Group 'B'. The American armour had passed round that flank and had brought about the collapse of the left wing of Army Group 'B'. Soon the US armour was driving along the German southern flank. Meanwhile, Anglo-Canadian forces were striking down from the north towards Falaise. The common objective of the Allied armies was to reach the Seine before the Germans did. If they could accomplish this the greater part of the enemy forces in north-west Europe whom they had already loosely encircled, would have been eliminated. The way would then be open for a swift advance into the Reich. Von Kluge, commanding Army Group 'B', was very aware of the danger of encirclement which faced his troops and issued discreet orders for certain units to move eastwards towards the Seine. These orders had to be discreet because only weeks earlier a bomb had exploded in Hitler's headquarters and many of those implicated in the plot had been army officers. The slightest sign of a lessening of moral fibre among the senior military commanders was taken by the Führer to be treachery and was punished accordingly. Von Kluge's carefully worded instructions directed the slow-moving, vulnerable and numerous horse-drawn formations of Army Group 'B' to move out of the pocket which was forming so that when the time came for the armour to withdraw, the panzers would find the roads clear of traffic. The collapse of the pocket came quicker than was expected and a great mass of formations belonging to Army Group 'B' was caught and destroyed in a battle which lasted from 12 to 21 August. When it ended the whole of the area from the River Orne in the west to Mount Ormel in the east and from Falaise in the north to Argentan in the south, was a cemetery of unburied dead. The stench of decaying bodies could be smelt by the pilots of light observation aircraft flying hundreds of feet above the stricken area. General Eisenhower described how it was literally possible to walk for hundreds of yards at a time stepping on nothing but decaying flesh.

The War Diary of Fifth Panzer Army, describing the conditions in the last days of the fighting, reported on the evening of 18 August: '. . . at the [eastern] exit of the bottleneck . . . no movement of any kind is possible due to the continual air attacks by fighters and fighter-bombers. These machines attack even individual soldiers. Nor is it possible to sort out the intermingled units . . . Communications have broken down . . . ' By the next day, although the encirclement was complete, along the eastern side of the pocket there were still a few gaps and some places where Allied forces were not yet in sufficient strength to repel any determined breakout attempts. The flexibility of the German military system produced plans for a mass breakout, even though those plans had to be drawn up under the most difficult conditions. Hubert Meyer was at that time GSO I of 12th SS Panzer Division. He wrote:

'Our divisional headquarters was a farmhouse in the area of la Londe, southwest of Trun. Also quartered there was the TAC HQ of 84 Corps under whose command was the remnant of our division ['Hitler Youth']. Unforgettable and typical of the situation as it was at that time were the conditions under which both headquarters were working. In one room of the farmhouse there was a long table on either side of which were benches without back rests. This room ran the whole length of the house and along one wall was an open chimney. On one side of the table sat Kurt Meyer, the divisional commander [of 12th SS Panzer Division 'Hitler Youth'] and I, his GSO I. On the other side was General Elfeldt, GOC 84 Corps, and his Chief of Staff, Lieutenant-Colonel von Kriegern.

'There were also a few aides-de-camp, runners and drivers, perhaps a dozen in all. We waited throughout the night, alternately dozing off and then waking up, expecting reports to come in that the [breakout] assaults by 3rd Para Division and by the [other] battle groups had been successful. There was almost no wireless communication. The 2 Para Corps attack had set off at 2330 hrs on the 19th, but as no report had been received by 0300 hrs on the 20th and as there were no sounds of firing coming from the direction of St-Lambert, we assumed that their break-through attempt had been successful. The 12th SS was given orders to move quickly, otherwise the hours of darkness would be too few to allow all the troops to escape. General Elfeldt and Lieutenant-Colonel von Kriegern joined our divisional head-quarters group and just before dawn we set out on foot to pass through the gap which had been made for us. The few remaining vehicles were left behind.'

The attack by 3rd Para Division to which Hubert Meyer referred, went in at 2230 hrs on the evening of 19 August. To the east of the Argentan–Trun road the leading groups took avoiding action to escape Allied tanks which were attempting to seal the bottleneck. During a fire-fight the Para divisional commander, Schimpf, was wounded and the Corps commander, General Meindl, assumed command. At 0030 hrs the River Dives was reached and crossed, about a kilometre to the south-east of Magny. The paras then came under fire from other groups of tanks which forced them to move eastwards in an attempt to break out of the Allied ring. By first light they had reached Coudehard at the extreme end of the pocket. Before him Meindl saw a commanding ridge, Mount Ormel, and as he watched a line of twenty enemy tanks drove up those heights. To his right there were two distinctive pieces of high ground: Point 262 on the right and Point 243 on the left. Meindl decided to attack Point 262 from the north even though without panzer support, and in daylight this seemed an impossible task to accomplish.

The Allied troops that occupied the high ground were from the Polish Armoured Division. They lay in that area which the trapped German units must take if they were to escape from the rapidly contracting pocket. On the German side panzer units from 'Das Reich' Division were attacking to create an escape corridor which Meindl and his Paras would then hold open for the trapped German units. The confused and bloody fighting for the high ground was fought with bitterness by the men of both sides; the Germans who had to break the Poles and the Poles who were determined to die rather than to give way.

The pocket meanwhile had become a killing ground in which Allied shell explosions and attacks by low-flying aircraft of the Allied air force killed or wounded without mercy. The German units were close packed in a shrinking area which had only the narrow exit at Mount Ormel. When Allied guns and tanks closed that last gap orders were given for the trapped units to make a major assault in order to break out. General Meindl, the Para Corps commander, wrote a letter to his son in which he described the situation of those days. In the attack the General, his runner and a small group of Jaeger had been cut off from the main body by Allied tanks and had only managed to avoid capture when a pair of 88s roared up, opened fire on the Shermans and drove them off.

'Our Paras and some SS men [who had been taking part in the attack] were astonished to hear us call from the enemy-held area. I nagged at my men for having carried out the attack across a flat and open field. Making our way back to our own lines was not easy as we had to pass through machine-gun fire and artillery barrages. For quite long periods we were forced to run doubled up to make smaller targets of ourselves. The enemy artillery bombarding us from three sides, was the worst thing we had to endure. By making a great detour by about 0930 hrs we had reached a small ditch near the road . . . In the same ditch (200 metres distant from Coudehard) was the Supreme Commander, SS General Hausser.

'The most difficult part lay ahead; we had to take the commanding heights east of Coudehard [Mount Ormel] on which sat a number of enemy tanks. To begin with I opened an attack upon the high ground about 200 metres ahead of us. I knew the ground. Then I moved northwards so as to bypass the enemy tanks and by evening we had accomplished this. The heat and the thirst were terrible. Luckily, one of the tanks at my TAC HQ was carrying a barrel of cider . . . I took the paras and the SS to the left [to the north] and put them into the attack while the army units were kept on the right [i.e., the south] of the road. Three or four tanks, two SPs, artillery without ammunition and about one and a half battalions of paras were my force to attack the heights. In very open formation the flank attack was carried out through hedges, ditches and clumps of trees. There were many anxious hours before we knew whether the attack had succeeded . . .

'Two enemy tanks in front of us caught fire. A pair of paras had knocked them out in close-quarter combat. Soon one Allied AFV after another was burning. The paras exploited the situation, stormed the heights and took over thirty prisoners. Only two tanks managed to escape. The enemy also withdrew from the neighbouring heights because he thought himself to be outflanked by another of our para units. Our opponents were Poles, excellent fighters who were supported by very good English artillery. Another miracle was the arrival of a panzer battalion of 'Das Reich' Division which attacked from the east into the rear of twenty Polish tanks and destroyed eighteen of them. By capturing the heights we were no longer under observation from the enemy artillery observers and as a result the fury of the barrages died down.

'By about 1900 hrs we could begin the evacuation of the wounded, including General Schimpf (GOC 3rd Para Division). I was on the high ground with my Fallschirmjaeger and, together with a heavy panzer battalion of the SS, kept open the escape gap which our attack had created. Army units, most of them without officers, streamed towards the gap, keen to get out of the pocket as quickly as possible. I moved my TAC HQ to Coudehard, which I knew would be easier to locate. By about 0030 hrs on 21 August, the SS Panzer Division rearguard reported that they were the last troops; there was no-one behind them. Two panzers were put in as a rearguard. The Poles were only 200 metres distant and because they fired at the slightest sound, I ordered a total blackout and no talking. Reports came in from our reconnaissance patrols, the last one at 0200 hrs. They all reported that movement had ceased. At 0200 I went through Coudehard, which was burning, to see Liebach, commanding 8th Para Regiment and gave him orders to pull in the flank guards on the eastern road. By 0300 hrs were were on the march with a small group leading, all machine-guns and Panzerfaust ready to fire. The whole group marched silently eastwards. At the end of 15 kilometres "Das Reich" Division took over the rearguard task from us and we loaded our wounded on to lorries. The road was marked by burning vehicles. Luckily, heavy rain then set in and not only deadened all noise but also reduced the watchfulness of the Poles. By the end of the 21st we were pleased – licking our wounds though we were – to have escaped.'

THE WOUNDED

The accounts of men who were in the breakout from the Falaise pocket read like fiction. One man, wounded in the shoulder, was carried by two of his comrades to a farm house. After food and sleep they woke him so that they could carry on with their march out of the pocket. Weak through loss of blood he could not walk. His comrades found a horse, tied him on with ropes and by evening the trio had reached the divisional concentration area. Another man wrote of how he had been wounded and had jumped from a half-track just before it crashed. Taken on board a small ambulance this too was hit and destroyed. After crossing the River Dives he faced the daunting climb up the ridge of Mount Ormel and while making the effort was fired on by a tank and wounded afresh '. . . but not in important parts of my body'. Hiding himself in some wheat sheaves he passed into unconsciousness and lay there until he was woken by an American soldier and taken prisoner.

Max Anger, at that time Adjutant of the 1st Artillery Battalion of the 12th SS Division, was in a panzer battle group. His description of the breakout is dramatic.

"Orders to break out of the pocket reached us in the Bois de Feuillet, north of Montabard. We were faced with making the difficult choice of what could be thrown away and what was absolutely necessary; what could be carried and how it would be laden. Hauptsturmführer Hagemeier told us, "Well, first we'll all have a bath and then put on our best uniforms so that we are well dressed if anything happens." He was joking, of course.

'During the morning of the 20th the columns began their march. Once we had passed out of the cover of the woods of Montabard we fanned out on a wide front and drove over the open flat ground. There was no enemy air activity although we presented a marvellous target. We were in good spirits and in some of our "Wasps" [light SP guns] the men were singing. It was a rare sight to see so many of our armoured fighting vehicles at one time. This was a luxury which normally only the enemy could enjoy. Next to our half-track Olboeter was standing in the turret of his panzer. We crossed the Route Departmental 916 heading for Chambois, but then came to a halt near Tournai. Every type of unit was there, mostly from the army and there was total confusion. I heard the cry, "Let the SS through!" We got through and drove farther east. We were suddenly bombarded from the northern ridge and suffered casualties. Between Chambois and St-Lambert we turned northwards and crossed the D 13. The enemy fire was unusually good and casualties began to rise. We drove uphill using a path which ran through lightly covered ground. The columns halted again. Hagemeier jumped out of our half-track and ran about 120 metres to a bend in the path. There he was hit by infantry fire and dropped. We loaded him on to an ammunition carrier. It was also here that I met one of the last battery commanders, Untersturmführer Rudolf Heller from Eger.

'I sent a couple of "Wasps" on both sides of the path and carried out my own observation as we were out of touch with everybody else and therefore had no command structure. I "weaseled" my way uphill through the undergrowth and there met SS General Hausser with another commander. He was the last person I expected to see in this place. It was now about 11 a.m. I had a number of targets to engage in order to keep the enemy's head down. Like a rabbit I sprang, crept and ran back to my vehicle and was under fire the whole time. From my vehicle I could make out the fall of our shells. They were spot on the targets on the ridge to the west of Mont Ormel. I tried to gain touch with our leading units but then we were struck by a direct hit. I had had it. Untersturmführer Korenegger from the 12th Artillery Regiment HQ brought me to a half-track and laid me on the floor. I was, therefore, not able to see any more of what then happened although I could hear bullets and sharpnel hitting the outside of the vehicle. We crossed and recrossed the ground for about half an hour under fire all the time looking for an escape route. Then all at once it was all up with us. Our half-track stopped and a few seconds later all the unwounded were dragged out. Our driver drove the half-track, under Canadian guard, to their main dressing station in Trun. The time would then have been about 1600 hrs.'

Oberst von der Heydte, whose 6th Para Regiment was one of those encircled, was scathing of the SS commanders.

'We [the paras] made attempts to escape from the Falaise pocket via Tinchebray which was being continuously bombarded by American artillery. Certain SS commanders tried to issue stupid orders or advice to the troops who had reached the village and in some cases these SS officers drew pistols to enforce their orders. Nobody took much notice of them. My runner asked me whether he could be spared for ten minutes. He came back promptly carrying a large model of a ship. He had promised to bring his little brother a souvenir from Normandy and had "organized" the ship before it and the toyshop were destroyed by the shelling. Once we had passed Tinchebray we knew that we had escaped from the pocket. We came across so many lightly wounded men of the Regiment that by the time we reached the Paris area our strength had risen to 800 men.'

FIGHTING THE REARGUARD

The battle of the Falaise pocket was over but somebody had to hold the line while the other units made their rapid retreat. The men of élite units, the Fallschirmjaeger, formed the rearguard whenever one was needed, or spearheaded desperate assaults to hold the enemy back. It was the combat skill of Meindl's men which made them the obvious choice to form the rearguard for Army Group 'B'. The exhausted para formations were put back into the line on 2 September, and held their ground while the motorized elements of Fifth and Seventh Armies pulled back. Meindl was critical of those commanders who placed his men in such situations. 'Panzer and Panzer Grenadier Divisions', he wrote, 'are able to move fast and far. Fallschirmjaeger fighting in a ground role cannot do this and thus they are caught by the advancing enemy. Near Mons on 4 September, the bulk of 3rd Para Division was taken prisoner through just such an incident and only a few of the division escaped captivity.'

The survivors of von der Heydte's regiment did not stay long in Paris. 'We moved to Nancy, the first stage of a march which took my remnant to the aerodrome at Gustrow in Mecklenburg where they were reinforced, rested and regrouped before being posted back to Northern Belgium.' After being alerted for the Arnhem operation, von de Heyde's regiment, now reinforced with extra men, was posted to Bergen op Zoom where a Canadian offensive was anticipated. 'The only opposition which the Canadians had met in recent weeks had been from coastal defence troops whose resistance, apart from a few units, had not been too difficult to overcome. For the Canadians to come up against a reinforced, paratroop regiment was a terrible shock. Their commanders decided upon an immediate attack made on a wide front. This collapsed in the resistance put up by my paratroops, but the Canadians mounted a new attack only three hours later and obviously using fresh troops. This assault, too, was brought to a halt just in front of our forward zone. I then launched a limited counter-attack which took us into the northern areas of two villages, Woondsrecht and Hoogersheide. The Canadians fought, I say this as a German, absolutely splendidly. Their officers, up to the rank of brigadier-general, stood side by side with their men in the front line.

'On 23rd October, I received two telegrams, one of which pleased me as much as the other saddened me. The first informed me that I had been awarded the Oak Leaves to the Knight's Cross. The second posted me away from my regiment to take over command of the Para Army weapons school where I was to train young officers. My last orders as commander of my regiment were for the units to move into the pill-box defences south of Bergen op Zoom. These had been built by the Dutch before the war. My last Order of the Day to my officers and men repeated the words I had used when the Regiment was raised at Wahn. 'Even if everything collapses and wave upon wave floods over our people, there will still be one Para of my regiment who, fighting against fate and amid the storm and terror, will hold aloft above the waves a banner on which will be inscribed in fiery characters the legend, "Greater Germany".'

ALL OR NOTHING: THE BATTLE OF THE BULGE

The combat zone in north-west Europe lay now between two great rivers: the Maas and the Rhine. These were the last barriers along which the German Army in the west could hold the imminent Allied offensive. Hitler's pre-emptive attack in the Ardennes, which has passed into history as the Battle of the Bulge, could not halt the advance of the Western Allies but could only delay it.

Although the senior officers of the attacking armies were critical of Hitler's battle plan, most German soldiers were optimistic and confident of success. This was, they felt, the big chance for the German Army in the west to alter the direction of the war and they were determined to gain the objectives which the Führer had set them. They would reach and capture Antwerp; divide the Allied armies and defeat them individually. One of the units which went into the Battle of the Bulge was 'Das Reich' Division, and the Commander of No 16 (Pioneer) Company described that last Christmas of the war:

'24th December 1944. Christmas Eve. The day dawned foggy and damp. The Regiment is to attack during the coming night in collaboration with 1st Battalion of 2nd Panzer Regiment. Our objectives: Manhay–Grandmenil and a break through westwards to Erezee. Part of the Company was told off for mine-sweeping duties and for reconnaissance patrols while the remainder were at the regiment's disposal [to be used as circumstances dictated]. In the early evening a patrol of Pioneers is to locate crossing places for panzer over the stream to the north-west of Odeigne. Another patrol is to recce towards the road crossing at Belle Haye.

'The weather changed. It was a bright moonlit night. The patrol reached Odeigne leaving the cover of the woods to the west of Belle Haye and then passed across undulating fields and meadows. It was not the nicest way to spend Christmas Eve, moving over open ground and without the protection of white camouflage clothing. The men could be seen as dark spots as they crossed the open ground and were soon under fire . . . An MG group acting as flank protection then went into action and covered by its fire the patrol withdrew bringing back three wounded; one of them serious. The enemy did not pursue. Two of the wounded could not walk and were carried while the third man, thought to be only lightly wounded, was sent to request stretcher-bearers and medical personnel. The lightly wounded soldier, a 17-year-old, reached my Company HQ and reported in the formal method of his training. In the middle of his report he collapsed. The miserable light in the dug-out had been insufficient to show how badly he had been hurt. The medical orderly told us that our young comrade had two bullets, one through the shoulder another through the upper arm and that a further five had grazed his body . . . How had he been able to march for more than a kilometre and a half through knee-deep snow to make his report?

'The bloody outcome of the recce patrol dampened our Christmas Eve. Our thoughts were with the mine-lifting group taking part with the main body in the attack upon Manhay. When the ration party arrived we found that it had also brought mail from home – bridges to link us with our loved ones. Our Company HQ was situated in the same house as the regimental TAC HQ. There was a piano in a large room and one of our comrades began to play a Christmas carol. There was some half-hearted singing, but we had no Christmas spirit in us – our regiment and the 1st Battalion of the panzer regiment were in action. Reports flowed in and during the night both Manhay and Grandmenil were reported taken. The enemy had offered the most bitter resistance and employed masses of artillery and armour. The Regiment had suffered heavy losses.

'25th December 1944. Christmas Day. The day opened with bright sunshine and strong frost. Sounds of heavy artillery fire came to us from both Manhay and Grandmenil. [The enemy's] fighter-bombers and artillery spotting aircraft clouded the skies without opposition. They swooped down and attacked any vehicle or movement on the roads or on the open fields. Odeigne itself was not attacked, neither by artillery fire nor from the air. Apart from those sections which were in action with the 2nd Battalion in Grandmenil, the remainder of the Company, which was at regimental disposal, did not go into action . . .

'26th December 1944. Second day of Christmas. We marched on foot and reached the TAC HQ of 1st Battalion, 2nd Panzer Regiment at dawn. Signs of heavy fighting and of enemy artillery fire were everywhere. Enemy artillery fire forced us to take cover. At about 0830 hrs we resumed our march to Grandmenil. About halfway there was renewed artillery fire which lasted for about an hour and a half. The road between Manhay and Grandmenil was under fire from both artillery and enemy tanks. We took cover behind a lone house behind which some men of the Regiment were sheltering, together with a few prisoners. Suddenly the enemy's fire stopped. We reached Grandmenil. Above us fighter-bombers were attacking the town. Just as we reached a point some 200 metres south of the place and were about to move into it the enemy barrage opened again. We took cover in the first house but did not stay there long as the Amis began to fire phosphorus shells and had soon set the house alight.

'During a break in the barrage we left that house and moved into another just up the road. There were a couple of panzers near it. In the house we found some forty badly wounded comrades of our 2nd Battalion. Suddenly there was a massive explosion just outside the house. The heavy ceiling of the cellar where the wounded were being treated was lifted in the air by the blast and came down without breaking up. That must have been a pretty sight for the badly wounded to see. We rushed out of the cellar to find out what had happened. The partially camouflaged panzers which had been standing on the road had been attacked by fighter-bombers. One bomb had fallen between one of the panzers and our house and had exploded leaving a huge crater. The panzer itself showed no signs of damage but the outside of the house had been torn away. The enemy bombardment continued to fall all round us.

'At about 1215 hrs it stopped . . . The Ami infantry then began an attack. There was the sound of battle to the north and to the west of us. The enemy struck with a mainly tank force along the road and to the north of it, aiming for Manhay. There was all hell let loose to the west of Grandmenil, but the enemy's furious attack was halted by our Regiment . . . We leaped over fences and across gardens to get to battalion TAC HQ and as we reached the smithy came under machine-gun fire from the right flank. A single enemy tank had broken through. I was on the road and reached the smithy in one huge leap . . . The tank stood in a garden about 125 metres away from us and the machine-gunner must have seen us for he concentrated his fire on the brick pillar at the smithy's entrance. He seemed to have an endless belt of ammunition. The pillar was about 40cm wide and machine-gun bursts tore whole bricks out. Then the tank's main armament opened up. The [armour-piercing] shots went right through the rear wall. Whenever the gun fired a door opened in the farm house and the heads of two of my comrades could be seen. They waved to me that I should join them. I couldn't do that. I would have walked right into the burst of machine-gun fire. I determined to wait until the enemy machine-gunner changed belts. The next shot from the tank's gun was a high-explosive shell. There was smoke, dust and then shrapnel whirled around. After that shot the machine-gunner stopped firing. I was intact. I raced to reach the farm door but landed instead in the midden. We three rushed round the corner waiting for the Ami tank, but it did not come. That HE round had been its last shot. A corporal from 2nd Battalion had attacked it with a Panzerfaust and had destroyed it.

'We reached 2nd Battalion's TAC HQ and I reported. The CO told me that the battalion was surrounded, that the Amis had attacked and captured Manhay. The battalion was practically out of ammunition and supplies.

Thank God, the Amis did not attack again although artillery fire continued to fall . . . In view of the shortages of ammunition, fuel and rations our attack . . . could not be continued. Severe losses and insufficient medical support forced the regimental commander to break off the attack. We would have to fight our way out of the encirclement. The non-walking wounded would have to be left behind with some medical orderlies. Radios and vehicles were to be destroyed.

'The CO gave the order to break out. A rear guard secured the battalion's withdrawal. In the event, we did not have to fight our way out. In the south there was a gap in the enemy's ring. By midnight the 2nd Battalion and the attached groups of No 16 Company were approaching the enemy lines. In a silent march we filtered through the gap, marched across meadowland, over a small stream and reached at last a large wooded area. In that wood we gained touch with our own troops. At dawn we moved north of Odeigne out of the forest and reported to Regiment . . . The Company was together again. Christmas 1944 was a memory . . . On the 28th the Company moved to a new battle area of Marcouray–Marcourt–Beffe–Trinal where it was grouped and employed as an infantry detachment.'

RECRIMINATIONS

The failure of the armies in the west to fulfil the Führer's plan to smash the Anglo-American forces, coupled with the destruction of Army Group Centre by the Red Army, left no room for doubt that Germany was going down to defeat and as the war neared its end the neurosis of the Party leaders led to the setting up of courts martial with frightening and summary powers. If the Führer decreed that a town or city was a fortress, any attempt to leave was considered to be desertion in the face of the enemy. Trials of those accused together with the judgements and executions were reported in both the local and national Press to warn readers that the Party was implacable in its pursuit of traitors and faint-hearts. Although the Reichsminister for Justice had only authorized the setting up of these special courts during the spring of 1945, drumhead trials had been sentencing and executing those found guilty of dereliction of duty very much earlier than that. Thus, the Party newspaper *Volkischer Beobachter* dated 11 February 1945, reported that Floeter, the mayor of Königsberg, had been condemned to death and hanged for leaving the city without permission.

The power of the flying courts martial was terrifying and did not consider war service, rank or medals. General Schlemm, commanding the German airborne Army along the Rhine, wrote of this. 'I had to think about the defence of the east bank of the Rhine in my sector. My proposal to withdraw the worn-out units to the east bank and to set my staff to the task of preparing defences there was turned down by those in authority. I was made personally responsible that no soldier who was fit for combat left the west bank. A "hanging Commando" was positioned at each crossing-point with orders to carry out a summary court martial on any offender.

'One highly decorated Fallschirmjaeger battalion commander, who had endured twenty-one days and nights of bitter fighting, brought back the exhausted survivors of his battalion to the east bank. It was only with the greatest difficulty that I was able to rescue him from the clutches of the "hanging Commando".'

RAISING THE VOLKSSTURM AND WEHRWOLF

In those times of trial and tribulation for the Third Reich every means was taken to increase the number of men on active service. As early as 25 September 1944, Hitler had issued the decree raising the Volkssturm. In its most dramatic form this meant the conscription for military service of those between the ages of 16 and 60, that is to say either old men or boys not yet of an age to be in uniform. The training was sketchy and the arms both few in number and poor in quality. And yet the Party demanded that these children and ancients, defend their hearths and homes with fanaticism. In fact it was often required for the battalions to fight in other towns, other provinces, sometimes other countries. One Austrian battalion was sent to Saxony and having spent a number of weeks in splendid isolation in the deep forests there, decided after a show of hands, to dissolve the unit and to return home. When the German Army pulled back, the Volkssturm men must have had bitter feelings as they watched panzer, heavy guns and well-equipped infantry retreating through their villages and knew that they now had to face the fury of their well-armed enemies. There is the story of one Volkssturm commander who, having seen the last military unit pull out, asked permission to disband his unit and let the men go home. The voice at the other end of the telephone told him that if he did that he would most certainly be shot. Whereupon, the Volkssturm officer with impeccable logic asked who would do this as the army had already withdrawn. The commander at the other end of the telephone line hung up.

With the Western Allies across the Rhine and driving through the heartland of Germany, the situation deteriorated and even more frantic efforts were made by the Reich's leaders to stave off inevitable defeat. The first day of April 1945, was Easter Sunday, and Deutschlandsender, the national radio station, announced the formation of a German resistance movement – Wehrwolf. The words used to proclaim the German partisan movement were hysterical but sinister.

'Hate is our prayer. Revenge is our battle cry. Those towns in the west of our country which have been destroyed by Allied terror raids and the starving women and children along the Rhine have taught us to hate the enemy. The blood and tears of our brutally murdered men, of our despoiled women and of our children beaten to death in the eastern provinces cry out for revenge. Those who are banded together in the Wehrwolf proclaim their determined, irrevocable oath, never to bow to the enemy's will but rather, despite difficulties and with only limited means, to offer resistance, despising bourgeois comfort and to go out, facing death proudly and defiantly to wreak revenge by killing the enemy for any misdeed which he has committed against our people. Every means is justified to strike a blow to damage the enemy.

'The Wehrwolf has courts which will decide the life and death of our enemies, as well as of those traitors to our own people . . . If the enemy believes that he will have an easy time . . . then he should know that in those areas of Germany which he occupies he will meet an opponent with which he has not reckoned, who is more dangerous because he is not tied by the limitations of bourgeois methods of warfare . . .'

The Wehrwolf call to action seems not to have found favour with all the civil population. A sergeant in a replacement battalion of 12th SS, which was positioned along the River Weser, described the reaction of the civilians to the fact that a battle was about to be fought around their village.

'The British [11th Armoured Division] began their preparations to cross the Weser in our area and I placed men in the fields on the outskirts of the village. From the positions I selected we would have had a marvellous field of fire which would have dominated the embarkation points on the west bank of the river, the crossing and for all the time that the British were building their perimeter on the eastern bank. That was my plan, but almost immediately a group of women came up to find out what our intentions were. When we told them they hurried away and returned with an elderly man who turned out to be the local mayor. He did not have the authority to order us to abandon the village but he and the women suggested that perhaps our positions could be dug a long way behind it, perhaps on the railway embankment, a mile away. It was very clear that the civvies were dead scared of Allied shelling and air raids. The women were the worst and got at my young lads with remarks like, "You have a mother of your own. How would you like her to be in our position?" The CO came up, listened to their argument and ordered us to leave the village and to take up positions on the railway embankment. Although there we had a very good view of the British infantry and Commandos crossing the Weser and taking up position in the flat fields on the eastern bank of the river I know, from experience, that had we stayed in the village we could have destroyed the river crossing attempt in our area.'

In the western area of the Rothaar Mountains the Americans were in action and an unknown civilian wrote of the events of Holy Week.

'On Maundy Thursday the Americans moved nearer to our village and the beaten German army flooded back through it. Hour after hour that tragic procession continued. Horse-drawn cars, smashed guns, shot-up tanks being drawn by tractors and finally the exhausted infantry. The Volkssturm, the last of all male persons between the ages of 16 and 65 who were still in the village, began to erect anti-tank barricades.

'On Easter Sunday the German Army moved into the village in strength and the inhabitants went down into the cellars, fearful that war would soon roll over them. During the night Easter Sunday/Monday the troops were reinforced. There were guns and ammunition lorries in every street . . . At 10 in the evening the guns opened fire . . . On Tuesday the Volkssturm was pulled back from its positions outside the village. German guns were brought into the woods and fields around the village. At 2115 hrs the first shell fell in the village and damaged a house. The shrieking of the shells, fearful explosions and terrible echoes filled the valleys. German guns replied . . . Wednesday the 4th, was a rainy day but from 8.30 am the guns fired non-stop . . . our soldiers tell us that not even during the Rhine crossing was the enemy's barrage so heavy. The German artillery can only fire short barrages as ammunition begins to run low . . . The civilians in the cellars have suffered casualties and some of the houses in the village are alight . . . Then fire from infantry weapons is heard and by the afternoon most of the German guns have been pulled out . . . The fighting grew louder as evening came on and then there was the sound of tank engines. The first Americans come into the houses searching for German soldiers whom they take into captivity. The sound of fighting moves away from the village but then the German artillery begins to fire upon the Americans. The population flees back into the cellars from which they had emerged only a few hours earlier . . . Sunday 8th April . . . This day is the one on which the young people make their first Communion, a sign that life is returning to normal.'

While life may have been returning to normal in certain rural parts of central western Germany, this was not the experience in the east where Soviet forces had entered the eastern provinces of the Fatherland.

EVACUATION IN THE EAST

The Red Army's summer offensive of 1944, brought about the collapse of Army Group Centre thus setting the stage for a Soviet offensive which would, eventually, thrust into the heart of the Third Reich. In the late autumn of that same year a Red Army offensive struck and split Army Group North. Within weeks of the assault's opening Russian spearheads had reached the

Baltic in the area of Memel while other Red Army formations spread out to encircle and to isolate East Prussia. There was then a temporary lull in operations while the Red Army fronts in the north, which had outrun their supplies, regrouped and reformed, preparing themselves for the next stage of Stavka's operational plan.

This was to be a twofold blow, the first of which, by 2nd and 3rd Belorussian Fronts, was intended to smash the German forces in East Prussia and Poland. The second offensive, to be carried out by 1st Belorussian and 1st Ukrainian Fronts, would drive from the Vistula to the Oder and create a springboard in central Germany from which the final Berlin offensive would be launched. Operations by other Red Army Fronts along the remaining sectors of the Eastern Front were to be subordinate to those blows. Within days of the opening of the first offensive, during the second week of January 1945, it was clear that Army Group North did not have the strength to withstand the assaults of the two Russian Fronts.

As the military units of Army Group North began to crumble fear grew among the civilian population. In most districts evacuation programmes had been worked out but had not been put into operation. Hitler was known to oppose any evacuation and Party officials lower down in the hierarchy were fearful of issuing movement orders lest they be considered lacking in moral fibre and condemned to death. Precedents such as the mayor of Königsberg existed. Conversely there had been cases where senior Nazi leaders had used the 'old boy' network to have themselves and their families appointed to posts in western Germany and had, thereby, abandoned the civilians for whom they were responsible. The most notorious case was that of Erich Koch, the Gauleiter of East Prussia, who had ordered the population not to evacuate. The Red Army, he claimed, would be halted in East Prussia. Most of the civilians under his authority had obeyed him. Others, living close to the Baltic and anxious to avoid the fighting which would soon break over them, began to 'trek', in defiance of his ban, towards ports and harbours from which they hoped to take ship to safety. The main ports to which the refugee columns struggled in the depths of that bitter winter were Königsberg, Pillau, Danzig, Gotenhafen and Hela. They were kept waiting in appalling conditions until Hitler, accepting the advice of Admiral Doenitz, authorized the evacuation of important factories, equipment and vital installations to western Germany. Once that authority had been given, refugees were also permitted to take ship. It was soon clear that a large-scale rescue operation was needed and within days the Kriegsmarine had planned and was evacuating the thousands of refugees arriving in the principal ports as well as in innumerable smaller harbours. It was clear that the Red Navy would show no mercy to refugee ships and the convoys were escorted by a miscellany of light naval craft. Some passenger liners relying upon their high speed sailed without escort and paid the price. At the end of January the worst sea tragedy in maritime history was suffered when *Wilhelm Gustloff* was sunk by a Russian submarine. How many went down with her will never be know because no embarkation lists were kept, but the number was certainly in excess of 7,000 and was probably nearer 9,000. Not only did the refugee convoys have to run the gauntlet of Russian submarines and dive-bombers but also had to endure the mass bombing of the reception ports by the air forces of the Western powers.

The shuttle service between the evacuation ports in eastern Germany and the reception ports in western Germany began in January and continued until May 1945. When the armistice was signed at Field Marshal Montgomery's headquarters on Lunenberg Heath, the commanders of the German ships anticipated orders to halt the 'taxi service'. Instead, OKM intensified the rescue operation and continued this until 9 May, when the final ceasefire came into effect. Despite the German Navy's heroic efforts, there were too few ships to take off all those crowded along the Baltic coast and waiting to be taken off. At Hela, for example, 60,000 civilians saw the last convoy leave without them, and military units which had hoped to be embarked moved from the quays back to their former positions in the battle line which a determined rearguard had been holding.

The story of that evacuation is almost unrecorded in the West, except for the US Official Naval History of the Second World War which describes it as perhaps the greatest rescue operation in the history of maritime war. Admiral Engelhardt, who was in overall control of the Baltic evacuations, wrote in his report that a '. . . total of 223 ships out of 366 employed, were lost by enemy action and though no accurate human losses can be given, an estimate of 30,000 lives, i.e., 2 per cent of those taken on board, were lost out of a total of 1,900,000 persons carried . . .'

RED ARMY'S REVENGE

This unknown story of the last weeks of the war in Germany's north-eastern provinces, known to many as 'The East German Passion', is one of misery, terror and degradation as well as heroism and self sacrifice. 'Within days [of the opening of the Red Army offensive on 12 January] there was terror in the land. It was said that Red Army men, encouraged by their officers and commissars, were robbing, raping and murdering civilians who had remained behind in their villages.' The terror to which Paula Hallhauser refers was instigated by a leaflet written by the Communist writer, Ilya Ehrenburg, which read in part, 'Kill! Kill! There is nothing of which the Germans are not guilty – those who are living; those yet to be born. Follow the orders of Comrade Stalin and smash for ever the fascist beast in his lair.' The exhortations of other Soviet writers may have been less inflammatory, but the end result was the same. The Red Army, in a terrifying wave of destruction, fell upon the luckless civilians of East Prussia who had been told by the Party to stand fast because East Prussia would not be evacuated. Had evacuation been permitted thousands would have been saved from the humiliation of rape and infection by the venereal diseases which were endemic in the Red Army. Among the reasons for not evacuating East Prussia was that the Nazi Party leaders considered the fighting will of the soldiers would be strengthened by the presence of German families.

When rumours spread in West Prussia, Pomerania and Silesia of the horror of what had happened in East Prussia, panic gripped the civilian populations, for it was upon them that the next blows would fall. Without waiting for orders those who could 'trekked' by cart or on foot to reach those ports where they hoped to find a ship and safety. Many 'treks', moving slowly through the deep snow, were overtaken by columns of Russian armoured fighting vehicles and crushed beneath the tank tracks. The reports of rape, indiscriminate murder and senseless destruction in Germany's eastern provinces make sad reading. 'My 15-year-old daughter was raped by ten soldiers. When she tried to escape the Russians caught her, kicked her and dragged her through the snow by her blonde plaits . . . Taken to hospital she died of her wounds. In the bed next to hers lay a 12-year-old girl whose internal organs had been torn open from repeated rapes.'

'We were taken from our trek . . . An officer came along and selected those who were to die . . . We others were ordered back on to our wagons and told to watch. An execution squad of ten soldiers shot the victims as they knelt in the snow begging for their lives.'

'The trek had to keep to main roads as all the side roads were choked with snow. We were a defenceless target and were attacked by Russian fighters and bombers. Our aim was to reach the Frische Nehrung, a narrow stretch of land along which we could reach harbours from where, so we had been told, we could get to Denmark.' Another trek moved along a narrow peninsula of land known as the Haff, with the Baltic on either side. In that bitter winter the sea was frozen over. Once the refugees had reached the end of the Haff they had to cross an open stretch of frozen sea in order to reach the tongue of land along which they would have to pass to gain the port of Danzig. Paula Hallhauser was one of those who made the terrible, mid-winter journey across the frozen ice. The 'treks', packed wheel to wheel on the narrow strip of land, shuffled slowly along and people fought to gain the few extra metres which would take them farther away from the advancing Red Army. 'We could move forward only a few metres at a time. Then there were long halts which seemed to last for hours. We spent one night camped out on the ice between the two tongues of land. This was the most frightening experience. It was clear that in parts the ice was thawing and throughout that long night the ice groaned and creaked. It was frightening because earlier in the day carts had broken through the ice and had been lost in the freezing water. In some cases the weight of the carts had broken the ice, but often this was done by bombs which were dropped by the Russian aeroplanes. When the planes attacked we had to stay and endure the bombing. We could not move forward and were unwilling to go back. The whole surface of the Haff was covered with dead bodies and the wreckage of carts. Dead people, dead animals and broken open suitcases marked the route of our flight. We shuffled slowly between low walls of dead things. It was a picture that could drive one mad.'

NAVAL BATTLE GROUP 2 AND *ADMIRAL SCHEER*

Admiral Doenitz, aware of how important it was for the Kriegsmarine to dominate the Baltic during the rescue operation, created Naval Battle Group 2 and placed it under the command of Admiral Thiele. The battle group was a powerful concentration of capital ships, including *Admiral Scheer, Prinz Eugen, Lützow* and *Admiral Hipper*, as well as destroyers and other small craft. The Battle Group's firepower was used to break up massive Red Army tank concentrations and to give heavy artillery support to the perimeters which the army still held along the Baltic coast. Herbert Dammert, an Army signals expert, was seconded to the cruiser *Prinz Eugen*. Dammert was one of the finest signalmen in the German services and was needed to maintain the wireless link between ship's guns and the army's forward observation officers on shore. The following are extracts from his diary:

'During the pauses in our bombardment I looked at the coast line through the artillery observer's high-powered periscopes. The beach was black with people who had all fled from the advancing Soviets and who were making their way to us on the little boats which they had found on the beaches. The fire of the *Prinz Eugen*'s guns helped to save the lives of many German people, to save them and at the same time, to stop the enemy . . . While we were anchored in Gotenhafen . . . I was told to report to my officer who ordered me to change ships and to sail with the *Lützow*. That ship was en route to the area from which the *Eugen* had just returned. She had been firing barrages from 2nd to 8th February . . . From the *Lützow* I was then transferred to *Admiral Scheer* which was en route to the Frisches Haff where the East German refugees were hoping to reach the ships which would carry them to safety.'

On 26 February, the Red Army launched a new, major offensive. The objective of this operation was Pomerania and once again, to cover the rear of the German Army which was being forced back towards the port of Wollin, the Naval Battle Group went into action. On board *Admiral Scheer* was a naval cadet, Edgar Pardy, who kept a log of the ship's final missions.

'18 to 22 January. We are lying at Pillau and are at 3 hours' readiness to move. The hospital ship *Berlin* has taken on board a number of wounded. The *Robert Ley* has also taken on board wounded and refugees . . . Hospital trains (they are really cattle trucks) arrive in the port. The wounded are lying on straw. The crew of the *Scheer* helps the wounded. In the icy cold we go from truck to truck dishing out soup to those waiting to be taken on board. The doors of some trucks have to be forced open. Inside them there is no sign of life. The wounded have all frozen to death. Women and children are now being allowed to board the ships with the wounded. Pillau is to be evacuated. Two more trainloads of wounded arrive. We help to carry them into the hospital ship. The scenes which I saw are indescribable. On the stairways and in the gangways stretcher-cases as well as women and children lie or sit huddled together. The ship is overfilled, but still more women and children pour on to her hoping to escape to the west. The enemy is at the gates of the city.

'25 Jan. The light cruiser *Emden* is anchored ahead of us. Midships there is the sarcophagus which holds the mortal remains of Field Marshal von Hindenburg, the saviour of East Prussia in the First World War. His estate in West Prussia, Neudeck, is already in enemy hands. The Tannenberg memorial, built in 1927, which had been von Hindenburg's final resting-place, had been blown up.

'26 Jan. . . . wounded continue to crowd aboard the hospital ship *Berlin*. All quays and piers in the harbour are prepared for demolition.

'27 Jan. Refugees, wounded and displaced people fill the piers. The streets of Pillau are jammed. Everywhere there is a sense of fear. The sound of gunfire is coming closer. The crew of the cruiser mounts day and night patrols of 20 men and an officer to keep order in the town . . . More train loads of wounded come in. The crew of the cruisers is given instruction in firing Panzerfaust launchers . . . We are trying to control the flood of people seeking to board the ship. Often the stretchers carrying someone on board are turned back and the men are laid instead in the snow. The young woman doctor standing by the ship's railing closes their eyes for these who are taken ashore are the dead whose places can now be taken by a living person.

'3 February. During the night we have loaded more 28cm ammunition for our heavy guns . . . At 0400 hrs we set out for the Frische Nehrung.'

From 4 February until 5 March, *Scheer* supported German ground forces in the Pillau and Königsberg sectors as well as at other ports in the eastern Baltic. On 6 March she took on board 800 refugees and 200 wounded and reached Swinemunde on the 8th. 'All around are ships which have been sunk or which have run aground; the victims of mines or torpedoes. Ghostlike their masts and upper works stand out of the water. I have identified one of the vessels as being the hospital ship *Berlin*.'

Once again *Scheer* sailed out into action in the eastern Baltic and upon her return to Kiel the cadets in the crew were posted away from the ship. 'We paraded on the pier when she steamed out again and in a farewell salute gave three cheers for our ship.' Pardy was then put into an infantry unit to defend the Danish island of Seeland. *Scheer*, from which he and the other cadets had been posted, was attacked by the RAF during the night of 9 April, and capsized.

BATTLES IN THE BURGENLAND, AUSTRIA

The preceding section traced the fighting in the northern sector of the line and it began with the words that the Red Army's summer offensive had brought about the collapse of Army Group Centre. One consequence of that disaster to German arms was that the battle line in the east consisted of major groupings in the north and south with only weak and unconnected formations holding the centre. This disastrous situation could not be repaired and continued throughout the last months of 1944 and until the end of the war. The Red Army was thus able to switch its forces in support of new offensives on either wing and, thereby, to destroy the German Army Groups in detail.

In the southern sector the situation was that, following the invasion of eastern Hungary during the first weeks of December, the Red Army had gone over to a major offensive by the 20th of that month. Budapest, the Hungarian capital, was besieged and fell after fifty-one days, and of the massive German/Hungarian garrison only 785 men reached the west. Hitler had, of course, launched attempts to raise the siege but these had failed despite the best efforts of Army Group South. Hitler then announced that without Hungarian oil the war was lost and ordered an offensive to regain the oilfields. This operation, in which three German armies took part, was mounted across low-lying, marshy ground in which the panzer formations could not operate. The offensive had little chance of success and after gaining some ground in the first days of March 1945, met increasing opposition from Soviet formations which had been rushed up to counter it. By the morning of 20 March, the strength of the Red Army in western Hungary had grown to a point where it could launch a general offensive whose repeated and heavy blows shattered the German formations. One of the divisions involved in the fighting was 12th SS Panzer Division 'Hitler Youth'. The savage battles of the previous weeks had so eroded its strength that some of its major formations had been reduced to battle groups. These fought on against Russian numerical and material superiority, but when Soviet advances forced divisional headquarters to flee into the deep woods around Oedenburg, there was no longer firm central control over its formations and these fought on almost in isolation.

Continual losses and no replacements weakened the 'Hitler Youth' and by the first day of April 1945, the 12th SS Panzer Division had been reduced to little more than a large battle group, with a strength of two battalions. One of the actions which reduced the strength of the division was a counter-attack mounted by 1st Battalion of 26th Panzer Grenadier Regiment on 31 March. That battle was typical of those in which the other divisional remnants were involved, and Martin Glade described the fighting in the heavily wooded eastern province of Austria, Burgenland.

'We [i.e., the battalion] left the protection of a little wood, some 300 metres from the village [Drassberg]. We moved quietly with our hearts beating fast. The first houses of the villages loomed up out of the dark. Only another 20 paces before we reached the first house. Suddenly the cry "Stoi!". Untersturmführer Degenhardt raised his pistol and fired. The red signal flares exploded in the sky. The Company split, some moved to the left – others to the right. We raced into the village. Bullets were flying about. Shouts. At a racing pace we charge through the village. Resistance is quickly broken. The Red Army men are taken completely by surprise – they break and run.

'By the time it was fully light the village had been cleared of the enemy. The villagers bring us hot coffee, sandwiches and coloured Easter eggs. We are suddenly aware that tomorrow is Easter Sunday. We rest in the village and take some boxes of German Army ammunition from a captured panje cart. The ammunition fits our carbines and assault rifles so the boxes are quickly emptied. At about midday we learn that the enemy has broken through in the direction of Vienna. Orders to leave the village find us, therefore, not entirely unprepared. Two comrades and I are ordered by Untersturmführer Degenhardt to cover the Company's withdrawal to the cover of a little wood. We set up our MG 42 in a ditch in front of the last house. The Russians have noticed that we are pulling out. A few groups of them start to move towards the village. At a range of about 250 metres we open fire. The Russians take cover. Some 50 metres to the left of us there is a haystack which suddenly catches fire. By the time that the advancing Russians are within 150 metres we have run out of ammunition. The village behind us is empty. There is not a soul to be seen. We pull back a short distance and take cover near a house. The Russians are suspicious of the quietness and do not pursue us. We are lucky and leave the village from the other side and reach the wood, which lies about 1,300 metres away, without trouble.

'Our comrades are in a clearing waiting for us. We [the battalion] have been cut off and set out to gain touch with our own troops. The Companies march out, correctly disposed, No 1 Company now in the rear of the battalion column. We move deeper into the woods so as to avoid the Russians. After a few hours we come across a road on which seemingly endless columns of Russian vehicles are moving; tanks, panje carts and infantry mounted in lorries. We stay under cover in bushes some 50 metres off the road and wait there for a break in the traffic so that we can rush across the road. Time passes. How long have we been here? We have no idea. At last there is a break. We reach the road and hear the sound of motor engines coming from the right flank. The wood swallows us up again. We move off quickly, then come to the end of the tree line. A little path takes us through another stretch of woodland and towards another road. This should be easier to cross as there is no traffic using it. About 100 metres away on the far side of the road there is more woodland. We wait. Evening comes. The leading files stand up, emerge from cover and cross the road. We, the rearguard, move forward and the leading files are practically on the road when from the right two cars come speeding along. We throw ourselves flat. A voice says "Don't fire! Let them through."

'One of the men loses his nerve and opens fire. The cars halt and try to turn round. We all know that the Russians must not be allowed to escape. What then happens is over so quickly. The cars are stopped by our fire. Nothing moves. We cross the road. Near the cars there are three dead Russian officers and two dead Russian women soldiers in uniform. We rest in the woods and then continue the march, across fields, woods and a rather wide stream into which some of the men fall. Villages, brilliantly lit up, are on either side of us. At about midnight we find ourselves in some deep woods. By moonlight we can see a road in front of us shimmering in the moonlight. Carefully we move forward. Suddenly a twig cracks and immediately there is a shout "Stoi! Stoi!"

'We stand like statues. It is dead quiet. Then the Hauptsturmführer gives the order, "Give a cheer lads and then charge across the road." His seems to be the only voice to shout hurray, but then others take up the cry and then we all start to move. What follows is a matter of a few seconds only. We reach the road. There are shots. In the shadow of the trees along the road there are lorries, motor cars, tracked and half-track vehicles. There is also a Stalin Organ [a multi-barrelled mortar]. The Red Army men who have been lying near their vehicles sound asleep are rudely awakened and reach for their weapons. We open fire on them, cross the road and dive into cover. The road is an absolute hell. The Russians are shouting, engines are started up, shots are fired. We leave them to it and move deeper into the trees. There we regroup and can see how few we are now in number. The Russians do not seem to be following us. We reach a deep hollow surrounded by trees and there we intend to spend the day. Dawn is breaking. We are able to rest for only a few hours. Towards midday we hear the Russians shouting to each other as they comb the woods. We lie still with our weapons ready. As the first shots ring out some of us turn and run. The Hauptsturmführer and Untersturmführer Degenhardt who are with our group order us to move quickly otherwise we shall be caught. As we do so I am wounded.

'The Russians are shouting behind us, "German soldier stand still!" but we ignore them. The enemy follows us at a leisurely pace. We reach the end of the woods. About 150 metres away there is a field and a strip of thick shrubbery. We race towards it, disappear into it, take up firing positions and wait. The first Russians appear at the edge of the woods, still shouting and firing. They see where we lie waiting to fight our last battle. But they turn away and do not come back. We can hear them for some time shouting in the woods but at last there is silence. We lie there for the rest of the day. The sun is pleasantly warm. We doze, and some of us sleep. We begin to realize how hungry we are.

'We move out at last light across fields and meadows. How long we marched I do not know. Then in front of us is a brilliantly lit town. Someone says "That must be Eisenstadt" [in Burgenland]. There is another road. How many is that that we have crossed. On the other side is an anti-tank ditch. We spend time looking for a crossing-place and then suddenly a lorry comes along with headlights blazing. We have no choice but to fling ourselves into the ditch. We find a place where we can climb out easily. The Hauptsturmführer tells us before we climb out "We'll shake off the Russians tonight. We shall move into the lake." Between Rust and Oggau the ground is spongy and eventually we are wading through knee-deep water. We move deeper into the lake and are soon up to our waists and then our chests. We are crossing the Neusiedler Lake. A rotten night lies ahead of us. The water is icy cold. There is a full moon in a cloudless sky and not a breath of wind. Sound carries a long way in such conditions. Very lights are fired in our direction. The Russians know where we are. We are so exhausted that we can feel nothing any more except hunger and thirst – thirst particularly, although none of us wants to drink the muddy water of the lake which stinks of rotting vegetation. All the time Very lights are fired towards us, but at last the moon begins to go down. In the east a new day is dawning. Daylight will force us to get out of the water and when at last we reach dry land we collapse on to it. We have marched most of the night through the lake and are at the end of our powers. As it gets lighter we find we are in a little vineyard.

'Our rest there is brief for suddenly there are shouts in Russian. These are coming from the direction of Purbach and from Breitenbrunn. They have cut us off. None of us wants to go back into the water so we shall have to infiltrate through the oncoming Russians. We reach a road. In front of us there is a high cliff. For men in our condition it is an impossible task to climb it. Our group – we are down to thirteen men now – run to the right. Some men seem undecided. Perhaps they no longer have the strength to move and just stand there. Another group breaks away to the left. Machine-pistols open fire. There are screams. We charge at the Russians, firing all the time, find a place where we can climb the cliff and move up it shouting to the others to follow us. But in vain. We run along the cliff edge waving to them, but they can do no more and drop into ditches or among the growing vines. The Russians close in and wipe them out. Some of us have run out of ammunition. I have only three rounds left. We move back into the cover of the bushes, discuss what we should do and then realize that there is no more noise coming from the road. I crawl to the edge of the cliff. On the road our comrades are lying dead and the Russians are emptying their pockets and taking off their wrist-watches.

'We pass through an orchard and, hearing the sound of the pursuing Russians coming closer, seek cover in a wood. Helmut Henn and I are a long way behind the rest of our group. The others wait for us and offer to carry us because he and I are so exhausted. Eventually, we reach a Fire Watch tower which has a small wooden hut at its foot. The comrades lift up some planks so that Helmut and I can creep inside and then bang them back into place with kicks from their boots. He and I are now alone. But not for long. Soon the Russians enter the hut and turn everything upside down. The sound of firing from within the woods draws the Russians away. We spend the rest of the day in our hiding-place and during the night break out intending to make our way through the Russian lines and to gain touch with a German units. After about eight nights of marching, some of which we spent in the Vienna woods, we give up the attempt. The Front lies too far away to the west. It was while we were in the Vienna woods that the end of the war came; on 8th May.'

FREEDOM ON THE ELBE

In faraway Berlin fighting for the city was concluded on 2 May and a great mass of Red Army formations, released by the fall of the German capital, drove westward to reinforce the Soviet armies lining the River Elbe. Eisenhower, the western Supreme Commander, had ordered the British and American armies to halt on the west bank of the Elbe, but the Soviets, fearful that the forces of the Western Allies would cross the river and advance into eastern Germany, built up the strength of their forces facing the Americans.

To German civilians the Elbe was a magnet. They were convinced that whoever managed to cross it and enter the US Zone would be safe from the Red Army and free. This is the story of one civilian, L. Gruenhagen, who made the attempt:

'Although I was not a soldier my story may be relevant to your book. At the end of the war I was ten years old and together with my family was trying to escape from the Russians. We were on a trek from our home in Pomerania and had been on the road for weeks. Conditions which had been bad to begin with grew worse and there was little of the Volksgemeinschaft – the communal spirit – by the time we reached the River Elbe. In a great many cases it was the strongest who got through and survived.

'We reached the eastern bank of the Elbe about 4th May and found there a great mass of people, refugees from many different parts of Germany, who had reached the river but who had not been allowed to cross to the western bank where the Americans were. We all wanted to reach their zone because we knew we would be safer with them than with the Red Army. I have since learned that the total numbers of people gathered on the eastern bank were in excess of two hundred thousand. We were all wet, cold, hungry and frightened, but we were civilians and the Americans would not let us cross. They were prepared to let German soldiers cross the river but the order that no civilians were to be let through was very strictly enforced and any refugees found mixing in with the military columns and hoping to escape were swiftly and not always gently taken back to the eastern bank.

'There was an agreement between the Americans and the Russians not to allow refugees to enter the American zone and the Amis of Ninth Army were determined to keep to the letter of the agreement. By the 5th or 6th May the crowd of refugees had become desperate. We knew that the Russians were coming; that they were only 30kms distant and that between them and us there was only German Twelfth Army whose soldiers we knew were just hoping to save themselves from becoming prisoners of war.

'Then on the 6th, when all seemed to be lost, a miracle happened. The Russian artillery opened fire. These Russian gunners had fought in Berlin and having regrouped were now driving towards the Tangermünde sector of the Elbe where they hoped to encircle and to destroy Wenck's Twelfth Army. They obviously made a mistake in believing that we refugees were part of that Army. They used their heaviest artillery and then backed this up with medium artillery. No! that was not the miracle. That was that the shells and bombs did not fall among us civilian refugees but flew across the Elbe and exploded among the American units on the west bank.

'The Russians took no notice of the Very lights which the Americans fired into the air. If anything the shelling became heavier as more artillery was brought closer to us. The Americans had a simple choice to stay and be killed or to withdraw. They pulled back for a distance of about 9 or 10kms and this left the west bank of the Elbe unoccupied. Almost immediately our soldiers took advantage of the situation and began to organize things. They launched every sort of craft that could float and brought these across to the eastern bank. These boats and floats were then loaded with civilians who were brought across to the western bank where they promptly vanished into the surrounding countryside. My family was lucky enough to get across very quickly and I can remember the drizzling rain, the boat very low in the water, the smell of the river and the faces of the soldiers who rowed us across the Elbe. We climbed the river bank and after a long walk a farmer gave us a lift in a cart. My mother was crying because we had had to leave everything behind on the east bank. We had been told that no luggage could be taken, that it was more important to rescue people than suitcases which took up room. How many refugees escaped across the Elbe to the west I have no idea, but it must have been many thousands. The Russians who found our abandoned suitcases and rucksacks must have thought they had entered Paradise because those piles of luggage on the east bank of the Elbe were all filled with family treasures.'

Collapse and Aftermath, 1945

SURRENDER AND HUMILIATION

Now it was all over. The first surrender was signed in Italy. Then it was the German forces in north-west Europe that capitulated. The main ceasefire came into force on the Eastern Front on 9 May, but in Yugoslavia the fighting continued for many days more. Eventually, and at long last, after years of fighting the German forces had laid down their arms and passed into captivity.

For some units the surrender took the nature of a formal ceremony with officers wearing gloves and carrying daggers at their wasts. This was particularly true of really élite formations which made the act of capitulation a ceremonial parade. Contingents of the Germanic SS, for example, drove into the American lines in Austria, with each vehicle spotlessly cleaned and immaculately serviced. Commanders leapt from their vehicles, formed up and marched in formation towards the place where the US senior officers were waiting to accept their surrender. It happened more than once that the tight-knit group of combat veterans was mobbed by groups of GIs and stripped of medals, decorations and awards by US soldiers, each of whom wanted a 'Nazi' souvenir.

On some battle fronts long lines of grey-faced men, exhausted by war, trudged into makeshift prison camps. For those on the Eastern Front kicks and beatings were followed by the selection and summary execution of hostages, a move designed to cow the survivors into submission. It was in the Balkans that the worst excesses took place. Mass executions, savage beatings and starvation were the norm. The cry of 'Vae victis!' did not just sound throughout Europe – it thundered out and the victors sat in judgement over the vanquished. They sat in judgement over men, women and children, for the US authorities sentenced to death or to life imprisonment young boys who had been condemned by courts martial as 'Wehrewolves'. The Red Army shot all the co-called 'terrorists' it caught and for years after the war's end hunted down the survivors in the Russian zone of occupation.

More than one German serviceman, recalling those first days and weeks after the end of the war, wrote of the humiliation of having to surrender to less worthy troops than themselves. Many wrote bitterly of the treatment they received because they had done their duty to the best of their ability.

In a subjective and punitive decision, the men of élite units were condemned as war criminals just because they had been members of just such a unit. That was the fate of the Fallschirmjaeger, the U-boat crews and, especially, those of the SS, some of whom were told that their sentence as prisoners of war would be for life. Many prisoners were subjected to physical or mental torture in an effort to break them. That the victor nations, fearing a resurgence of German nationalism, should seek to contain this by imprisoning the men of élite arms of service, was understandable as a short-term measure, but it seemed, in the first post-war months, as if this was no short-term policy but a long-term plan. The Cold War caused the Western Allies to rethink their policy *vis-à-vis* the former enemy – a rethink that had already been carried out in the eastern Zone. The prison camps were emptied of all but the most senior members of the SS and even their sentences were reduced in length. But before that change of policy came about a cynical manoeuvre changed the status of prisoners of war in American hands to that of Disarmed Enemy Forces. Under the terms of the Geneva Convention, prisoners of war have to be fed the same rations as the soldiers of the captor nation, Disarmed Enemy Forces do not. The consequence of that name-change was the death of nearly a million German servicemen from starvation and hunger-induced diseases.

In their zone of occupation the French had 'fleshed out' the depleted ranks of the Foreign Legion by recruiting former SS men. Thereby the French Army gained first-class soldiers and the SS men who survived their period of service with the Legion acquired French citizenship. The Russians, to begin with, treated all German servicemen as criminals because they had invaded the Soviet Union, and put them to years of hard labour. Only Great Britain did not take reprisals against the former enemy, although the government of the day considered its prisoners as additions to the work force in mines and on the land, and kept them until the end of 1947.

In his history of 12th SS Division 'Hitler Youth', Hubert Meyer wrote 'The soldiers of the Waffen SS and a few "selected" personnel of the Wehrmacht who were in POW camps in West Germany, were released from prison camps under a Military Government Directive of 1 November 1946. They were then immediately re-arrested under the terms of the "automatic arrest" law and became civil internees. On 12 January 1946, the Allied Control Commission issued guide-lines to facilitate the removal of National Socialists and Militarists from the administration and other sectors. The American law of 5 March 1946, announced . . . release from civil internment camps was only permitted after "denazification". This law defined all commanders of the Waffen SS as "criminals". All other members of that organization were "contaminated" . . . The fact that a man had received decorations for bravery in the face of the enemy or had been promoted for that reason, counted against him . . . All those who were released from the internment camps had to undergo some sort of "penance". This took the form of labouring in the internment camps, financial penalties, being excluded from one's former occupation or trade as well as the loss of voting rights either for a fixed time or for life.'

Reinhold Hoffmann, a former Fallschirmjaeger, wrote of his treatment:

'At the end of the war we prisoners were divided into one of three groups. The 'A' Group contained the anti-fascists. 'B' Group was made up of those who had supported the regime and the 'C' Group held those who were considered to be dyed-in-the-wool Nazis. The dirty work of deciding to which group one belonged was carried out by deserters from the German forces. One of these, a lieutenant, categorized me as "C Plus", because so far as he was concerned for me to have gained the "German Cross in Gold" at my rank indicated that I was worse than the worst SS swine.

'Because of that categorization I spent a year in Punishment Camp 282 at El Daba in the desert. At that place we received only half-rations and had to attend re-education classes in order to de-Nazify us. Those classes, too, were run by deserters. My father had been a life-long Social Democrat and not one of my family belonged to a Nazi organization. For me to be considered as a "C Plus", was the worst punishment that could have been inflicted.

'Like every other soldier in the world we had carried out our duty as the law demanded. Two of my brothers and two of my uncles fell in the war; a war which brought only loss and destruction.'

ESCAPE

There were some German servicemen who sought to escape from their country's enemies by fleeing to neutral countries – not always successfully as Erich Kassel wrote:

'A soldier's life plays him many tricks, but none could have been a worst trick than that which was played upon those men who were interned in Sweden at the end of the war. The convoys of ships which evacuated the civilians and soldiers from the eastern provinces of Germany usually came under air or submarine attacks and were dispersed. It happened quite frequently that ports in west Germany at which individual ships arrived were often not those for which they had set out. The vessels of some dispersed convoys were driven so far off course that they arrived in Sweden, although, of course, some deliberately set course for that country.'

Kassel, who had served in an assault gun unit on the Eastern Front, was one of the survivors of a brigade which had reached Danzig and which was then sent to Hela to be evacuated.

'Our Brigade did not sail as a single group, for at this stage of the evacuation only small ships were still operating. One fairly large group of the brigade boarded a river steamer. Two other groups were carried on ferries and landing craft to a west German port where they were taken prisoner by the British. The group on the river steamer arrived in Sweden and was interned as were the other German soldiers who reached that country. They all assumed they would be held in internment until things had settled down in Germany, but in that belief they were disappointed. In November/ December 1945, that is to say six months after the end of the war, the Swedes handed over to the Soviets all the German servicemen in their country. I do not know whether this was a contravention of human rights as many have claimed, but it was certainly moral cowardice on the part of the Swedes. A soldier's fate plays him many tricks. Those who were taken prisoner by the Western Allies had all been released by about 1947. Those who reached Sweden and, as they thought, safety did not return from the Soviet Union for a great many years.'

UNREPENTANT

The question that remains is, what did the German serviceman think of his time under arms? This is a complex question for much depends upon the unit with which he served, the privations he underwent and his post-war recovery from the shock of Germany's defeat. With very few exceptions, those whose words are contained in these pages are proud to have fought for Germany. Among the correspondence that arrived too late to be included in an earlier book, *World War Two Through German Eyes*, was an item from Ulrich Luebke, who admitted he was an unrepentant nationalist.

'I thought it might be worthwhile to put the viewpoint of my type of German. Unlike many of my countrymen I do not agonize about the Second World War not make excuses that we fought it. I regret that Europe had to tear itself apart twice in my lifetime, but the fault was not Germany's. We did not declare war on you: it was you who declared war on us.

'I am now over 80 years old so that I was born when we still had an Emperor, although I have almost no recollection of those days. What I do have is a very strong recall of the misery of post-war years under the Weimar republic. My formative years I recall as time of personal deprivation and national humiliation. There was widespread unemployment and Germany was saddled with the burden of reparations because she was blamed for starting the war. I remember very well the electric charge that National Socialism gave to Germany and as a Party member I was proud to belong to a movement which exercised leadership and to a nation which was strong.

Once the National Socialists were elected we Germans seemed to regain our national pride and soon had a strong army, navy and air force. Germany, once again, was a powerful voice in Europe.

'I enlisted voluntarily into the army, and joined an infantry regiment, one which carried on the traditions of an élite Prussian grenadier regiment. I saw service in Poland but not in France during 1940, and remember the sense of uplift which that successful campaign brought about. We were all convinced that the war was over – all of us from the lowest to very highest in the land. After the French campaign a start was made to demobilize the older age groups, but that initiative was reversed when we made our pre-emptive strike against Russia.

'During the fighting for Smolensk I was wounded and when I rejoined my unit it was to find that the CO had decided that those of my age group were too old (at 32) to serve in a rifle company. Those who were affected were to be posted back to the depot in Prussia, where we would serve as instructors. The Ivans had other plans for us. On 8 November 1941, they made a massive attack along our sector of the front.

'It was shortly after midday and I was making my way from the front line to TAC Regimental HQ, which was about two kilometres away. It was bitterly cold and although there had been no heavy falls of snow there was a shallow covering on the ground. The hours of daylight in November are few, and the day was overcast with heavy clouds. I trudged along silently up the track towards RHQ from where I would go by lorry to the railhead and there take a train back to Germany. Suddenly, without warning, the barrage started. Shells crashed on to our forward positions and then crept across country towards me in waves of explosions. There was nothing to be done but wait until the fire and destruction had passed over me. When it did I was shaken but unwounded and stood up and began jog-trotting back to my old Company position. I knew the Company would be under pressure and that every man would be needed. As I trotted along a group of horsemen raced over the brow of a hill immediately to my left and some of them were so close that they almost ran me down. One of the Cossacks swung his horse towards me and struck at me with his sabre. It was a powerful blow to my upper left arm, just below the shoulder and it knocked me to the ground. It felt as if my arm had been broken and I saw there was blood on my gloves after I had touched the numbed area.

'I reached the Company positions – barns built round a sort of central courtyard in which a battle group from the Company preparing to go into a counter-attack. A sergeant saw me, took one look at my bloodied overcoat sleeve and called for the first-aid men. In the MI room when they removed my overcoat and jacket they must have realized that there was little that the Medical Officer could do. I would have to be evacuated to a main hospital and the medics warned me it was almost certain the arm could not be saved.

It had been so deeply cut that it was half-severed. Surprisingly there had been no great loss of blood as might have been expected and I did not feel dizzy or weak at all. It was probably the bitter cold that had reduced the flow of blood from the wound. The Medical Officer injected me with a drug which knocked me out and during the time I was unconscious I was evacuated and flown home. My left arm was amputated in a Leipzig hospital and that ended my active part in the War.

'I am not bitter that I lost an arm. My generation was brought up to believe that no sacrifice was too great for the Fatherland. The philosophy we were taught was that Germany must live, even if we had to die for it. Accepting that philosophy we believed, and I still believe, that we had to fight to break the ring which the capitalist nations of Europe had cast around us.'

PROFESSIONALS

There were some who, in the words of the late Harry Gold, a Luftwaffe soldier in the anti-aircraft artillery, wished that 'the cup might pass from me'. The wounds that he had received in the last months of the war and which were not dealt with properly must have contributed to his early death at the age of 60. All Gold had wanted from life was to live in his North German home town, working as a bookbinder. When war came he was not immediately conscripted, but was called up early in 1944 and badly wounded in an air raid upon Berlin later that year. The amputation of his left leg might not have been necessary had the German medical service had the sulfa drugs and the penicillin available to the Western Allies. They did not and amputation was the only option open to German doctors to save a patient's life. The cup did not pass from Harry Gold and the bookbinder died prematurely.

The last words are those of Colonel Glasl, the commander of 100th Gebirgs Regiment. One day while making an inspection of the positions held by his men in the first days of the battle for Cassino, he turned to Helmut Hermann, the regimental adjutant who was accompanying him, and remarked, 'Do you know, I should very much prefer to be the Abbot of this Monastery than the commander of a regiment.' It is this attitude of carrying out to the best of one's ability a dangerous and distasteful task that is, I think, most typical of those men and women of the German services whose stories fill this book.

List of Contributors

Max Anger
R. Buchbinder
Georg Cordts
Herbert Dammert
Rolf Dittman
Roman Geiger
Martin Glade
A. Glasl
Hermann Goetzel
Herr Graber
Emil Grohl
E. Grosser
L. Gruenhagen
P. Hallhauser
Peter Hansmann
E. Hauber
Franz Heimann
Helmuth Hermann
August von der Heydte
Max Hildebrandt
Reinhold Hoffmann

Erich Hoppe
Oswald Jahnke
Paul Kamberger
Erich Kassel
Harry Keilhaus
Heinrich Kiss
Traute Kren
Odilo Kumme
Franz Kurowski
Rudolf Lanz
Ulrich Luebke
Heinz Macher
Hubert Meyer
J. Meyer
R. Pichler
R. Pohl
F. Puechler
Johann Radl
Günther Resch
Albert Richter
Günther Rolf

Heid Ruehl
Wolf Schirrmacher
Herr Schmokel
Gerd-Dietrich Schneider
Edeltraude Schranz
Thomas Schulze
Hans Schumann
Hans-Ulrich Schumann
L. Schumman
Alfred Spies
A. Stahlberg
Richard Stahlmann
R. Stahlschmidt
Rolf Steiner
Heinrich Stolz
Adolf Strauch
Hans Teske
Herr Valentin
Otto Weidinger
H. Werner

Index

WAR
MACHINE

WAR MACHINE

A Yellowthread Street Mystery

WILLIAM MARSHALL

THE MYSTERIOUS PRESS

New York • London • Tokyo

The Hong Bay district of Hong Kong is fictitious,
as are the people who, for one reason or another,
inhabit it.

This book was originally published in Great Britain
by Hamish Hamilton Ltd.

Copyright © 1982 by William Marshall
All rights reserved.
The Mysterious Press, 129 West 56th Street, New York, N.Y. 10019

This Mysterious Press edition is published by arrangement with the author.

Printed in the United States of America
First Mysterious Press Printing: February 1988
10 9 8 7 6 5 4 3 2 1

Library of Congress Cataloging-in-Publication Data

Marshall, William Leonard, 1944-
    War machine.

    (A Yellowthread street mystery)
    Reprint. Originally published: London : Hamish
Hamilton, 1982.
    I. Title. II. Series: Marshall, William Leonard,
1944-   Yellowthread street mystery.
PR9619.3.M275W37   1988   823   87-42711
ISBN 0-89296-198-8

Night-Jar

At 4.15 a.m. at the seawall on Beach Road, Detective Inspector Auden screwed up his face and listened.

Nothing.

There was a storm building up somewhere out in the South China Sea and he flexed his shoulders under his shirt as the air around him built up and became sticky and close.

Still nothing.

He screwed up his face and cocked his head to put his ear in the direction of the sea. There was a dull roar of thunder a long way out and, somewhere off to his right, the sound of a small outboard motor as a fisherman in one of the western inlets of Hong Bay either went back to his boat after a long night or started off from his boat for a long day, but apart from that...

... nothing.

In the open back of the Army radio directional van, Corporal Tong pulled back his earphones, rubbed at his ears with his fingers, and catching Auden's eye, shook his head.

Persistent reports of gunfire...

Fifty yards away, walking the deserted sidewalk by the seawall, Detective Inspector Spencer asked The Fireworks Man, 'Anything?'

The Fireworks Man said quietly in Cantonese, 'I can't hear anything except the water.'

Spencer glanced at his watch. There was a crackle from his walkie talkie and he put it against his ear to hear what was being said to the RD van from the Water Police.

Sergeant Lew of the Water Police, a hundred and fifty yards out in the harbour, transmitted in Cantonese to the Army Corporal,

1

'Nothing. How about you?'

The Army Corporal looked at Auden and shook his head.

Persistent reports of gunfire. It was 4.18. Auden said, 'We might as well pack up. Tell Lew—'

Lew's voice said, 'There! I heard it! It's coming from—did you get it?'

Auden looked at the Corporal.

The Corporal shook his head.

Lew's voice said between bursts of static, 'Sorry. It was thunder. I should have been counting the time between the lightning and the rolls. The storm's about two miles out. My coxswain tells me the time's right for it to be thunder.' The sound came rolling in across the miles and rumbled over Beach Road.

The Fireworks Man said to Spencer, 'It's thunder.'

There was another explosion and then another.

Auden said to no one in particular, 'Thunder.' He saw Spencer approaching him and he went forward to meet him to decide to call it a night.

Night noises. Things that went bump in the night.

Auden called out, 'Bill, this is a waste of time. It's probably just a lot of little lonely old ladies ringing up to get attention.' He looked out at the dark sea and wiped his face with his hand, 'It's a waste of time. It could have been anything.'

'Two nights in a row?'

Auden said, 'It's almost half past four. All the reports were in by three both times.' He looked at The Fireworks Man, 'It could have just been some idiot with a few fire crackers.' He looked up as another roll of thunder crashed above him, 'Summer's the time of year for thunder. It could have been—'

The Fireworks Man heard it first. The Fireworks Man said suddenly, 'That's a gunshot.'

And then another. The Fireworks Man said, 'That's not fireworks, that's a gunshot!'

From his van, the Army Corporal called out, 'Sir! Gunfire! I can hear it in the phones!'

Lew's voice was on the R/T. Lew said from his boat, 'Shots! I

2

can hear shots!'

Auden yelled to the Corporal, 'Where?' The muffled cracks were echoing across the water, coming from—from where? Auden called, 'Where are they coming from, the sea or the shore?'

The Corporal said, 'The sea! They're coming in from the sea!' He snapped the radio link open to Lew on the police launch.

Lew was saying, 'Fifteen ... no, twenty degrees ...' He realised the link was open, 'They're coming out to us from the shore!'

Auden wrenched the microphone from the Corporal's hand. Auden said quickly, 'Are you taking fire?'

'No, we can just hear them. They're not aimed at us. They seem to be coming from—from where you are.'

'The Army says the shots are coming in from the sea!'

There was another shot, and then another. The sounds seemed to be echoing above their heads. Spencer said urgently to The Fireworks Man, 'Come on, you're the expert on explosions. Where are they coming from?'

'I'm the expert on fireworks and they're not fireworks.' The sounds seemed to be ripping directly above The Fireworks Man's head. He had done his work. The sounds were not fireworks. It was thank you and goodbye time.

Lew's voice crackled on the radio, 'No, they're hitting Lamma Island. The sounds are travelling across the Channel and bouncing off Lamma Island and then they're—' Lew said, 'No, the wind's changed and they're—and the sound's echoing off—' Through the link Auden heard Lew's coxswain shout out something in rapid Tanka and then Lew cursed, 'They're changing direction! The wind out here keeps changing and the sounds are—' There was a fusillade of shots, 'It's impossible! First the sound goes one way and then the other!' Lew said, 'They've got to be coming out from the shore! Are you getting any muzzle flashes?'

Spencer had a stopwatch in his hand counting the seconds between the shots. They were coming bang—pause, bang—pause—exactly one and a half seconds apart. Spencer said urgently to The Fireworks Man, 'Are you sure they're shots? They're regular.'

'No, I'm not sure they're shots, but they're not fireworks!' At seventy one, he was too old to duck. The Fireworks Man said, 'They're shooting at us!'

At the van, Auden had his hand on the Corporal's shoulder. On the roof of the van the directional antennae were turning first one way and then the other. The Corporal said in protest, 'They're moving! The shots are moving!'

Spencer said, 'They're only one and a half seconds apart. They can't be moving.'

'I tell you they are! I'm catching the echoes. They're moving as far as three miles apart. They're muffled. It's almost as if—' The Army Corporal said with an odd look on his face, 'As if they're being broadcast.' The Army Corporal said desperately, 'Look, I need at least two other vans to triangulate this and at least—'

At sea, Lew said, 'I just had a clear sound. It seemed to be coming from somewhere behind you, high up.' He asked again, 'Are you getting any muzzle flashes?'

Auden scanned the area behind him with night glasses. He glanced at Spencer. Spencer was still timing and counting. So far, there had been twelve shots in eighteen seconds exactly. Spencer said, 'It's like some sort of machine. It's firing every—'

Auden saw only lines and lines of skyscrapers. Back from the sea shore, Hong Kong was lit up at its usual level of Gone With The Wind premiere intensity and if there were flashes they were invisible in the brilliance.

Spencer said at his side, 'What are they shooting *at*? How many are there?'

Lew's voice cut in on the radio, 'Did you hear that one? I heard it clearly. It must have been straight on in my direction. It sounded like—'

Auden demanded, 'Where the hell are the bullets going?'

Lew said, 'It sounded like a blank. It had that softer slower sound to it like the blanks you use at gun handling practice.' Lew's voice said suddenly, 'Something just landed in the water beside

4

us!'

Spencer's stopwatch was going tickticktickticktick...

Lew's voice said quietly, 'It's sunk. Whatever it was, it's...'

From the shore, everyone around the van heard the dull thump, then rushing across the sea, unfettered and unmuffled there was a sharp detonation that rolled and echoed with the thunder.

Lew's voice said curiously on the radio, 'About fifty feet away. Deep. Something deep in the water's just—' Lew said in very rapid, furious Cantonese, 'Sir, under the water—and there was a brilliant white light!' Lew said incredulously, 'I think it was a fucking *depth charge!*'

The Fireworks Man, looking hard at Spencer looking out to sea, said anxiously, 'Inspector? *What the hell's going on?*'

There was a silence.

At 4.20 a.m. on an oppressive Summer's night, for the third time in succession, that was what everyone wanted to know.

Hong Kong is an island of some 30 square miles under British administration in the South China Sea facing Kowloon and the New Territories areas of continental China. Kowloon and the New Territories are also British administered, surrounded by the Communist Chinese province of Kwantung. The climate is generally sub-tropical, with hot, humid summers and heavy rainfall. The population of Hong Kong and the surrounding areas at any one time, including tourists and visitors, is in excess of four millions. The New Territories are leased from the Chinese. The lease is due to expire in 1997, but the British nevertheless maintain a military presence along the border, although, should the Communists who supply almost all the Colony's drinking water, ever desire to terminate the lease early, they need only turn off the taps. Hong Bay is on the southern side of the island and the tourist brochures advise you not to go there after dark.

Persistent reports of gunfire.

At exactly 4.21 a.m. and thirty seconds, with the expenditure of precisely one hundred and twenty three rounds of ammunition,

5

the shooting stopped.

Out to sea where the underwater light had been, the water stopped foaming, and, receding into ripples, became again eternal and undisturbed.

1

Out of a clear blue sky...

On the fourth floor girders of a half completed building across the street Mr Muscles was at it again. It was a little after 7.15 a.m. and Detective Senior Inspector Christopher O'Yee, in the peak of condition and almost at the stage of being able to hold his first cup of Yellowthread Street police station coffee in his hand without trembling with the effort, said in shaky admiration, 'Yep, he's definitely working on his gastrocnemius with side benefits to his planters and biceps femoris.' He looked at Detective Chief Inspector Harry Feiffer working on nothing more spectacular than the monthly crime reports and said in explanation, 'Calves, feet and rear thighs.'

Feiffer said, 'Oh.'

Through the open window of the Detectives' Room, O'Yee could see Mr Muscles' chest rippling through his Tee shirt as he moved on from his gastrocnemius and, flexing his glinting chest expanders, decided to have a quick go at his serratus magnus. O'Yee said, 'You know I've watched that guy. He gets over there about 6.30 and he goes through his exercise routine for about an hour, then he goes down to the ground, waits for the other rivetters to turn up at the time clock and then, when they take the elevator cage, he runs up the stairs.' He shook his head and sipped at his coffee as Mr Muscles stopped for a moment and flexed, 'And then he does twice the work of any two men.' Mr Muscles was a squat Southern Chinese of, to say the least, healthy appearance. O'Yee said, 'What do you think he's up to?'

In the last three years, let alone the last month, the total haul of illegal firearms was two pistols, one rusty revolver, a sawn-off

7

shotgun, a starting pistol and two cap guns converted to fire live ammunition. And no live ammunition. If there was someone running around at night shooting off at least half a dozen rifles and a hundred and twenty three rounds of ammunition at a time then he hadn't found them lying around on the street. Feiffer said without interest, 'I don't know. Maybe he's found an undetectable way to commit suicide.' And according to the phone-in reports of the night, not only had the half dozen guns and hundred and twenty three rounds of ammunition come from nowhere, evidently, they were also being fired from nowhere. Reports of the gunfire ranged from Hop Pei Cove to the west as far north as Singapore Road and then east out to the New Hong Bay Cemetry. Feiffer said wearily, 'If he succeeds let me know and I'll join him.'

'People like this guy don't die, they live to be six hundred and three.' O'Yee looked down into the black glutinous swamp Constable Yan had the gall to call coffee and then to his cigarette in an ashtray by the window. O'Yee said, 'Do you realise that while we're standing around here letting our systems go to hell that guy is up there getting *fit?*' Mr Muscles stepped into his expanders and made a straining motion like a bird pulling a difficult worm out of the ground. O'Yee could almost hear the creak, 'Your body is like a finely tuned watch. You should look after it.'

There was an ordnance map of Hong Kong on Feiffer's desk. He put it on top of the monthly returns and looked at it for a moment. Feiffer said with a groan, 'I even went so far as to ring up the Hong Kong representative of the Chinese People's Army to ask him if there'd been manoeuvres on the border and after he'd got over the shock that I knew his secret number he said he didn't know and gave me the secret number of British Intelligence so I could ask them.'

'... mind you, my grandfather lived to be eighty nine and he used to drink like a goddamned fish and smoke eighty Burmese hand rolled cigarettes a day.' O'Yee looked down at his ashtray and took up the cigarette, 'His theory was that it wasn't good for you to be too fit. You know, like a racehorse. They're always shooting them because they get so delicate.'

Feiffer said, 'Like a finely tuned watch.' He looked at his own and found it had stopped, 'When are Auden and Spencer due back on?'

'At nine.' O'Yee said, 'They've gone out on their own initiative to the cove to have a look around for spent shell cases.' The body-builder, having dealt with the gastrocnemius and biceps femoris had moved on to doing neck exercises, ' Do you think we ought to get up earlier and jog or something?' O'Yee said, 'Mind you, I had a friend in San Francisco who jogged and he got a heart attack and died.' Mr Muscles was building himself up into The Incredible Hulk. O'Yee said, 'I don't cough or anything in the mornings, do you?'

Feiffer put the map down and lit a cigarette.

O'Yee looked at Mr Muscles.

Feiffer said, 'Hmm.' He took up his coffee and tried it again. Once you got used to it it wasn't too bad at all. O'Yee said, 'No, it's all in the blood. My grandfather lived to be eighty nine years old and the only reason he isn't with us still is that he tried to cross a road outside the chest hospital when the brakes weren't working properly on his iron lung.'

The storm had passed over a little before dawn and it was a lovely cool morning and if anyone was ever going to die of anything, today was just not the day.

7.21 a.m. As O'Yee turned away, across the road Mr Muscles began flexing his way down the steel stairs to the ground floor to await the arrival of his less energetic, elevator-riding colleagues.

There was a temporary supply shack near the stairs on the third floor and, with a flourish, Mr Muscles leant his still glittering chest expanders against it as he passed.

Coming from under the door of the wooden shack there was a faint stream of black oily smoke, but Mr Muscles, grunting and groaning, had his fist in his face to exercise his triceps and forearm extensors and totally failed to notice it.

*

9

There was definitely something black, sludgy and infinitely horrible moving along in the dark on the ground behind him. In the bowels of the Hop Pei Cove storm water drainage system, Auden stood up to his gumbooted ankles in slime and God knew what, up to his nostrils in stench, up to his spine in cold shivers, shone the flashlight quickly into the mire behind him and said, 'Yugh, it's moving!'

Spencer said, 'It's only a rat. They're harmless.' He shone his own light down into the slowly swirling water and saw that it wasn't. Either. Spencer said in a gasp, 'God, it's alive!' He flashed the light upwards as something oozing disengaged itself from the roof and fell in a twisting motion onto his boot and then breast-stroked away, 'Ugh! Whatever it was, it was—' He backed up against the wall of the giant drain and at least half a dozen other things went squelch, whistle, plop, scuttle, flurry as they unglued themselves from the material, went flailing down through the fetid air, hit the water and sank and then—snakes alive—got up again and dashed off. Auden said, 'Oh Christ—' He reached down for his Colt Python in its shoulder holster and had a horrible picture of blowing down one of the walls and releasing into the world— Auden said, 'Christ, Bill, I'm beginning to wonder if this is a good idea!' The Senior Inspectors' Examining Board interviews were only a week away. Auden said quickly, 'No, it's a good idea! It shows initiative getting up early and coming in here on our own time and—' The light illuminated something from an alcoholic's nightmare. Auden said, 'God! What in hell's name is that?'

Whatever it was was swimming purposefully in Spencer's direction. The tops of Spencer's gumboots were open where he had tucked his pants into them. The thing's beady eyes battened on them and thought it had found the Ideal Home Exhibition. Spencer drew back his boot and kicked it to the next stand.

The next stand was Auden's boot bungalow. Auden said, 'Ahhggh!' and stomped on it.

It was a great life in the exotic East. Auden said, 'Right, first principles. If the gunfire can't be located because it's travelling all

10

over the Colony then it's clear that it isn't being aimed in any particular direction. Right?'

It was a lizard with wings. Definitely. Spencer stepped back. His flashlight battery dimmed for a moment and he panicked. Spencer said, 'Right, Phil! Right! Right! Whatever you say!'

Auden sidestepped the flying lizard. The lizard galumphed into the water and didn't surface. 'I didn't say it, we both did. We came up with it in concert.' There was plenty of Senior Inspector's gold braid to go around. *Wasn't there?* The lizard still hadn't surfaced. Where the hell was it? Auden said, 'So therefore, the shots weren't aimed at anything. Right?'

'Right!' Spencer peered down into the mire, 'Because they were blanks.' Spencer said tensing, 'Right!'

'Right.' Where was it? What was it doing down there? *Where was it going?* Auden said, 'And since the shots seemed to bounce off the islands and the islands are just a little above sea level, then the shots had to come in a straight line from the shore here to—' It surfaced. Auden saw its head. It had turned from some sort of lizard into some sort of bat. Auden stepped back, 'So they're probably shooting from cover at sea level and since there are buildings everywhere in Hong Kong from any point in a straight line to the harbour they have to be either shooting from a beach—'

Spencer ducked. There was nothing there, but he ducked. 'Right! And we know the Water Police would have seen the flashes if they'd been shooting from a beach, so they're— They're shooting from in here, but they're not aiming outwards, they're just standing in here in the drains shooting blanks along the pipes and the noise is being projected outwards.'

Auden said with feeling, 'They must be mad.'

'And since no one's reported any lights they stand in here at night in the darkness.'

Auden said, 'They must be completely around the fucking twist!'

Spencer said, 'So all we have to do is wander along the three or four miles of interconnected pipes along the beach front until we find some evidence.'

11

Auden said nothing.

Spencer said, 'Even if it takes all day.'

Auden swallowed. In the enthusiasm stakes he was not going to be found lacking by the Examining Board. Auden said between clenched teeth, shining his light onto something bubbling, 'And night.'

Spencer said, 'Right.'

'Right.' From the dark recesses of the far end of the pipe something groaned. Whatever it was, it wasn't human.

There was a silence. Spencer said, 'Mind you, Phil, if they were ejecting their cartridges straight into the ooze then we could be just wasting out time and we'd be better off getting the Sub Aqua Squad in here with metal detectors and underwater—'

It groaned again. It wasn't much. Just something minor. A Minotaur maybe or a Cyclops getting out of bed and reaching for the morning papers, or— Auden, stepping backwards, said, nodding, 'Or firecrackers. I mean, The Fireworks Man could be wrong and they could have been firecrackers and all the burned paper, by now, would have just floated out and—'

Spencer said with a disappointment in his voice, 'In which case we would have seen it at one of the entrances and the case would have been solved.'

The news in the morning's paper obviously didn't suit the Cyclops. There was a retching sound followed by a long drawn out gurgling.

Auden said, 'Exactly so.' He was about to say, 'Lead on.' Senior Inspectors didn't say "Lead on", they led. Auden said to the Examining Board as they gasped at his dedication and sniffed at the stench on his clothes that five hundred years in a non stop Chinese laundry would only faintly begin to remove, 'I'll go first, shall I?'

Squelch, whistle, plop, scuttle, flurry, scuttle, whistle, plop, squelch—ROAR! . . . gurgle.

There was plenty of gold braid to go around.

Auden said, stepping back, 'I know, let's split the difference shall we, and go together?'

Team spirit.

Auden said to the Examining Board, 'I'm all in favour of that.'

How he was going to spot ejected shell cases in opaque muck by dimming flashlight with his eye tightly shut he had no idea, but he thought, as did Spencer, that if he got really lucky, somehow he might manage it.

Something wet brushed against his leg on its way to Spencer's gumboot and Auden opened his eyes to see what it was and wished he hadn't.

*

In the Detectives' Room, Feiffer stubbed out his cigarette in frustration and said, 'Damn it, Christopher, it's impossible. There just aren't that many unlicensed guns in the entire Colony!' He had a copy of the Anti Triad Squad's report for the half year and he held it up and waved it in O'Yee's direction, 'Even the Chinese secret societies haven't got half a dozen guns and a hundred and twenty three rounds of ammunition. And as for brilliant white lights or depth charges or whatever it was that landed near Lew's launch—'

O'Yee said, 'It's kids. It has to be.'

'Kids doing what?'

'Kids being kids.' O'Yee had his second cup of Yan's invigorating coffee. Even if life was short that was no reason to deny yourself its little pleasures. Even if the pleasures made it short that was still no reason. O'Yee said, 'Just kids. The Policeman's Friend. Just put down "Kids" in the report and the crime computer will gobble it up, think about it for a while and then spit it out in the Minor Juvenile Disturbances column.' O'Yee said, 'It's not as if anyone's actually shooting *at* anyone. Just put it down as kids.'

Feiffer looked at his watch. It had started again of its own volition. He hesitated.

O'Yee said, 'Look, Harry, it's been going on for three nights now. It's like lights in the sky. It's just one of those things you can't explain and if you could it'd turn out to be something so bloody stupid that you'd wonder why you bothered about it in the first place.' O'Yee said, 'Put kids.' He asked, 'Can you smell this coffee?'

'Another Constable Yan Special Brew?'

'He's improving. After the first mouthful your stomach doesn't even clench.' O'Yee moved back towards the window and glanced across at the rivetters standing chatting to Mr Muscles. It was a beautiful day. What could possibly happen?

He was getting nowhere. Feiffer said, 'Yeah, why not?' "Kids". He looked down at the map with all the crosses reporting the sound of gunfire in the night. Feiffer said, 'If there was anything else happening we probably wouldn't even bother with this sort of thing, would we?'

O'Yee said, 'No.' He went out to have a word to Yan to get the percolator and his his magic recipe working again. O'Yee said from the door, 'Did I ever tell you about my grandfather? He was eighty nine when he died and he'd be with us still if his kidney machine hadn't caught fire on his way out of his girlfriend's house.'

Feiffer looked down at the map.

O'Yee went to get the coffee.

Across the street, Mr Muscles' colleagues took the elevator and Mr Muscles took the stairs.

*

There was a round area of scorched greyness on the ceiling of the pipe where all the ooze, slime and primeaval swamp seemed to have been cleaned away in a single stroke.

Spencer shone his light up to it and tried to stretch up to get a better view. Auden said, 'What is it?'

'I don't know.' Spencer shone his light along the roof and saw another cleared patch a few feet back in line with the first.

And then another.

The patches, like the footprints of a giant roof walking spider,

14

marched away into the darkness.

Auden sniffed. The faintest smell of something different was there. Something that reminded him of—

Both he and Spencer flashed their lights down into the ooze simultaneously and there, a little beneath the surface, like a single golden eye, something glinted at them.

*

Mr Muscles, grinning, made it to the third floor supply shack first. He flexed, waved to his colleagues in the elevator, reached down for his expanders, and called out abruptly, 'Hey! The shack is on fire! There's smoke coming out!' He looked at his expanders in horror, 'The shack's burning and all my copies of *Asian Bodybuilder* are in there!' The door to the shack was shut.

Mr Muscles called out urgently to the foreman as he stepped out of the elevator and came over, 'Quick, bring the keys! All my stuff is in there!'

On the second floor some of the rivetters had already begun work and the foreman waved to them to compliment them on their industry and, reaching into his back pocket took out his ear protectors to insulate himself against the noise.

Mr Muscles said, 'Hey! Hey! The shack's—' He tried the door but it was solid.

Mr Muscles yelled at the top of his voice, 'Hey! All my bodybuilding stuff is in there!' The smoke was coming out in increasing volume. From inside the shack there was a thump.

Mr Muscles yelled out, 'Hey, there's someone in there with matches or something and he's playing with my equipment!'

There was a hissing sound from under the door and then suddenly, another.

Mr Muscles yelled out at the locked door, 'Hey! *Hey*!!' He yelled, 'Hey! You'll smash all my—' The rivetting was pounding in his head. Mr Muscles yelled, 'Hey! All that gear cost me—' The rivetting was going non-stop. Mr Muscles shrieked in desperation, 'Hey! Stop! *Stop*!'

15

In the briefest of brief pauses in the rivetting, from inside the shack there was a single click and for one glorious, wonderful moment, Mr Muscles thought that whoever was in there had had second thoughts and was going to come out and—

8.11 a.m. At the third floor shack Mr Muscles pounded on the door and yelled, 'Hey! *Hey*—!!'

*

In the drains, Auden turned a corner and said in a gasp, 'My God, the place is full of them!' He had the brass cartridge case from the mud in his hand and as he shone his flashlight into a glittering garden of the things, he dropped it back into the slime and turned his light upwards. The long pipe stretched two hundred yards in a straight line towards Hop Pei Cove and on the ceiling of almost every one of those yards there were the spotless giant spider's footmarks where the muzzle blasts from the guns had scorched away the slime of decades. The cartridge cases were everywhere, in piles, in lines, forming half completed circles and rectangles and, in one or two spots, poking out from the mire like volcanic islands. Auden said, 'My God, Bill, there must be a thousand of them.'

Spencer had one in his hand. He turned it over. The top of the long open necked object was pleated. Spencer said, 'They're blanks. You can see where the neck was turned in by a machine to close it off.' He held it out in his palm for Auden to examine as he bent to pick up another, 'They're all blanks. Every one of them.' He looked up at the marks on the ceiling, 'They must have held the guns at an angle and blasted them off in the direction of the roof.' He got up again and scraped at one of the scorches with a case. A fine rain of burned cordite came down. The scorch marks, as far as he could make out, all seemed to be the same size, 'They must have walked backwards and forwards with their rifles aimed up at the ceiling just banging away until—'

Auden said, 'Until what? Until they ran out of amunition? And then left?' Auden weighed a dozen of the cases in his hand, 'There must be a small fortune in brass in here and they just left it?' He dug around in a mound. Every one of the cases was a blank. Auden said, 'These are definitely rifle cases. I can't make out the headstamp, but they were definitely fired by a rifle.' He heard Spencer say, 'One ... two ... three...' and he glanced back to see him picking up cases and examining them in the light, 'What are you doing?'

Spencer said, 'Four ... five ... the same again ... six ... seven...'

He was examining the different firing pin and extractor marks on the cases. Auden said, 'How many guns do you think there were?'

Spencer's voice had gone quiet. He was still counting. Spencer said, 'Ten, eleven...'

'But they're all bloody blanks! What the hell for?' Auden said, 'Kids. It's got to be kids. Who else would—'

Spencer picked up another few cases from the mound and looked at them. He found something else among them and he brushed the mud from it carefully with his finger. Spencer said softly, 'Phil—' He held the object out for inspection and looked up at the muzzle blasts on the ceiling.

Barring one, there was no conceivable reason on Earth why anyone would spend his nights in a storm water drain firing blank cartridges up at the ceiling and leaving the empty, valuable cases where they lay.

That one reason was that he was practising for something and that as well as having an unlimited supply of blank practice rounds for the purpose, somewhere, ready for the proper occasion when he was good enough, he also had an unlimited supply of—

Auden said in a gasp, 'Oh my God—!' He took the object from Spencer's hand and peered at it in the light to make sure there was no mistake.

There was no mistake.

Spencer reached down into the mud and brought up a handful of cases.

They were all live, not crimped, but loaded with long pointed

17

bullets.

There was a slapping sound as something crawling along the roof decided to let go its slimy hold and fall directly into Auden's gumboot, but in the interval between letting go and landing Auden and Spencer were gone, running through the slime into the open air for a telephone, and the creature, falling onto a mound of cases, dislodged them and was buried under their weight.

*

The foreman had gone. The elevator was going all the way down to the ground and in the rivetting he could not hear Mr Muscles' shouts. Mr Muscles heard a clicking sound in the shack in a pause in the rivetting and he put his ear hard against the woodwork and heard another and then another. The smoke smelled of burning rubber and the door was solid and immovable.

There was a window on the other side of the shack, but it was on the side facing the street and he could not get to it.

Mr Muscles tried to look through a crack in the wood, but he could see nothing.

The smoke was increasing as if something inside the shack was burning through. Mr Muscles got down on his haunches and tried to look under the door jamb.

The smoke was thick and rubbery and he got up again and put both his mighty paws on the door itself and began straining. Mr Muscles said over and over, 'You bastards ... you bastards ... I'll show you what a strong man is ...'

He heard a click and then a sort of snapping sound as something inside the shack gave way. Mr Muscles said between sobs, 'Oh, no, please, please, don't—' and at that moment the rivetting stopped and from inside the shack there was another, louder snap and a click and as the window facing the street was blown out in a shower of disintegrating spinning glass—in one and a half second measured volleys—the shooting started.

*

18

On the phone, Auden yelled above the noise, 'Live rounds, thousands of them!' He shook his head to clear the noise and thought it was the sound of the rivetting being carried to the Station by the wind, 'Guns! They've got at least ten or eleven of them and they—'

O'Yee's voice shouted back, 'Do fucking tell!' The bullets were flying in the window and ripping into the masonry behind him. He saw Feiffer on the floor reaching for his revolver and he got down as a bullet smashed into the desk above his head and sent a shower of flying splinters into a filing cabinet and scarred it from top to bottom. He heard Auden shouting, 'What? What are you saying? I can't—' and O'Yee screamed into the phone, 'We're taking fire!' The last remaining shards of glass in the window jamb went and showered the room with shrapnel. O'Yee yelled, 'We're under—' He looked and the phone was flying outwards and upwards and disintegrating into bits of coloured airborne plastic. O'Yee fell backwards with the receiver still in his hand. He saw Feiffer look up and he went towards him yelling, 'Harry, keep down!' as Feiffer ducked a bullet that gouged out a corner of the desk and span it across the room.

The firing was non stop. Feiffer shouted above the sound, 'It's coming from the building across the road! I can see the muscle builder! It's coming from the supply shack on the third floor!' There was a series of heavy thumps as the shooters raised their elevation and ripped bricks out of the outside wall above the Station window, 'I'm going to try to get to—' He saw O'Yee staring at him with the telephone receiver still in his hand, 'Get on to the Emergency Unit and get some counter-sniper gear up here!'

The firing lowered again and blew the entire window jamb out spinning into the room. In the street Feiffer could hear the screaming as people ran to escape. Feiffer yelled, 'Use the bloody telephone, man! What the hell do you think it's for?'

It was for scrap. O'Yee held the shattered instrument up and then brought it down again as someone took it for a moving target and missed it by a millimetre.

19

O'Yee saw Constable Yan standing at the door of the Detectives' Room looking down stupidly at the remains of the coffee percolator in his hand. O'Yee said, 'Yan—!' as a hand from behind swept the smashed percolator onto the floor, span Yan around and shoved an Armalite rifle into his arms. It was Constable Sun. Sun yelled at Feiffer and O'Yee, 'You stay here! We've got a clear exit out through the charge room onto the street!' and then as if by magic another Armalite appeared and he slid it hard and fast across the floor into Feiffer's grasp.

Feiffer yelled, 'It's the supply shack on the building across the street!' and Sun yelled back something in acknowledgement and shoved Yan hard in the middle of the back to get him moving.

At the shack Mr Muscles shrieked, 'What are you doing to my gear?! What are you bastards doing to my *equipment*?!' His great muscles were shaking with the effort on the door and he got his shoulder against it and roared with the exertion as he applied every ounce of his strength to get it open. The shooting was roaring and echoing in the street. He saw people running.

The door to the supply shack flew open. Mr Muscles said, 'Oh, no—!'

He looked down to the street and saw two uniformed cops scurrying out of the Station with rifles in their hands. Mr Muscles said, 'Oh, NO!' and in that instant all the noise stopped and there was only a gentle click, click, click sound coming from inside the shack.

He saw the cops looking up at him with their rifles raised and Mr Muscles, his hands all empty and gentle, held out his arms like a Buddhist priest about to give a blessing and said with a curious look on his face, 'No, it's—' It was all too much to understand. Mr Muscles half turned his body slowly and pointed into the interior of the shack.

Mr Muscles said...

There was a single click and then the faintest of popping sounds and Mr Muscles said in a sad, lost voice, all his work over so many years all gone for nothing, 'No, it's just not fair...' and then, in one single roaring, flaming, vapourising explosion, he, the shack, and everything around it for a distance of thrity feet was gone forever.

*

8.21 a.m.

Out of a clear blue sky.

In the charge room of the Station a telephone began ringing insistently, then, after a little while, stopped as the caller decided perhaps he would try again later.

2

On the third floor of the half completed building, the Government
Medical Officer, Doctor Macarthur, took an elbow from his
collected exhibits on the laid out door of the shattered supply
shack and asked the foreman evenly, 'Is this him?' The elbow had
half the forearm attached, the forearm flexor muscle standing out
on it like whipcord.

Feiffer had his hand on the foreman's arm, steadying him. The
foreman said, 'Yes.'

'And this?' Macarthur lifted up part of a shoulder, 'You can see
the development of the deltoid—'

The foreman nodded. 'Yes.'

Feiffer said quietly in Cantonese, 'Take it easy.'

The foreman nodded. He had a cone shaped roll-your-own
cigarette in his left hand and he pursed his lips and looked down at
it and thought that if he put it anywhere near his mouth he would
throw up. Doctor Macarthur moved back a little of the burned
and ragged skin around the muscle with a probe, 'The level of
development suggests—'

The works foreman said, 'Yes. He was a bodybuilder. He was
going to enter the Mr Asia contest in Macao in the—' He closed
his eyes and Macarthur withdrew the probe and the skin flopped
back like a piece of wet canvas. The foreman, nodding, looked at
his cigarette. It had gone out. The foreman said again, 'Yes, that
was him.'

The door had mounds of human tissue and bone laid out on it
like a giant jigsaw puzzle. The awful stuff covered every inch of it
and spilled over onto a section of planked flooring. The foreman
said with an effort, 'I'm trying to be helpful, but I don't know any

22

of the others.' He turned to Feiffer and saw the man smile at him encouragingly, 'If you had a face or two—'

Feiffer shook his head.

Macarthur selected something else. It was part of a lung.

The foreman said quickly, 'I don't know.'

'The development is good.'

'I don't know.' The foreman said again, 'I'm, I'm trying to be helpful, but I—I really didn't know him that well. I—' He put his hand to his face, 'I—I couldn't recognise his lung.' He looked at Feiffer, 'Could I?'

'No. It's all right. That can all be done at the Mortuary.'

'I won't have to—' The foreman said, 'His name was Shuk. He was a good worker. He wasn't a special friend of mine or anything, but he worked hard and he was—' Down in the street, Inspector Sands of Ballistics was using a portable jack hammer to break bricks out of the Station wall in order to collect spent bullets. The foreman said, 'I've checked and all my workers are accounted for.' He went to indicate the human debris on the door and found himself pointing at what looked like a severed penis, 'I just don't know who all these other—who these other people *are!*'

Feiffer said, 'And the supply shack door was locked?'

'Yes! No! It was just a shack for keeping things in and for people to cook themselves up a meal or—' The foreman said, 'It must have been jammed or—' His hand indicated a human leg, 'Or one of the people inside must have held it closed.' He saw Auden and Spencer pick up something from a truss section on the floor that looked like a length of sausages. They were human intestines. The foreman said, 'All I heard was him yelling something at me and then the shooting started.' He became aware of an awful smell coming from the remains, growing in intensity like bad meat. 'He got the door open and then he saw your policemen in the street and he held up his hands to show he wasn't one of them and then—' The foreman said, 'I've seen a few industrial accidents in my time, but—but in those they always had the faces left.' He got the dead cigarette up to his mouth in a trembling hand and drew in on the extinct tobacco, 'I've never seen people blown up before.'

23

He looked away down into the street, 'I heard one of the cops say he thought it was kids. Was it?'

'We don't know.'

The foreman said, 'I've got children of my own.' He shook his head, 'They just went mad and started shooting with guns and then—and then they accidently blew themselves up? Or what?' Spencer came over and put the plastic bag containing the intestines on the plank near the door. He had something else in his other hand. It was a shoe. The foreman said quietly, 'I don't know!'

Feiffer asked, 'Is that the only one?' and Spencer nodded and went back to where Auden was looking at something between two girders. The foreman said again to the shoe, 'I don't know!'

Macarthur selected a section of white cranium and turned it over in his hand. The scalp still had a few tufts of black hair adhering to it. Feiffer said quietly before he could show it to the foreman, 'All Chinese have black hair,' and Macarthur, pausing for a second, said, 'Oh, yeah,' put it down and reached in under the mass and brought out a hand.

The hand still had a digital watch strapped to its wrist. The watch was still going, flashing its little seconds light like a pulse. The foreman said, 'I don't know! I just don't know! Is it one of the kids'?' He looked at the giant wrist, 'It's his, isn't it? And the pieces of skull, they're his too. Aren't they?'

'Yes.' Feiffer indicated part of a leg. 'And that?'

The muscles were like whipcord. The foreman said, 'Yes!'

'And that?' Part of a back, with the latissimus dorsi like a great—

The foreman said, 'Yes!' His body was shaking from one end to the other. He felt his mouth tighten, 'And that—' He nodded at another section of chest, 'And that's him too!' The remains covered the entire door. There was enough there for twenty humans. The foreman looked at the dozen sections of cranium laid out like a half done jigsaw puzzle at the top of the door, 'And that, that's him too! And that! And that! The foreman said with his breath coming in short, sharp gusts, 'It's all him, isn't it! All of it?

All this—this is all just one person, isn't it? There isn't anyone else. This is all that's left of just one person, *isn't it?*'

Feiffer said softly, 'Yes, we think so.'

The foreman saw Spencer lean down to get something adhering to a girder. When it came up in his hand it was the colour of vinegar. The foreman yelled to him, 'Yes! Yes! That's him too! What the hell's that? His heart or his liver or his—' His hands were shaking uncontrollably. The foreman yelled, 'It's all him! There isn't anyone else here! It's all just—*him!*'

Macarthur said, shaking his head, 'There isn't anything else.' He looked up at Feiffer, 'That's all. Leaving aside the face and part of the stomach we've got everything.'

The foreman's eyes were full of tears. The foreman said on the edge of hysteria, 'He doesn't need his face. What does he need his face for? He's dead. He's just butcher's stall offal. He doesn't need a face. Only people need a face and he isn't a person anymore, is he? He's just—' The foreman said desperately, 'What am I going to do? I've got a wife and children and I can't tell them I stood here doing this!' By the smashed cranium there was a mound of grey jelly. Brains. The foreman, gagging, said, 'Oh, no!'

Feiffer turned the foreman around to face him, 'You're sure you didn't see anyone else around the shack either before or after the shooting started? Anything? A shadow? Anything at all?'

'The door was shut! He couldn't get in! If anyone had come out he would have seen them!' The foreman said, 'I know it's true, but I just can't believe it.' He put his hand to his forehead and tried to form words, 'I know there's only one man there on the door because you've told me, but I—it looks like so many—' He put his hand to his own stomach, 'All that, inside—all that—' Auden and Spencer stopped for a moment at a girder and exchanged a few words. The foreman saw them shaking their heads. The awful thing in the plastic bag was bouncing a little against Auden's leg. The foreman said, 'But if there was no one inside the shack and when the explosion came the only person who was—was hurt— was—was—him, and this is what it did to him—'

Macarthur said quietly to Feiffer, 'It looks like you've got a

25

sniper on your hands who knows how to set up remote controlled gunfire. Maybe two or three.'

'Yeah.' The thought had occurred to both Auden and Spencer. Feiffer saw them pause to look upwards to the other floors and then unbutton their coats to have quick access to their revolvers. Feiffer said, 'Yes, it definitely looks that way, doesn't it?'

The foreman's eyes were staring at the pile of remains on the door. Trying to comprehend it, he shook his head. The foreman said, 'What can I tell my family?' The smell was rising, clogging his nostrils. The foreman looked down again at his cigarette, but it was out. The foreman said quietly to Macarthur, 'Sir, if this is just one man—all this—'

Macarthur said, 'Yes?'

The words cascaded into the foreman's mind like a torrent and then tumbled over and over. Everything he had ever been told or thought he knew or had seen on television or at the movies or read about, it was all—

The foreman said in a shriek, *'My God, what must a war be like?'*

He was about to find out. Far across the girdered and planked third floor on the east corner of the building there was another, identical supply shack with its window facing directly at him.

There was the faintest of snapping sounds and then something inside the shack began hissing softly.

There was another snapping sound and then another, and, too far away on the floor to be heard, the hissing increased serially and urgently in volume.

It was 12.06 p.m. and the sounds were, as they had been planned to be, dead on time.

*

They fazed him. By the shattered hole in the wall that had once been one of the Detectives' Room windows Inspector Sands of Ballistics turned his collection of shell cases, cartridges and spent bullets over in his hand and shook his head. He rattled the objects together in his hand and pursed his lips.

They fazed him.

He looked again and went through the objects in a logical order: six undistorted fired bullets from the Station wall, all in good condition, jacketed and with firm deep striations from the lands and grooves of the barrels that had fired them, (he separated one of the bullets and felt its weight—about 125 grains), four empty blank shell cases from the drains, (he took one up and flicked at the spread open crimp with his thumbnail), and finally, two live, bulleted rounds also from the drains, bullet weight about one hundred and twenty five grains, in perfect condition, commercially made, and without the slightest trace of identification anywhere on or about its entire length.

Sands looked at the silver primer at the base of one of the live cartridges.

It was an axiom that every commercially made cartridge had its calibre, nomenclature or at least date of manufacture on its base.

He shook his head.

These had none.

There was a blue band painted at the base of each of the blank rounds, but what it represented, Sands had no idea.

He thought he knew just about every round for every gun that the mind of man had ever thought of, but he had never seen one like this. He had a pocket micrometer in the top pocket of his coveralls and he took it out and measured the bullet.

About seven millimetres.

Maybe it was a wildcat round loaded by some enthusiastic home gunsmith. If that was the case the enthusiastic home gunsmith would have had to have used a standard cartridge case and neck it down and the standard cartridge case would have had markings on it.

He looked at one of the fired blanks. The star crimp at the neck that had been forced open by the charge of powder was black and scorched with the blast—the bang when it came must have been of tremendous power.

Why? For a blank round?

Sands looked up at the half completed building across the street

27

and watched absently as Auden and Spencer stopped by a girder to talk. Sands' mind was far away, flipping through cartridge manuals, getting nowhere.

If only he had got to see one of the rifles before the explosion in the supply shack had turned them into dust. Sands said to himself, 'Fuck it, what are they?' He looked again at the blue bands on the base of the blanks, 'What the hell are they *for?*'

Nobody made cartridge cases that looked like this anymore. Even the design: the straight sided cylinder neck narrowing gracefully to the bullet was inefficient. Everybody knew these days that the best design for a rifle case was straight sided and—

Sands said suddenly, 'These days!' He looked up at the building, 'These days!' He saw O'Yee coming out of the Station with a pair of binoculars to scan the third floor and Sands said louder than he had intended, 'These days, Christopher! *These days!*'

The blue band around the base of the blank. . . .

Sands said, 'These days . . . these . . .'

A single blue band around the base of an unmarked cartridge . . . His mind went flick, flick, flick through a thousand pages of technical manuals in an instant.

He found the right page. He found the right reference, the illustration. He found . . .

Sands said jubilantly, *'Right!'*

The full implications of his discovery struck him and he said in a gasp, 'God Almighty, it isn't possible . . .'

O'Yee was scanning the building with binoculars, one hand a little inside his coat where his shoulder holster hung, and before he put down the glasses and saw him standing there, Sands slipped the cases and the bullets into a plastic evidence bag and, determined to say nothing until he was absolutely sure, stuffed the bag into his pocket along with his micrometer and went back to examine the walls minutely for more bullets.

*

28

In all the western movies, they always said something like, 'Quiet? Yeah, it is. Too quiet.'

It was. There was something strange and a little uncompleted about it, something—

By the main door of the Station, O'Yee scanned the ground floor of the half completed building with his binoculars and then moved to the elevator. It was up, on the third floor: he could see the cables hanging down below the cage, slack and waiting.

Auden and Spencer were in the centre of the floor, poking at something with a steel rod. They came up empty. He saw Spencer shake his head and look around for somewhere else to search. There was no wind: the air was still and silent. A faint pall of smoke hung over some of the girders and billowed lazily from the west to the east corner of the building.

The crowd behind the cordon was beginning to break up and from behind him, O'Yee heard Sands chipping away at the bricks, not with his pneumatic drill, but with a little hand held bit head.

On the third floor, the foreman had evidently fallen silent. He was looking down at his shoes, hanging his head, quiet and thoughtful, and Feiffer a little way from him, was writing in his notebook and alternately nodding to Macarthur.

From where he stood O'Yee could hear no voices and he had the feeling that, somehow, up there, now, there were no voices to be heard.

'Yep, pard, jest too quiet.' Outside the town, in the cut away shot, he could feel the distant rumbling under his feet as the cattle milled and grunted as the prelude to a stampede.

He was being stupid.

Nerves.

He put down the glasses and turned to go back into the Station and stopped at the front door.

The front door was full of ragged bullet holes and there were long strips of wood hanging down, about to give way at the slightest touch.

Something... He had seen the building every day for the last month in one stage or another of its construction and there was

29

something just not right about it.

He turned back and looked up to where the supply shack had been.

That wasn't it. It was something else.

All the workmen had gone. Each of the other floors below the third was empty and skeletonised, like a deserted ship's engine room.

But there was something.

Something...

He heard Sands curse softly to himself as a sliver of brick cut his hand and O'Yee shook his head and said softly to himself, 'No, you're being stupid.'

The next thing would be astrology.

He said aloud, 'No, there's something wrong. I can feel it.'

But what?

He turned again and glanced at Sands to see if he was watching him making a fool of himself.

It had been kids. Kids with guns had gone mad and blown themselves up and killed someone and that was—

O'Yee raised the binoculars and scanned the second floor.

Nothing.

Something.

He scanned the third again and saw the tableaux of Auden and Spencer in their little knot and then Macarthur, Feiffer and the foreman in theirs.

He could almost smell it. It was...

O'Yee yelled suddenly, 'Smoke!' He saw Sands spin to see him, 'Smoke!' O'Yee shouted, 'There's another supply shack up there and it's in a direct line and it's smoking!' He saw something at the window of the shack flash and then shatter and then—he saw Auden and Spencer look up, in direct line. O'Yee yelled, 'Smoke! It's smoking! It's happening again! The first one was a come-on bomb!' He saw Sands running towards his Ballistics truck to get a weapon and O'Yee reached back into the Station behind him, got an Armalite from just inside the door and pulled back on the cocking handle in a single motion, 'There are more of them in the

second shack and they're—'

He heard the first shot roar out over the third floor. He saw—

It was happening in slow motion.

He saw the flash, the smoke, the muzzle blast as the window disintegrated fully in a single blast of light and motion. He saw Spencer look up and then to one side. He heard him say—

He saw Auden look down at his chest. He saw—

The shooting began in a single uninterrupted burst as the machine gun inside the shack began working.

He saw Spencer say—

He saw Auden fall.

He saw him die. He saw—

O'Yee and Sands had their Armalites up simultaneously.

He saw bits flying off the shack as the bullets went in.

*

Spencer yelled, 'It was a blank! He wasn't hit! It was a blank!' Feiffer saw him on the floor reaching for Auden and drawing his revolver with his other hand as the bullets ripped over his head and ricochetted off girders in a shower of sparks. Macarthur was standing over the door with his mouth open and Feiffer yelled at him, 'It's happening again!' and wrenched the man to the ground. He looked around for the foreman and saw him a little ahead behind a pile of girders, keeping his head down. It was a medium machine gun: the bullets came out in an uninterrupted stream and sparked off the girders like bombs.

Auden was on his back, rolling around trying to unlimber the barrel of his giant gun from its holster. His shirt was still white. There was no blood on it. Spencer yelled out as Feiffer got up into a crouch and then ducked again as the fire seemed to swivel back to him, 'It was a blank! It blew the window out! The first round was a blank!' He was shouting something else, but the firing drowned him out.

The sound was shattering. Bits and pieces were flying off the roof of the shack as the fire came up from the ground. Through a

31

hole in the planking Feiffer saw O'Yee and Sands standing side by side in the middle of the street spraying automatic fire up from their Armalites. The clip came out of Sands' gun as he fired the last burst in the magazine and he had another one in and was firing back before Feiffer even saw him cock the bolt.

People were scattering in the street. Feiffer heard shouting and then a car horn blow. There was someone on a bullhorn warning people in Chinese to get out or get down—Yan, or Constable Sun—and then there was a fusilade of poppings as they got their revolvers up and shot rapid fire into the shack.

It was a machine. They had found only one body. It was some sort of machinery. Auden had his big gun out and was banging at the shack and shaking with the recoil. Feiffer saw one of the big bullets strike the corner of the shack and rip an entire plank out with the concussion. The firing was going on in an unceasing burst. Spencer had his gun out, trying to get a bead on the window as he rolled to avoid the bullets.

Feiffer shouted, 'There's no one in there! It's a set-up! There's no one in there!' as a stream of bullets from the shack passed over his head and whined off metal into the air.

The foreman got his head up and looked back. A shower of sparks hit him in the face and he got down again, shaking his head and yelling something.

Feiffer yelled, 'Don't fire! It's a set-up! There's no one in there!' The shooting from the street had assumed war battle proportions. There must have been at least half a dozen Armalites and revolvers all firing at once. Feiffer yelled above the din, 'Don't shoot! We want what's in there before it—' and then a line of bullets ripped up a plank by his hand and traversed without pause in the direction of Macarthur and the door.

Macarthur shouted, '*Jesus!*' and got himself down with his hands over his ears. A bullet struck his long silver probe on the planks and propelled it like a lance into the air.

Feiffer yelled, 'Stop firing! We have to—' The machine gun stream seemed to move away. The gun inside was evidently jumping wildly and spraying in alternate directions. He got up and crouched to run. He saw the foreman shouting at him, but there were no words.

The firing from the street was continuous.

The foreman yelled, 'No! No one else! No one else!' and rolled to one side as a stray bullet from the street ripped through the plank he was lying on and made it jump.

The machine gun had stopped. There was only the firing from the street. Feiffer got up and yelled down, 'No! Cease fire! There's no one in there! *Cease fire!*'

The shooting stopped. The foreman was on his hands and knees saying over and over in Cantonese, 'No ... no ... What can I tell my family? No ... no ...' He saw Feiffer getting into a crouch to run past him for the shack. The foreman said, 'No! No! Not twice!'

There was smoke coming from the shack. The foreman saw Feiffer coming towards him and stood in his way like a blocking forward. The foreman said—

'*Get out of the way!*'

'No!' The foreman screamed, 'No! Not twice! *No!*'

The shack was smoking heavily. A black oil spume was flowing out of the smashed window and through the holes in the wood.

The foreman yelled to Auden and Spencer, 'Get down! Get down!' He saw Feiffer almost on top of him with his gun drawn and he reached out and caught the man by the shoulder and dragged him down. The foreman yelled, 'No! I'm not going to let it happen twice!'

The smoke from the shack became a cloud. Feiffer wrenched at the man's grasp and ordered him—

Auden and Spencer were on the ground.

Auden said, 'Christ, it was a—I thought I'd been—'

The foreman, holding Feiffer in a grip of steel, was shaking with purpose. The foreman said between clenched teeth in a supplication to the gods, 'No ... no ... I need to have something good to tell my—'

The explosion from the shack came in a single overwhelming roar and scythed down every single stick in its construction to the ground.

33

The foreman, totally deafened for the instant, said, 'I just—' No sounds came out. He saw Feiffer's face an inch from his own. He was shaking his head and saying something over and over. Whatever it was it was in English and the foreman could not make it out from the movement of his lips.

Feiffer said in English, his eyes looked as if they still had not quite comprehended, 'Thank you. Thank you ... very much.' He was gasping for air.

'All right.' The foreman, still deafened, failed to hear his own voice. The foreman, looking at what lay on the door behind him, said louder in case no words were coming out, 'All right.' The foreman's eyes were filling with tears.

At last, he had something to tell his family.

The foreman, patting Feiffer on the shoulder over and over and staring back at what was left of Mr Muscles on the door, said over and over with the tears streaming down his face, 'All right. All right. *All right!*'

*

In the street, O'Yee said in the sudden stillness, 'Christ. Holy mother of—Christ Almighty!' A phone rang in the charge room of the open Station and he went in, rubbing his forehead and put the Armalite by the charge desk, and took up the receiver.

There was a pause and then a giggle and then a voice said something barely audible in Cantonese.

O'Yee said, 'What?'

The voice said again, slower, 'I have a divine mission to eradicate all the uniformed forces of colonial repression in the world and I have now made a beginning.'

The hot weather brought them out like beetles.

O'Yee heard giggling in the background.

O'Yee said, 'What?' A heavy black pall of smoke was drifting in through the Station door.

Out of a clear blue sky...

Far away in the mountains, O'Yee could still hear the echoes of the gunfire rolling and echoing like thunder.

He was trembling.

O'Yee yelled, 'You stupid, time-wasting—*fucker!*'

12.47 p.m.

He slammed down the phone and went back outside.

3

There was a ragged coolie wandering about on the roof of the Hong Bay fishmarkets looking for somewhere to put down the load of bamboo scaffolding he carried and have an afternoon sleep. At 2.06 p.m. the sun was over Hanford Road on its way towards Wharf Cove in the west and the coolie shaded his eyes and looked up at it. He wore an enveloping cotton labourer's veil over his head and shoulders and he put his hand inside the veil and rubbed at the back of his neck where the bamboo lay. The roof of the deserted fishmarkets was flat and covered in seagull droppings and the bones of long dead fish and the coolie looked down to place his sandles carefully to skirt them.

The load looked heavy. He rotated his shoulders and shifted the weight a little as he walked. The bamboo poles were tied together in a bundle with rattan and the coolie rotated his shoulders again and shifted the biting knots on his collarbone.

He walked to the edge of the roof and looked down two storeys into Cuttlefish Lane. The street was full of traffic and people going about their business and he felt alone and above them. He could smell the sea and the suds the filleters used in the markets to wash down their boning boards, and the disinfectant the floor cleaners had used to hose down the floors and steel tables before work ceased punctually with the last basket at noon.

Across Cuttlefish Lane, a parking warden was clearing a waiting driver out of the driveway to an ambulance sub-station, not being obnoxious about it, but from the gestures he made to the driver, firm. The parking warden waved his hands: he was not going to give the driver a ticket this time, but NO PARKING AT ANY TIME also meant NO STANDING and the traffic warden

36

pointed to his watch and indicated that it also meant 'No hanging around talking to Traffic Wardens hoping your passenger will come back before you have to move on'.

The traffic warden put his fingers to his forehead and then waved whatever the driver said to him away. There wasn't one he hadn't heard twice already ranging from 'My little girl had to find a toilet and she'll be frightened if I'm not here when she comes back' to the standard 'I had a blackout and I thought I'd stop for a while because I was becoming a danger to my fellow drivers' to the highly exotic, 'Someone slipped me curare and the only thing I can move until it wears off is my mouth.' The traffic warden, seen from the roof mimed, 'No,' and made a few well meant remarks concerning the driver's responsibility to his fellow parents, black-outers and curare victims to ensure that they could be reached by ambulance in other NO PARKING spots.

The coolie looked at the doors to the ambulance sub-station. They were closed and there was no sign of an ambulance through the glass windows. He listened. No sirens. The coolie unlimbered his bamboo and squatted down with the veil still hanging over his face. He touched his fingers to his lips and watched as the car pulled out of the driveway watched by the traffic warden and the traffic warden drew a deep breath, congratulated himself on his maturity in not losing his temper, and looked down the street for more evil-doers.

The coolie undid the rattan around one end of the bamboo sheaf and looked again at the sun. It was directly behind him. The coolie put his hand under his veil to his neck again and felt the warmth coming through the cotton material onto his fingers.

The coolie's left eye was blinking a little. He put his hand onto the lid and wiped away perspiration and the tic stopped.

He heard a siren a long way off. Traffic was flowing freely up Cuttlefish Lane and spilling out onto the two way lanes in Canton Street going either in the direction of Yellowthread Street, or, to the south, down to Beach Road and the shoreline.

The coolie sat back on his heels and reached down to the bamboo.

He pulled out a long, well polished rifle and held it below the level of the cement railing that served as a rain run off for the roof. He looked behind him. The roof was flat and deserted.

He took out something resembling a squat metal cup from inside the bamboo and affixed it quickly and efficiently to the rifle with a wing nut.

He took out a piece of chalk from his trousers pocket and still squatting, his eyes flickering back and forth from the roof to the traffic warden and the ambulance station, wrote in a series of grass characters *Divine mission to eradicate all the uniformed forces of colonial repression.*

It interested him not at all. He had promised to write the words and he had.

He looked down at the characters with a faint derisory sneer and, putting the chalk back into his pocket, reached inside the bamboo sheaf and took out a single black cannister that fitted exactly into the cup on the muzzle of the rifle.

The knuckles on his left hand began to tingle and he put the rifle and the loaded grenade down onto the roof and leaning forward a little, rubbed at the knuckles with the palm of his other hand until the tingling stopped.

It was 2.07 p.m. on a beautiful, warm, balmy day. Inside the sheaf of bamboo poles there was one more object and the coolie took it out reverently and, like a priest kissing a holy item before dispensing a blessing, put his lips to it and closed his eyes.

It was a brown, cotton cap, heavily sweat-stained with a single star on it as its insignia.

The coolie drew a calming breath.

Just one, single inch...

Lying down full length behind the cement railing, listening to the far off siren, a blue banded blank cartridge on top of the others in the magazine of his rifle, he chambered it, and settled down to wait.

*

38

It was impossible. *All of them? All of them* had been... At a reloading bench in the shuttered Police Armoury at Headquarters, Inspector Sands read the words again in the reference book spread out open in front of him and said aloud, 'All of them? Every last one?'

It was impossible.

It was true.

It was in front of him on the page in black and white, complete with photographs and drawings. Sands said, 'All of them? Every one?'

Sands shook his head.

It was impossible.

He looked at the pile of cases from the drain and the bullets from the walls of the Station and picked them up one by one and measured them with his pocket micrometer.

He looked down at the figures and dimensions laid out in the technical manual in front of him.

'*Hong Kong Shipment.*

These weapons, all of which were...'

The words swam in front of his eyes.

Sands said aloud in the empty room, 'Jesus *Christ*! All of them?'

It defied comprehension.

Sands said, 'Jesus Christ in Heaven!'

He reached for the phone and began dialling the number for Yellowthread Street as rapidly as his trembling finger could find the numbers.

*

In Cuttlefish Lane the ambulance driver turned off his siren and flicked his indicator lever to signal a left turn into the double doors of the sub-station. A little known fact was that, by and large, the only time ambulances used their sirens was when they wanted to get back to the station for lunch or out of the station to do a last call before going home. The ambulanceman smiled to himself and, as he saw the driveway approaching, turned off his flashing lights as well.

He was doing O.K. It had been visiting day in the bronchial ward and he had scored two cartons of cigarettes from the visitors' gifts confiscated by appalled elderly Sisters and Matrons, one bottle of brandy from the fruit basket in the alcoholic ward, and since it was Monday, his usual tame undertaker's retainer of fifty Hong Kong dollars to continue telling him the names and addresses of DOAs before the opposition found out.

The ambulanceman had a long standing arrangement with the parking warden to keep the driveway clear and he saw the man doing his duty for him and slid one of the cartons of cigarettes and the bottle of brandy under his seat so the usual daily pay-off would stay at reasonable proportions.

It was definitely the ambulance driver's winning day.

He felt like a game of Chinese chess. He thought he might ask the traffic warden in for a while.

He reached the driveway, pressed a button on the dashboard of his ambulance and the big double doors opened automatically to let him in. He saw the traffic warden turn in his direction and start walking towards him.

The ambulance driver waved, drove in with the doors still open, and getting out and walking around to the back of his vehicle, opened the back door wide to let the smell of his last passenger out.

The ambulance driver had the carton of cigarettes in his hand. He broke open the seal, ripped the foil from the first pack with his thumbnail, and taking out a gold cigarette lighter, lit a relaxing smoke and began walking towards the warden to discuss chess and corruption.

On the roof of the fishmarkets the coolie took his veil off and put it in his pocket.

He blinked.

Just one, single inch . . .

His hand touched the stock of the rifle.

*

On the phone in the Detectives' Room, Feiffer said incredulously to Sands, 'What do you mean, "all of them"? How many are there?'

He saw O'Yee look over.

Feiffer said in disbelief, '*How many*?! It's a *what?*'

He said softly into the phone, the smashed and still smoking building across the street visible in the hole in the wall where one of the Detectives' Room windows had been, '*Oh, my God!*'

*

It was happening. At last it was happening. It was happening. He saw it. He felt it. He knew it. It was in every part of his body, tingling, shivering, building up, roaring, *increasing*... The coolie said, 'Yes!' He felt the trigger break and then the concussion, the thump as the stock of the gun hit hard in recoil against his shoulder. He saw the flash, the smoke, the black apple-like object go sailing free and fast in a parabola down into the open back of the ambulance. He saw it disappear into the blackness. He saw the faint light coming through the windows of the ambulance— the ambulanceman half way along the street with the traffic warden turn and mouth something in surprise—he saw the objects in the back of the ambulance: cylinders, a stretcher, some sort of white box, something made of stainless steel, something...

The coolie, frozen in time, began shaking. He felt the rifle come snaking back towards him and his own hand touch at the wing nut on the barrel and start to twist it free. He felt the metal cup come off...

It was happening easily. It was happening the way he had always—it was happening...

All the right things.

All the right things.

Everything was...

Just one inch ... just one...

He saw the smoke. He saw...

41

Just one inch...

The cup was off the barrel. He was putting it into the bamboo sheaf. Seconds. Seconds were ticking away.

It was all, all happening just the way...

The seconds were all used up. He saw the ambulanceman start to...

Moments, fractions, milliseconds...

*

In the Detectives' Room, O'Yee said in a gasp, 'Christ Almighty! What was that?'

*

It was gone. The ambulance sub-station was gone in a great gout of roaring, burning stark white flame that knocked people down in the street and smashed plate glass windows from one end of Cuttlefish Lane to the other.

Just one inch, just one inch, just one inch... The coolie was on his feet with the rifle in his hands. He felt the blast come racing up at him and he stood hard in it ferociously as it tore at him and tried to knock him down. It was a giant wind. He stood firm in it and drew his lips back over his teeth and grinned at it. He felt the rifle jump in his hands—he held on to it and yanked it back down again as the racing air tried to wrench it from his fingers.

The coolie had his cap on. He put his hand hard to the back of his head and pulled it down tight. He saw the ambulanceman and the traffic warden on the ground scrabbling to get up and he saw their silver buttons glint in the sun and then fade as someone ran past them—then glint again as the someone got clear.

He saw the ambulanceman's stupid face open its mouth and then close it again and he saw—

The coolie yelled at the top of his voice, 'Hey!!' and the ambulanceman looked up and saw him.

The coolie saw his mouth open. The coolie saw him see. The

coolie saw him.

The traffic warden was looking up. He was saying . . .

Just one single inch . . .

The coolie raised his rifle and fired.

He saw the bullet pass between them.

A single inch.

He saw the bullet miss by a single inch.

The coolie yelled out, 'Hey! Hey! Hey!'

He saw his enemy.

The coolie drew a bead on the ambulanceman as he tried to get up, and shot him cleanly through the knee.

*

Sands yelled into the phone, 'I'm telling you, the guns are from a fully operational Japanese Second World War arsenal! Complete! Intact! Untouched! And there's more! There's—' He yelled into the phone, 'Hullo, hullo! Is there anybody there?'

*

He shouldn't have shot to— He shouldn't have shot to—

He saw the ambulanceman writhing on the ground.

He shouldn't have shot to hit. He should have—

Just an inch.

He should have missed by an—

Something had happened. With the shot something had happened. The coolie's hands were shaking. The coolie said, 'Yes. Yes . . . Yes . . .'

The coolie said, confused, 'I—I—I—' He felt a surge, a great wave pass over him and the "I" was gone. The coolie said— The coolie said—

He touched the trigger. The ambulanceman jumped. The coolie said, '*Yes!*'

He saw the traffic warden try to get up and the coolie killed him with a single shot through the head. He saw a spray of blood and

43

bone cover the man's shoulders and then the body was going down again, jerking and— The coolie screamed, 'Yes!' The ambulanceman looked up. Blood was coming from his leg and he looked up and then the traffic warden's body jerked as another bullet went in and the ambulanceman—

The coolie shrieked, '*YES!*' Flame and smoke were still coming from the scythed down sub-station. A burning tyre burst out from the hissing flames and rolled down the street.

The coolie saw the ambulanceman move.

The coolie said, 'Yes!' and killed him with a single shot.

The coolie shouted, 'Yes! Yes! Yes! *Yes!*'

People were running.

The coolie began shooting at them. He brought a man down by the side of his car, a middle aged Chinese, and then his wife, and then someone in the doorway of a shop, cowering. The bullets were flying off the roadway and smashing into window displays and exploding their contents out into the street. He saw a man try to scoop up a radio from the pavement as he ran and the coolie brought him down with a shot in the hip.

The ambulanceman was still moving. The coolie shot him again and then swung onto a running woman and sent her spinning with a bullet through the ankle.

He saw the traffic warden twitch. The bullet hit him dead centre in the chest and he thumped backwards onto a wall like a lump of meat. The echo of the explosion was coming back from the mountain and rumbling up and down the street.

The coolie heard screaming and the sounds of battle and felt the hot, burning air in his nostrils.

The coolie fired again, and the gun clicked open empty and he reloaded another magazine and went up and down the street with the sights shooting everything that moved.

The coolie said, 'Yes! Yes! *YES!!*'

At last. At long last. After all those years—

*

44

Sands shouted into the phone in a vain hope of raising someone, 'It's an entire Japanese arsenal from the Second World War! I'm trying to tell you, it's entirely possible he's some sort of bloody Japanese *hold-out*! A soldier! A—' He shouted, 'Is anyone there? Can anybody hear what I'm *saying*?'

*

His life had reached its consummation. Holding aloft his rifle in victory as the street burned, the coolie said, '*Yes!! YES!!*'

Beneath the faded Sergeant's cap of the Japanese Imperial All-Conquering Army his face was shining with glory.

He put his free hand to the back of his head to set the cap more squarely on his—

The coolie said, 'Yes! Yes! YES!'

The gun would go back into the bamboo sheaf and the cap into his pocket and he would put the coolie's veil back on and as he went back into invisibility in the city, no one, not a living soul would ever know ... would ever know ... *anything*!

The street was burning fiercely. He heard the screaming and saw the blood. He saw flags, flickerings, movements. In his mind he heard again bugles and the sound of men advancing and the joy of comradeship and the acts of fire and steel. It rose in him like a great storm, building up, pressing out, wanting to burst.

His moment had arrived.

The coolie yelled, '*YES!!!*'

At the top of his voice, the words echoing across the flat roof of the fishmarkets and down into the bloody, burning street, the coolie at last himself, shouted in Japanese, 'Yes!'

The coolie, the veins in his temple and neck throbbing with ecstacy, shouted, 'Banzai! *Banzai!* BAN—*ZAI*!!'

45

4

On the phone to the Detectives' Room the Commander's voice said incredulously, 'He was a what? And he yelled out what?'

His coat and shirt still smelled of smoke. Feiffer changed the receiver to his other hand, 'Banzai. It's Japanese. It means—'

'I know what it means! It means "Ten thousand years" and that about sums up how long it's been in this part of the world since anybody in his right mind's ever actually said it!' The Commander said irritably, 'It isn't enough that bloody Sands rings me up on the edge of hysteria telling me there's an entire Japanese arsenal hidden away for forty years in this bloody town, now you're telling me—what? That there's an eighty year old Japanese arsenal keeper going around shooting at people and discharging phosphorous grenades into empty ambulances?'

Feiffer said evenly, 'And killing people. I've just come back from the scene and apart from the two who were killed outright there are at least three others who aren't expected to live and one other who, if he does live, is going to be permanently paralysed from the waist down.'

'I'm not denying what this character did. What I'm denying is the rising feeling that he's some sort of Japanese hold-out sitting on his keg of bloody gunpowder just awaiting the resurrection of General bloody Tojo!' The Commander said reasonably, 'Harry, this isn't some sort of uninhabited Pacific island on the edge of nowhere full of high grass and hidden booby traps, this is one of the busiest, most densely populated cities in the world.' His reason faltered, 'Jesus Christ, all some mad bloody geriatric Nip would have to do to know the war was over was look up—any time of day or night—and see Japan Airlines coming in wing by friendly bloody wing with TWA, bloody British Air and bloody QANTAS! Or turn on a transistor radio and listen to Downtown Tokyo Radio playing American hard rock and humburger commercials!' The Commander said dismissively, 'No, it's ridiculous. And the fact that he seemed to be wearing some sort of Japanese kepi is just as ridiculous—in that case half of bloody Hell's Angels would be Adolf Hitler with rejuvenating pills.' The Commander said, 'No. Advice from on high. Final. You've got some sort of murderous maniac on your hands with access to Japanese guns from World War Two, but what you haven't got is any hold-out World War Two Japanese soldier! The end.'

'All right.'

The Commander seemed to hesitate. 'How could it be? How old would he be? Where would he have been all these years?'

Feiffer said tonelessly, 'How old are you?'

'I was about eighteen years old during the Second World War and whatever I might have done then or had done to me is over and forgotten! It was forty years ago—and for the last forty years I've been getting on with my life!' He said as a barely audible aside, thinking of Ballistic Experts ringing him up raving about Japanese arsenals, 'For the last thirty of them I've been here putting up with all this.' He became efficient again. 'From what I could make out from Sands' mixture of gunpowder and gabbling the shells your people picked up in the drains and the bullets he got from the walls are something rare. Is that how you understand it?'

'They're from guns made at the Nambu Rifle Manufacturing Company in the mid thirties. Evidently they're an early version of an assault rifle capable of semi and fully automatic fire issued to the Japanese Army—'

The Commander said tightly, 'Then he's got that wrong too. The Japanese Army didn't have assault rifles. They had Arisaka bolt action—'

'—on an experimental basis for use in Manchuria, but never adopted. The shell cases didn't have identifying headstamps because they were a consignment hand-built for the tests. After

47

Hong Kong fell in 1941 the rifles were brought here for reshipment back to Japan, but they were never despatched. According to Sands, the factory records list two hundred and twenty trial pieces consigned and almost half a million rounds together with accessories like grenade launchers, cups, blank cartridges for the grenades, bayonets, cleaning kits, spare parts—'

The Commander said, 'And whoever's found them has got the lot in mint condition, right? All nicely packed in grease and put away in waterproof banded boxes.'

'Evidently, yes. Sands suggests they were stored in an arsenal here which was probably sealed by bombing or landslip and they've been here undiscovered ever since.'

The Commander said warningly, 'But not with their little Japanese quartermaster though—left there alone and bloody friendless in the dust. Right?'

'If you say so, Neal.'

'I don't say so. Common sense says so.' The Commander said tightly, 'Listen to me, Harry. We've got good relations with the Japanese these days and they want to forget the bloody war even more than we do, and we don't want it all dredged up again with the popular press reprinting bloody atrocity stories that find their way into the nearest Datsun or Mitsui or bloody Mitsubishi office. The Japanese who run things these days aren't the same gang who ran things when they had a mad urge to take over the rest of the world and if you think you've seen the Chinese react wildly when they think they've lost face you just haven't seen anything until you've witnessed the Japanese version.' The Commander said carefully, slowly, 'I hate to sound like a politician, but it may come as a shock to a lot of people to know that if it wasn't for Japanese financial partnership and investment in this Colony we'd all be in a lot worse state and quite probably considering asking the Chinese Communists to send us food parcels to keep us all from starvation.' The Commander said finally, decisively, 'No. Whoever it is, it isn't a hold-out Japanese soldier, and anyone, anyone who suggests it is, especially within hearing of the gutter press, is going to find himself getting very Japanese indeed and

48

trying to find out where he can take a few quick hara-kiri lessons!'
The Commander said, 'I trust I make myself clear?'

'Yes.'

There was a pause. 'Harry, we don't want it all brought up
again, can you understand that? I don't know how much you
know about the history of Hong Kong under Japanese
occupation—' He asked, 'How old can you have been? Eight or
nine?'

Feiffer said quietly, 'I was evacuated to Australia. My father
was a cop in Shanghai. He was shot by a firing squad in 1940
during the Sino-Japanese War.'

'Then you know what I'm talking about!' The Commander said
quietly 'There were things that happened in those days...' His
voice trailed off. 'China was split. The Japanese were fighting here
for years before Pearl Harbor, before any of that. It wasn't just
split into the good guys and the bad guys—the Japanese invaders
and the poor suffering, defending Chinese masses: it was split into
the Japanese and the Communist Chinese and the Nationalist
Chinese and the Chinese–Japanese collaborators and the secret
societies and the Communist collaborators and the Nationalist
collaborators—it was split into bloody pieces. When I first came
here as a young Inspector just before the Korean War we were
still, still finding people in ditches with bullets in the back of their
necks and their so-called crimes engraved bone deep into them
with razors. The War Crimes Tribunals were still in force, even
the—' The Commander said earnestly, 'It was a disgusting, evil
few years and I don't want the families of anyone who was
involved—on either side—having to hear it all brought up again
and all the old hatreds resurrected.' The Commander said, 'I
want this down as a mad sniper who's taken on a police station
and an ambulance depot because he likes chalking stupid bloody
messages on fishmarket roofs, or a demented gun freak who likes
guns and using them on people, or a gang of kids with a pet
arsenal, or even the lead-up to the Third World War between the
Chinese and the bloody Russians, or even, if you like, the Kurds
and the bloody Persians, but I do not want it down, under any

circumstances, as a Second World War Japanese hold-out bloody soldier! *All right?*'

Feiffer paused for a moment.

'*All right?*'

The pause continued. Feiffer said evenly, 'Neal, at the moment, apart from a vague description of a figure on a roof top, all I've got to go on are the guns. I have to get in touch with someone and tell them they're Japanese even if only to find out where they were hidden.'

'I've no objection to that.' The Commander said with uncharacteristic obstinacy, 'If they were never used by the Japanese Army then they're not Japanese Army guns. Get in touch with whoever you like, provided he isn't Japanese.'

'I just don't see how anyone else would have found them. If they'd been turned over by an earth mover or in the course of land reclamation or—' Feiffer said reasonably, 'Neal, unless he had them buried in his back garden I don't see how any one man could have found them—' There was a silence from the other end of the line. Feiffer said carefully, 'I don't want to sound like a politician either, but with land in this Colony at a million dollars a square yard, an arsenal of the size you're talking about, presumably with living quarters for the staff, would have to be so big that—'

The Commander said tightly, 'No one has come back to claim them. The guns were found accidentally by a local.'

'There just isn't that much free land in Hong Kong. And if it was sited near the waterfront as it probably would have been and it was sealed by bombing—' Feiffer said, 'I just don't see how anyone could have dug their way in without someone hearing about it. Not *in*.'

'What the hell are you suggesting?'

'I'm not suggesting anything.'

'*What the hell are you suggesting?*' The Commander roared into the phone, 'My God, man, are you seriously suggesting that after forty years—*forty years*—someone in that arsenal has dug himself ... out? Are you—' The words would not come. The Commander said, 'My God, are you— Like ants coming out from a—'

50

The Commander said over and over, not giving an order, but resisting something, 'No! No! No! Harry, *no!*'

*

In the arsenal, the Bannin closed the steel door behind him and looked up at the hurricane lamp burning on the cement ceiling of the war room. The ceiling was white and powdery with dryness and there were dustwebs clinging to it, swaying faintly in the disturbed air from the burning lamp. The Bannin's eyes were full of tears and he wiped them with his gloved hand and stood silent for a moment, listening.

Through the thick concrete and rock of the walls of the room the sound of the sea a long way off rolled and thundered and shook dust loose from the last of the masonry adhering to the cement. He heard a crackle like small arms fire as somewhere in the tunnels rocks fell, and then a louder, deeper vibration that shook and trembled in the stale, urine-smelling air and then dissipated into echoes.

The Bannin looked down at his uniform and saw it was in tatters. He brushed at it with his hand and a little piece of rotted material broke loose from the weave and fluttered to the ground.

He looked back to the steel door and bit his lip to hold back the tears.

The other man in the room said gently, 'Bannin? (Watchman?)' and the Bannin swallowed and took something from his pocket and handed it to him.

It was a little metal Army issue cigarette box and the other man opened it carefully and looked at the lock of hair and fingernail parings it contained and then closed it again.

The other man in the room said quietly, 'Cuttlefish Lane, Bannin. There were people killed.'

'*Asi wa arauku tame ni arimasu.*'

The other man said gently in Cantonese, 'I don't understand.'

'One's legs are there in order that one may walk.' The Bannin said quietly in the holy place, reverting awkwardly to Cantonese,

51

'It was my Sergeant. He has fought his last battle and his end was glorious according to the code of Bushido. I assisted him at the last and he died without a murmur.' The Bannin said sadly, 'I have no way of returning his personal momentos to his family in Japan, but I have made arrangements with his enemies that his last battle be recorded.'

The other man said softly, 'Bannin, please. I'm a technician. This doesn't have to happen. I can do a set-up like the one in Yellowthread Street any time and your section—'

'My section are soldiers.' The Bannin said without anger, 'I don't expect you to understand this, but it is not something they want to do, or I want them to do, it is something they are all entitled to do.' He gave The Technician a thin smile, 'After forty years, it is the very *least*.' The Bannin said, 'He tried. The Sergeant. Before he committed seppuku, he told me he tried to reward your friendship—to assist you in your plans—he tried to miss *by one inch*, but, after all those years—' The Bannin held his gloved hands together like fists straining to explain something inexplicable to others, 'But the freedom, the great stirring in him as he—as he liberated the weapon—as the sword leapt from the scabbard—' He smiled again, 'I don't expect you to understand, as a Chinese.'

'Bannin—please—'

'No.' The Bannin said, 'We are all going to die. You must accept it. The entire section. It is our duty.' He heard the sea a long way off thundering against the solid rock on the other side of the war room wall, 'It is our glory. Like the sea, our inevitability.' He listened for a moment.

'Bannin, I have only just found you!' The Technician said, 'Please, won't you still help me?'

The Bannin listened.

The Bannin said after a moment, 'Yes.' He looked down at his uniform, his rags. The Bannin said with a strange, sad smile, 'The Sergeant was dressed in the clothing of a Chinese coolie when he fought his last battle, but he still wore—he still wore—' The Bannin said, 'I have made arrangements.' He looked back at the steel door anxiously, 'You know where the guns are.' He became stiffly correct. Major (Quartermaster) Juzo Takashima of the Japanese Imperial Army 38th Division in Hong Kong said formally, 'You will excuse me now. My command is not yet exhausted and after they and I have completed the formalities with our dead comrade, there are orders to be given.'

The far off force of the sea was shaking at the walls and roof of the underground chamber and The Bannin paused for a moment listening to it, the nodding, turned and opened the steel door and went through.

After a moment, there was the sound of a scratchy record coming from somewhere inside the room, being played on an old hand-wound player.

It was the Kimigayo: the Japanese national anthem, and about it, the rest of the command were silent, in mourning for one who had been lost to them.

The Technician said softly to himself in desperation, 'Please, do you have to keep on killing people?' His eyes fell on the closed steel door and he heard the music stop.

There was nothing to be done.

The Technician took down the hurricane lamp from the ceiling to go to the gun store and plunged the dry, ancient room back into darkness.

*

Up on the roof of the fishmarkets Sands collected the last of the expended shell cases and gazed down at the chalked message. It was in cursive, grass script and he could not read it.

He looked down at the cases in a plastic freezer bag in his hand. They were the same as the others.

Across the street he could see the firemen still spraying the ambulance sub-station with foam to make sure that the last of the phosphorous from the incendiary grenade was out and would not suddenly flare up again.

Over the last two nights, the expenditure of ammunition had

been approximately three hundred and ten rounds of blank, and on the third floor of the building in Yellowthread Street, counting both the rifle fire and the automatic gun, a minimum of four hundred live rounds.

There were eighteen empty cases in his freezer bag.

Three hundred and ten, plus four hundred, plus eighteen, plus one rifle-launched phosphorous grenade, plus an allowance for error, plus—

Not a spit in hell.

Starting with a base supply of two hundred and twenty guns and half a million rounds, they represented not even half a spit in hell.

Under his coveralls Sands wore a stubby stainless steel Detonics Mark VI .45 combat automatic in Condition One: cocked with the oversized safety ready to be flicked off as it came out of the leather.

He felt its weight under his armpit.

"... *The carrying of firearms by police, apart from their purely defensive function, is designed to give confidence in a situation where otherwise the officer might be reluctant to engage upon a course of action consistent with his duty...*"

Sands' duty was the open, exposed flat roof.

He glanced down into the street below where the ambulances had taken away the dead and the dying and found that his gun gave him no feeling of confidence at all.

There was a high building in direct line with the roof—over on Stamford Street—and something glinted momentarily on a sixth floor window and made him start before, at 3.05 p.m. in the afternoon, he realised with relief that it was only the sun.

*

It was there, faded with the sun. At the back of the fishmarkets, Auden said curiously, 'What is it?'

It was on the far side of the giant flat building, held by a length of tattered material with a knot. Auden said again, coming closer,

'What is it?' It was facing East, the last direction he would have expected the sniper to take if he had been escaping from the north side of the roof in a hurry.

It was a length of thick material, folded over like some sort of money belt or sash. It fluttered a little in the breeze from the sea.

Whatever it was, it seemed to have stitches in it in no apparent order, serving no apparent purpose.

Spencer said quietly, 'It's an *obi*, a Japanese ceremonial belt.' He touched at it gently and one of the coloured stitches in the material gave way and broke into ragged threads. Spencer said quietly, 'It's a thousand stitches obi given to Japanese warriors and suicide pilots for good luck.' He turned it over gently on the wall and the length of material fluttered briefly like a pennant.

Auden said quietly, 'Bill?' He saw the man squint at a line of faded characters written by hand along a seam of the stitches.

Spencer said, 'It's a name. I can't read it except for this one character here.' He indicated a single character evidently written a little later or with more pride than the rest, 'Sergeant.' Spencer said, 'And this bit here, I can make that out a little. It says 38th Division and these two characters here are the Japanese for Hong Kong.' He looked harder, 'And this, this line of characters is the way the Japanese do the date.' He began reading aloud, 'Sho-wa—' He said quietly, 'I can't make it out.' He said suddenly, 'Yes! 1942. Showa ... ju ... hachi...' Spencer said quietly, 'Nineteen hundred and forty two.' Something else fluttered in the breeze behind the obi and Spencer leant forward quickly and caught it before it fell to the ground.

Spencer said, 'And this too. 1942. The Japanese Imperial Army 38th Division in Hong Kong.' He read without expression, 'Sergeant Quartermaster—I think ... something...'

Auden said with sudden irritation, 'It's a bloody joke!' He saw Spencer look back to the faded characters on the obi again.

Spencer said, reading the obi, 'Sergeant Quartermaster—' Spencer said, 'Is it?'

'Of course it is! How the fuck can it be from 1942? It's something somebody's tricked up! You can get this stuff anywhere. There's plenty of this stuff around. People collect it. If you want a bloody World War Two obi all you have to do is—'

Spencer said quietly, 'What about this?' He held the second object out and let Auden see it. It was a piece of card with the characters clear on it, written as if yesterday or kept carefully from a long time ago and protected against the light. Spencer said with sudden anger, 'And where the hell do you think he got this?'

He turned it over in front of Auden's face.

Auden said softly, 'Christ!'

It was a photograph of a man in Army uniform standing with his wife and child outside an army barracks and smiling as they glanced up at a sign in Japanese reading *Quartermasters' Training School, Hiroshima.*

Auden said, 'It's a fake, isn't it?'

Spencer said, 'No.'

Far off in the distance, you could see the domes and buildings of the city destined to be the first victim of the Atomic Age. Then, in 1942 or earlier, when the photograph had been taken and the man on the roof had put it in his pocket to keep all these years, that city had been completely, totally, and obviously ... intact.

Auden said again softly, 'Christ...'

He touched at his gun under his coat, but it seemed a very insignificant thing indeed, and he took his hand away and looked back to the fluttering obi and shivered.

*

There was a flash at the window again and Sands clenched his fists together and said, 'Damn it, it's the sun!'

There was nothing there.

He saw another shell case on the roof and, picking it up, glanced back again and ordered himself, 'Keep your mind on the job!'

3.28 p.m.

He just wanted to get back to his Police Armoury and close the door behind him.

*

The phone rang. It was him. At his desk O'Yee felt himself stiffen as the voice said evenly and unhurriedly in Cantonese, 'I have a divine mission to eradicate all the uniformed forces of colonial repression in the world and I have now made two beginnings.' O'Yee stayed silent. There was nothing more from the voice, but the line was still open.

Feiffer was outside in the charge room with the Uniformed Branch and there was no one else in the Detectives' Room but O'Yee.

'O'Yee said with no emotion in his voice, 'Anata wa nihongo wakarimas' ka?'

There was a silence.

The words meant, he thought, 'Do you speak Japanese?' The words were in Japanese.

O'Yee could hear the man breathing at the other end of the line.

He could hear the breathing coming in gasps.

O'Yee said—

There was a single click as the caller suddenly hung up, and then, in the burring of the dial tone that went on and on in O'Yee's ear for a very long time, nothing.

*

On the ground below the obi there was yet another object. It moved as Auden stepped back and touched it with his shoe.

It was a single three quarter inch ball bearing, and, since there were no machines in the fishmarkets, just as there were no Japanese soldiers left in Asia, it also had no right to be there.

The ball bearing was brand new, with a fine sixteenth of an inch hole drilled all the way through it like the worm hole in an apple.

It had not been meant to be found. It had fallen out of someone's pocket and in the confusion either the sniper had not noticed it or it had rolled away and he had not been able to find it again.

57

Or perhaps he had not even cared.

The ball bearing was nickel plated.

Like the window in the sixth floor building across from Sands on the roof, it glittered brightly in the mid afternoon sun.

5

In the silent underground vaults of the Historical Archives Store
under Icehouse Road, The Keeper Of Secrets looked at Feiffer for
a very long time before answering. His office was bare,
windowless and without even a picture or a sign of personality in
sight. The Keeper Of Secrets said, 'I don't speak the language,
but I read it,' turned his face and the glassene envelope encased
obi away under a desk lamp and put on his glasses. He said, 'My
name, for your records, is Mr Owlin.' He looked back with the
glasses on his face and waited for the inevitable comment, then,
when it failed to come, turned the obi over carefully in long
scrupulously clean hands and read, 'Sergeant Quartermaster
Seichiro Tanino, Japanese Imperial Army, Thirty Eighth
Division in Hong Kong, the equivalent of nineteen hundred and
forty two.' His face, in the soft light, looked Chinese. He turned
back slightly and all the bone structure went and, except for the
black hair, it was a European Nordic face. He took off his glasses
and the bones changed again and became Korean. The Keeper Of
Secrets said, 'It's a thousand stitches obi from the Second World
War probably taken from a living man.'

Feiffer looked curious.

The Keeper Of Secrets said, as if it was simplicity itself, 'No
blood.' He turned the transparent envelope over carefully. It
made a crackling noise. 'And very little evidence of sweat, so it
was washed regularly and removed from the owner while he was
calm and not in battle.' There was a single thick file on his desk
marked *Events At Leighton Hill, Feb–April, 1897—not to be opened
without Written Authority* and The Keeper Of Secrets looked at it for
a moment, then put the obi carefully down on his desk. The

Keeper Of Secrets asked without expectation of a reply, 'Can I ask where you got it?'

'At Cuttlefish Lane.'

The Keeper nodded. He glanced back behind him to a single locked door to the main records store.

Feiffer said, 'What were they used for?'

'As stomach warmers. And as good luck talismans. The wife or mother of the recipient stood on a street corner in Tokyo or Osaka or wherever her relative was billeted and asked passers-by to insert one single stitch into the material as a sign of good wishes and luck for her relative's forthcomig death. When she had a thousand the obi was presented to the soldier as a sign of his countrymen's hopes for him to die well in battle.' The Keeper of Secrets could not have been more than thirty five years old. He said with the authority of one who had been there at the time, 'This man was a soldier late in life or he was a regular soldier. If he had been inducted into the Forces at the time of the Sino–Japanese War or after Pearl Harbor he would have gone in as a private and the belt would have been presented to him then. In which case his previous rank would have been erased or crossed out when he became a Sergeant. The date 1942 was the date on which he was given the obi and the 38th division was the unit he was attached to at the time.' There was the faintest movement in the young-old man's face. The Keeper Of Secrets said, 'The thirty eighth division was the unit based in Hong Kong who cut down all the trees.'

'Pardon?'

The Keeper Of Secrets offered the obi back. There was the feeling of tenseness about the otherwise gentle move. The Keeper Of Secrets said, 'The thirty eighth division atacked Hong Kong from across the border on the morning of the eighth of December, 1941 and fought their way across Kowloon to Hong Kong until the General Officer Commanding, Major General Maltby, was finally forced to surrender on Christmas Day of the same year. And then Hong Kong was occupied until Liberation in August, 1945.' The Keeper Of Secrets said softly, 'During that period the

Thirty Eighth Division cut down every tree on Hong Kong for firewood, including cypresses and junipers and oaks planted by the first settlers a hundred years before.'

'I see.'

The Keeper Of Secrets said, 'The cypress and the juniper are symbols of longevity to the Chinese. As well as the commercial aspect, it was a political move to subjugate them,' The Keeper Of Secrets said, 'My family has been on the China Coast for five generations, first at Macao and then, when it was founded, here in Hong Kong. My family planted some of the trees.' He asked, 'Do you like trees, Mr Feiffer?'

'Very much.'

'All of the old trees were replaced after the war by quick growing varieties. I helped plan some of the plantings.' He looked down at the obi, 'But, like the philosophy that created your obi-wearing Sergeant all the old, solid, ancient things have gone.' He gave Feiffer a faint, sad smile and looked down at the floor of the windowless, air-conditioned room, 'I miss them. The old trees before the war.'

'You couldn't have even been born before the war.'

'No.' The Keeper Of Secrets said, 'But the records were.' He moved his hand back to the closed door behind him, 'All the records were. They were all here underground and they survived, all of them.' He looked up, 'This room and the rooms behind it will survive a nuclear explosion, so they will always be here.' The Keeper Of Secrets said, 'I can go in there and take out files and records and photographs and there never was a war. I can take out a map and a guide book and I can walk down all the streets and through all the villages where my family planted trees to last forever and I can even read their letters to nurserymen asking advice and their receipts for payment and their shipping invoices as each one of the oaks and the junipers and the elms and the larch trees came in. I can read how many inches each tree grew each year—'

The man's face was pale and bloodless. Feiffer said gently, 'Do you ever go out?'

61

'No. The world above me is not the one I—' He stopped. The Keeper Of Secrets said with a quick, nervous, embarrassed grin, 'Like some burrowing mole I could survive down here in the past forever, dreaming my own dreams and—'

'Do you have the records of where the Japanese military establishments were during the Occupation?'

'Some of them, yes.'

'The arsenals and the—'

The Keeper Of Secrets said, 'No.' He paused for a moment, 'My predecessor kept these records all during the Occupation and the Japanese didn't even know he was here. But he, unfortunately, because of it, was hardly in a position to file away military secrets.'

Feiffer said with alarm, 'Do you mean he was here undetected?'

The Keeper Of Secrets nodded.

'For four years?'

'And one day.'

'How did he live?'

The Keeper Of Secrets smiled.

'Is it possible to—'

'Certainly.' The Keeper of Secrets said with a secret, mad smile, 'This place is bomb proof, like all—' He leaned forward at his desk, 'Do you think that in Europe, for example, when they hid the Mona Lisa and the Rembrandts and all the important things of the world that they didn't make arrangements for the hiding to outlast the temporary aberration of *war*?' The Keeper Of Secrets said, 'In France there was a case where a group of soldiers were entombed in a block house for almost twenty years!'

Feiffer said barely comprehendingly, 'And when they came out?'

The Keeper Of Secrets said, 'They were all mad. Of course.'

Feiffer waited.

The Keeper Of Secrets said with triumph, 'But their philosophy was intact.' The Keeper Of Secrets said, 'And that, in the long run, in the movement of time, is all that matters.' The Keeper Of Secrets turned his face away from the light and stared hard at a blank wall and saw—God knew what. The Keeper Of Secrets said, 'The trees, they are the only transitory things of this world that I miss, but if I wait long enough, even they—'

Feiffer said evenly, 'The Thirty Eighth Division, what happened to them after the war?'

'Nothing.' The Keeper Of Secrets said, 'They were transferred to another posting in early 1943—to Guadalcanal. They were all killed.'

'All of them?'

'All of them.' The Keeper Of Secrets looked down at the obi in its little stapled envelope.

Feiffer felt a cold shiver up his back.

The Keeper Of Secrets fixed him with a fierce, strange look and thinking of the trees, said quietly, 'They were all cut down.' There was a faint, unidentifiable, other wordly look on The Keeper's face. The Keeper said after a moment, still smiling, 'Weren't they? Just like the trees. They were all—all of them—*felled*.'

Behind him, through that closed door, there must have been miles of corridors and shelving and acres of folders filled with papers and memories and photographs all straining to be free of the timeless order in which they were arranged and classified and fossilised, but as The Keeper Of Secrets kept smiling, from behind the door there was not even the faintest rustle to indicate their presence.

*

HONG KONG. FINAL MESSAGE.

The General Officer Commanding authorises me to state that the white flag will be hoisted and all British, Canadian and other military operations against the Japanese Army will cease forthwith. You will consider yourselves prisoners of war. Issue orders to all those concerned to cease fighting.

For:

GENERAL OFFICER COMMANDING, British Forces in China.

God Save The King!

Hong Kong, 25th: 12:1941.

63

The Keeper Of Secrets looked at him.

The obi was in Feiffer's hand.

There were one thousand stitches in it exactly, each lovingly placed there a lifetime ago.

Sergeant Quartermaster Seichiro Tanino, Japanese Imperial Army, Thirty Eighth Division in Hong Kong, 1942...

Feiffer saw The Keeper Of Secrets still looking at him silently, and, in the deep, air-conditioned room he put the object back carefully onto The Keeper's desk and, through the sealed, tagged, glassene evidence envelope, felt it cold and dry, like death.

*

The telephone number of the Japanese Embassy was 4–50153.

The only country left in the world, leaving aside Switzerland and Andorra, without a standing offensive army.

Anata wa nihongo wakarimas' ka?

It was the only Japanese O'Yee knew.

And it was probably wrong at that.

O'Yee looked at the replacement telephone on his desk and tried to think who he knew who spoke the language. And who he could trust.

The telephone number of the Japanese Embassy was 4–50153.

The Emergency Unit were moving sandbags in to cover the broken windows and laying out bullet proof vests on the floor around him and he found it hard to think.

*

He was committed. He had no choice. In the engine room of the moored police launch in Fisherman's Cove, The Technician worked in the failing afternoon light with his rifles. Through one of the portholes by the twin diesels he could see the upstairs room of the double storied building where the Police were having their afternoon conference before changing shifts. There was no one around. It was the same theory as speeding in the exact five minutes between the change of shifts of traffic cops, and even the Constable at the open wire gates to the wharf area was inside changing into civilian clothes and thinking that he had earned a good day's pay for a very easy day's work.

He saw a movement on a disused wharf a hundred feet away and for an awful moment thought the cops knew he was there and were watching him through binoculars to catch him in the act.

The Technician crawled on his hands and knees to the porthole and shot the cuff of his mechanic's coveralls quickly to check his watch.

The shift was still changing and The Technician, short on time, squinted hard at the thick glass of the engine room porthole to try to make out who it was.

He knew him.

The man was wearing a fisherman's smock and a wide boat people rattan hat to cover his features, but The Technician knew who he was.

The Stores Corporal.

It was Corporal Sakutaro Ozawa. For a moment the wind caught his smock and The Technician saw his thousand stitches obi around his stomach.

The Technician said softly in Cantonese, 'No...!' and looked back to his set-up.

The Corporal had been carrying something long and dark under his arm, wrapped up to look like a length of wood under a medium mesh fisherman's net.

The Technician, hurrying, glanced back through the porthole and the man was gone.

*

5.59 p.m. By a disused warehouse facing the sea, the Corporal paused. There were ball bearings in his pocket, together with a few coins and bits and pieces of screwed up paper.

By the warehouse there was a public telephone booth for the use of fishermen and their families and, going to it, he stood looking down into the dark water at his own reflection.

The ball bearings were no longer of any interest to him.

Dropping them into the sea, one by one, he saw his reflection at first ripple then distort, then, in the disturbed water, pass from reality altogether.

He touched at the rifle hidden in the rolled up medium mesh net and smiled.

*

On the phone in the Detectives' Room O'Yee said, '*What?*' He changed into Cantonese, 'I can't understand you. *What?*'

The voice at the other end of the line was old, croaking, it seemed to be coming from a long way off. Somewhere in the background O'Yee could hear what sounded like a faint wind pulling at the voice and taking it away. There was a ship's siren, noises and sounds of time and distance and—

The voice said, '*Eigo o narau tame ni Eikoku no husu o kikimas—*' It made a harsh cackling noise.

He listens to English ... in order to ... learn English... O'Yee heard the word, '*but*'. O'Yee said desperately, 'I can't speak Japanese! I don't know what you mean! I know you speak Cantonese! I—'

It wasn't the same voice.

O'Yee said, 'Eigo wakarimasu ka?' Do you understand English? It wasn't right. It should have been—

Far off behind the voice he could hear the sound of the wind and—

O'Yee said, 'Tanino! Sergeant Seichiro Tanino. Are you—'

'Ie.'

He knew that word.

It meant, 'No.'

66

The voice said slowly, an old, old man's voice coming from a long way away, 'Ozawa. Sakutaro Ozawa.' There was a burst of numbers and technical words that could have been some sort of serial number and rank. The voice said something that sounded like, 'Bushido.' It said something that sounded like, 'Seppuku.'

O'Yee waited.

Outside, it was becoming night and the darkness was moving in through the holes in the wall over the grey sandbags like seeping gas at a parapet. There was no one else in the Station.

Behind the caller's breathing, he could hear a faint wind taking all the words away.

O'Yee said...

Night. Outside it was becoming dark, secret night.

O'Yee said—

There was a silence and then, to someone a long time ago, perhaps someone in a place long gone and a time never to be returned to, the caller said sadly in Japanese, 'Goodbye.'

The voice said softly and sadly, not to O'Yee, 'Sayonara ... sayonara ...'

It sounded for a moment as if he was crying.

O'Yee said—

Outside, it was dark, black, friendless night.

O'Yee yelled into the phone a moment before the line went dead, 'God damn it, *who are you? What do you want?*'

"I have a divine mission to eradicate all the uniformed forces of colonial repression and I have now—"

That? Why hadn't he said that?

The night was dark and full of terrors.

O'Yee said desperately in the empty Detectives' Room, surrounded by the sandbags and flak jackets and guns, 'My God, how many of them are there?'

*

The ship's name was the *Osaka Maru*. On its way out to sea it passed across his line of vision with all its running lights on and its

67

leaving port pennants fluttering in silhouette in the wind. He saw some of the crew leaning on the fan tail looking down into the foaming water.

It was going home.

There was nothing now to go home to.

He was crying a little.

Corporal Sakutaro Ozawa of the Japanese Imperial Army 38th Division in Hong Kong, high up on the roof of a disused warehouse facing the sea, slipped the photograph of his long dead parents safely inside his thousand stitches obi, rested his hand on the waiting Nambu M1935 Experimental Assault Rifle by his side, and settled down to a dreamless, final sleep.

There was a cheap, mass produced, Japanese Army issue watch on his wrist, held by a frayed and cracked black leather band.

At exactly 6.03 a.m., its mechanism all clogged and old, without warning, it suddenly stopped.

6

At the 5 a.m. Headquarters news briefing this morning a police spokesman reaffirmed that the weapons involved are .303 Lee Enfield rifles abandoned by units of the defending Canadian Army during the battle for Hong Kong in 1941.

The spokesman went on to strenuously deny reports given by eye-witnesses to this newspaper that the sniper wore the uniform of a Japanese Army officer and that the grenade which destroyed the ambulance sub-station in Cuttlefish Lane was of a type stored in Japanese arsenals during the Occupation.

He also refused to confirm that counter sniper units had been attached to regular police patrols and that there was increasing Emergency Unit activity on the streets.

The Spokesman said the police were treating the shootings as purely criminal incidents without political motive.

A spokesman from the Japanese Embassy said late last night that in the absence of an official approach from the Government his office could make no comment on the incidents.

A further news conference had been convened by police for this morning when more information is expected.

Following the death early this morning of one of the victims of the Cuttlefish Lane shootings the condition of the other victims in St Paul de Chartres' Hospital is said to be stable . . .

*

There was a ragged junk making its way back into harbour through the lightening purple dawn, its stern auxiliary motor popping and bubbling a wake that flowed against the side of Lew's police launch and set it bobbing slightly against its moorings and

69

Sergeant Lew, shivering a little in his coat, kicked his boots against a bollard on the wharf, thought of clean open seas and seagulls and looked away as a human turd surfaced in the phosphorescence and then sank again like a submarine. At the stern of the junk there was a wooden circle with a hole cut out of it set out over the wake—the Chinese junk fisherman's mod cons—and one of the fishermen using it. "Jaws" nothing. In Hong Kong harbour you ran a bigger risk of being crapped to death than eaten. A sampan passed a little behind the junk, well out of range, and there in the absence of a wooden seat there was a splash as someone threw over an entire plastic bag full of something.

Lew heard the bag seethe as it went straight down to the gutters of Atlantis and the Atlantean street sweepers, seeing it, made bubbling noises and went instantly out on strike.

Lew had been educated in an English speaking Catholic missionary school on Kowloon. Knowing he came from a long line of boat people one of the Brothers had set him to learning Masefield's 'I Must Go Down To The Sea Again' and Lew, watching as yet another turd surfaced said quietly to himself in English, 'Give me a tall ship and a star to steer her by . . .' There were no stars. Pre dawn, it was dark and overcast. And no tall ships. Just shit. Lew looked full at Constable Pan at the door to the engine room and said, irritated, 'Pan, if you haven't got the fucking wit to open a door I'll fucking find someone who has!'

At the varnished door to the engine room, Pan said back, 'It's locked.'

'That's why you've got the key.' Maybe, on balance, being a sea turd wasn't so bad. At least you had the place to yourself. Lew said, 'Take the key in your hand, place it carefully in the lock, give it a little turn while at the same time maintaining a steady pressure on the door handle . . .'

Pan said, 'I've done all that. It's locked. Someone's locked it from the inside.'

'The door leads to the engine room. Engine rooms are not locked from the inside because if they were and something terrible happened then the engineer inside—' Lew said, '—who is you—

70

might be stuck in there and he might drown.' Briefly it was a thought that did not lack appeal. Lew said with an effort of sweetness, 'Look, Constable, the night patrol is due in in three minutes and we're going to look a bit silly if we can't get our door open, aren't we? So try again, would you?' The coxswain was in the wheelhouse taking the night covers off the instruments and Lew hopped down onto the deck, glanced up at him, and seeing that at least everything was all right in there—that he hadn't forgotten to order a goddamned wheel or anything—went down to the engineer and took the key.

Pan said, 'I'm only new, Sergeant. When I trained we had the newer type of launch. It had a combination lock on the engine room door.' He was a big moon-faced ex fisherman, probably still counting his luck that he had a toilet that flushed and a helmet that protected him against those who didn't. Lew said with a shrug, 'O.K., as a matter of fact, this door does get stuck occasionally.' He put the key in and gave it a turn.

It turned.

Lew said, 'There. It must have been a sea water warp or something.'

He pulled at the door handle and nothing happened.

Constable Pan said, 'See?'

The junk passed off to starboard, going pop-pop-pop and then, yet again—the entire crew must have waited through the vast South China Sea for the exact moment they passed the Water Police moorings—plop-plop-plop. Lew said, 'What's that smell?'

Constable Pan said, 'It's the wind. It's blowing in the—'

'No.' Lew leaned forward, 'On the door.' He got up close and put his nose against the varnished timber and sniffed, 'It smells like acetone or—' He saw the coxswain and two of the deckhands lean out from the wheelhouse and smile at him and he roared, *'Which one of you bastards has put Super Glue on the engine room doors?'* He took hold of the handle and wrenched at it in a fury, *'If one of you bastards thinks this is funny you'll be thinking it from the other side of the Police Disciplinary Board carpet!'* Lew shouted, 'Are you out of your minds? The night patrol boat has got a Chief Superintendent on

71

it—it's Superintendent Allison—and when that man hears about this there won't be enough left of any of you to use for shrimp bait!' Lew said in a trembling mutter as he pulled hard at the door to free it, 'Holy Mother of—' He ordered Pan, 'You! Get around to the porthole and see what the hell's holding it. It better not be glue! It'd better be an oily rag stuck in the jamb—which is only two month's suspension—it had better not be glue, which is instant gladdamned *death*!' He saw Pan staring at him like a moron waiting to be told which foot to put forward first in order to walk. Lew ordered, 'Get around to the porthole and have a look in!' He saw the man start off in the darkness, 'And take a flashlight, you nincompoop!'

The door was stuck. He heard Pan tip toe around the edge of the boat with all the nautical grace of Moby Dick in his death throes and he called out, 'Well? Can you see anything?' It was Super Glue: Lew could smell it.

Pan called out, 'No. I can see the door where it says something about a divine mission and the usual ship's blessing, but I—'

Lew said, 'What?'

Pan said, 'But I can't make out anything else for the smoke.'

Lew said, 'The what?' He thought his ears must have— Lew said, 'The *what*?'

Pan said, 'Yes, I can. It says, "to eradicate all the uniformed forces of—"'

Lew's voice was a gasp. Lew said, 'Is this a *joke*?'

'No. No, it says—'

The night patrol launch was coming in. Lew heard it. Lew shouted to the coxswain, 'Get off! Get off the boat!' He saw Pan coming around, smiling at him and playing the flashlight on the ground to make patterns. Lew shouted at him, 'Get off! Get off the boat!' He saw the night boat coming in. All along the wharf there were police boats and auxiliary craft moored in a single unbroken line. Lew shouted, 'Clear the area. It's a set-up! Clear the area!' He saw the coxswain and the two deckhands start to come towards him, not sure of what they had heard and he took the first deckhand by the scruff of his neck and threw him overboard into the sea.

The coxswain heard him shout again, 'Set-up!' and as Lew went past him leapt a full twenty feet from the deck onto the wharf and began running.

Lew shouted, 'The moorings! Cast off the moorings!' as Pan and the other deckhand followed and made for cover.

The diesels were self starting. Lew pushed the two buttons and they roared into life. He heard someone shout, 'The moorings—' and he yelled back, 'Cast them off!' waited not a moment later and putting the engines into Full Ahead ripped the wharf to matchwood and put the vessel at top speed into the centre of the harbour.

He smelled smoke.

It came from under the door of the engine room. He saw it seeping up through the decking in the wheelhouse.

The night boat was coming in.

He saw them come about to hail him. Lew shouted—

It was no good. It was too far away.

There was an electronic loud hailer on the ceiling of the wheelhouse and Lew flicked it on and yelled out a single word in Cantonese that carried past the junks and the sampans to the night boat and rose above his roaring engines.

That word was *'Bomb!'*

*

On the roof of the disused warehouse facing the sea, Corporal Ozawa awoke.

He had been in a long, deep sleep. He touched at his thousand stitches obi and began to undo it.

Like a sudden dragon, he awoke.

*

Coming across the harbour from Lamma Island, Lew saw a ferry. It was full of people. The night boat had turned off and was

73

pacing him, coming up a little astern as he put the bow of the boat out towards the open sea and kept the throttles forward. Something was burning through: he saw the black oily smoke coming up through the deckboards.

The engines were roaring, racing, without their water jackets filled glowing red hot and warping out of true, buckling, going wild.

He heard a click. It came up through the boards, then there was more of the smoke and then something hot and fast pushed up and made a whoomph sound under his boots and one of the smaller fuel tanks gave and spilled oil over the engine room floor. Lew could see it in his mind as the black oozy stuff flowed unstoppably towards the glowing engines.

Something inside the engine room was burning and making pinging sounds. They came as punctuation in the roaring of the engines. He could feel the boat glowing, going faster, becoming bright like a light bulb about to burst.

He heard it. He heard a solid, loud bang as something like a gunshot went off inside the hull. He knew something had gone, been fired, done something. He knew that whatever was happening had started to happen and he was—

Seconds.

Less than seconds. He got the wheelhouse door open and then ducked as it smashed back with the speed and all the glass went.

The boat was going for the open empty sea. He saw the night launch behind him in the wheelhouse mirror chasing him, its bows cutting twin white knives through the rolling sea.

Lew said at the top of his voice, forgetting all his Catholic education, 'T'ien Hou, Goddess of the Sea, protect me now!' and spinning the wheel hard to port to break the boat's back propelled himself out through the smashed door and into the foaming dark, enveloping sea.

*

He awoke. From a long, deep, dark sleep, he awoke and he was young again and the rifle was by his side.

Bushido.

The code of the warrior.

It was fast becoming dawn and he could see across the water and he had his rifle.

Corporal Ozawa stood up.

*

The boat was on fire. The engines stopped and it began drifting. In the water, Lew said over and over, 'Oh, God, oh God, oh, God...'

If he had been wrong...

The boat was drifting back, turning in circles, intact, its back solid and hard. It made a one hundred and eighty degree turn and he saw it and then, less than two hundred yards away, what he had done to the wharf and the moorings.

Lew said, 'Oh, God, oh God...' and wished that his sodden clothes would pull him down into the sea.

The boat was burning in great rolling billows of white and black smoke, floundering as it turned and then came about again and then, rudderless, turned again and began drifting back towards the shore.

Lew saw the night patrol boat cut its engines and come to a stop in the water: he felt the ripples wash over him and then abate and then stop altogether and he was floating in a still, Limbo sea as the night boat and Superintendent Allison came towards him with murder in his eyes.

He saw them all lined up on the after deck of the boat, one or two of them with boat hooks ready to pull him out and Lew, treading water, touched at his holstered gun and thought, 'That's ruined too. All my uniform and equipment, it's all ruined because of an oily rag in the—' He thought, 'No...' He touched his head and felt something warm on his temple and he thought with great, happy gratitude, 'I'm hurt. I must have banged my head so at least I've got a wound to show them.'

His boat was turning in slow circles, the smoke fading and whispering out into white puffs.

Lew thought, 'I believed that idiot Pan. It was all a joke and I believed him.' He touched at his head and could have wept that at least they had to be sympathetic to a wounded man. He saw Superintendent Allison's face and he was afraid to wave at the man to signal the pick up in case it showed he wasn't really hurt and—

The fire on the boat had gone out.

Lew said, broken hearted, 'Oh, no...' The boat was drifting back in the water, all the fires out, not a mark on her except the broken wheelhouse door he had smashed himself.

On what was left of the wharf Pan and the coxswain would be saying, 'Me? No, I didn't know anything about it. He just went crazy and threw me overboard and then he started running back and forth like a lunatic telling everyone to get off—'

Back to the goddamned junks and the aft shit seat. Lew said softly to himself, 'You've screwed it up. You've screwed it up...' The boat was drifting back to the shore, less than a hundred yards away from the wharf and he struck out for it as the night boat came to get him and a voice hailed, 'This way. Swim this way!' and Lew, crying, shook his head and made for his own craft to salvage it.

There was a puff of smoke from the engine room area.

The night boat started its engine and came about at dead slow to cut off his path.

They were all drifting back to the shore.

Lew said with salty tears running down his face, 'I'm sorry ... I'm sorry...' He heard a faint pop from his drifting boat and as he struck out for it in a fury, Lew said with blood all over his face, 'No!' Not twice! Not again, you bastards! *Not twice!*' and then, in a sudden swelling of the timbers there was a great pressure inside his boat—he actually saw the plankings bulge—and then in a sudden, roaring, blasting, liberating boiling explosion the boat disappeared from the surface of the sea and sent him down into the sea in a gout of boiling water and matchwood.

He felt a terrific whack in the shoulder as he sank and he thought—

He looked up from the darkness below the surface, sinking, and he thought for a moment that the entire sea was on fire.

*

The windows went. All the windows in Beach Road went and came crashing down in shards and splinters and entire sheets of plate glass into the street.

In the Detectives' Room, O'Yee said, 'Christ! It's happening again!' He saw Feiffer and Auden and Spencer go for their Armalites. Sandbags had collapsed from the shored up windows and the room was a flurry of papers and bits and pieces of wood and sand and material.

The explosion was rolling, echoing, never ending.

O'Yee said, 'Christ! It's happening again!' O'Yee said over and over, trying to find his Armalite, his flak jacket, anything, in the mess, *'Christ, it's happening again!'*

*

His eyes were bright and shining.

He awoke.

After forty years, the rifle was at his shoulder and it had living men in its sights and, after forty years, he awoke.

He pressed the trigger and it was like a great gust of clear clean revivifying air and, at last, again, he was himself.

*

On the night patrol boat, Superintendent Allison said, 'Jesus!' He saw the windows in his wheelhouse go and then something hard smash against it in a splash of blood and then reel back again and disappear from sight. Bullets were ripping the woodwork

77

around the wheelhouse to pieces. He saw a flash from the shore—the sounds were echoing out in the roaring reverberations from the falling pieces of Lew's boat—and for a moment he thought he saw Lew surface in a circle of blood and then go down again and he shouted to one of the deckhands, 'Take the wheel! Take the—' and then the man was down and kicking on the deck as a spout of blood ripped through him like a lance and cut him in two.

Bullets were flying off the metalwork. Allison saw a shower of sparks as a davit buckled and then something hard came down from the superstructure and scudded along the deck.

He saw the engineroom door open and a head come out. He actually saw Constable Ling in there open his mouth to say something and then look surprised as a bullet cut him through the throat and almost decapitated him.

On the ferry, a long way off, there was screaming: he heard the old engine thumping in the craft as the Captain issued an order the engineer had never heard before in his life and then a bullet hit the flare locker on the police boat and a cauldron of white and red and green boiling fire covered Allison and burned through his hair.

He was on fire. He saw something fly off the woodwork an inch from his hand and then the pyrotechnics burned into his face and he thought, 'Oh, my God, I've been disfigured and I—' and then something hard hit him in the centre of the stomach like a sledge hammer and he went over backwards and felt water on his back and the taste of salt.

Engines. He heard engines. He looked up from the water and all the fires on his face had gone out. There were sampans coming, and junks. He looked around for Lew and saw nothing.

Two of his men went down on the deck and then someone came out from below decks carrying something and a bullet took him in the chest and dropped him like a ninepin and Allison screamed out into the water, *'You're killing all my people!'* He saw Lew. He reached out for him. Something hard hit the water beside him and for a single mad moment he thought it might be a duck or a nightbird hunting for minnows.

78

The dawn was coming up. He saw a flash from a warehouse on the shore. The flashes were coming from there.

Crazy. Crazy. Allison, underwater, reached for his gun.

He saw Lew's hand, reaching out for him: a claw covered in blood and he grasped it and thought—

Something touched the side of his head: a great unstoppable metal weight, but so lightly that he thought he had not been touched at all, and with his hand still grasping Lew's, he floated still and dead in the water with only the faintest look of curious surprise on his face.

On the night boat they were all dead and it drifted for a little before the other boats arrived, then, slowly, holed and torn in secret places out of sight, it began to wallow like a raft, and washing the blood and tissue on its decks regularly and evenly out through the gunwales into the sea as if, sure of salvage, there was all the time left in the world.

*

Dawn. Corporal Sakutaro Ozawa of the Japanese Imperial Army 38th Division in Hong Kong saw, for the last time in his life, the glory of the rising sun in the east.

It gave him great joy and happiness and, at long last, at its closing, sliding the rifle back into the rolled-up net and beginning to move, he regretted his life not at all.

7

'Radio Hong Kong. News at Nine . . .'
All the news was bad.

*

On the phone the Commander's voice asked with concern, 'Did you know him? Allison?' He must have had the same batch of ghastly photographs on his desk that Feiffer had. One of them showed Allison floating with half his head blown away and globules of water on his cheeks that made him look as if a moment before the bullet hit he had been crying. The others, of the wreckage of his boat and the dead deckhands, showed . . .

'Yes, I knew him. As a matter of fact—' Feiffer turned the photograph on his desk face down but the image remained. Feiffer said, 'Look, Neal, I've been reading the statement Lew made in the ambulance and I get the distinct impression from what he says that the first bang he heard wasn't a fuel tank exploding at all, it was a blank cartridge being fired in the engine room. I've been in touch with Forensic on the scene by radio and they say they've located the engine room door and as well as having Super Glue on it it's got a bloody great ragged hole blown through it surrounded by powder burns.' Allison had had two children, one of them the same age as Feiffer's pre-school son. Feiffer said, 'I get the feeling that whoever set up the arrangement in Lew's boat wanted to give him time to get clear before it went up and that Allison's coming on the scene made him nothing more than just—'

'Than just what? A convenient target?'

'No.' Feiffer paused. 'For the person who set up the blank

80

cartridge and the explosives I don't think he was any sort of target at all.' The dead deckhands had been laid out in a row on the swamped launch for the photographers. Feiffer said, 'I think whoever set the charges could have quite easily have given them an instantaneous fuse set to ignite the moment the door was tried, and I think, even if he hadn't the wit or the equipment to do that, he could have shot every one of Lew's men off the deck like ninepins while the launch was still at the wharf. By the time the shooting actually did start Lew's people were about six miles away and still running.' Feiffer said cautiously, 'Neal, I hate to sound like Nero Wolfe sitting in his barricaded house in New York growing orchids and solving cases by remote control, but I think there are at least two different courses of action going on and at least one of them we don't understand at all.'

The Commander said with heavy irony, 'And one of those courses was Corporal Sakutaro Ozawa that well known geriatric Jap, who, like his mate, Sergeant Seichiro Tanino, late of the Cuttlefish Lane fishmarkets, so conveniently left us his obi and family snaps for our delight and inspection. 'Right?' He waited for Feiffer to say, 'Yes.'

Feiffer said, 'Am I allowed to say yes?'

The Commander said, 'What is the other one?'

'The other one is whoever keeps ringing us up telling us what imperalist pigs we are. The other one is someone who either doesn't or won't realise that in the Colonial repression stakes the Japanese Imperial Army only ran a close second to Julius Caesar and Adolf Hitler combined.' Feiffer said quickly, thinking of Allison, 'The other one is the one who set up rifles across from us that in the course of firing Christ knows how many rounds didn't hit a single living human being, and the other one is the one who loads the first link of his machine gun belt with a blank so even bloody Auden has the time to realise he hasn't been killed and get down under the field of fire.' Feiffer said, 'And his mates, the Japanese soldiers—'

The Commander said, 'No.'

'The alleged Japanese soldiers—'

'Not even that, Harry.' The Commander said, 'So far so good.'

'What, the logic or the politics?'

The Commander said, 'Go on.'

Feiffer said, 'I think that someone's found a Japanese arsenal and he's decided to use it. I think all this bullshit about colonial repression is just a mask to cover whatever he's planning to use it for—'

The Commander said, 'Kids? Are you saying that kids found this dump and they—'

'No, I'm not saying it's kids. I'm saying that the arsenal came first and he sat down and decided how best he could use it and he came up with a primary idea and that the notion that the best way to go about achieving that idea was to convince us that he's some sort of Masked Anti Imperialist Avenger and that—'

The Commander said with gratitude, 'Anything that lets the Japanese angle out. Anything that—'

Feiffer said, 'And I think that he found something else in that Arsenal that—'

The Commander said warningly, 'What? A few old photographs and obis and—'

'No, some *one*!' Feiffer said desperately, 'What else have we got to go on? According to Christopher O'Yee—'

The Commander said, 'I can't ask the Japanese for the location of their secret arsenals during the Second World War (a) because I can't ask the Japanese anything, and (b)—'

'I know. And (b) because all the papers giving their locations were destroyed.'

'They were. Most of them were kept in Tokyo until the bombings and then they were moved for safety to Nagasaki. And those that weren't went with the 38th Division to Guadalcanal.' The thing about diplomacy was that there were always reasons to say no. The Commander said, 'And if the arsenal is still here some forty years later it must have been bombed so we wouldn't find it anyway even if we had the location. And with redevelopment in this Colony—'

Feiffer said, 'Neal, I think our non lethal kid or maniac or whatever he is is being followed around by whoever else lives or was found in that arsenal!'

'Not by a bloody Second World War hold-out Japanese soldier!'

'No.' Feiffer said, 'No, *by a whole bloody section of them!*' The picture of Allison would not go from his mind. Feiffer said, 'Neal, please, can't we get the Japanese Embassy in on this? Would it hurt so much?'

'Yes! It'd hurt so much!' The Commander said violently, 'I'm not the bloody ogre in this. I've got my orders. Politicians have given me my orders and the economic advisers have given me my orders and the bloody London government have given me my orders!' He paused for a moment in frustration, 'Just let them thank God that they, unlike me, don't have to go around this morning and tell Allison's wife and his children what those bloody orders have led to! And they can thank God that—'

Feiffer said quietly, 'I was best man at Allison's wedding. I've already told them.' He paused with his hand on the photographs, waiting.

There was a long silence, then the Commander said with a sigh, 'Harry, do you know anyone at the Japanese Embassy?'

'O'Yee does, yes!'

There was a long pause.

The Commander said, 'Then ring them.'

'Neal, no one official need know. All of it can be kept totally—'

The Commander said fiercely, 'I don't give a damn! Ring them. And that's an order!' There was a silence as if the Commander, for a moment, listened to hear a tap on his line.

The Commander said again, clearly, not caring who heard, 'Ring them! *Ring them!*'

*

On the phone Mickey Okuno at the Japanese Embassy said happily in English, 'Christopher, everything I have is yours: my wife, my hibachi, my holiday house in the clear fresh air beneath the chimneys of the Mitsui leather tanning factories, the shirt from my back—but if you're after a free ticket to the Tokyo-Nagoya baseball final this season you can forget it.' Okuno's accent, after a Master's in Political Science at Berkeley was as perfect as Berkeley could make it. Okuno said, 'Tell me what you want, oh honourable flatfoot, and it shall be yours.'

O'Yee said evenly, 'I want a Japanese interpreter with a knowledge of nineteen forties military slang and usage and the mentality that went with it.'

There was a silence, then Okuno said, just as evenly, 'Is that you, Christopher? For a moment I thought I had a crossed line and I was talking to a cop or something.'

O'Yee said coldly, 'This is a cop and I'm making a request for—'

There was a brief pause and then Okuno said, 'And this is the Information Officer at the Japanese Embassy, Hong Bay, in the British Crown Colony of Hong Kong and those fucking rifles, asshole, are English or Canadian or something and have got nothing to do with us!'

'Mickey—'

Nothing.

O'Yee said, 'Mickey, we're in a lot of trouble. We've lost—' He hesitated. 'We've lost five of our officers and half a dozen bloody civilians and I get this bastard ringing up in Japanese and—'

Okuno said, 'No, you don't. You don't get any bastard ringing up in Japanese and that's official, and if you do it isn't a Japanese bastard, it's just some bastard who speaks Japanese!' Okuno said, 'Forget it. The war's been over a long, long time and we're not like the Germans going around suffering guilt pangs about it, we just want to forget it!' Okuno said, 'You want someone who speaks a few words of Japanese nineteen forties slang? O.K. 'Tora! Tora! Tora!' How's that?'

'I'm not trying to resurrect the war.'

'Good! Because it's staying buried!' Okuno said, 'Detective Senior Inspector, if you've got an official request to make to this Embassy then you have your Government make it and my

84

Government will consider it and then my Government will inform your Government—'

'I need someone who can talk these bastards in!'

'Talk them in where?'

'In! Safe! Someone who can make them understand—'

'Who the hell is "them"?'

'The spokesmen. The two who ring up. The spokesmen for the rest of them! The—'

'The rest of what?' Okuno said in a gasp, 'God, they're true, aren't they? The rumours. There's a hold-out, isn't there? There's a World War Two hold-out Japanese soldier on this island from forty years ago and he—' He stopped. 'What do you mean, "the rest of them"? *How many are there?*'

'*We don't know.*'

Okuno said, 'You don't mean there's a platoon of them, do you? You don't mean there's a—'

O'Yee said, 'A private interpreter, that's all I'm asking. Just someone the Embassy can recommend. A Chinese, for Christ's sake—'

'Oh, great! What the hell do you think we Japanese go around learning Chinese and English for? A Japanese speaking Chinese who understands the military slang of the nineteen forties—' Okuno almost shrieked, 'Under what circumstances do you think he would have learned it?'

'No one's asking to bring up the actrocity stories all over again!'

There was a hard silence, then Okuno said in a brittle voice, 'Oh. Were they atrocities? Were they? According to our code, is that what they were?' His voice became tight, 'Sorry, did we commit atrocities? Sorry, haven't we become westernised fast enough for everyone? Sorry. The dirty cruel Nips have done it again.' The conversation was going all bad. Okuno said, 'Yeah. Right. Shit. Just like Berkeley. Atrocities. Right. Just hang on a second while I put in my buck teeth dentures and settle my pebble glasses and then I can say in my hissing tone of voice, "Ah, dirty White Race" while I stick a few bamboo slivers up your fingernails.' Okuno said, 'Find your own fucking interpreter! And when you do, make sure you tell him to remember to tell the hold-outs that on the orders of General Macarthur the Emperor isn't a god anymore, but just a nice old man who lives in his Palace studying marine biology—*all right?*'

O'Yee said quietly, 'I'll do that.'

'Good.' Okuno said. 'Do you intend to make an official request? If you do I'll log it.' His voice was formal, stiff. 'Well?'

O'Yee defeated, said softly, 'No.'

There was a silence then Okuno said, 'Don't mistake it, Christopher, never, never mistake it. You're like me: the product of two worlds, but, at base, I know exactly who I am.' Okuno said, 'I only sound like an American, but what I am is a Japanese. You, you look almost like a Chinese and you are—what?' Okuno asked, 'Do you know?'

'Right now, what I am is mud.' The Commander had been right. O'Yee saw Feiffer looking at him with concern on his face.

Okuno said in a strange, sad voice, 'O'Yee-san, hazimete o-me ni kakarimas' . . .' (Mr O'Yee, I meet you for the first time.)

'I don't understand.'

Okuno said quietly in English a moment before he finally hung up, 'No, I know you don't. And the pity of it is that I'd never, never realised it until now.'

*

In the underground arsenal The Technician sat on a stone arms shelf facing The Bannin transferring blocks of explosive from their tattered khaki bags into hessian sacks. The explosive was dry and intact and he broke a little off like chocolate and smelled it. Behind the Major the steel door to the other room was shut. The Bannin had his head bowed in thought, touching at the top of one of his polished leather boots and worrying at the flap. The Technician said without looking up, 'Corporal Ozawa?'

The Bannin said in Cantonese, 'He's dead. Like Sergeant Tanino.' A short disembowelling sword was across his knees and he rested his gloved hands on its scabbard and drew a breath,

'They were both old men. At their respective moments they died like birds, without murmur, and their souls—' The Bannin said, 'We have all resolved to die in battle, those of us who are able, and the rest—'

The Technician, still looking at the explosives, said quietly, 'All right.'

The Major said sadly, "One Hundred Million Will Die Together." That was what the Emperor promised.'

'Yes.'

The Major said, ' "The survivors will them engage in general battle." '

It was no use at all. The Technician said, 'Those people on the boat—'

The Bannin said, 'Enemies.' He brightened up, 'Corporal Ozawa's obi and his family pictures are by now on their way to his home and his family—'

The Technician said quietly, 'You promised to help me.' There was no emotion in his voice. He was merely probing. The Technician said, 'The divine mission to eradicate the uniformed—'

The Bannin made a hissing sound.

'I see.' The Technician clenched his mouth for a moment to hold back the anger and the tears. The Technician said with a sniff. 'It seemed all right to you when we talked about it. When we finally found each other—'

The Bannin said, 'Things have changed.' He looked down at the sword, 'All my people are old. All my—' He said quickly, 'Private Masuo Morishita will be next to go with you. He wants to be next. Ozawa was his friend and he wants to be next.'

'Nobody has to go! Nobody has to die! Nobody has to die!' The Technician said in sudden vehement anger, 'Nobody has to—'

'Everybody! And then when everybody but me has gone, then I will go.' The Bannin touched at the sword and then held it. 'And you, you have promised to assist me at the end so I can find a glorious soldier's death! You, you have promised me—'

'And what about your promises to me? What about the—'

'Children's talk!' The Bannin started to stand up, drawing the sword. The Bannin said, 'All this colonial—all this—we were the colonists! We held Asia like a trembling butterfly, but we—Honourable death is not a course or a choice, it is a necessity!' The Bannin said, 'Private Morishita will be next and you will lead him to the place.' The Bannin pulled at the steel door and was gone for a moment before returning with a rolled up object in his hand. The Bannin said, 'Here! This is our banner. It will be burned so as not to fall into the hands of the enemy and then we will do as you ask and fulfil your little plan and at the same time, culminate our own!'

It was all no use. The Technician said, 'Bannin—'

It was all no use. Totally, utterly, no use at all.

The Technician said, 'All right.' He heard the sea start to thunder against the rocks, as at 9.40 a.m. the tide change began.

The Technician said again, 'All right. If that's what you want. You can rely on me.'

The Bannin nodded. 'You are a good Chinaman and you will be rewarded.'

Cain and Abel. It came back to The Technician from Bible Study class he had once attended in the English Middle School in Hanford Road. The Technician said in Japanese, 'Thank you very much, Major Takashima.'

The Technician looked hard at The Bannin's eyes, but somehow failed to find them. They were not looking at him and The Technician thought that if he was going to do anything it had to be done today, before the man made everything go wrong.

The Technician, resolved on a course of murder, touched at the explosive charges between his knees.

He looked hard at his brother's polished leather boots and only concerned himself now with the best means by which to do it.

*

In the intensive care unit of St Paul de Chartres' Hospital Lew said so softly that Spencer had to lean over his bed to hear him,

'Did he get everybody, Mr Spencer?'

Spencer glanced at Auden. Auden was standing near the end of the bed with something in his hand, shuffling awkwardly from foot to foot. The smell of antiseptic and post-operative vomit and sputum was very strong in the room.

Spencer said quietly, 'Yes, I'm afraid he did.'

'And Allison?' There was pain in Lew's eyes. The pupils seemed to be swimming through a mist that kept building up and then, as the man grimaced, receded and then built up again.

Spencer said, 'Yes.'

'They're all dead except me?'

Spencer said with a smile, 'You're not going to die. You've got a broken shoulder and a little bit of extra ventilation in your uniform, but you're going to be all right.'

Lew said with effort, 'I didn't see a thing. The smoke—'

'We know. Your crew have made statements and—'

Lew said, 'Stupid goddamned Pan. He said he couldn't read the words because of the smoke. He said—' The pain in his eyes welled up and he had to pause, 'I thought for a moment that I'd—' Lew said in a gasp, 'I want a medal for him. I don't care who I have to see or who I have to beg: Allison came over to save me and I want a medal for him.' He was on the edge of tears. He asked again, 'Is he dead? Are you sure he's—' He saw Auden's hand as the man brought it to his face to try to clear some of the smell from his nose. Lew said, 'Is that them?'

Auden brought his hand down quickly.

Lew said, 'In that bag you've got. Is that them? The bullets? Are they the—'

Auden said, 'Yes.' He lifted up the plastic bag.

Lew said in Chinese, 'So many? Did he use so many? To kill—everyone?'

Spencer said softly, 'You're O.K. now. It's just a broken shoulder. You were lucky.'

Lew said, 'Which one of those did they take out of me?' His grip was going and he was drifting away with the effects of the drugs. Lew said, 'I want it. I want the bullet. Which one of the bullets is

89

mine? I want the bullet and I want it reloaded and I want a gun that'll fire it and then I want—' His eyes lost focus and he couldn't seem to remember what he was saying.

Auden said softly, 'Come on, Bill.'

Lew said vaguely, 'The bullet—'

Auden said, 'Sure. You've got my word on it. It's yours. Just as soon as we've finished with it—'

Lew said, 'I can't. I can't hate whoever did it. I can't keep thinking of him long enough to hate him. I just keep thinking of Allison and how I never liked him and how—'Lew said in a sudden blaze, 'I want that bullet!'

Spencer said quietly, 'Lew...' but the man was already asleep and Spencer, straightening up, looked at the package in Auden's hand.

There were only some of the bullets in the package. The rest were still in dead men laid out on steel trays in the Mortuary in body bags and they still had to be recovered.

Lew's bullet, at least, had come out of a living man.

If it had been a bullet at all.

In fact, it had been a single three quarter inch ball bearing with a hole drilled through it, and, because he thought it was something special and it made a pair with the one from Cuttlefish Lane, Auden had it not in the packet with the rest, but bagged, labelled and safe in his inside coat pocket.

He looked at Lew's face on the pillow and touched at the bulge the object made in his pocket with his hand.

*

In the charge room of the Station, Ah Pin the cleaner swept at a mound of white masonry from the ceiling and scooped it up in his cut open five gallon drum scooper. No less than eighty years old, he was bent over from a lifetime of sweeping and Feiffer could swear that he had one arm which was longer than the other from leaning forward to simultaneously sweep, scoop, then scoop again.

Ah Pin said abruptly in a clear Cantonese enunciation that surprised Feiffer, 'Not far from here, during the Occupation, there was the Murder Verandah.' He went on sweeping, not looking up. 'During the Occupation, the Japanese Secret Police used to tie spies they'd caught in chairs and sit them out on the verandah of a hotel and torture them as an example to others.' He looked up at the ceiling where the masonry had come from, and at the bullet hole that had brought it down, 'Important spies and saboteurs: people who picked up twigs off the ground for firewood and people who painted their coal white and used them as paving stones to store them secretly for the winter, and people who—' Ah Pin said abruptly, not looking at Feiffer or anything but the dust, 'On the waterfront, that was a Japanese gun. I've heard them before.'

Feiffer said quickly, 'Those particular sort of Japanese guns?'

'No, just Japanese guns.' Ah Pin said, 'I've heard them before.' He looked through to the Detectives' Room where O'Yee was on the phone talking in Cantonese to someone from the Tourist Office about someone who might speak wartime Japanese and no, he couldn't explain why he wanted to know, but was it possible, was it possible that they knew someone who—.

Ah Pin said quietly, 'The Fireworks Man speaks Japanese.' He was an interpreter at the Murder Verandah hotel for the Japanese.' He looked up. He was at least eighty. There was something in his face that made Feiffer pause. Ah Pin said, 'But in reality he was a member of the BAAG—the resistance.' Ah Pin said, 'In those days a lot of people learned to speak Japanese.'

Feiffer said, 'Do you? Do you speak Japanese?'

'No.' There was no expression in Ah Pin's voice. It could have been true or false, but it was never going to change. Ah Pin said philosophically, 'That's why he prospered after the war, why he got his fireworks licence. He trained in Japan—with his displays and his fireworks—and the Japanese brought him back here after the invasion to interpret for them.' He said again. 'He was a member of the resistance. After the war he was checked carefully and his good deeds outweighed his bad so he was allowed to live.' He gave Feiffer a cracked smile, 'We all got government jobs after

91

the war or we got special consideration for licences and trading concessions when the British came back—everyone who was in the resistance and who wasn't a Communist. We were called the British Army Aid Group, the resistance. Good Chinamen. Good loyal subjects of the King.' He went on sweeping, 'Depending on what we did or what job we had.'

'Will he help?'

'I don't know,' Ah Pin said. 'He was never any more than an interpreter. At his trial he said he often lied to the Japanese about what people said so some of the spies they caught escaped, but—' Ah Pin said with no trace of irony, 'It was all a long, long time ago and now we are all in our assigned, trusted places depending on what sort of men we were then.'

Feiffer said, 'What were you?'

'Now, I am a sweeper of police stations.'

Feiffer said nothing.

'And The Fireworks Man who was a fireworks man before he was an interpreter is back to being a fireworks man again.' Ah Pin said quietly, 'He may help you. But nobody wants to remember.'

Feiffer had seen the man every day of his life for so many years he had lost count. He had always been old. Feiffer said, 'Ah Pin, is there anything I can do to get you back your old job?'

'No.' Ah Pin smiled at him, 'I have it. Before the war, I was also a sweeper of police stations.' Ah Pin said, 'Sixty one years and not once have I missed a day's work.'

Ah Pin said quietly, 'During the war I was an engraver. I left men's crimes engraved with a razor in their bodies.' He saw Feiffer's face and looked down at the broom, 'I was loyal and as you can see, I have been returned to my proper occupation in life.' Ah Pin said, 'I am well satisfied.'

Ah Pin said, 'Ask The Fireworks Man. He knew the war-time Japanese. Ask him.'

He went on sweeping.

Feiffer looked into the Detectives' Room.

He could see O'Yee looking upset about his friend at the Japanese Embassy, Mickey Okuno, but in that moment as Ah Pin

went on sweeping, Feiffer could think of absolutely nothing to say
to him to make it seem right.

*

11.03 a.m. As The Technician drove the stolen furniture van
onto a deserted hill in a public park overlooking the harbour he
leaned out of the cab and glanced up at the position of the sun.

He was early. He knew where Private Morishita would stand
and he was early.

He was resolved.

The spot he had chosen was well away from the paths and the
lunchtime crowds would come nowhere near him.

11.04 a.m.

The Technician waited.

He had his fuses and his paraphernalia in the cab alongside him
and he knew exactly, when the time came, how they would act.

11.06 a.m. He leaned out of the cab again and looked at the
position of the sun.

He waited.

8

Once at the drains, lucky. Twice...

Standing in dejection at the entrance to one of the gaping black holes on the seafront, Auden said quietly, 'That bastard on the roof shot me. He blew all my chances and he shot me with a blank.' He had the two ball bearings in packets in his hand and he clicked them together and took a mental blood-oath. Auden said, 'He blew it for me whoever he was. I was doing fine with the cases we found and then some bastard had to set up something on a roof and shoot me with a blank.' He clicked again, 'I was doing O.K. I was just starting to think like a senior officer and now all I can think of is getting hold of whoever did it and blowing his fucking head off.' Auden said, 'What have I got to redeem myself? Two fucking ball bearings.' He said in utter despondency to Spencer, 'I'll never get to make senior inspector, I'll just spend the rest of my life like Buster Keaton being shot over and over by blank cartridges while the entire Police Mess sit around laughing at me.' He reached the nadir, 'And then, after the Examining Board have finished I'll be going around saying "Yes, sir" even to you.'

There was a half dead minnow flopping around in the sand at Spencer's feet trying to get back to the water. Spencer gave it a gentle push and it made it. Spencer said, 'No, you're a good cop. We found the cartridges together. If it hadn't been for you I wouldn't have even gone in there.

Auden said, 'If it hadn't been for you yelling to everyone that it was only a blank I'd have looked even stupider by starting to do my dead act on the fucking roof.' Auden said reasonably, 'I thought I'd been shot. Anyone would.'

'Sure.'

'Well, *you* didn't! *You* knew it was a blank!' Auden said, 'What the hell have we got? Two ball bearings and that's it, one from Lew and the other one—the other one could have been dropped by anyone.'

'They've both got holes drilled through them.'

'For all I know every ball bearing on Earth has got a hole drilled in it!' Auden said evilly as, for some mad reason, the minnow flopped back to suffocate and he watched it gasp, 'I don't think I'll worry about the promotion. I think I'll just let all the clever buggers solve all the cases and then I'll just come in at the kill like some dumb fucking blunt instrument and beat people up!' Auden said, 'Maybe that's why I haven't been promoted before. Maybe I'm just too dumb.' He looked down at the dying minnow and couldn't bring himself to punish it by prolonging its life. (Spencer gave it a gentle nudge with his shoe and it went back into the water.) Auden said, 'According to Harry, there may be two courses of action happening at the same time: the bloody Jap snipers and the inoffensive little bugger who sets up blanks and safe fields of fire to—' He protested to the heavens, 'Why am I falling back on what Harry says? Why haven't I got any ideas of my own?'

'You have a lot of ideas.'

Auden said, 'Leaving aside putting a .357 through the gut of the guy who shot me with a blank, name one!'

Spencer said, 'Well, um—'

The fish came back to the sand. Auden stomped on it. Auden said, 'I'll put a hole through someone's little ball bearing—!' He looked down at the fish and saw it drill its way back to the surface. Spencer bent down and put it back in the sea. Auden said, 'Hey, if a ball bearing is solid nickel steel and it's meant to protect the moving parts of a steel machine from wearing out, how the fuck do you drill a hole in it? With more steel?'

Spencer felt embarrassed. Spencer said, 'With a diamond tipped drill.' The minnow was definitely looking on its last legs. Spencer said gently, 'I wish you wouldn't keep—'

Auden said, 'You don't drill a hole in a ball bearing! It's crazy.

What for? A ball bearing spins—it turns : It isn't a disc turning on an axis, it's a ball that runs round and round and—' Spencer put the minnow back into the water and it climbed out again. Auden said, 'Unless you—' He got one of the objects out of its plastic bag and tested its weight in his hand. Auden said, 'Unless you—'

Looking at the crushed fish, Spencer made a tutting sound.

Auden said, 'Look!' He scraped his fingernail across the nickel of the ball that had come out of Lew's shoulder and a tiny sliver of nickel flaked off and showed grey underneath. Auden said, 'This isn't a ball bearing at all! It's fucking lead nickeled over to look like a ball bearing! That's how they drilled the hole in it. It's only lead!' He got out the other one, 'They both are!' The minnow came up for air and he kicked sand on it.

Spencer said, 'Listen, leave the fish alone!'

Auden said, 'What?' He looked down at it and then at Spencer's face. Poor bastard. Spencer was just never going to make it to the higher reaches of his profession. Auden said, 'You stupid bastard, that isn't a fish, it's a crab without a shell. Don't keep putting it in the water. It lives underground.'

So did the man who had drilled out the lead ball bearing.

Auden said, 'Shit! I've got it!' Auden said, Queeg-like, 'Click, click, click . . . I've fuckingwell got it! *I even know what it is!*' He held the two balls lightly in his thumbs and fingertips, pinching them slightly by the nails and said, tapping them together, 'Yeah? A section of Japanese soldiers from World War Two, is it? Yeah? Is it?' He went click, click, click, Auden said, 'Yeah? Is it really?' Auden, the senior inspector, demanded, holding the balls up on invisible strings, 'Well? Quick! What is it?'

Spencer said, 'Newton's Cradle. It's part of Newton's Cradle. It's an executive *toy*.'

Auden said with the sweetest of grins, 'Isn't it though? Isn't it though?' He could have kissed himself, Auden said, 'Isn't that, just exactly, precisely, what it is?' Auden said in triumph, '*Yeah!*'

Spencer glanced down at the shell-less crab on the sand.

In fact, it was a minnow, but the odds too much against it, it decided instead to become a corpse and expired on the spot.

*

He had been careful. The furniture van had come from the rear of a shop specialising in the restoration of heavy antique furniture for rich Europeans on the Peak and The Technician, knowing what was inside, calculated the position of the sun and parked it carefully in just the right spot.

He had time to spare.

He thought of Private Morishita watching with his rifle and his rolled up flag and he contemplated his destruction.

The Technician felt a pang of sorrow for someone he had never had a chance to know, but it was nothing the someone would return so he put it from his mind.

The Technician said quietly, 'Bannin, you were never any brother of mine.'

Divine mission to eradicate all the uniformed forces of colonial repression in the world.

It had seemed such a good idea at the time.

The Japanese.

Maybe all the stories about them in the war were true.

No, he *knew* they were.

And, in the end, they were going to make him a very rich young man indeed.

*

In the Detectives' Room, O'Yee said to no one in particular, 'My grandfather lived to be eighty nine years old and the only reason he isn't with us still is that he couldn't stand the suspense of waiting for the end so he killed himself to spare himself the worry.'

11.47 a.m.

The telephone on his desk was silent.

He lit a cigarette and put the burnt match carefully into his ashtray so as not to dirty up Ah Pin's nice clean floor and, glancing at the photographs of the dead from the launch Feiffer

97

had left on his desk before he went out, wished he had had his grandfather's foresight.

*

In his underground vaults The Keeper Of Secrets said softly to himself, 'Come on, Owlin, *how*? How? *How*?'

He was in the labyrinths. As far as he could see in the dimly lit corridors there were papers and books, runs of periodicals, letters, diaries, reports, White Papers, everything the Colony had ever known since—

In the heavy silence Owlin's voice said, 'Come on, how? *How*?'

How to find a buried Japanese arsenal on the waterfront using trees?

How, with only one side of the story did you find the other?' How?

A buried arsenal.

Buried by what?

By bombing? None of the Japanese papers from that period were there and the Hong Kong Occupation news sheets would never have been allowed to print that the glorious Imperial Empire was at last under attack from the skies, that—

Nineteen hundred and forty two. By forty three the Thirty Eighth Division was gone to Guadalcanal where they were slaughtered.

Nineteen hundred and forty two.

Owlin went to a shelf packed with yellowing single sheet newspapers headed *Occupation Newspapers And Official Proclamations Issued To Hong Kong Residents 1941 to 45, File Only, Not To Be Removed. For Office Consultation Only.*

He leafed through the pages.

Sunday August the 25th, 1942, Wharf Cove, Hop Pei Cove, Reservoir Bay—

Blackout.

After that Sunday there had been a blackout imposed.

98

That Sunday the first American bombers had hit.

... Wharf Cove, Hop Pei Cove, Reservoir Bay...

Monday September the first, 1942:

The blackout was extended to Hong Bay East, the area surrounding Beach Road and...

RESTRICTED AREAS.

The Japanese Government in Hong Kong informs residents that certain reconstruction works will be carried out in the Wharf Cove and Reservoir Bay districts beginning Wednesday, September third and that any persons found in these restricted areas or in possession of military objects from these areas will be shot.

Long Live The Greater Asia Co-Prosperity Sphere!

(Signed) Area Officer, Engineers

Imperial Japanese Army in China.

The military objects were bits and pieces of American bombs, and what?

And bits and pieces of damaged underground arsenals.

Owlin said quietly, 'Well, well, well...'

All he needed was a bombing map.

He walked to another labyrinth, flicking overhead lamps on as he went until he came to a section marked, *AIR FORCE, U.S.*

He even had the flight briefings of some of the pilots who had led the raids.

He touched at the first diary on the shelf and, opening it at the first page, felt the paper and, knowing that once, once that page had been made from a living tree, felt for the first time in his life, a strange, revengeful pleasure.

*

On the phone Feiffer's voice said curiously, 'Christopher, are you sure the address you gave me for The Fireworks Man is correct?' He paused for a moment and it surprised O'Yee that there was absolutely no sound of the city behind his call, 'I mean, *our* Fireworks Man. You're sure you got the right address from the files?'

O'Yee said, 'Where are you?'

'Well, I'm out at Maltby Point which is a bit like saying I'm out at the Eddystone Lighthouse.' Feiffer said, 'I had to leave the car at the end of a pebble road and then I spent twenty minutes wandering along the perimeter of what I assumed was at the very least a nuclear missile base before I realised it was the fence of a fireworks factory.' Feiffer said, 'The address you gave me is Maltby Point. I assumed it was probably a row of shanty houses. There's a bloody great sign saying that anybody who attempts to pass a point here carrying matches, metal or explosive or inflammable substances is liable to about five hundred years under the Dangerous Substances Ordnance, not to mention High Treason, and I thought before I handed in my boy scouts' tinder box and gun I'd better find out who the hell I was handing it in to.' Feiffer said, 'I'm ringing from a phone box a little way from the main entrance that's so isolated that not even the vandals have found it.' Feiffer said, 'It's incredible. The place is huge. Apart from the wooden two storey office building there are rows of wooden factory buildings and wooden storage huts and—would you believe, wooden cranes? We have got the right man, haven't we? I seem to remember The Fireworks Man as that rather disreputable bugger in a singlet and shorts that Auden and Spencer dragged out with them when they went listening for gunshots. What's his actual address?'

O'Yee said, 'Maltby Point is his actual address. He owns the whole shebang. That disreputable bugger in singlet and shorts is worth a cool couple of million dollars in terms of land alone.'

Feiffer said, thinking of Okuno, 'How are you feeling?'

'Fine. How should I be feeling?'

'You should be feeling fine.' Feiffer asked, 'No more calls?'

'No.'

There was a pause and then Feiffer said, 'O.K. I'll hand in my six shooter and silver mounted Bill Durham tobacco pouch.'

O'Yee said, 'That's *Bull* Durham.'

'Oh.' Feiffer said, 'Well, you should know.'

100

'*Why* should I know?'

'You're the resident American, not me.' Feiffer said, 'You did know though, didn't you?'

'Look, I'm not feeling bad about Okuno. All right?' O'Yee said, 'Thanks anyway, but—'

Feiffer said, 'It never ceases to surprise me how you can wander down a street in Hong Kong avoiding people who look like ten cents and never know they're worth—'

O'Yee said with irritation, 'Well, that's the bloody Chinese for you, isn't it? They don't like advertising their wealth!' O'Yee said, 'Look, I appreciate what you're doing, but you don't have to ring up and tell me what a good guy I am because Okuno has got me thinking I'm a shit, because I don't think I'm a shit!' O'Yee said, 'I made a boo-boo and lost a friend, that's all. You know better than I do about the bloody Chinese and it hasn't surprised you one iota that the local tramp is the official money lender to Howard Hughes because you've been here longer than I have and in the first place you wouldn't have made the mistake of ringing up bloody Okuno anyway! You'd have had more sense!' O'Yee said with difficulty, 'My grandfather lived to be eighty nine years old and the only reason he isn't with us still is that—'

Feiffer said, 'His friends all got around and smothered him with misconceived concern. Right?'

O'Yee said, 'That's right!'

Feiffer said, 'Look, it was my fault. When the Commander said we could ring someone at the Embassy I automatically thought of your friend Okuno—'

O'Yee glanced at the clock. It was 12.06. Ah Pin was in the charge room, out of earshot. O'Yee said, 'Harry, what are you doing—worrying about me?'

There was no reply.

O'Yee said, 'Are you there?'

There was another silence and then Feiffer said with a clucking sound, '*Bull* Durham. I'll remember.'

O'Yee said quietly, 'I appreciate it.' 12.08. There was no one else in the Detectives' Room. O'Yee said in his best Texas drawl,

'Say, pard, thanks for droppin' by. It gits a mite lonesome out here on the prairie when there's nary a—'

Feiffer said, 'O.K., I'll take my Bull Durham and I'll wander over to the Marshal's office here and deposit my hog's leg.'

'You haven't got a hog's leg! A hog's leg is a long barreled Single Action Army—' O'Yee said, 'Forget it.' He looked down at his desk and smiled. O'Yee said with a grin, 'You know, with you around, maybe my old grandad might have made it to ninety.'

12.08 p.m.

He lit a cigarette and looked around for the ashtray and found that somehow, secretly, to cheer him up, Ah Pin had slipped him the cleanest one in the place.

*

Outside *Technotrex Toys And Games* in Wyang Street, Auden said urgently to the ticking of Spencer's stopwatch, 'I can take it out, Bill.' He watched the silver balls clicking in the shop window next to a display of chess computers and nickel plated toy Blondins balancing on metal wires designed to soothe the executive mind and said again with emphasis, 'There's just enough time if I see the smoke to get to his set-up and take it out before it starts working. I know there is.'

The clicking balls, five of them, were suspended from a central pivot by what looked like fishing line. The idea was that you drew back one ball and let it go and, miraculously, on a principle discovered by Isaac Newton, the force was transferred through the other three and caused the fifth, the one at the far end, to click out like a pendulum. It was supposed to soothe the minds of frazzled executives. Auden said, 'What he has to do is draw back the last ball and set it with some sort of fuse or string and then burn it through to make a timing device, then when the ball hits, it transfers the whack through to the trigger of the set-up rifle and fires it.'

Spencer said, 'The rifle must be set upside down with the trigger guard taken off.' He watched the balls clicking with one eye on the stop-watch. 'It's very reliable.'

Auden said, 'And then the principle is that the last ball clicking back again hits the next in line and transfers the force back to the first which flies out and then hits the one next to it and repeats the process.' He said, 'That's how he gets the gun to keep on shooting. The ball keeps going back and hitting the trigger every time until it—' He asked, 'What's the timing between hits?'

Spencer said with a wary shake of his head, 'Less than one and a quarter seconds. If they were using the technique down in the drains then it was taking longer.' The balls in the shop window display were the same size exactly as the ones in Auden's pocket. Spencer said, 'I don't think you should make too much of what timing the one in the window's got. There's the question of recoil when it's tied up to a gun and you don't even know how far out the first ball was pulled to start the pendulum effect.' Spencer said, 'We know how it's done. That's something anyway. Sooner or later—'

Auden said, 'Sooner or later he's going to use it again.' He looked earnestly at Spencer. 'I cane take it out, Bill. After the smoke there's a period of time before the fuse or whatever it is burns through and then there's a blank before the live rounds start so that gives me—what? Three plus say two plus say two seconds before the first round—that's all of nine or ten seconds.'

Spencer said with alarm, 'That's seven!'

Auden said, 'Christ, in seven seconds an Olympic runner could get—'

'You don't happen to be an Olympic runner.' Spencer said, 'If anything, I could run faster than you. I'm thinner—'

Auden said, 'Yeah, but you don't have the motivation to do it.'

'Of course I don't have the motivation to do it!' Spencer said, 'The Army Bomb Disposal people are the ones who have the motivation for this sort of thing, not us—they've got remote control gadgets that can dismantle a bomb without anyone being within fifty yards of the thing!'

Auden said, 'In eight seconds?'

'Seven!' Spencer said, 'It's bloody *seven!*'

'Look, if I know the first live round's coming next all I have to do once I get into the hut or shed or wherever it's been set up is just to get to one side and—'

Spencer said, 'And if by any chance it's been set up with instantaneously—' Spencer said, 'Can I remind you that after the set-up goes fizz, fizz, click, click, bang, bang, it then goes ka—BOOM? Can I remind you that—'

Auden, not hearing a word of it, had his gaze fixed firmly on the swinging balls, Auden said, 'Well, what do you think?'

'I've just told you what I think! I think it's crazy!'

Auden said, 'I can do it. I know I can. I'm quick. I've got fast reactions.'

Spencer said in a mutter, 'You'll need them.'

Auden watched the swinging balls. Spencer's watch going tick, tick, tick, tick, echoed the click, click, click, click in his brain.

Auden said, 'And then we'll have all the evidence we'll need: the entire set-up, fingerprints, everything. Leave the Jap thing to the political experts and we'll just come in with all the hard evidence and dump it on their desks and come out whiter than white covered in bloody braid.'

Spencer said, '*We?* Where do I come in when you're doing your imitation of a hazy blur?' Spencer said seriously, 'No, Phil, don't even consider it.'

Auden said, still watching the balls and mesmerized by the steady clicking and ticking, 'No, I'm not considering it, I've decided.' Auden said, 'They get me once on the blank trick, but not twice.'

'What if that's the way they're thinking too and the first round isn't a blank?'

Auden said, 'No, don't worry.' He turned and crossed the road to go to the car, almost being knocked down twice, and, still clicking and ticking and dreaming dreams of glory said to Spencer's alarmed face, 'I'm really light on my feet. I can have the door to a shack down with my shoulder in about half a second flat.' He was smiling and nodding to himself and as he took off straight into the stream of traffic without an indicator light he missed a taxi by an inch and went decisively down towards Yellowthread Street to the stalls to put himself ready to await Starter's Orders.

*

All the names had been changed. The American pilots had been using the names of features on the island used before the Occupation and then the names had been changed by the Japanese during that Occupation and then, after the Occupation, in order to wipe out old memories and commemorate new ones, the toponomists—the namers of streets and features—had changed them again.

And they were only the names in English.

In Chinese all the names of all the streets and all the features and all the landmarks were different and always had been.

And, during the Occupation, the Japanese had changed them too, and then, after the Occupation, the Chinese again, had changed them back, and then—

In the vaults Owlin looked at a bewildering array of maps and briefings and government reports and tapped on his desk with his fingernail.

12.19 p.m.

Somewhere, on one of those maps or in one of those reports or mentioned in one of those briefings, the location of the arsenal awaited him.

As he always did, he set to work from the beginning and began doing the job minutely and slowly, a piece of evidence at a time.

Occasionally, he met a temporary dead end in his researches, but it bothered him not at all and, in the interests of accuracy, like any true scholar, he merely went back to the beginning and, undeterred and unhurried, began again.

*

There was no equivocation. In his picture windowed office

overlooking the harbour at Maltby Point The Fireworks Man said, 'No.' His face was set like cement. There was a sign on a door leading from the wooden office to the main factory complexes reading in both English and Chinese, *Absolutely No Unauthorised Persons Past This Point* and the sentiments and finality of the sign were mirrored exactly on The Fireworks Man's face.

The Fireworks Man, sitting at his surprisingly large mahogany desk in his well cut suit and expensive Thai silk tie, said at the helm of his surprisingly large enterprise, 'No. Not again. Not a word of the language. Never again. No. Not for anything anyone can offer me. *No!*'

*

He saw him.

Private Morishita.

He was dressed as a delivery coolie. Carrying a rolled up bolt of cloth he moved across the park to take up his position behind an old World War Two pillbox preserved and sealed in the park as a monument.

The Technician smiled.

The Technician got back into the cab of the van and moved it a few feet as if he was worried that the wheels sat on less than solid ground, and then, getting out again, satisfied, looked at the sun, entered the back of the van carefully, and unhurriedly completed his labours.

9

The Fireworks Man looked at the walls of his office and out through the wooden framed picture window across the compound to the wooden firework assembly huts. Everything in the place was either wood or cement. Feiffer noticed that all the pens and paperclips and even the scissors on his desk were either brass or bamboo—nothing that might cause a spark. The Fireworks Man touched at his own lined face—he wore a single jade ring—and said again, 'No.' He had a strange look on his face, midway between sadness and a smile. 'I'm seventy one years old—you're telling me these people are left-overs from the Occupation?' He said with force, 'I'm a left-over from the Occupation. Not only do these people, according to you, shoot, they *run!*' The Fireworks Man said with heavy irony, 'What have they done? Missed all the stresses of modern life and all the dangers of eating the wrong food by living in their caves for forty years?' He paused for a moment, 'And why are they running and shooting now? Why not ten years ago? Why not twenty?' The Fireworks Man said with rising age-wisdom anger, 'Why not *thirty?*' He looked hard at Feiffer and saw a man in his early forties whose eyes had not even begun to dull with the true comprehension of life, 'Have you any idea how long forty years is? Does it mean anything to you? It's your entire *lifetime.*' The Fireworks Man said slowly, looking down at his ring and twisting it, 'The other night on television—totally by accident, at the home of a business acquaintance—I saw a film about the Second World War.' He paused and his eyes came back to Feiffer, 'In the film which was made recently all the people had a modern cut to their clothes and their haircuts were all modern, and the attitudes they all had were cynical and up-to-date and—'

The Fireworks Man said, 'But it wasn't like that, the reality. The reality is that it was forty years ago. The reality was— The reality was that, now, now—in modern terms—it was all old-fashioned!' He saw Feiffer's face and thought he was simply not getting through to him. The Fireworks Man said, 'Don't you understand? It wasn't just another time—it was another *world*!'

Feiffer said nothing. He watched as The Fireworks Man's gaze strayed out the window again.

The Fireworks Man said quietly, 'We wouldn't do it again. Not like that. Not for the things we thought were important then, not—we wouldn't do it like that again because "we"— everybody—us, the Chinese, me, the Japanese—we're all old men!' The Fireworks Man said, 'No, I won't talk to whoever it is speaks Japanese. Use an official interpreter.'

Feiffer said quietly, 'An official interpreter, like your war film, could only talk in the modern idiom. We want someone who was familiar with the idioms of the time as well as the military—'

The Fireworks Man said, 'Someone has told you about the Murder Verandah, haven't they?'

Feiffer said, 'They told me you pretended to help the Japanese while at the same time working for the British Army Aid Group: for the resistance.'

The Fireworks Man said with a trace of irony, 'Did they? Is that what they told you? Who was that? Someone who was there? Or someone who just—'

Feiffer said, 'Someone who was there.'

'Another old man.'

'Yes.' Feiffer said quietly, 'You've helped us in the past. The other night you helped my two officers on the beach with the gunshots—'

The Fireworks Man said easily, 'That was for my licence. Every year my fireworks licence has to be renewed and I need a good character from the police to get it.' He nodded to himself, 'I'm a businessman.' The Fireworks Man said, 'I began my career in Japan. It was where I learned my trade. Before the war. I export seventy percent of my products to the Japanese.'

'No one has to know.'

'Of course people have to know! If these men are what you claim them to be who is going to stand up in Court next to them and interpret?'

Feiffer said, 'An official police interpreter.'

'You just said—'

'When we get them it doesn't matter who talks to them or whether the cut of their clothes is modern or old fashioned. Before that—'

The Fireworks Man said, 'No.' He shook his head. The Fireworks Man said, 'I've forgotten. It's the truth. I've forgotten the language.'

'Then how do you export to Japan? Do you let one of your juniors do it?' There had been no sign of any other office of comparable size in the ground floor corridor leading to The Fireworks Man's office. Feiffer said, 'This is your own business. If you built up any contracts in Japan before the war the last thing you'd do is insult them by passing them on to a junior—'

The Fireworks Man said, 'Very well, you know about the Chinese business mind!'

Feiffer said, 'And you know the Japanese military one.'

'Stop cajoling me!' The Fireworks Man said, 'Are you asking me or telling me? This business only exists because I have a licence to manufacture explosive substances. All the police have to do is—'

Feiffer said, 'I'm asking you.'

'*You have no idea what those times were like here in Hong Kong!*'

'No.' Feiffer said quietly, 'That's why I'm asking you.'

The Fireworks Man put his hand to his face.

'I understand that you—'

'You understand nothing!' The Fireworks Man said, 'To hear it all again—to see them come out of the ground like resurrected corpses—to bring it all back...' The veins in his neck were standing out. He looked like a very old man. The Fireworks Man said sarcastically, 'Maybe they can still shoot and run—after all, they were better men than us. That was what they always told us.

Maybe the great Japanese code of Bushido had a built-in longevity that we poor ordinary men—' The Fireworks Man said, 'I was married to a Japanese girl before the war, did your informant who was there tell you that?'

Feiffer said, 'No. My informant only—'

'Oh, your informant knew all right. Who was he? One of the BAAG men? One of the good loyal Chinese who my masters tortured on the verandah? Someone who helped try me after the war? Illegally!' He said suddenly, 'Yes, I was tried! Not by a War Crimes Commission, but by the Chinese vigilantes! By the righteous representatives of the people! Did you know they had executioners who—even after they'd killed you—stood over your body and cut your crimes into your body with a razor? Did you know that?' The Fireworks Man pulled the sleeves of his shirt up melodramatically. 'But do you see any scars on me?' He leaned forward and dragged at the collar of his open-necked shirt, 'Do you see any healed bullet wounds in my neck?'

'No one suggested you—'

'*Didn't they? Didn't they?*' The Fireworks Man shouted, 'Of course they did!' They just didn't prove it, that's all! They proved that I spoke Japanese and they proved that in order to keep my business intact—to keep my land out of the hands of the Japanese—to curry their favour—I interpreted for them! They proved that! And they proved I had a Japanese wife who had relatives in the Occupying Army! They proved that too! They proved that sometimes I lied to the Japanese about what some of the Chinese spies and saboteurs they caught said to me—they proved I helped—they proved I helped the Chinese more than I helped the Japanese! Or did they?' His breathing was coming in fast, hot gasps. The Fireworks Man said in a sly, provocative voice, 'Or did they merely prove, did they simply prove that I made sure a few captured spies were still alive at the end of the war to say that I was on their side and that the greater proportion—the ones who would have said I helped the Japanese more—had all been killed off and were not in a position to prove anything?' The Fireworks Man said, 'The Resistance, when they tried me in their little cellar on Wyang Road—all standing around with their looks of hatred and their captured officers' pistols and their razors—all they ever proved about me was that there was nothing to prove!' The Fireworks Man said quietly, 'But they killed my Japanese wife.' He paused, 'The moment the news came through that the atomic bombs had fallen and that the Emperor had issued his Imperial Rescript telling the Japanese to lay down their arms, they killed her all right.' In the wooden, uninflammable room, it was as if The Fireworks Man looked around on his desk for a cigarette. The Fireworks Man said, 'Yes. She was easy. No doubt about her. She was Japanese. So they killed her.'

Feiffer said softly, 'I'm sorry.' People had been killed too in Cuttlefish Lane and in the harbour and on the half completed building across from the Station. Feiffer said, 'I have to ask.'

The Fireworks Man said softly, 'They asked me what she was like and I said, "She's a Jap" and that satisfied them. At the time, that was enough.' The Fireworks Man said, 'I married again, after the war. This time, a Chinese woman, and I have a son. A Chinese son.' He shrugged. 'So, after the war, that was all right.' He said with a bitter smile, 'My Chinese son, when I am dead, will get none of this.' He looked out at the compound, 'When I feel near death, everything I have here will be sold and all the profits given to charity for my soul and the soul of—of others—and nothing, nothing of what all this cost me will be left.' He said with heavy sarcasm, 'And then they can make an heroic film about the brave battles of Hong Kong and they can give me a younger face and a modern suit and with-it haircut and they can concentrate on making all the bodies of the too-young actors look attractive and they can forget the ugliness of the soul.' He demanded, '*Can't they?*'

Feiffer waited.

The man's eyes were dim and full of memories.

'I wasn't attached to the Army units, I was with the Kempeitai.' He smiled at the window and shrugged. He wiped at his eyes. 'You know, the Japanese Secret Police—the Gestapo.' His eyes stayed staring at the glass. 'On that verandah they tortured over fifteen hundred people and then the ones they decided were spies—which was most of them—they shot.' The Fireworks Man closed his eyes. 'Several of the spies and saboteurs were people who had forgotten to salute a Japanese flag as they walked past it, which was a capital offence.' The Fireworks Man said, 'In one or two cases I got them set free by saying they were simpleminded and that what they said—even in Cantonese—didn't make sense.' He swallowed. 'And I got one or two of the resistance people off—one or two of the important ones, some of the executioners—by saying that they were part of my own little spy ring and that, if the Japanese let them off then they'd lead them to bigger fish.'

Feiffer said nothing.

The Fireworks Man, a long way away, said, 'Shooting is a very quick and clean method of killing. Do you find that?'

'No, not particularly.'

'A little cleaner and quicker, however, than sending men to their deaths by stealth and wrong information against them.' The Fireworks Man said quickly, 'Oh, they supplied the names—the Resistance—they had a list of people who could be eliminated in place of their own men. The only proviso was that I had to make sure the Japanese thought they would resist them to the death so they'd be killed outright and, rather than break in on them to capture them, they would come in shooting.' The Fireworks Man said, 'Which didn't matter anyway because the resistance had already killed them with Japanese weapons and wired their houses with grenades to make sure.' The Fireworks Man said, 'This man who told you about me, I know who he is. I've seen him in the Station. Did he tell you what he did during the war?'

Feiffer nodded.

The Fireworks Man said quietly, 'He is serving his penance too.' The Fireworks Man said reflectively, 'Ah Pin. The "Ah" as you know, simply denotes that he is a servant, a labourer for someone or something.' He paused, 'That was all he ever was.' The Fireworks Man twisted his jade ring, 'But he still wonders, I know he still wonders. I've seen him lately, each of us in our respective ranks, with our respective prosperity, and I know he still wonders about me...'

Feiffer said quietly, 'About whose side you were really on?'

The Fireworks Man looked on the verge of tears. 'Yes.'

'No one is still after you.'

'Maybe I am still after them.'

'Are you?'

The Fireworks Man said with a smile, 'No, anything that happened now would be murder. Then, on the other hand, it was glory.' He looked hard at Feiffer with a strange, hard expression on his face. The Fireworks Man said, 'Wasn't it?' He smiled. 'Yes. It was glory. Of course it was. I saw it all on a film on television, just the way it was. It was glory.' He looked at Feiffer with a strange, pitying look, 'The film was full of young men doing young men's things and it was made, my friend who follows these films tells me, by young men.' He asked, 'How can it not be true? Young men never lie.' He waved his hand at the picture window, 'Whatever I say or do, you will grant me the licence because you are a young man. All this is true. Surely.'

Feiffer said firmly, 'This has nothing to do with the licence and provided you haven't contravened any safety regulations the licence will be granted.'

The Fireworks Man said, 'Sure. Of course I believe you. I believe everybody: the Japanese, the Resistance—'

Feiffer said irritably, 'During the war, whose side *were* you on?'

The Fireworks Man said, 'I will speak Japanese to your hearty cave dwellers. I will tell them to come in in the idiom of the time.'

Feiffer said, 'I have my own reasons for wanting to know!'

'Why? Did you lose someone too? A father perhaps? An uncle? Someone who—' The Fireworks Man said between clenched teeth, 'Wonder! Think about it and watch your television films and read your books and think your own thoughts and—at the end of it—maybe when you are as old as me—*wonder. Wonder about it!*'

Far below, in the old cellars and air raid shelters beneath the fireworks factory at the end of Maltby Point they were testing some of the new run of heavy display fireworks.

The explosions in the contained, safe rooms, rocked and reverberated against the thick rock of the point, but, insulated from them in the fireproof, silent room, neither The Fireworks Man nor Feiffer heard them and they went on, unnoticed, until the test pieces were consumed and became extinct.

*

The pill box in the public park was a memorial to the men of the Royal Rifles of Canada and the Winnipeg Grenadiers who had fought during the seventeen day defence of the Colony in an heroic attempt to stave off inevitable defeat.

So the little brass tablet on the sealed structure read.

In the languages of the country, French and English, it commemorated the thousand or so of those men who had died during the defence or later from their wounds.

The pill box was pock marked with bullet and shrapnel holes and around the meshed-off gun slits, burned a deep brown colour where perhaps once, or perhaps at the last, it had been seared by a flame thrower or a phosphorous grenade.

With its Roman characters, the tablet meant nothing to Private Morishita and, glancing down at the rear of the furniture van as The Technician finished there and nodded to himself, he took off his thousand stitches obi and tied the frayed tapes carefully and reverently to a jagged piece of masonry and knelt down in the direction of the Imperial Palace in far away Tokyo to make an act of dedication.

The Rising Sun flag of his Quartermaster Unit was folded on the ground beside him, signed with many names, and he touched at it and then the rifle beneath it and spoke an ancient prayer for the last time.

2.04 p.m.

The sun was behind him, over his shoulder and, as The Technician had intended he would, he had a clear unimpeded view of the back of the furniture van and the ground behind it.

The uniformed forces of colonial repression.

Morishita smiled to himself.

2.06 p.m.

All he had to do was wait.

*

In Icehouse Road, Feiffer pulled his car over to—amazingly—
an empty parking spot near the entrance to the Public Records
Office and thought for a moment of going in to ask Owlin—

What?

About the Occupation? The Japanese? Arsenals?

About his own father?

The only photograph he had of his father showed a tall, fair
haired man standing in his old fashioned Shanghai Municipal
Police uniform somewhere on the Bund with ships and sampans
and tenders in the background.

In the picture, it seemed to be raining.

After the war Feiffer had gone back to Shanghai with his mother
from Australia and his uncles there—

His uncles there had never told him anything.

It was said that beneath the streets of London, if you dug deep
enough, first you would come upon signs of the medieval city and
then, even deeper, the Roman, and then, if you kept on digging,
going deeper and deeper, you might find...

The streets of Hong Kong, like the buildings, all looked new
and modern, clean and up-to-date and sure of themselves, and as
if they hid—

Exactly nothing.

2.13 p.m.

After whatever happened next, The Fireworks Man said he
would come to await the phone call.

After whatever happened next.

There were people everywhere in the city and the streets were
moving like serpents, imperceptibly changing and twisting and
coiling, swallowing them up.

Out of a clear blue sky...

115

Feiffer felt cold.

He started the engine of the car a moment before someone behind him honked for him to either get out of the car or get the car out of there and, still thinking of an old, old photograph and old, old streets, drove directly to the Station to wait.

Tick, tick, tick, tick, tick, tick, tick . . . eight seconds. At his desk in the Detectives' Room Auden pressed the lever on the stopwatch down hard and said to Spencer with a fierce nod, 'Eight seconds.'

Spencer was standing at a pile of sandbags looking out through the hole in the wall at the streets. Spencer said without turning around, 'It's—'

'I know. I know. Seven.' Auden said, 'I'll try again.' He saw O'Yee looking at him and grinned.

Spencer said, still without turning, 'It has to be less than seven. Seven is from first warning to finish line. Seven is the absolute—'

Auden snapped the stopwatch in his hand to reset the timing. O'Yee was still looking at him. Auden said, 'I don't know how far I have to run, do I? For all I know I could be right on top of it from the moment I start!'

O'Yee asked mildly, 'On top of what?'

Spencer said, 'Seven isn't a measurement of distance, it's the time you get from the first reliable warning to the end.' He turned around, 'You should be already there when you start thinking in terms of seven seconds!'

O'Yee said, 'Already where?'

'Well, I've got to assume that!' Auden said, 'How the hell can I tell where I'll be when I've got seven seconds if I don't know where I'm starting from?'

O'Yee said, 'Starting to do what?'

Spencer said with a curious look on his face, 'Forget it, Phil. There are just too many imponderables.'

Tick, tick, tick, tick, tick . . .

O'Yee said, '*What's he doing?*'

Spencer said with a sigh, 'Running.' He looked at Auden sitting at his desk with his eyes closed and a look of strain on his face, 'He's bloodywell *running*, isn't he?'

116

O'Yee said, 'Is he?'

Auden stopped the watch. 'Seven exactly.' He looked at O'Yee. O'Yee looked back. Auden winked at him and said with a nod, 'I'm off cigarettes for the rest of the day. They slow you down.'

Spencer came forward. He still looked cross, like a Mary Poppins nanny tired of explaining that umbrellas went up, not down. Spencer said a word at a time as if to a moronic child, 'You haven't got seven seconds! You don't know how long you've got whatever you do! For all you know you could start the seven seconds when you're still eight seconds away from it and then you've got minus one second and you haven't got anything!'

Auden said, 'It'll work,'

O'Yee said, 'What will?' He waited for an explanation, but none came. O'Yee said mildly, 'Excuse me for asking—'

The phone on Feiffer's desk rang and all three of them went for it at once, but it was only someone ringing up to report an act of gross indecency in a public park off Beach Road and O'Yee gave him the number of Vice and told him to get them to pass the message on to one of their patrols.

2.15 p.m. exactly.

Tick, tick, tick, tick, tick, tick . . .

The voice reporting the indecency had sounded muffled, as if it was someone trying to disguise his identity with a handkerchief over the mouthpiece. It was the usual thing with Vice jobs.

Tick, tick, tick, tick, tick . . . Auden said in triumph, 'Six seconds!'

Maybe it was some sort of new English game, like unemployment.

O'Yee said quietly to himself, 'I don't know . . .'

Tick, tick, tick, tick, tick, tick, tick . . .

He wondered why Spencer seemed to look so worried about it.

*

In the labyrinth of archives, The Keeper of Secrets, Owlin, moved to a shelf marked *Pacific War, Underground Bunkers Used By*

Japanese In.

One of the bunkers found on the island of Iwo Jima during the fighting had been no less than fifteen hundred feet long, cut thirty feet deep in the ground, and the American Marines who had entered it had discovered no less than seventeen concealed entrances and exits in the crazy subterranean jigsaw of the place.

The bunker had held three hundred men and enough food and supplies for them to hold out, if necessary, for up to three and a half months.

On the evidence, the Hong Bay arsenal held a single Quartermaster's section, and the size of a complex on an island the size of Iwo Jima compared to that the Japanese might have built in a garrison the size of Hong Kong...

Owlin did his sums.

It was unsummable.

It had to be huge: a complex for something the size of Hong Kong, against the unthinkable event of invasion by—

God, it had to be *enormous*.

It had to be at least—

It had to be...

On Iwo Jima parts of the complex had been destroyed by bombing and naval gunfire and become sealed off. Parts of it were so massive that at first the Marines, fighting for their lives gallery by gallery had thought there was not one, but a dozen, complexes, all—

Not one, but a dozen...

But it had only been one, and—

And, on wartime Iwo Jima—

And—

Owlin said in a fury at his own blind stupidity, 'You stupid *fool!*'

—And in peacetime Hong Kong, years ago, it had to have *already* been found!

*

They came. The Technician had made his call and they came.

118

The first of many. In plain clothes, they came.

One of them was a young Chinese woman. Morishita saw her clearly as she got out of the car and glanced around the park.

There was a man with her, still in the car—a European—and she was nodding at the van and asking him to do something about it.

He saw the man nod, then lean forward in the car to take up the radio telephone to ask Despatch for further information while the woman waited.

The man and the woman were in plain clothes.

Morishita waited for the uniforms.

The sun was directly behind him.

Even if they looked straight at him, they would see nothing.

2.35 p.m.

Appositely, it all hinged on the sun that was commemorated on the folded up flag that lay by his waiting rifle.

Concealed by the sealed-up pillbox, Morishita waited.

10

At the van Detective Inspector Winter touched at the flat Walther PPK concealed under his flowered shirt and said soundlessly to Woman Police Constable Minnie Oh, 'O.K.' He nodded, 'Open it.' He saw Minnie's long fingers close around the handle on the cab door and gently pull it down to free the lock. She wore flat shoes and slacks: Winter saw the muscles in her thighs tighten as she had to stretch to reach the handle and he sighed inwardly.

The door came open without a sound and he looked in.

Nothing.

There were a few candy papers and a street map of Hong Kong on the offside seat and the usual collection of dust, grime and bits and pieces of assorted truck driver effluvia on the driver's seat. The key was still in the ignition.

Minnie glanced back into the park. The sun was in her eyes and she could just make out a war time pillbox a hundred yards away and, behind it, a stand of trees.

Winter sniffed.

There was the faintest smell of something old in the cab, but whatever it was it wasn't something he recognised.

He sniffed again and the odour of it bit at his nostrils: something sharp and a little sour, like old canvas that had got wet mixed in with something more pungent—a smell of vinegar or some sort of acid.

Truck driver's effluvia. Winter nodded and Minnie closed the door a little without a sound.

There was no sound from inside the back of the furniture van and he crouched down—tried hard not to think of Minnie's legs under the grey slacks—and looked along the bottom of the truck's chassis to the rear wheels.

The wheels were still and if there was a brothel in full blast inside the back of the truck then they were being remarkably non-bouncy about it.

Minnie put her ear to the side of the truck.

Winter looked at her thighs as they tightened.

Minnie mouthed. 'Nothing.' She looked slightly annoyed and touched Winter on the shoulder to shepherd him a few feet back from the truck to where they could whisper. Minnie said softly in English, 'It's a hoax.' The side of the truck had a small discreet legend in English and Chinese painted in the typography Chinese merchants imagined small discreet legends should be painted in: a sort of elegant Georgian lettering that the Georgians, most of them barely literate, would have found almost impossible to read.

The sign read *Quality Furniture Restorations* and gave a phone number. Minnie said softly, still looking around, 'I've heard of this firm. They repair furniture for the rich taipans up on the Peak.'

Winter nodded. The smell was still in his nose. He was Dutch by parenthood and the smell reminded him of something he had smelled when his parents had been posted in Java. (Or more particularly, when his parents had been expelled from Java when the Javanese had decided they wanted it back.) He associated the smell with his father. His father had been a Colonel in the Dutch Marines—maybe it was just the smell of the canvas from the tents out in the jungle or...

Winter said softly, 'What's that smell? Does it remind you of anything?'

'What smell?'

Winter said, 'I'm not sure.' He looked at the back of the truck, 'What do you think? Do you want to call Stolen Cars and have them run it or shall we turn it over ourselves?'

Minnie looked at the wheels. Those shock absorbers were not absorbing any shocks. Minnie said, shrugging, 'I suppose it could be a gambling set-up and whoever telephoned was a big loser...' She seemed unconvinced. She shrugged again, 'We may as well have the arrest if there is one.'

What the hell was that smell? Even ten feet from the closed cab Winter imagined he could still smell it. He couldn't. He had it somewhere in his memory and it kept niggling at him and coming back as if it was real. Winter said, 'There's no probable cause. We can't even open the back of it without leaving ourselves liable to—' He looked at the legend on the side of the van, 'I'm not having someone say we got our dirty pawmarks all over their Louis Quinze commode.'

Minnie said, 'Their Louis what?'

Winter said with a smile, 'Or Tang pot or something.' What was that smell? Winter said, 'I'll give it the old "We know you're in there, Murphy" routine, but if that doesn't draw any reaction—'

Why were they whispering? Minnie said uncomfortably, 'Why are we whispering? There's obviously nothing in there. Just give it a kick and if there's nothing we call the Uniformed Branch and be rid of it.' She looked at her wristwatch, 'We've got to be in Court at 3.30.' The shock absorbers were still. The van simply sat there. It was obviously empty. Minnie said, 'It's all this business with the sniper. Everyone's going around being careful. Let's just turn it over and be done with it.'

Winter paused. He sniffed.

Minnie said, 'Will we?'

Whatever it was ... Winter said, 'Yeah, let's do it.' He was still whispering. He listened and heard a slight rustling in the trees a long way off. Across the park he could hear the sea against rock.

He could still smell that odour in his nose.

Minnie said, 'We'll do it now, will we?' She was still whispering.

Winter said, hesitating, 'Sure.' He stayed where he was.

In Java once he had ... He stopped again. A group of his father's Marines had been sitting around in a jungle clearing doing something with knives and canvas bags. Eating? No. Opening something? It was all a long time ago and he had only been a child ...

He tried to think.

He tried to get it straight in his mind...

He had gone down a little path out of the base and there were half a dozen of his father's Marines squatting around getting something ready for a—

That was it. *Getting something ready.*

The old, "Come out Murphy, we know you're in there" trick.

The truck was still, unmoving, anchored to the grass, becalmed.

Minnie said with a frown, 'David?'

Something he should have been a long way away from. They were doing something he should have been...

Winter said abruptly, 'All right.' Whatever it was, it was gone now.

Minnie said softly, 'Good.'

Still frowning slightly, she stood back a little as Winter flipped the restraining strap off his shoulder holster and went around to the back of the truck to do a little standard stentorian Murphy-flushing.

*

In the Detectives' Room, Feiffer said, 'He'll come. Once. He'll listen to him once and if he's a Japanese soldier...' He looked at Auden and Spencer. 'The Fireworks Man. He speaks Japanese.'

O'Yee was silent.

Feiffer said, 'After that, provided we issue him his good character for his Fireworks Renewal I don't think he'll ever help us again.' Feiffer said, looking a little embarrassed, 'Not our day, Christopher, is it?'

O'Yee said, 'No.'

Feiffer said, 'No.' He went into the charge room to smoke a cigarette and, standing there as O'Yee came after him with the recleaned clean ashtray, for a moment, seemed a very long way away indeed.

*

In the forty years since the end of the war the Public Works Department must have closed up more holes and tunnels in Hong Bay than the entire world's population of ants.

In the Archives Owlin came to yet another list of sealed-off, made-safe or cemented up tunnels, air raid shelters, bomb craters and assorted holes in the ground and said softly to himself, 'Damn it . . .'

If there was only one gigantic catacomb like Iwo Jima, then all the little holes led, like a honeycomb, to a central core.

If the gigantic single catacomb *was* a gigantic single catacomb and if, like Iwo Jima . . .

He had a map laid out on a table in front of him, held down by the yellowing pages of survey and construction gang reports and he began drawing little marks where they had sealed off each hole or repaired each cavity or made safe each abyss and hoped that sooner or later, just like a jigsaw, they might make one central picture.

'*Southern side of Great Shanghai Road, Hong Bay: Entrance to Japanese storeroom, impassable after ten feet due to bomb damage. Filled with cement and resurfaced for road works, Feb 5th, 1947.*'

Owlin ticked it off and made a little cross.

He looked at the map.

All the marks he had made were crosses. They stretched erratically almost the entire length of the old shoreline like some part of spreading, growing graveyard, some sort of giant unstoppable necropolis.

The centre. He needed the centre.

'*South-east Beach Road, Hong Bay: March 8th, 1947 . . .*'

Owlin made another cross.

*

His fist froze on the rear door of the truck.

In the jungle clearing the Sergeant came over to him and gently

124

shepherded him away, glancing back at the men squatting on the ground with their canvas bags doing...

He could still smell the smell, the smell of canvas and damp and the smell of the stuff they were using that was seeping a little in the heat and giving off...

Winter said without looking away from the doors, 'Minnie, I don't think we should touch anything.' He looked at his fist an inch away from the doors and brought it down slowly, 'I think we should—'

The stuff the Marines had been using was TNT. He had smelled it.

Winter said, 'Minnie, I think we—' His mouth was dry. He swallowed.

The next morning he had seen the photographs on his father's desk of what they had set it up for. His father, grinning at the Sergeant, had seemed very pleased about it.

Winter said in a dry voice, 'Minnie, I'm not absolutely sure, but—'

The charge had decapitated the infiltrator. His head was in pieces on the ground near what was left of the tripwire and the—

Winter said in a croak, 'I don't want to make fools of either of us, but I think we should get on the radio and—' He turned his head slowly to look at her, but she was not listening.

Staring at him, she seemed rooted to the ground. She seemed to be trying to get her breath.

Minnie said in the same strange voice as his own, 'David...' She nodded at something written in chalk above the rear numberplate of the truck.

Divine mission to eradicate... It was written in small, joined up characters and Winter had to strain to make it out.

2.46 p.m.

The sun, moving west, was directly behind Morishita's right shoulder. It was in a clear blue sky and, in the absence of cloud, at its clearest and brightest as he took a preliminary sighting on the rear of the truck and worked the cocking handle to slip the first round in the magazine into the breech of his rifle.

125

He did it slowly and quietly and as Minnie and Winter began walking quietly and carefully across the grass to the car, their hands touching like lovers', there was only a single, muffled—
...*click*.

*

In the war room, The Technician looked at the closed steel door in front of him. The door was two inches thick, bombproof, grey and, to the touch, cold and unyielding.

He raised his hurricane lamp to it and it seemed suddenly to glow with warmth.

The Technician said quietly to the door in Cantonese, 'Damn you ... damn all of you ...'

The war room was the centre of a honeycomb of passages, all leading off in different directions.

The Technician closed his eyes and heard the hissing of the lamp as it glowed at the door and gave it life.

The Technician said quietly, 'Damn every last one of you ...'

Private Masuo Morishita, Quartermaster's Section, 38th Division, Japanese Imperial Army in Hong Kong.

The Technician shouted at the top of his voice in the empty, echoing room, '*Damn you all!*'

Divine mission to eradicate all the uniformed forces of colonial imperialism ...

Just given half a chance, it could have worked.

The Technician said softly, 'Juzo...' but his brother, the Major, was no longer there and there was nothing but silence in the stone room.

The 38th Division of the Japanese Imperial Army in Hong Kong ...

In the war room he thought he heard a noise in one of the passages behind him and he raised the lantern quickly to see what it was.

It was nothing.

He looked at the steel door.

126

He was alone.

In his pocket he had two cartridge cases from the gun Morishita had taken with him to the park and he took them out, considered them for a moment, and then threw them away into the corner of the room.

2.51 p.m.

In the hissing of the lamp, unafraid, he took one of the passages and, moving quickly through it, made for the surface.

*

On the radio Despatch said without urgency, 'Yes, Car Victor Four?'

Winter saw Minnie's long fingers on the car door beside him. She was standing, watching. He saw her mouth tighten.

Despatch said again, 'Yes, Car Victor Four, go ahead, please.'

They were both right out in the open.

He saw Minnie look at him and force a smile.

Nothing but park and an old war memorial and a stand of trees, and between them and the truck, nothing.

Winter, swallowing, said as calmly as he could manage, 'Instructions, please, Despatch. We believe we have an emergency situation developing . . .'

Between them and the truck there was only their car: potential red hot tearing shrapnel, and the windscreen, a square yard— maybe more—of blasting, slicing, searing glass.

Winter said as calmly as he could manage—

The truck was just sitting there, unmoving, waiting—

Winter said in a sudden snarl, 'Despatch! God damn it! Acknowledge!'

*

If they wanted it, it was theirs, but they couldn't have anyone else—anyone—for at least an hour, maybe more. It was unbelievable. On the phone in the Detectives' Room, Feiffer said,

127

aghast, 'Are you serious? You want me to take my people out into an open expanse that hasn't even been searched, into a situation you know is potentially lethal, and you say I can't have anyone to back me up for—' He couldn't credit what he was hearing, '*For how long?*'

The Commander's voice was tight, breathless. 'They have to change, Harry. They have to change into civilian clothes and then they have to get transport for their equipment and—'

'The damned bomb squad aren't in uniform! They wear coveralls and helmets and—' Feiffer said, 'Uniforms. Right?'

'Right.' The Commander said, 'And the Emergency Unit in their Land Rovers and their flashing lights and their bloody sub machine guns and—'

'*All right!*' Feiffer glanced at O'Yee watching him, 'What about securing the road? The park stretches along Beach Road and down into—' The Commander knew all that. Feiffer said reasonably, 'At least they could secure the street and keep the park bottled up.'

'They are. I've got all the uniformed men I can spare from North Point going over to do that, but if it is a set-up—'

'According to what you told me, Winter thinks the van's been stored there for later use. According to you he says the keys are still in the ignition!'

The Commander said, 'And the first two attacks were directly opposite a police station.'

'There's no evidence the attacks were directed solely at people in uniform. We weren't in uniform when he had a go at us and half the people in Cuttlefish Lane he dropped were about as uniformed as—'

The Commander said, 'I can't take the chance. It may be exactly what whoever's behind it wants. The calls say "the uniformed forces of colonial repression"—'

'The calls are bullshit!'

'All right, then it's your damned Japanese! In either event, it's aimed at bloody symbols and as far as I'm concerned, before anyone goes out and makes himself a target he's going to divest

128

himself of every one of his bloody little shiny symbols and go out there looking like Elmer Cluck the well-known amateur lepidopterist!' The Commander said suddenly 'quietly, 'Harry, these people are bloody suicidal. It's well known. Documented. For all I know, I could run a line of bloody EU men and Bomb Squad right across the park and these bastards wouldn't give a damn about mowing them down like bloody hay! Because they don't give a shit what happens to them next!'

'What bloody people? You've been drumming it into me that this Japanese business is just a smokescreen for some sort of gun-happy psychotic!' Feiffer demanded, 'What bloody people?'

'The people who left the van there.' The Commander said reasonably, 'I agree with you. I agree that they wouldn't have left the van in the park with the keys still in it unless they intended to move it somewhere else, and I also agree with you that if the keys are in it they're not far away, but I also agree with my bloody self that it isn't a Japanese kamikaze force, but I have to take the reasonable way out and not put anyone at risk I don't have to put at risk!' The Commander said earnestly, 'No one will blame you if you don't touch it, but it's our only chance to get one of these set-ups intact and find out for once and for all who's behind it—Japanese or other.'

'Can you give me a helicopter overfly to at least survey the possible fields of fire?'

'*No!*' The Commander said, 'How low would he have to be? We don't happen to have our own Hong Kong Police satellite a hundred and fifty miles up in bloody space, we've got a few traffic choppers marked all over COP—SHOOT ME and to spot a sniper they virtually have to get down to tree top level and—you're the only plain clothes unit I've got in the area familiar with the situation. I'm not asking you to disarm the thing, I'm only asking you to—'

Feiffer said, 'To do what?'

'To bloody well go out there and get Winter and WPC Oh in if nothing else!' He said suddenly. 'They haven't shot at *them*, have they?'

That's because they may be waiting for *us!*' Feiffer said, 'Neal, I've got my own people to think of. I can't just—Look, I'll go myself. How's that? I'll go and relieve Winter—that's all you want anyway, isn't it? If they're not going to shoot two plain clothes officers they're certainly not going to shoot one. Get on the radio and they can leave just as I arrive.'

'No. The area has to be secure. I can't have civilians wandering onto—'

'I fail to see how the hell the area is secure in the first place since there are only two of them—' It was hopeless. Feiffer said, 'Bullet proof vests and aprons, can we at least—' He saw the vests and aprons on the floor. About the only thing they didn't have on them to identify them as police property was a large target pinned over the heart area and a few sighting gauges so the sniper could get his aim right before he left the aprons and vests completely alone and went straight for the head. Feiffer said, 'All right. One hour. We'll hold the area—if we can—for one hour and then, by God, the Royal bloody Emergency Unit Ballet had better have changed out of their working clothes into their bloody tu-tus or the only emergency they'll be handling for the next six months will be *me!* What sort of weapons do Winter and Oh have? I assume since we're trying to look like anything but cops we can't take our Armalites so what sort of firepower can Winter and Oh provide us with on the spot?'

'Winter's got a sidearm, I suppose.'

'Vice Squad's sidearms are little Walther PPKs! I meant, in the car?'

'I don't know.' The Commander must have had a print out in front of him. He said after a moment, 'Yeah, you're right, a Walther is standard issue ... and in the car nothing, not even a shotgun.' He paused for a moment, 'WPC Oh has got a—'

O'Yee said quietly in the background, 'A twenty two calibre derringer. I've seen it.'

The Commander said, 'Harry, Winter and the Oh girl have been there now for—' He paused, 'For too long. And they're close to it, trying to keep it under surveillance and they're—' The

Commander said quietly, 'Harry, Winter sounds very frightened indeed.'

Feiffer said, 'So am I. That makes it a clean sweep for everyone, doesn't it?'

'*Godammit, I've telephoned my wife to bring my civilian clothes from home but it's going to take an hour with the fucking traffic!*' The Commander demanded, 'What can I tell you? Reinforcements will be there, I promise you! I know you're worried about your people, but I assure you that reinforcements will be there!'

Feiffer glanced around the room. He saw Auden touch at the big Colt Python under his arm and heft it as if he was testing its weight. Spencer had a stopwatch in his hand, turning it over and over. He saw Feiffer looking at it and put it carefully on his desk then looked surreptitiously at Auden.

The Commander said, 'I don't want any heroics, Harry. I just want you to hold the area until reinforcements arrive.' Put reasonably, it sounded more reasonable. The Commander said, 'The van isn't live. According to Stolen Cars it was only taken a few hours ago. No one's heard a sound from it or seen smoke or—' He said, 'It's safe! The whole area's safe!'

'All right!' Feiffer said, 'All right, so it isn't a Japanese suicide mission, O.K.?'

There was a silence, then the Commander said with difficulty, 'I'm in Despatch. I can actually hear Winter on the radio—' He hesitated. 'He's doing all right, but he—'

The Python was too heavy. For some reason, Feiffer saw Auden swap it with Spencer for Spencer's airweight Detective Special. He saw Spencer, looking less than happy, glance at the big gun for a moment and then put it into his waistband. The stopwatch was still on the desk. Spencer touched at it and then slid it quickly out of sight into his drawer. O'Yee had one of the bullet proof aprons in his hand. He looked at it for a moment and then stacked it on a sandbag.

2.58 p.m.

The Commander said, 'An hour. I promise you, *one hour!*'

2.59 p.m.

131

Through the minutes, the van, and whatever else was in the park, waited solely and exclusively for—

3.00 p.m. and thirty seconds.

For whatever it was waiting for.

*

The crosses stopped. By 1955 the war had been over ten years and the novelty or the satisfaction had worn off and the Public Works Department hardly thought fit to mention less than an accidentally exhumed mass grave.

In the archives, Owlin, staring at the incomplete map—the crosses without pattern—said to the final secret hidden beneath the lines of streets and grids and contours, 'You bastard, where are you!' He looked hard at the map and the collated pile of useless reports, 'You rotten bastard, *where the hell are you?*'

Where else? Where else could he find anything?

The thousand stitches obi. Was there anything on it that might—?

Anything?

Feiffer had left it with him in his office for study and Owlin, staring at the maps, rubbed at his glasses with his handkerchief and, before going back to his office to look at it, racked his brains for everything he knew about them and wondered if there was anything about it he might have missed.

*

He was in the heart of the system: the centre hub of all the tunnels. The Technician touched at his throat and felt the warm dry air catch at him and make him want to cough.

He had stopped sweating. Under his shirt his chest seemed to be covered in a fine, white, dry dust.

He saw something glint in one of the side rooms of the main tunnel and he raised his lantern and saw the eyes watching him.

It was one of the Major's section—a Private, his rifle across his knees—but the Technician didn't recognise him and, still touching at his throat and chest, passed on.

*

Morishita touched at the rolled up flag and raised his head a fraction above the pillbox to see the man and the girl by the car.

They were standing there together, unafraid, waiting, doing their duty.

Morishita nodded.

In his own way, he admired them.

He touched at the flag.

He knew about duty.

Far off, the engines getting louder as they approached, he heard the cars coming.

He touched at the flag.

11

Out in the open, perspiration was standing out on Auden's forehead. He was behind one of the two parked cars, the real or imagined protection of the engine block between him and the furniture van. Auden's fingers were drumming on the roof of the car. They went thumpety-thumpety-thump, thump, thump...

Auden said, 'Harry, the shots have got to come out of the back of the van, right?' He looked over at Feiffer on the other side of Spencer and Winter and got no reply, 'Right? But there isn't anything to shoot at in that direction so it isn't set up to shoot.' Next to him, Minnie Oh looked at him curiously and Auden dismissed her with a thumpety-thump on the roof, 'So even if—'

The van moved. There was a wind coming in from the sea with the tide change and the van moved a fraction. Winter said to Feiffer, 'Sir—'

'It's the wind.' Feiffer said with his eyes still on the van, 'Was the handbrake on when you looked inside?'

Winter said, 'Yes.' He looked to Minnie for confirmation and she nodded, 'And it was in first gear with the keys still in the ignition.'

Auden said, '—so even if there's a charge set up to blow the back doors open so they can shoot it probably isn't even armed yet—or if it is it's probably just a few ounces—'

Winter said with alarm, 'It's TNT. I smelled it. It only *takes* a few ounces!'

'Then a few bloody grammes then! In any event, it won't be enough to do any real damage because if it did it'll put the rifles in there off their aim so even if I got the doors open and the charge went off—'

134

Feiffer said, 'Phil, for the fourth and last time: we'll wait.'

'Harry, I could do it!' Auden said to Spencer, 'Tell him: I could, couldn't I?'

Spencer said, 'No.'

'What do you mean, no? You timed me. I've got at least three seconds to spare on the twelve seconds you said it'd—'

Spencer said, 'Seven seconds! Seven! Not twelve, not ten, not even eight, but *seven!*'

Winter ran his tongue across his lips. Auden's voice was a series of words and sounds but they were not forming themselves together in his mind into any meaning. Feiffer touched him on the shoulder, 'Have you done a walk around or have you stayed here with the van?'

Minnie said, 'We stayed with the van.'

Something moved. Auden said, 'Is that smoke?'

It was a leaf. Feiffer said quietly, 'Fine. You did the right thing. I want you to keep staying here and at the faintest sign of activity I want everyone down behind the car engine blocks. Then, if the shooting starts, I want everyone out of here.' He saw Auden about to open his mouth, 'It's a leaf.' Feiffer said, 'Phil, you're in charge of the retreat. At the first sign of anything you're to secure all the personnel here and evacuate them to a safe distance that-a-way.' He jerked his thumb vaguely in the direction of China, 'Understood? You're the senior man here and I'm relying on you to—'

Auden said reasonably, 'Harry, I can take it. I know how the guns work and I can disarm them.' He asked suddenly, 'Why am I in charge? I'm not the class bloody cut-up the teacher puts in charge to make sure he's got a responsible job! Where the hell are *you* going to be?'

Feiffer said, 'I'm going to take a walk around the perimeter of the park.'

'*And what if there's a bloody sniper?*'

'Then he'll shoot at me, won't he?' So far, if there was one, he hadn't shot at anyone. Feiffer looked at his watch. The changing-room brigade were still at least forty minutes away from arriving.

Feiffer said, 'I just want to make sure the area's secure before we—'

Auden said, 'It moved! The van moved!'

Winter said, 'It's the wind.'

Auden snapped, 'How the hell do you know it's full of TNT anyway? What are you—the big local TNT expert?'

'I've smelled it before.' Winter said, 'Have you?'

'Of course I've smelled bloody TNT before!' Auden tried to think where. Auden said to Feiffer, 'At least take Minnie with you. It'll look more natural if you've got a girl with you.' He looked at Feiffer's face and said with a beaten, 'All right, all right, I'll do what I'm told.'

Winter said in an undertone, 'At least I don't go around getting shot dead by blank rounds...'

Auden said, 'What did you say?'

Feiffer said, '*Auden!*'

Auden said, 'All right! All right!' He saw Feiffer draw a breath and step out from behind the car to start walking. Auden said, 'If anyone should do that, it should be—' He saw Spencer looking at him with that disapproving look of his. It was the same look the Examining Board gave him every year before they turned him down for promotion yet again. Auden said, 'Seven seconds, right? I remember. O.K? Seven seconds. Not eight or even seven and a half, but seven—right?'

Spencer said, 'Right.'

Minnie said quietly to Feiffer, 'Harry...?' She moved a step forward.

Feiffer stopped and turned around. He saw her face. One tiny .22 derringer hidden somewhere in her handbag. Feiffer said, 'Stay here.' He smiled, 'If you come too I'd never be able to keep my mind on the job.'

Minnie said quietly, 'Is it true about the Japanese soldiers?'

The van was moving slightly in the wind, rocking on its shock absorbers as the breeze pushed under the chassis and billowed against it like a lifting surface of an aeroplane. There was the faintest rustling from the stand of trees behind the sealed off pillbox and the noise of the sea as it changed tidally and washed against rocks and sand.

Feiffer said, 'Yes, it's true.' They had to get to the set-up this time before it went off and turned into vapour. Feiffer said with a wink, 'Don't worry, this time we've got the element of surprise and it'll be our game.'

He looked again at his watch and, heading for the perimeter of the park where a railing separated it from the rocks and cliffs leading down to the sea, at 3.23 p.m. with the sun behind the van in his eyes making him blind, began walking.

*

Sergeant Quartermaster Seichiro Tanino, 38th Division, Japanese All Conquering Imperial Army in China, killer of ambulance stations.

At his desk in his main office Owlin took off his glasses and looked down at the spread out material in the protective glassene envelope on his desk.

Sergeant Seichiro Tanino ... nineteen hundred and forty two... In the temperate air-conditioned room, Owlin bent down and sniffed the envelope and looked puzzled.

Sergeant Seichiro—a thousand stitches obi. The work of a wife or a mother or a sister or a friend who had made the long sash like object with care and then stood on a street corner or in a market square or a railway station somewhere in Hiroshima day after day until each of one thousand people had listened to her pleas and each, carefully, with expressions of luck and best wishes for her son or brother's health and glorious death in battle, inserted a single crude stitch in the fabric and then passed on their way.

A thousand, like-minded, unyielding people to whom the notion of defeat was unthinkable.

In the days when the Emperor had been a god. In the days before General MacArthur, that unmaker of gods, had decided, by simple decree...

Owlin bent down and sniffed at the envelope and still looked puzzled.

The envelope was labelled EVIDENCE—DO NOT OPEN and he took the label in his hand and tapped it against his thumbtip thoughtfully.

Sergeant Seichiro Tanino...

*

In the archives, there was nothing.

It was slightly moist in the office, suitable for people rather than paper, and there were a few drops of moisture condensing on the inside of the envelope and blurring slightly at the strange, ancient, totemic object inside.

The smell, somehow, reminded him of trees.

There were two staples holding the long transparent envelope shut and as Owlin flicked absently at one of them with his thumbnail, it came away and a section of the lip of the envelope fell open.

*

Behind the pillbox, Morishita said quietly, 'I am prepared.' He saw the tall man near the railing walking slowly and casually, looking around, his hand resting loosely against the open flap of his coat where his holstered gun was. The man was a long way off, walking the edge of the park, looking first ahead and then back into the park and then, casually, over the railing down to the cliffs and the sea. The man wore no uniform, but he was, nevertheless, the enemy.

The others would come.

In the slight wind coming across the park, Morishita could see the van rocking a little. He thought of what was inside. Morishita said softly to all the people who had sent their wishes to him in the stitches of his obi, 'I am prepared to do you honour.'

The girl was still there behind the cars parked fifty yards from the van, still looking worried.

He wondered why the uniformed people were taking so long.

He thought of The Technician.

He trusted him.

He said softly, aloud, 'No.' It was no mistake. He trusted him.

Private Morishita, still watching Feiffer, said with self encouraging determination, 'I will achieve success and I am fully prepared to die here in this place to achieve it.'

He touched at his flag and found either it or his hand was moist with what felt like perspiration.

*

Into the Valley of Death... On the phone in the Detectives' Room O'Yee demanded, 'What do you mean, "another three quarters of an hour"? You said one hour! That's an hour from the time of the call to the time the goddamned Cavalry arrives on the scene with their shiny little bugles blowing! The call came through to us at least forty minutes ago and you must have had it even earlier than that! What do you mean, another—'

'O'Yee!' The Commander said in a snarl, 'You're forgetting who the hell you're talking to!'

'I'm forgetting nothing! I'm sitting here watching the clock go around and I've got plenty of time to remember just about everything starting from the Book of goddamned Genesis to the last thirty episodes of goddamned Perry Mason!' O'Yee said, 'Three of my friends are out there waiting for you to get the proper equipment to them before some mad bastard starts shooting at them—and what do you mean by telling me that—' O'Yee said suddenly tightly, 'What the hell's going on? Have you told the Emergency Unit about the Japanese sniper or not?'

There was a pause.

O'Yee said, 'All right, then the goddamned South American sniper or the goddamned Lesotho-land sniper or the goddamned—*Have you told anybody that there's a*—' O'Yee said abruptly, 'You haven't! It's orders from on top, isn't it? There isn't any sniper, is there? The idea is that if you leave it long enough—'

The Commander said, 'There isn't any Japanese hold-out sniper!'

'You hope!'

'I'm not discussing it with you!'

'You are! You are discussing it with me!' O'Yee said, 'Or fucking else!'

The Commander said, 'What did you say?'

O'Yee said quietly, 'I said, You lying bastard, you had better not have taken your orders from on high and sent my friends out there in the hope that if there's a bloody Jap sniper they'll clean him out for you before anyone finds out—'

'Are you threatening me, O'Yee?'

'They didn't even take a goddamned rifle!'

'You had better not be threatening me, Detective Senior Inspector.' The Commander said, 'I had better not have heard what I just heard.'

O'Yee said, 'Yes, you had. You had better have heard it—otherwise, if anything happens and I come looking for you—'

'That's enough!' The Commander said suddenly desperately, 'Damn it, it isn't *me*! What the hell do you think? That it's *my* idea?'

'The goddamned Emergency Unit and all the rest of them have their civilian clothes with them at their bases! They could have been changed in about—'

There was a silence.

'They could have changed in about—'

'Don't you think Feiffer knows that?' The Commander said, 'Don't you think I know that? Don't you think—'

'Bloody goddamned Japs! Bloody goddamned sensitive, two-faced goddamned *Japs!*' O'Yee shouted, thinking of Okuno, 'Who the hell won the fucking war anyway? *Them?*'

'Christopher, I'm standing here in bloody civilian clothes ready to go. I've got my orders too!' The Commander said, 'Christ, don't you think I want to go too? Don't you think—'

O'Yee said in a snarl, 'Twenty minutes! Whistle blowing time is in exactly twenty minutes! In exactly twenty fucking minutes I'm going around there with enough firepower to bring down the whole of Tokyo and the fucking Japanese Second World War Imperial Army and the Pearl Harbor attack force combined! In twenty minutes exactly—'

'Good, then you can meet me there!' The Commander said, 'I've given them fifteen! In fifteen, bloody career or no bloody career—'

The clock on the wall went *click*.

3.41 p.m.

O'Yee said softly, 'Christ, Christ...' He tried to keep the phone firmly in his hand, but his hands were covered in sweat and the instrument kept slipping from his grasp.

3.42 p.m.

His stomach was turning over.

O'Yee said softly into the phone, over and over, 'Christ ... oh Christ...!'

*

At the parked cars, Auden said quietly to Spencer, 'Bill, if that truck starts to go ...' He looked at Spencer's face, 'If it starts to go...'

Feiffer was a long way off along the railing of the park. He was starting to turn inwards towards the truck from the far corner of the point.

Auden said, 'Bill ...'

'All right.' Spencer nodded.

'I can take it.'

Spencer ran his tongue across his lips and touched at the big magnum in his waistband.

Winter said softly, 'I did smell TNT. I know the smell. I—' He looked at Feiffer, the only figure in a still, silent landscape, 'I saw someone killed by it once when I was a child.' He looked at Minnie.

Minnie said softly to Auden, 'I don't need anyone to tell me

141

which way to run.' She touched at her handbag, 'All I've got is a little—'

Spencer said quietly, 'There's an Ingram M-10 sub machine gun in the back of the car, under the rear seat.' He looked quickly at Auden, 'I put it in there while Harry was—' Spencer said, 'If there is a sniper.'

Auden said to Winter and Minnie, 'I can take the van. I know how it works. I can take it.' He looked across at Feiffer, walking slowly like a man thinking of something that had happened a long time ago. Auden said, 'The Japanese shot his old man in Shanghai, did you know that? Christopher O'Yee told me.' Auden said, '*I can take that van.*'

Feiffer stopped. He bent down and seemed to pick up a piece of grass and look at it for a moment.

Auden said, 'They're not coming, you know that. They're not coming until they know for sure that there won't be an international incident about it.' He looked hard at Spencer, 'Bill, you've timed me. You know I can do it.'

'Yes.'

Auden said, 'Minnie? The Ingram?'

Minnie said, 'I know how to shoot one.'

'Winter?'

'Yes.'

3.50 p.m.

Auden said, 'One move, one sound, one little vibration . . .'

Spencer said with an unsuccessful smile, 'You'll be a Senior Inspector yet.'

Feiffer had the piece of grass in his hand. He began walking again. Auden said, 'On my own merits. No one moves me up to fill dead men's bloody shoes!' He looked hard at Feiffer and clenched his fists, '*No one.*'

Spencer said helpfully, 'Maybe it's just as everyone says and it's been left here and absolutely nothing's going to happen at all.'

Auden said, 'Sure.' He looked at Winter and Minnie and saw their faces. Auden said quietly, 'Do you believe that?'

3.51 p.m.

Spencer said, 'No.' Spencer said with a tremor in his voice, 'Eight seconds, all right? Eight seconds.'

He saw the look on Auden's face.

Auden said, grinning, 'Seven. You got it wrong. It's seven.'

Spencer said, *'Whatever!'*

He touched at the gun in his belt.

And, closing his eyes for a moment, waited.

*

Wah ... wah ... *wah* ... *wah*! ... WAH! It was rising in him: the old war cry of the warrior, growing, coming closer, reaching culmination. Minutes, seconds. It was coming, reaching fulfillment, becoming greater than the ability of his chest to hold it in—it was arriving, the moment: coming, rising, reaching pitch ... shaking at him, surging ...

He saw him. He saw the man in the park look over and drop something from his hand—grass, a piece of grass. He was coming closer, looking, searching, trying to find him, knowing he was there—walking, walking ... Morishita said ... he said ... he said ...

3.56 and a half ... It was now. The time was right. The Technician had said that ...

The uniforms were not coming.

The man walking towards him was his enemy.

It was coming. The war cry, the ultimate moment, clenching at him like a fist, constricting his muscles. On the ground next to him the furled up flag seemed to be pulsing, the hidden sun on its face beginning to burn with life like a star coming back into existence, all the painted rays emanating from its centre going blood red and shimmering ...

Wah ... wah ... *wah* ...

He was too close. He was coming, cutting across the park, his hand resting loosely near where the holstered weapon was waiting to— He was coming, too close.

He was coming, reaching, drawing nearer ...

143

The sun was behind Morishita. He saw the man's face. He saw him look up at the sun. He saw him move over a little to the left to cut it out. At the car the others were standing there just...

He saw.

He saw.

Wah ... growing, growing...

He saw Feiffer see him!

He heard Auden shriek, 'Jesus Christ!' He saw the van smoking.

He heard something loud inside the van go *CLICK!*

*

The obi... Open, taken out of the glassene envelope, it was...

Unbelievably, it was...

Owlin said, '*No—!*'

It was vanishing.

Before his very eyes, with the smell strong and pungent biting at his nostrils and making him cough, the whole thing was simply *vanishing!*

*

In the Station, O'Yee shouted at the clock, '*No!*'

On the other end of the phone, The Fireworks Man said, 'What was that?'

O'Yee shouted, 'Get here! Get here! It's happening again!'

He heard the shooting from the park.

He heard it.

O'Yee said, 'Oh, Jesus Christ!'

Too late. It was all too late.

3.58 p.m.

Helplessly, hopelessly, O'Yee slammed down the phone and said in the sandbagged, secure, safe, too far away room, 'Oh Christ! Oh, Holy Mother of God! *Oh Christ!!*'

*

Auden was running.

Feiffer shouted, 'No!' He saw the truck smoking, burning, the black oily stuff pouring out through the cracks in the rear doors. There was a burst of fire and from somewhere. Minnie had gotten hold of an Ingram and she was pouring fire at the pillbox. On the ground, Feiffer saw bits and pieces of grey masonry and dust coming off the structure in puffs. He saw Spencer out in the open.

He shouted, 'Run! Run!' and then the sniper was up again as Minnie changed magazines and a fusillade of bullets ripped tracks in the grass beside him as he got out his own gun and tried to get off a shot.

Spencer was out in the open with Auden's big, long barreled gun, firing aimed rounds through the slits of the pillbox.

There was no one inside. Feiffer saw a wedge of cement fly off as one of the bullets smashed itself to pieces again and then Spencer was shooting again, the big gun kicking high and hard in his hands. There was a crackle of dull fire as Winter got off a rapid fire clip on his Walther and then another burst as Minnie began spraying in three round series, searching, flicking at the pillbox with the big .45 rounds and tearing squat chunks out at a time.

The sniper was behind the box and not one of them could see him.

Feiffer yelled, 'Behind! He's behind the box!' He saw a flash as the sniper snapped off a shot at him from a sort of half leaning position and the air around him exploded into dirt and grass and he got his head down and tried to shoot back.

In the barrage his gun hardly sounded as if it went off at all.

Auden reached the van. The smoke was pouring out in his face. Auden said, 'Five, six, six and a half ... six and three quarters...!' The doors were stuck. The first one was a blank, always ... the first one was a blank that would blow the doors open ... Auden got his hands on the handles and wrenched.

Nothing.

Spencer shouted, 'Ten, eleven!' He was timing it to the gunfire. His gun clicked empty and he got in another load with a speed loader, all six rounds at once, and snapped the cylinder closed and had the hammer back in the same motion.

He tried another aimed shot.

There was nothing to aim at.

The doors were jammed. Auden shouted, 'Bastard! *Open!*' Newton's cradle. It was inside there, burning through, getting ready to swing. Auden, wrenching, yelled, 'Open! *Open!*'

It was happening. Morishita saw the ground around the tall man detonate and go upwards like a suddenly sprouting flower. He was safe. All the bullets were hitting the pillbox and he was safe. The van was burning, smoking. He tried to get in a shot at the man wrenching at the back of it, but a burst of fire ripped across the top of the pillbox like steel raindrops and he got his head down and reached for his flag.

The man on the ground was getting up.

Morishita flicked the flag and it came out open, the rising sun on it burning with life. He saw the man on his knees shouting at someone to do something and he levelled the rifle and got a clear shot in at the man's face and pulled the trigger.

Something happened. Nothing happened. The rifle failed to kick. It was jammed, stuck. Morishita jerked back the cocking handle and the empty brass shell case came out glittering like gold and fell onto the open flag. A hole. There seemed to be some sort of tiny hole in the case and he let the bolt fly forward and chambered another round and tried to get in an aim.

The man at the van almost had it open. The doors were giving.

Where was the explosive charge? It should have gone off? Like a man shooting ineffectually in a nightmare, Morishita caught sight of the man on the grass getting ready to run and pulled the trigger again and nothing happened.

He ejected the case. They were all duds. Nothing was happening. The case came out empty and fired and the bullet had gone somewhere, but the man on the grass was still living and he was—

Tiny holes: all the ejected cartridge cases seemed to have tiny holes in them. Morishita screamed, 'Wah! Wah!' and stood up to get in a shot.

Seventeen, eighteen, nineteen... Auden shrieked at the doors, 'Come on, you bastards!' He turned like a monkey climbing a frame and saw someone standing up at the pillbox behind him—a blurred figure washed out by the glaring sun. The door was coming—he felt it give.

Spencer yelled, 'Minnie, behind! He's behind the box, not in it—behind!' He saw Feiffer standing up as the figure, lost in the sun, got up and for a moment he saw a flag and a cap and a— Spencer shrieked, 'It's a Jap! It's him! It's a Japanese!' He shrieked at Minnie, 'Kill him! Cut him in half! *Kill him!*' The Ingram's magazine was empty. He saw Minnie snap it out onto the ground and reach into the car seat for another. Feiffer was running, his gun drawn, straight towards the blurred figure. Spencer saw the flag. Spencer yelled— Winter's little automatic was popping away, but all the bullets were going low. Spencer yelled— He got Auden's big magnum up and thought— He shouted at Auden, 'It's too long! It's more than seven seconds!' and then Minnie had the magazine in and was drawing back the bolt, and Spencer yelled, 'Don't spray them! You'll hit Harry! *Don't spray them!*'

It came open. One of the doors came open. A fraction.

Then more.

And then the other one.

Something gave and they were coming open. Auden said, 'Come on, come on...' Something was holding them... 'Come on, come on...!'

It was happening in a nightmare. He was shooting, aiming the rifle, doing his honour and his duty and—and it was a nightmare. The gun was not shooting, it was simply making popping noises, like blanks, and all the bullets were going—nowhere. Morishita wrenched at the gun again to clear yet another useless case from the breech and saw in the magazine the live round come up and go into the breech. He saw the silver bullet in its end. He saw. The tall man was coming at him, running. He was twenty yards away. He had his gun out, not a military gun, but an ignoble, squat barrelled little— Morishita yelled in Japanese, 'Work! Function!' and got the rifle up to his shoulder and drew a final pulverising aim onto the man's face, directly into the forehead, and began pulling the trigger. Morishita yelled—

The world exploded into bright, burning, searing light. It was a mirror. There was a giant mirror in the back of the van.

Morishita said, 'Ai!' as the light swamped him and drowned him and seemed to— The sun was directly behind him and the mirror had it all and was blinding him and burning out his eyes. Morishita said, 'Aai—!' Somewhere the man was coming at him. All the shooting had stopped. He saw the tall man for a moment in the glare turn back to the van and—

Auden shouted, 'Got you, you bastard!' and with Spencer's gun coming out in the fastest draw he had ever done in his life killed the reflected image of the Japanese sniper in the mirror with a single slot that exploded the mirror into a million fragments. Auden said, 'Oh, no. . .!'

The drowning pool of light was gone. Feiffer said, lost. . . 'Where are. . .' He was on the ground, rolling. He saw for an instant through the light and—

Winter shrieked, 'Auden, get out! The TNT's—'

The van was loaded with the stuff. Winter heard Spencer shout, 'No!' It was like a scene from an execution. He saw Feiffer half crouched on the ground with the sniper's gun barrel actually touching his forehead and Spencer yelled, 'No! No! No!' He saw—

'Oh, Christ. . .' Feiffer had a sudden picture of his father dying on the ground in Shanghai with all the gun barrels smoking and lowering like— All his breath was gone. . . He heard Winter shouting . . . and in the overwhelming, disintegrating blast Feiffer fell backwards and thought he somehow floated away with a bloody, torn up face looking down at him and some sort of flag with a picture of the sun on it flowing all around him like a shroud, and he was drifting, hearing things, going backwards. . .

Spencer shrieked, 'The gun's blown up! The gun's gone up in his face!' He saw Winter out at the van wrenching and dragging Auden out of it and he yelled at Auden, 'He's blown his gun up!

It's his blood, not Harry's. He's got blood all over his face and—'

Auden shrieked as Winter pulled him off, 'I shot a fucking reflection! I've done it again and I've shot a fucking reflection!' Auden shrieked—

Spencer yelled, 'Get him over here!' He caught Auden by the shoulder as Winter grabbed him and clapped him hard on the back. Feiffer was on the grass, moving, alive. Spencer saw the Japanese stagger, his face all torn to pieces and he yelled at Minnie with the quick firing Ingram, 'Finish him! Finish the bastard! Don't worry about police regulations—shoot him before he can—'

He saw the Ingram come up. The Japanese was out in the open, starting to run, easy, a perfect target.

Spencer, out of control, shrieked, 'Kill him! Kill him! *Kill him!*' and at that exact moment the three hundred pounds of TNT The Technician had carefully placed in the van behind the mirror, a hessian sack load at a time, exploded in a single ball of blasting flame and blew him completely off his feet and onto the grass.

*

4.07 p.m. There was nothing left of the van but a burnt out chassis and, by the time the other units began to arrive—eight minutes early—no sign of the wounded sniper but his unfurled flag lying on the ground where he had dropped it next to the shattered rifle.

By his side, Auden said apologetically to Feiffer, 'Harry, I'm sorry. I shot a reflection...' He looked on the verge of tears.

Feiffer's hands were still shaking. He tried to get something out, but no words came.

Auden said, 'I'm really very, very sorry ... I suppose this is the end of all my promotion chances...' He looked up sadly, like a little boy caught out.

Feiffer said, nodding, 'Yeah, I suppose it is.' He patted Auden hard on the shoulder. Feiffer said with difficulty, 'You'd be posted to another Station, you know, if you were—if you got

149

promoted...' He kept his hands together in an attitude of prayer on his chest and tried to stop them shaking.

Feiffer said, still trembling, 'And then, Phil, what the hell would I do without you?'

The Emergency Unit squads were running across the grass from their civilian vehicles—a motley array of totally un-believable fake delivery trucks and station wagons—coming to see the flag, but before they reached it, glistening with moisture, it seemed suddenly to fray apart and turn into a picture floating on a saucer of water like a transfer and then, as if it had never been, the flag totally and completely and utterly ... disappeared.

For a brief moment there was a very odd smell, like decay, and then, with the flag, all at once, it was gone.

12

In his best suit, The Fireworks Man came into the charge room from the street and looked at Ah Pin. In his torn khaki shorts and holed singlet, Ah Pin was still sweeping.

The Fireworks Man asked in Cantonese, 'Did they get him?' He waited for an answer.

Ah Pin stopped sweeping. Ah Pin said with the faintest narrowing of his eyes, seeing who it was, 'No. This time he got away.'

He held The Fireworks Man's eyes for a long moment, but after all those years there was nothing that easily to be read in them and he turned away and went on with his work.

*

He had travelled from one time to another and he was free. It was like fresh air, cool and new and wonderfully light and—and he was himself, living in the time he lived in when everything was new and modern and fresh and clean. In his car by the isolated telephone box at the harbour, The Technician lit a menthol cigarette and drew in the smoke gratefully and let it out in a long, relaxed, easy stream. He closed his eyes.

His head was resting on the back of the driver's seat and he felt his lungs empty the old stale air of the tunnels and fill with the sharp tang of the sea. He had made it: he was only a few easy steps away from the end and he had made it.

Across the point, past where the junks and sampans were, he could see the pall of smoke from the furniture van turning from black to grey and then white as the last of the chassis burned down or the Fire Brigade doused it with their foam hoses.

It was over. He felt new and young and optimistic, and everything, everything was all right and linear and well-planned and certain.

One more call.

He had just one more call to make and everything would be just the way he had planned it.

Tanino, Ozawa, Morishita: they were all just memories. All dead and forgotten.

Away from the tunnels and the death and the warm, rotten air, all that was yesterday and none of it meant anything to him anymore. He had set all his charges and that was the end of all that too.

And guns and grease and oil and the stink of cordite and age and weapons: all finished, something from a war. He had returned, alive, uninjured and the war was just something, sometimes, he might think about. But it was not real anymore.

The technician said softly to himself, 'I shall be very, very rich.' He made a clucking sound and felt all the tiredness go from his body.

He felt his eyes filling with tears. 'I'll be well again. I'll be well and strong and hopeful and everything I want—' The thought was getting harder and harder to hang onto. 'It was all worth it! I made mistakes, but in the end it was all worth it!' He opened his eyes and saw his own face reflected back at him in the car windscreen. The Technician said with sudden force, 'He never did anything for me! Why should I care what happened to him?' The Technician said, 'No.' He felt encouraged. 'It's every man for himself in this world and no one ever gave me anything!' He would become one of the ever-rich, ever-young, ever-happy people he saw on television. The Technician touched at his shirt. It was light cotton. 'Silk shirts and women—anything I want! It's mine by right and whatever I did, I only did it because it was all denied to me!' He thought for a moment of the Major—The Bannin, like some sort of awful, squirming slug . . . Something the ever young, ever rich never thought of. 'No, it's mine by right!'

152

The smoke from the burning van in the park had stopped and The Technician cursed it, and Morishita who had died there, and all of them, 'Rot! Go back to dust and rot!'

There had been love between him and The Bannin. At least, he had thought so.

4.39 p.m.

No, there had been no love.

The Technician looked hard at the telephone and tried to bring his mind to his future reality by concentrating on the bright colours, the plastic and the aluminium.

One more call.

One last call and he was free.

A little behind him, on one of the cliffs was one of the entrances to the tunnels and he looked back in its direction in his rear view mirror and saw, crawling out from the time warp, *nothing*.

One more call.

Uniforms. Lots and lots of uniforms.

The Technician got out of his car and, spinning a twenty cent coin in his hand for the phone call, looked across at the horizon above the harbour and saw in it nothing but hope.

A long way behind him, at the edge of the cliffs, something moved, but he was temporarily mesmerised by the spinning object in his hand, and The Technician, in absolutely no hurry at all, did not notice it.

Dead men rising.

At the tunnel entrance on the cliff, all the dead were meeting, watching.

He saw The Technician talking to himself and grinning as he flipped the coin again and again easily and happily into the air.

The little spinning object was spinning, rising and falling, glinting dully in the light.

At the tunnel entrance all the dead were whispering incessantly in Major Takashima's ear.

The Major was listening.

... watching.

Nodding ...

On the phone in the Detectives' Room the Commander said, 'Either he was a genuine bloody seventy five year old hold-out soldier or he wasn't! You saw him. What the hell was he? Didn't you see *anything*?'

Feiffer said, 'No! I saw a bloody great flash when the mirror got the full light of the sun and I saw a rifle muzzle and I saw— All I saw was about two seconds left before he blew the top of my head away and then after that all I saw was his face covered in blood. For all I know, it could have been anybody!'

'Did he at least *move* like an old man?'

'He was behind a pillbox. He didn't have to move at all, Neal, all I saw was—'

The commander said, 'Was the mirror flash.' He made a tutting noise.

'I'm sorry. I'm lucky to be alive. If it hadn't been for Phil Auden shooting the mirror to pieces—'

The Commander said, 'And the flag—'

'Evaporated.' Feiffer said, 'And the obi—'

'It's genuine. I've had it translated and it belonged—belongs—to someone called Private Masuo Morshita of the 38th and it's genuine, and as for the flag, according to Forensic it was just so old and rotten and dry that it just—fell to dust.' The Commander said, 'Harry, it can't have been a bloody real, live Japanese! Any seventy year old man taking the full force of an exploding gun would have had a heart attack and died on the spot!' The Commander said, 'Why? Why wasn't the van set up the way all the other situations were? Why the hell if someone had gone to the trouble to steal a van with a bloody great Victorian dressing table mirror set up in it, why the hell didn't he point it at his enemies instead of at his friends?'

'Why the hell didn't the uniformed people who were supposed to be sealing off Beach Road catch him?'

'I don't know! Because he didn't come through.' The

Commander said at the end of his patience, 'Because like his fucking flag, he just disappeared into thin air. Because if he is some bloody Jap who's managed to survive here for forty years he's like a bloody ghost and—' The Commander said, 'Have you had your follow up phone call yet? Maybe, the way things are going, you're not even going to get one!' The Commander said hopelessly, 'Harry, what the hell do these people want? If it was just a sniper job or even a few hold-outs I could understand it, but there are these phone calls as well. And evidently, someone who wants to kill the so-called Japanese snipers in the bloody public parks even more than we do. And these calls: one lot from someone pretending to be what? A political terrorist? And the other—from whom? From a Japanese speaking what?' Lost, he demanded, 'Someone tell me what the hell's going on!'

'I don't know what the hell's going on.' Feiffer said, 'We've got a Japanese interpreter here, but if he doesn't ring then I don't know where we even start to make sense of it.' Feiffer said, 'So far, we've had three full attacks and the one in the park and we're at bloody bedrock.'

'The Japanese arsenal must be at fucking bedrock! There isn't any Japanese arsenal! It would have been found!' The Commander said, 'Have you got anyone working on it at all?'

'I've got Owlin at Archives trying to—'

'Him? You mean the tree-nut?' The Commander said, 'Is that the best we can do?'

'No, the best we can do is take the names of the soldiers we've got from the obis and feed them into the Japanese Defense Department computer in Tokyo and then feed that into the US and British War Records computers and then, when the names come out—'

The Commander said angrily, 'And do what? Get onto all the still living relatives of bloody dead men—all the people in the photos—and say without getting them too upset, "Excuse me, but if your husband or son who died in 1942 might happen to be still alive in a bloody arsenal in Hong Kong have you any idea which particular arsenal it might be?"' The Commander said, 'And what then? After we've calmed their bloody hysteria—get down on our knees and beg them not to give the story to the newspapers?' The Commander said, 'No. Like hell we do.'

'Then we're still at bedrock.'

'I don't like it Harry. It's happening too quickly.' The Commander said, 'Put it all together and it's been happening so fast we haven't even had time to take it all in. It's almost as if—' The Commander said, 'No, I just can't believe it's a lost section of soldiers—and this other person, this one who rings up in Cantonese, the anti-colonial terrorist or whatever he claims to be, who the hell is he?'

Feiffer glanced at The Fireworks Man sampling some of O'Yee's Constable Yan made coffee and said nothing.

'And why did this man Morishita's gun blow up? Does anyone know?'

'Sands has got it for examination—what little there was left of it.'

The Commander said, quoting, ' "The uniformed forces of colonial repression." What uniforms? There wasn't a uniform in the park anywhere and still he started shooting. And who the fucking hell made a report to the Vice Squad and why?' The Commander said, 'No, it's not right. It's not how the Japanese Army used to do business. If they wanted you dead then they didn't mess about, you were just dead.' The Commander said, 'No, it's this other fellow, this one who rings up.' He asked, 'Have you got a trace set up for his call? If he makes it.' He answered his own question, 'Yes, of course you have.' The Commander said suddenly, 'The Japanese computer thing, no. We can't—not just yet.' He seemed to think for a moment.

The Commander said, like everyone else, at bedrock, 'Jesus Christ, bloody Johnny Appleseed Owlin! *Is that really the best we can do?*'

*

4.52 p.m.
The Technician looked at his watch.

Whispering, hissing, whispering: the voices were insistently rustling in the Major's ear.

The Major was listening, nodding.

His eyes were blank.

The Major—The Bannin, the watchman—

He was listening to the voices.

*

He had it. He looked at the residue on the desk where the obi had disintegrated and he had it at last.

He knew at last how to find the arsenal. There was the faintest smell of something old and bitter in the air-conditioned room and Owlin, staring down at the desk and grinning, knew exactly where the thing had come from.

Owlin Family: Records Of Tree Plantings On The Island Of Hong Kong, 1853 To—

He knew that smell.

Owlin said, 'Oak.'

A barren rock with scarcely a tree upon it. That was how Hong Kong had been described after the Opium Wars when the first of the ships had sailed to it from Macao and the first of his family to establish himself there had sent for seeds and nurtured them and walked the length of the island in search of good ground from which to grow—*oak.*

Owlin Family: Records Of Tree Plantings On The Island Of Hong Kong, 1853 To—

Owlin said in victory, 'Got you, you bastards. After all these years, my family has got back at you and I've got every record of every tree ever planted here and I know where your dirty little obis and your dirty little guns and your axes are—I know just how to find out where you stored them!'

He was the last of the line. After him, there would be no more members of his family in Hong Kong.

He knew that smell.

Firedamp.

157

What miners called firedamp.

Methane, slightly impure, mixed with—

All the crosses on his big map went nowhere. They just meandered and wandered around the circumference of an unfindable circle and they—

The obi came from the centre of that circle and it smelled of firedamp.

The reason he had been unable to locate the centre of the system was that he had been expecting straight, man-made lines when in fact the tunnels were built around natural fissures in the granite and the smell about the glassene envelope and the obi it had contained came from—

The question was not where the Japanese Empire forty years ago built an arsenal in Hong Kong to store their weapons; it was simpler than that.

It was, where had the Owlin family a hundred years ago, out of love and hope for the future, planted their oak trees?

Owlin smiled.

It was almost unncessary to go back into the Archives to look.

It was his life.

He already knew the answer.

*

On the phone in the Detectives' Room, Inspector Sands of Ballistics said, 'In case you're feeling you've had your entire life's supply of luck doled out in one glob you haven't. The rifle was sabotaged to blow up.'

Feiffer said, 'How?'

'By the simple method of drilling little holes in three or four of the cartridges in the magazine and draining off a proportion of the powder, then following them up with a live, undrained round.' Sands said, 'The first round fired and jammed the first bullet about fourteen inches up the barrel, then when the second followed suit and fused itself to the first and then the third did the same what you had inside that barrel was a pipe bomb. Then,

158

when the next live round came up with a full load of powder, its bullet couldn't get out and the whole bolt assembly got blown back and the receiver sides just disintegrated like tissue paper.'

Feiffer said eagerly, 'So he's hurt? Seriously? The sniper?'

'Maybe. I've recovered most of the bits, including long splinters of wood from the stock that went up in the bang, but it's possible that a tiny piece of metal got him—but unlikely.' Sands said, 'The general idea, I think, was that the bolt itself would be blown back into his face like a spear, but with a hand-made gun, particularly one designed to handle experimental pressures—'

Feiffer said angrily, 'His face was covered in blood! He *must* have been hit!'

'Maybe. Or it could have been gas blast, or burned varnish from the stock, or some other part of the gun—the blueing—or maybe even—'

'Or maybe even what?' Feiffer said incredulously, 'Are you saying a bloody rifle blew itself to pieces and the man behind it didn't even get a goddamned *nosebleed*?'

'I'm saying it was a very good rifle!' Sands said, 'And before you bother to ask me about fingerprints—'

Bedrock. Everything was barren, worthless, valueless, useless bedrock. Feiffer said, 'Who the hell are these people? The fucking *Samurai Immortals*? All this stuff you're telling me is useless!'

'You're bloody lucky one of the samurai immortals decided he didn't like the other one or the only way you'd be shouting at some poor bastard doing his best to help you would be via the goddamned Celestial Phone Box! It's not my fault. I was the one who told you about the guns in the first place! What the fuck do you think I was doing while you people were being shot at in the park? Sitting on my hands? I was ready to go. Bloody Headquarters stopped me! It wasn't my idea, it was theirs! I'm an Inspector, not a bloody Commissioner. When I'm standing there in civilian clothes next to my bloody civilian car ready to go and I'm told I have to dress in civilian clothes over the next hour and then spend another forty minutes looking for a civilian car I don't say "What the fuck are you talking about?" I say, "Yes, sir!" I would have been there! I was ready to go! Bloody WPCs shooting Ingrams!' Sands said angrily, 'That's my fucking job! I would have been there.'

'Yeah.' Feiffer said suddenly calmed, 'Yes, I know you would. I'm sorry.' Feiffer said quietly, 'Look, have you got anything else at all?'

There was the slightest of pauses.

Sands said sadly, 'No, not a thing.' He asked, 'How about you?'

4.58 p.m.

Feiffer said, 'No.' He fell silent for a moment then put the phone gently back on its receiver and saw The Fireworks Man looking at him curiously.

*

4.29 p.m.

At the entrance to the tunnels, his eyes never leaving The Technician, The Bannin waited.

The voices beside him had all stopped whispering.

The Bannin touched at his face and found he had Morishita's blood on him.

5.00 p.m. exactly. From somewhere behind him on the headland, The Bannin heard a siren howl to signal the end of a work shift. He saw The Technician look at his watch and then get back to his car to wait.

The Technician had been spinning a little coin up in the air over and over. It had glittered dully.

The Bannin also had something made of metal in his hand that glittered in the sun.

Brightly.

He felt its sharp edge and narrowed his eyes.

*

At the door, Ah Pin looked hard at The Fireworks Man at a desk near the sandbags and then to the tape recorder and tracing

160

extensions on O'Yee's desk. O'Yee looked up and smiled at him and Ah Pin, his eyes still on The Fireworks Man, nodded back.

It was a minute after five, past his quitting time.

Ah Pin, drumming his fingers out of sight on the door jamb behind him, hesitated.

O'Yee, still smiling, said lightly in Cantonese, 'You know, my grandfather lived to be eighty nine years old and he'd be with us still if it hadn't been for the overwork.' He looked pointedly at the clock and, in case Ah Pin was waiting for permission to leave, nodded at him encouragingly.

The Fireworks Man's face was bland.

All so long ago...

The Fireworks Man's suit was expensive and well cut.

At the door Ah Pin smiled back at O'Yee and then, after a moment, went back into the charge room in his torn shorts and singlet, to go home.

*

Running across Hong Bay, directly through all the overlaid crosses and marks on the map, there was a natural tunnel in the granite.

In the centre of it, long before there were detailed geological maps to be had, Owlin's family had planted a forest of ash trees.

In their deep, dead, decomposing roots, those long dead trees now grew Japanese obis and methane gas.

He was the last of the line.

In his silent room, Owlin ran his finger across the coloured strata of time and change and looked for where the tunnel, linking generations, came out into the present.

*

5.05 p.m.

By his car The Technician closed his eyes and tried to focus dreams.

161

One more call.

Behind him, the siren was still howling, running down and he thought that in less than three hours it would all be over.

He tossed his coin casually onto the bonnet of his car and it made a tinkling sound as it struck, rolled a few inches, then, losing momentum, lay flat in front of him, waiting.

13

The two nickel-plated balls in Auden's hand went click-click-click... Auden caught The Fireworks Man looking at him and opened his hand to show the man what he held. Auden said, 'They're lead balls, plated.' He drew an imaginary filament from the balls with his fingers, 'They hang on strings from a central point and when you hit one against the other they click. It's an executive toy. It's called a Newton's Cradle.'

The Fireworks Man was sitting at O'Yee's desk. In front of him was the telephone with a tape recorder and extension wires attached. The extension wires ran to Feiffer's telephone and the one on Spencer's desk. The Fireworks Man looked first at that and then at the sandbags and the bullet proof vests. Auden had been speaking in English. He thought the man had not understood and began again in Cantonese.

The Fireworks Man said, 'I understand English. It's a pendulum device invented by Sir Isaac Newton.' He seemed worried. He watched as Auden smiled and nodded at him and then went back to clicking. The Fireworks Man said quietly, 'Like most things they are originally a Chinese invention.'

Sencer looked at Auden and shook his head. The sounds were clearly upsetting The Fireworks Man. Spencer said in explantion, 'It's part of the device used to set off the rifles.'

The Fireworks Man said, 'Originally, it was designed as an amusement. Gunpowder was originally designed as an amusement!' It was warm in the Detectives' Room and The Fireworks Man took out a white handkerchief from his inside coat pocket and dabbed at his face. Feiffer was at his desk going through photographs and folders, getting something ready. The

Fireworks Man said with a trace of desperation in his voice, 'I don't know that I even remember the sort of Japanese soldiers speak. It's not the same as commercial Japanese—'

O'Yee said, 'You'll be fine.' He connected something from the telephone into the tape recorder and touched a button to test it. A light came on on the recorder and he switched it off again. O'Yee said, 'All you have to do is keep him on the line. The last time I tried Japanese on him it gave him such a shock that he was stunned into total silence for about thirty seconds and—'

Feiffer had a folder assembled. He brought it over and put it on the desk in front of The Fireworks Man. Feiffer said, 'Here's everything we know about them—the names, everything.' He waited, but The Fireworks Man went on looking into his face. Feiffer said gently, 'There's no problem about your good character. I've told you you can have it whether you do this or not.'

The Fireworks Man's face seemed to be melting. The Fireworks Man's mouth formed a word, but nothing came out. Behind him, he could feel the invisible presence of Ah Pin in the charge room. The Fireworks Man said, 'What did he tell you? Ah Pin. The executioner? What did he tell you about me?'

Auden said, 'The what?'

Feiffer said, 'Nothing. He told us what I told you.' He pushed the folder a little closer, 'You're our last chance.'

'*Why* am I your last chance ? I don't ask you to do my job for me, why should you ask me to do yours?'

O'Yee said, 'We can't get anyone else. There's no one else who can speak the Japanese slang of that period and—'

'*How in the name of heaven can they be Japanese soldiers?*' The Fireworks Man said, 'Look at me! I'm their age! Can you imagine me with enough courage to go into battle now?'

'No one's asking you to go into battle.'

'Why am I doing this? To convince a cleaner after forty years that I was a loyal Chinese?' The Fireworks Man said, 'Look at me, I'm rich! Why should I have to convince him of anything? I—I was standing there in my—in my best suit and he in his dirty,

164

ragged—and he—' The Fireworks Man looked down at the folder and pushed it away. The tape recorder and extensions were on the desk in front of him. All of a sudden, The Fireworks Man said, 'No!' He shouted at Auden, still clicking, 'Stop intimidating me! It's all over! It's finished! I was tried and it's all over! Why should I lose any more?'

Feiffer said, 'There are people dead!'

'There are always people dead!' The Fireworks Man said, 'All right, I believe you: you're an honest man. You're the only honest man I've met in almost eighty years on this Earth—you said I could have my good character for my licence renewal whatever I did—all right, I'll do nothing—now give me my good character!'

Feiffer said, 'At least read the file.'

'You said I could have it! I want it!'

'At least look at the names! At least give us *something*—'

The Fireworks Man said, 'No!' He shook his head. 'No.' He challenged Feiffer with a look, 'You said you'd give me my good character, now give it to me! I won't have anything more to do with this and you can tell your cleaner that if—' The Fireworks Man said, 'No!' Give me the character! Let me finish my life and sell the whole filthy factory for the peace of my soul! *Give me the good character!* Let me be rid of myself!'

Spencer came forward to rest his hand on The Fireworks Man's shoulder. Spencer said gently, 'Look, you're just a little upset—'

'You *boy!* You fresh-faced, stupid, unknowing *boy!*' The Fireworks Man demanded, 'What's the worst thing you've ever done in your life—*stolen money from your mother's purse?*' He saw Feiffer's hand on the folder and he swept it away, 'I don't want to see the names! I don't want to have to read them! I don't want to have to remember! I don't want to even—' His hand closed around the folder to fling it to the floor, but Feiffer's hand was on his wrist.

Feiffer held him. Feiffer said suddenly, 'What the hell are you holding back?' His face had gone hard. He looked down at the folder and then back into The Fireworks Man's face. Feiffer said over his shoulder to O'Yee, 'Give him his good character. Type it out and sign it.' The Fireworks Man's wrist in his hand was surprisingly strong. Feiffer said with his eyes still on The Fireworks Man's face, 'You know something. Don't you?'

'Nothing. I know nothing!' The Fireworks Man wrenched his hand free. He turned his eyes to Auden, 'You, playing with your little toys and telling me—' He looked at O'Yee, 'And you, you *Eurasian*, you with your little wires and your—'

Feiffer ordered him, 'Read the names!'

'I know the names!'

'Read them!'

'I know them!' The Fireworks Man grabbed the folder and held it up in his hand, 'Who have you got so far? What have you got— their thousand stitches obis? You asked me in my office if I knew what a thousand stitches obi was. Yes, I know what they are! I knew the people who wore them! I was married to a Japanese girl who made one! Yes, I know what they are!' He turned to Spencer, 'You, is your family rich?'

Spencer said, 'Well, no, of course they're not—'

'Are they poor then? So poor that they steal from garbage bins to stay alive? So poor that they sell what they steal rather than eat it themselves? So poor that—'

Feiffer said, 'Nobody is suggesting that during the Occupation—'

'I wasn't poor during the Occupation! I was rich! Being poor was a choice! I had no choice! I had a Japanese wife and I had no choice at all!' The Fireworks Man said, 'Even now I have no choice!'

'You have a choice! You don't have to do this.' Feiffer said evenly, 'But if you know something and you're holding it back—in a murder investigation—then God help you when—'

The Fireworks Man said, '*Tanino*! Am I right?' He looked down at the folder, 'Sergeant Quartermaster Seichiro Tanino of the thirty eighth division in Hong Kong. Am I right?'

Feiffer said in astonishment, 'Yes.' He had thought the man had meant only that he knew the names figuratively. He had thought— Feiffer said, 'Yes, he was the one in Cuttlefish Lane—'

Auden said, 'And the boat?'

The Fireworks Man said, 'Corporal Sakutaro Ozawa.' Tears were beginning in his eyes. The names were coming out like old unhealed wounds. The Fireworks Man said, 'Private Masuo Morishita.'

Feiffer said, *'How do you know all these names?'*

The Fireworks Man looked hard at Spencer's unlined face. The Fireworks Man said quietly, 'And their leader, Major Quartermaster Juzo Takashima, called by those who knew him well or those who loved him, "Bannin", Watchman—because he once, during his student days, took a job where he—' The Fireworks Man said quietly, 'You see I know all the names already. I know them. I know every one of them—and some of the others, some of the others who were temporarily attached to his section, but who—' The Fireworks Man said in a sudden explosion, 'I don't have to look at your file! *I know all their names already!'*

Feiffer demanded, 'How? How do you know all their names?'

Spencer said softly, 'My God, they really are Japanese soldiers!'

The Fireworks Man said with the faintest of bitter smiles, still looking at Spencer's face, 'Yes, they really are.' The Fireworks Man said quietly to Feiffer, 'I know the names of every one of them. Even after all these years, every one—'

'*How?*' Feiffer demanded, 'How? How do you know their names? How? After all these years, *how* do you know their names?'

Ah Pin was long gone, but The Fireworks Man still felt his presence behind him and the invisible presence of other things. His best suit was merely a sham: an old man dressed up. He touched at it and felt his eyes brim with tears. The Fireworks Man said, 'How? How do I know all their names?'

There was silence in the room.

The Fireworks Man said quietly, 'Because almost forty years ago, one night, September the first, 1942, I, not the bombs, but I . . . I killed them.'

5.17 p.m.

As, on the headland, The Technician got out of his car to make his call, The Fireworks Man looked at all the faces in the stilled room in Yellowthread Street and said softly, 'The Bannin—Major Takashima—was my wife's brother. The Resistance ordered me to kill him to save her and I did.' He touched at his suit and shrugged, 'But then, because she was Japanese, after the Liberation, they killed her anyway.'

The Fireworks Man looked down at the telephone in front of him.

The Fireworks Man asked the room, 'What do I say to a ghost?' Tears were running down his face. The Fireworks Man said almost inaudibly, 'That I'm—that I'm *sorry*?'

*

JAPANESE SOLDIERS IN HONG KONG?

Persistent reports reaching this newspaper that recent shootings in the Hong Bay district were carried out by hold-out Japanese soldiers from World War Two were again denied by the police in a statement issued late this afternoon.

The Press Officer at the Japanese Embassy in Hong Kong, Mr Michael Okuno, when questioned by reporters from this newspaper, refused to confirm or deny that recent police investigations had centred around nationals from his country, but said that, following a request from various sources, his Embassy would be releasing a statement aimed at clarifying the situation sometime tomorrow morning.

Mr Okuno refused to be drawn on what the contents of the statement might be.

*

Outside, dusk was coming. Feiffer said quickly, 'Then where the hell's the arsenal now? If that's where you killed them, then where the hell is it now?'

The Fireworks Man said, 'I don't know and that's the truth. That night, when the bombers came I went in and planted charges along the passage that led from Wyang Cove, but Wyang

Cove isn't there anymore. When the bombs fell and the charges went off there was nothing but rubble.' He looked at O'Yee and held out his hands in a gesture of helplessness. 'Wyang Cove isn't even there anymore. Not even by name. After the war when the Public Works people sealed off all the old air raid shelters and the tunnels the entire area was covered as part of a reclamation scheme and Wyang Cove became part of the new Beach Road.' The Fireworks Man said, 'The next morning when the Japanese inspected the damage they thought it had all been done by the bombs and they never even once suspected—' The Fireworks Man said, 'My brother-in-law, The Bannin—Major Taka-shima—he was never involved in the torture and the exe-cutions, but the Resistance decided he was one of the few Japs they could kill and get away with it and they were trying to impress the Communists and the Nationalists to send them arms and money and they needed to show that they'd at least killed somebody.' The Fireworks Man said, 'They needed confirmation that a real live Japanese with a name and a family had died—and they got that from me—someone they trusted—they let me go on working for the Japanese, because he was a—' The Fireworks Man said, 'And then, after the war, they killed my wife and they— *Because they never knew which side I was really on!*'

Spencer said anxiously, 'Whose side where you on?'

'Don't ask me that!' The Fireworks Man said, 'I was on the winning side! Can't you tell? Look at me! See how prosperous and happy I am! I was on the winning side!'

Spencer said after a moment, 'And which one was that?' All of a sudden he no longer felt fresh faced and young. Spencer said, 'Which was the side that won? The one that lost the fewest people it loved?'

The Fireworks Man said to Feiffer, 'I don't know where the entrance to the arsenal is. There were many. It was one giant system. All I did was destroy one little part of it.' The Fireworks Man said, 'I don't know. At first, when nobody was purposely hurt—on the building over there—when only one man was accidentally killed according to the newspapers—I thought it

169

could have been children and then, in the papers, it hinted that it was some sort of anti-colonial terrorist gang and then—' The Fireworks Man said, 'I waited to hear about a flag.' He looked at Auden. Auden had the two balls in his hand. He looked down at them and put them gently on his desk. The Fireworks Man clenched his hand, 'Before their last hopeless battle, before they all committed suicide, the Japanese always burned their flag to stop it falling into enemy hands, but I—I haven't read about flags so I—' He asked, 'Has there been a flag?'

O'Yee said, 'Yes.'

The Fireworks Man said, 'Then they've come back.' The Fireworks Man closed his eyes. The Fireworks Man said quietly, 'Hanabi San: Mr Fireworks.' He smiled, 'My brother-in-law— Major Takashima—that's what he called me.' He said quietly, 'The Bannin—The Watchman.' He looked down at the telephone and said quietly, 'My brother-in-law—The Bannin—he's come back for *me.*'

*

He had had to go. It was obvious. He had had no choice in it. It was obvious. At the telephone, The Technician paused, gazing out across the harbour. *It was obvious and he should have no regrets about it because it was obvious!*

The Technician said quietly, 'Bannin . . .'

It was obvious and he had had to go.

An inch. All he had had to do was miss a few people by an inch and everything would have been all right and all this Japanese shit would have been— The Technician gripped the telephone receiver in his hand in a fury and cursed, 'Damn it! All you had to do was just what you were told and you could have had half! But no, you had to have all this Japanese shit and—'

—and sooner or later everyone would have been caught and it would have all been for nothing. An inch, just one inch. All he had had to do was—but no, that was too straightforward for a goddamned Jap and he had to start shrieking Banzai and killing people and—and Morishita had died in the park in the set-up and all The Technician hoped was that his face had been so thoroughly shot to pieces by the cops that it was just a pulp! The Technician said, 'Curse you! You could have had half!'

'Divine mission to eradicate all the uniformed forces of colonial repression....' Would they still wear it?

They had to. It was too late to change. It might just last long enough until...

The Technician, hesitating in the phone booth said in a fury, 'Damn him! He deserved to die!'

The 38th Division of the Japanese Imperial All Conquering Army in China—it was the goddamned methane gas or marsh gas or whatever it was down there. It had sent him insane. The Technician said, 'I had to kill you! I had to!' The Technician said to the plastic and aluminium telephone, 'You could have had half! I found the tunnels and I found you and you could have had half with all my blessings!'

He said in a fury of frustration at the telephone, *'Fuck you! You could have been my brother!'*

By now, the first of the incendiary charges would have gone off.

The Technician put his finger to the dial and began ringing the number for Yellowthread Street.

A hundred yards behind him, his face covered in blood, a ghost from forty years ago stood up at the cliff side.

The Technician had his back to him in the phone booth, dialling a number.

The long, razor sharp bayonet flashed in the ghost's hand.

His boots made no sound on the grass as he went forward.

*

The Fireworks Man said helplessly, 'No, you don't understand! If it's him...If it's the Major...'

Feiffer said desperately, 'Please, just one word...'

All the tracing apparatus and the recording devices were attached to the phone. The Fireworks Man said, pleading, 'If it's him come back—'

Feiffer said, 'People are dead! We've got nothing! All we've got is you!'

The phone was ringing.

Feiffer said in a final appeal to the Fireworks Man, 'Please ... *please!*'

*

The final map in his collection was a geological chart of the Hong Bay region, complete with seismic soundings and surveyed, accurate strata formations and—

And he found it.

The tunnel went—

He found it.

Maltby Point. It came out in at least eight places on the cliffs and under the—

Owlin said softly, 'Got you!'

He had found it.

At least one of those natural tunnel exits would have been used by the Japanese engineers, possibly two or three, and at least one of those exits was still there because the Public Works Department, after the land had been sold, had only given cursory attention to the sealing up of old craters and—

He had found it.

He flipped back the canvas backed chart and overlaid it with a modern street map and stopped.

One of the tunnels, if all the maps and his calculations were right, came out under the—

The tunnels were filled with what? With guns. Shells? Explosives?

The Keeper Of Secrets stared hard at the street map and then flipped it back to expose the survey chart.

One of those tunnels came out directly under the—

It went right past where the old oak forest had been, directly under—

172

Owlin said, 'Oh, my God!'

One of those tunnels packed with guns and dynamite and TNT and God knew what else—one of the tunnels the Public Works Department had missed—came out directly under— Under the modern, fully operational Maltby Point fireworks factory.

Owlin said softly, again, 'Oh, my God...'

He flipped back to the first map again to make absolutely sure he was right.

*

Feiffer said in a whisper with his hand on The Fireworks Man's shoulder, 'Please, just one word...'

The Fireworks Man said, 'I mined the entrances and the air vents. The Resistance knew the bombers were coming and I had a pass to move around at night and I—I mined the spot where Major Takashima and his men were asleep and they—' The Fireworks Man said, trying to make someone understand, 'It was me! It wasn't the bombers, it was me! I killed them—my own brother-in-law, everyone—the whole eleven man section! I killed every last one of them!' The Fireworks Man said, 'No! It can't be true! *They're all dead!*'

*

He was coming. Across the grass, the Major was coming. He touched at his face and his hand came away bloody and black with the burned powder from the exploded rifle. The bayonet was in his other hand, held low. He looked down and saw his cracked leather boots crushing at the grass as he walked. The Technician was ahead of him in the phone. The Major said softly, over and over, 'Traitor ... traitor ...' He lifted up the long steel bayonet and it glittered in the sun.

The Technician had his back to him. His muscles tightened against his white shirt as he held the receiver hard to his ear, listening about to speak.

173

All the voices of the dead were whispering in the Major's ear. They came as wind in from the sea, coming across flat water in the dying light.

They were whispering, cajoling, working on him, hinting, entreating. The Major felt his breath coming in hard gasps. The Technician was in front of him. He saw the muscles in the man's back flicker as he moved in the booth and cocked his head slightly against the phone receiver to say something.

The Major's boots made no sound on the grass.

The Technician was moving, leaning closer to the phone, readying himself for his lies and dishonours and his—

The Major said softly, 'Traitor ... *traitor!*'

He raised the bayonet and it flashed in the light.

The Major's hand was tight and hard on the haft. His arm was full of life and power. He felt his bicep tremble with anticipatory force.

His boots made no sound on the grass as he approached.

*

On the phone, O'Yee shrieked, 'Who the hell are you? *What the hell do you want?*' He heard Feiffer snap, 'Christopher—!' and O'Yee shouted, 'You lousy bastard, what the hell do you want?'

'I have a divine mission to—'

'Bullshit! Bullshit!' O'Yee saw the Fireworks Man's face and shouted, 'What the hell are you doing to my people? What the hell do you think you're doing to everyone? You're killing people! You lousy, rotten, stinking bastard, you're killing people!'

'—*divine mission to eradicate the uniformed forces of*—'

'No!' The Fireworks Man said, 'No! It's him! I know it is!'

Auden yelled, 'Pick up the extension!' He thrust it into The Fireworks Man's hand and The Fireworks Man pushed it away. Spencer said desperately to The Fireworks Man, 'Please, just one word! Just hold him long enough to—' He was already on the other phone dialling the number for a trace. Spencer said, 'Please, wouldn't you just—'

174

'—divine mission to eradicate—'

O'Yee shouted, 'No, I don't want to hear it!' He glanced at Spencer. Spencer was through to the exchange and he was reading off the number to them to get the engineers working. O'Yee said quickly to Feiffer, 'I can't hold him—' He looked hard at The Fireworks Man.

The Fireworks Man said—

'—colonial repression and I have—' He stopped. Behind him, The Technician heard something. In the phone booth he turned and saw death. The Technician said in Japanese, 'Bannin! *No!*'

He heard it. From across the room, he heard it. The Fireworks Man said, 'No, it can't be—' Auden still had the extension in his hand. The Fireworks Man said—

Auden thrust the phone into his hands and ordered him, 'Talk! Say something! Hold him until we can—'

'Bannin! Ie! *No!*' The Technician said hysterically, not knowing which way he was talking, 'I have a divine—Bannin! No!— mission to eradicate—'

O'Yee shouted, 'Who are you? *Tell us who you are!*'

Spencer was onto the engineers. He was saying, 'Yes, yes ... yes...' as they narrowed down the call street by street. Spencer said, 'Yes ... yes...'

Feiffer shouted at The Fireworks Man, 'Damn it, don't kill anyone else! Help us!' The Fireworks Man had the phone loosely in his hand. Feiffer gave him a shove in the back that almost sent him crashing against Auden's desk, 'Talk to him! Talk to him in Japanese!'

The Technician said, raving, '—uniformed—' The bayonet was glittering in the Major's hand. The Technician said, '—to eradicate all the—' He heard another voice on the other end of the line say in Japanese—

The Technician said—

'*Kwan Yu!* Kenneth!' The Fireworks Man said, not in Japanese, but in Cantonese, 'It's you! Kenneth, it's you! *Isn't it?*'

'It's Shozo, father, it's *Shozo!*' The Technician said, losing power, fading away, 'It's Shozo ... they were all Shozo.... I ...

175

it was...' The Technician said, 'It was mine! My birthright! I didn't do any of the things you did and it belongs to me when you're dead, not your soul!' The Major was standing next to him in the phone box, cramped close, his breath on The Technician's face, smiling, his eyes lightless and blank. The Technician said, babbling, 'Father, it was all mine ... you had no right to ... you have no right to ... to ...' He saw the bayonet come up, 'No right to deny me my .., my ... *my*....' He saw the bayonet come up. The Technician, The Fireworks Man's son by his second, Chinese wife, shouted in extremis, 'Father, *help me*—!'

Spencer said, 'Maltby Point! The call's coming from Maltby Point!' From near the—!' He looked hard at The Fireworks Man, '—from near the fireworks factory!'

There was a silence. At the other end of the line there was nothing but a silence.

The Fireworks Man said, 'Kenneth? Kwan Yu? *Kenneth?*'

He heard someone breathing.

He heard a hissing sound.

It was Shozo. It had all been Shozo...

The Fireworks Man said into the phone, 'After the war started I got you out, away—I got you away to Japan to stay with your mother's family ... I did right!' There was only a silence from the phone.

The Fireworks Man said, 'I thought it was the one good thing I ever did! I thought it was the one good thing—' The Fireworks Man said, desperately, changing to Japanese, 'I didn't want to kill him! *I had to!* It was either that or your mother and then, after the war, they killed her anyway!' The Fireworks Man shouted desperately at the son he had never wanted back, 'I got you away to Japan when you were just a baby! I thought it was the one good thing I ever did!' The Fireworks Man begged, 'Shozo! *Answer me!*' The Fireworks Man said, pleading, 'You were my first born son! Understand what I did for you! And then, after the war, I thought if they ever found out I had a Japanese son still living they'd take the factory back! Everything I had! I thought you wouldn't ever want to see me again after I killed your mother's brother and

176

your—I thought—' The Fireworks Man begged into the phone, 'Please, Shozo, *please!*'

O'Yee said quickly to Feiffer, 'I can't follow it all, but it's his son! It's the son of his first marriage to a Japanese woman! It isn't a hold-out at all, it's his son! It's someone from now—it's someone who's come back and made some sort of alliance with the other son, the Chinese one, and—'

The Fireworks Man shrieked into the phone, 'Where is my second son? What have you done to Kwan Yu? To Kenneth? *Where is my second son?*'

'*Here!*' The Major's voice said in a sudden old man's croak, 'Here! With us! With all the men you killed! With me! With The Bannin! Your son is here! *Hovering!* Waiting! *Rotting!*' The Major said, 'Your son—all your sons—all your family, everyone you ever touched—they are all—'

The Fireworks Man heard his second son say in a gasp, '*No. . . !*' There was a terrible thump.

The Bannin said, 'Dead! Where we all are since you murdered us! All—long ago . . . all of us—*dead!*'

*

It was burning. The first of The Technician's charges had gone off in the underground testing chambers and the fireworks factory was beginning to burn.

*

5.45 p.m.

In his office in the Archives Owlin tried for the third time to ring the Station.

There was no one there. The phone just went on ringing and ringing.

Above him, in the streets, he had no idea whether it was night or day and he had to look up the times of sunset in an almanac before, drawing a breath to venture into the outside world, he

177

knew that there was at least an hour and five minutes before the city became dark.

*

It was burning. The factory was burning. All his enemies were coming. At the entrance to the tunnel on the cliff The Bannin heard the sound of sirens and klaxons as, from all over Hong Bay, uniformed men came to consecrate the last battle of the 38th Division of the Japanese Imperial all-Conquering Army in Hong Kong with their deaths.

The factory was burning.

5.59 p.m. The factory on Maltby Point was burning.

In the coming dark the flashes and detonations lit up the sky.

The sirens and klaxons were coming.

The Bannin was ready.

He went to inform his men that their victory, at last, was momentarily upon them.

14

In the car Auden shouted above the roaring of the engine and the blast as one of the wooden fireworks storage rooms went up, 'It's The Fireworks Man! He was after The Fireworks Man! He was going to kill him under cover of shooting at bloody uniforms in the fire so he's got to have a set-up still in there!' The locked wire gates to the compound were racing towards him. He saw a pothole in the road, swerved to avoid it, and saw the night shift running along the grass inside the fence looking for a way out. The wire gates were padlocked. There was a man trying to climb it and Auden wound down the window and shouted in Cantonese, 'Get away from the gate!'

Spencer yelled, 'He can't hear you!' The man was half way up on the wire like a monkey, trying to fling a leg over the top. Spencer yelled, 'Hit the fence! Hit the fence a little way down from the gates!' Auden hit a pothole and Spencer went flying inside the car and grabbed hold of the dashboard to steady himself. A fireball exploded low and racing across the compound it ignited a second wooden shack. It burned for a moment, then, as the flames caught, the gunpowder stored inside disappeared in a flash and a billowing blast of grey smoke. It was like an old black powder cannon salvo: the smoke rolled and turned white and got in the open window of the car.

Behind him, Spencer could see the Commander's car coming to a skidding halt at the telephone box and then the Commander, in full uniform, was out with Feiffer and O'Yee waving the fire engines to a stop and ordering someone to take cover. Another blast roared out from the factory and incinerated first one, then another of the small shacks, then like giant's footsteps, the

179

explosions erupted in a steady line. Spencer yelled, 'Mind the people at the—' and Auden hit the wire fence with the front of the car and smashed it down. One of the shacks went up and rained down sparks. Spencer shouted to the running men inside the fence, 'Get out! We've brought the fence down! Get out through the opening!' They didn't have to be asked twice. Spencer, out of the car, bent double against the heat, yelled, 'Through here!' and ducked to one side as the workmen went past him running for safety. Spencer yelled, 'They're clear! Get the car started!' He saw Auden get out with his big gun in his hand and yelled, 'He's dead! He's up by the phone box! We've got everyone out—'

A shack detonated and almost blew him off his feet. Auden yelled back, 'He was after The Fireworks Man! He was going to kill him before he sold his land! Look at all the bloody uniforms up there! There's goddamned fire and ambulance and the cops and—' A small storage shack of maroons and rockets went off like machine gun fire and sent burning powder cascading fifty feet into the air. Auden shouted. 'He's left a set-up in here! He's set his bloody little executive toy and his bloody little guns to get The Fireworks Man when the uniforms came in to stop the fire!' Auden looked around and saw the administration buildings fifty yards in front of him, still unburned, all the windows glinting in the last rays of the setting sun. Auden shouted, 'It's somewhere opposite the offices! That's where The Fireworks Man would have been helping with the hoses or—'

Spencer yelled, 'So what?' All the workers were safe and running towards the police and the fire brigade. Spencer yelled, 'He's dead! So what if he's—'

'*He's fucking shot me once and made me look stupid twice!*'

Spencer yelled, 'So what?' A shack went up and staggered him with the blast. Spencer shouted, 'This place is turning into—' He saw Auden's face, 'Phil, he's dead it doesn't matter any more! The Fireworks Man isn't in his office—he's safe! Back there! With Harry!' All the words had no effect. Spencer yelled, 'Safe! Harry! All right? Everything's—' He saw Auden's glazed eyes. A shack went off in a fountain of yellow and white sparks and rolled a billow of smoke down and covered them. Spencer heard Auden shout, 'Just once! Just once I'm going to—' and then there was a secondary blast that cleared the smoke and when Spencer looked Auden was gone.

One, two, three, four seconds ... five, six... He saw Auden running towards the administration building with the giant gun still in his hand. Auden turned for a moment with a fierce look on his face, then staggered as a blast caught him sideways and spun him around. All the buildings were wood: a shower of planks and splinters came down at Spencer and ricochetted off the car and smashed through the windscreen. Spencer yelled, 'Phil—!'

Auden mouthed something. It could have been, 'Nine seconds...!'

Spencer shouted back, 'Seven, goddamn you! It's seven! Seven! Seven!!'

All the workmen were safe. The fence was down. All the buildings were wooden. Spencer yelled—

Spencer yelled, 'Seven, curse you!' and began running after him into the fires.

*

At the telephone, the Commander roared through his bullhorn, '*Nobody*! Nobody enters that compound!' He heard an engine start as one of the firemen decided that the time had come to earn his money. The Commander thundered, 'Nobody and that's an order! The first man, fire brigade, ambulance or cop who moves one millimetre farther forward will be on charges!' The engine stopped. There was a steady roaring coming from the fireworks factory. The Commander shouted, 'Everybody stays here until the fire is out!' The engine started again and he wrenched the Chief Fire Officer next to him by the shoulder and shouted, still through the bullhorn, 'Is that place sited safe to burn, yes or no?'

The Chief Fire Officer said, 'Yes!' He looked at the fires with longing. The Commander's grip on his shoulder turned into a vice, 'Yes! It's safe! It's sited safe. We can let it burn!'

181

There were uniforms everywhere. The Commander ordered everybody, 'Nobody moves! Everybody stays here! Let it burn—nobody gets shot! And that's an *order*!' He saw the Emergency Unit counter sniper platoon setting up behind a fire engine, unlimbering their guns and looking for something to counter snipe at, and the Commander, turning the funnel of the amplifier on them, ordered them, 'Set up here! If there's someone around here who thinks he's a goddamned Jaanese soldier set up here and protect these people!' If there was someone around who thought he was a Japanese soldier then he was well hidden. There was nothing but grass and cliffs and smoke. The Commander thundered out, 'Keep your eyes out for a tunnel!'

*

At the phone box, The Technician had taken a single thrust through the throat. There was no trail of blood—he had gone down and died without a twitch where he had been hit. Feiffer, with his hand on The Fireworks Man's shoulder demanded, 'Where is it? The tunnel? Is it in the factory?' The Fireworks Man was on his knees over his dead son, his hands moving above his face gingerly, afraid to touch him, too late for love. Feiffer demanded, 'Where? Where is it?' Behind him he heard Doctor Macarthur say to Sands, 'It's an obi. I can read a bit of it. It says Major—something—Takashima of the—' and Feiffer shook at The Fireworks Man's shoulder and rapped at him—

The Fireworks Man said, 'I don't know! It's here! It used to be here! It used to be everywhere—all over the island! It used to go from the beach right through here and come up—but it's all been bombed or filled up or—' He tried to touch his dead son's face, but his hands were trembling too much. The Fireworks Man said, 'I don't know!' He heard a gigantic rumbling explosion as one of the underground testing chambers caught and detonated, and he shouted, 'I don't know! I should have been in there! At this time of day when the shift starts I'm always in my office doing the accounts! All this is for me!' He looked down at his son's face and

182

it, dead, reacted not at all, like wax. The Fireworks Man implored at him, 'I did it for you! It's all bad joss—all jinxed, ill-fated! I did it for you!' He looked up at Feiffer and tried to make someone understand, 'It was all tainted—all the money! I thought during the war that the things I did to earn this place were all worth it, but they weren't! I learned that in old age!' He looked back to his son and it was all too late, 'You could have made your own way! My money was tainted!' The Fireworks Man implored Feiffer, 'Understand! I wasn't being hard! He was only my second son and I—' The Fireworks Man's face was running with tears and soot from the billowing, acrid smoke. The Fireworks Man said, 'He did all this for the money! He was going to kill me so the land could all be his!' He looked down at his son with desperation, 'He was just like me! He did it all for the money!'

Sands said suddenly, 'Jesus Christ, it's gone!' He had a piece of the obi in his hand and it was decaying literally before his eyes. Sands said, 'Doc, what the hell's—'

Macarthur touched at a piece of the material and it crumbled. He saw Feiffer looking at him. Macarthur said, 'It's dry. It's desiccated, like—' He looked down at his hand and the material had gone to dust. Macarthur said in a whisper, 'Where the devil has it been kept? *In an Egyptian pyramid?*'

Wrenching at The Fireworks Man, Feiffer said again, desperately, 'Where the hell is the *tunnel?*'

*

In the main compound, Auden shouted, 'Here! Here it is! That's it, isn't it?' A fountain of exploding sparks burst out from one of the shacks fifty yards away and fell fizzing to earth around him. The two storey office building in the compound was the only one in the place still undamaged. All the wooden framed windows were still intact. Auden yelled, 'That has to be it! That has to be where The Fireworks Man had his office!' He looked around quickly and avoided a piece of burning wood that threatened to set fire to his pants leg. Auden said, 'Look, what was supposed to happen was that we'd all turn up and use the compound here as a base and we'd form a picket line here and The Fireworks Man would have—' His brain was working overtime, 'And we'd keep him back here and then the set-up—' Auden looked around. The compound was full of what looked like old derelict wooden barns and storage shacks, 'And then the set-up would start opposite here—there! And kill the bastard!' The stopwatch in Auden's brain was going like a Swiss chronometer. Auden said, 'There! One of those shacks there! He must have set up in one of those shacks there to catch him in the line of fire!' He began moving. Spencer said, 'So what? It's all over! The Fireworks Man is safe and—' and Auden shaking his head, said with an evil grin on his face, 'And the smoke hasn't even started yet so I've got all the time in the world!' He went quickly to the first wooden shack and kicked the door down and dashed in.

It was wrong. The logic was all—Spencer glanced around the compound and tried to see how everyone would have placed themselves and it was all— Spencer said, as a blast from a far shack erupted sky high like a volcano and showered him with sparks, 'No! Phil! It's all wrong! It's too easy! How could he have actually hit anyone—?' He saw Auden come out of the shack looking disappointed and he shook his head and said again, 'Phil, it's all wrong!'

Seven seconds. No little puffs of smoke. No trick mirrors. No blanks to make you fall down clutching your chest and thinking you were shot on the roofs of buildings. No—

Spencer yelled, 'It's all wrong! It isn't the way it would have been done!'

Auden ran to the next shack and, the fierce grin still on his face, turning bright red in the glow of the burning shacks, kicked the next door down with a look of pure delight and anticipation.

*

At the phone, Feiffer said, 'I don't know. I don't know where he is! For all I know, he's nowhere or fifty bloody miles away!' The counter sniper unit had lowered their rifles and they were watching the fire and enjoying the show. Feiffer said, 'I know he's here, but I dont know how to—' He saw the Commander's face. Feiffer said, 'I don't know! *Under us!* He's somewhere bloodywell under us and I haven't got the faintest bloody dog's idea where to even start sniffing!' He saw O'Yee grab one of the fleeing workmen on his way past and spin the man around to ask him a question and Feiffer demanded, 'Christopher, where the hell are Auden and Spencer?'

O'Yee was questioning the man in rapid-fire Cantonese. O'Yee said, 'They're still in there! They left the car and went in to get—I don't know!' The workman shook himself loose, ducked as a gigantic explosion lit up the darkening sky and got free of O'Yee's hold on him. O'Yee called out to Feiffer, 'They've gone in to look for more people—I think!' The workman ran towards an ambulance, found it closed and himself uninjured, and just kept on running. O'Yee yelled to the Chief Fire Officer, 'Is there anyone else in there?'

The Chief Fire Officer was ticking off numbers in a notepad as the workmen came by. The Chief Fire Officer said, 'Two more.' He saw them running towards him. He ticked them. The Chief Fire Officer said, 'No, that's everyone!' He saw the Commander's face set, 'Sir, when the hell can we go in and put out the fire?'

The Commander ignored him.

The Chief Fire Officer said, 'Sir! Commander—?'

The Commander was looking down at the ground. In a Japanese arsenal, below ground, packed with war material...

The Chief Fire Officer said again, 'Sir, when the hell can we go in and put the bloody fire out?'

The Commander said, 'Harry, where the hell's that goddamned *tunnel?*' He saw the Chief Fire Officer about to open his mouth again and he snapped at him, 'Shut up! Just shut up, will you!'

Feiffer said, 'I don't know. *I don't bloodywell know!*'

*

All, all for nothing. By his dead second son, The Fireworks Man was crying quietly. All, all for nothing.

He should have let someone, a long time ago, kill him.

All, all too late.

The Fireworks Man looked at the waxen, set, dead face and shook his head.

All, all too late.

He couldn't even remember what the boy's voice sounded like. He had never heard it.

He touched at the blood on the neck and it was still warm and he fell down over the body and wept.

*

'*Phil!*'

Auden shouted, 'Let go!' He spun around and got Spencer's hand off his collar. Auden said, 'This is it! This is the one! Look!' He stabbed a finger in the direction of the two storey office building. 'I've got it taped! We would have all been there and The Fireworks Man would have been—'

'We've got to get out of here!' Spencer ducked as a series of explosions rumbled at first deeply beneath his feet, then cascaded up through one of the far shacks and detonated in an ear-splitting crack, 'This is all just small stuff! The big stuff could be going off any second and for all we know the entire administration building could be wired and that's made of concrete!' Auden's mind was somewhere else. Spencer yelled, 'Phil!' Spencer said, 'The bloody Japanese tunnels are under here somewhere! They could be full of bloody TNT!'

'*No!*' Seven seconds. He saw another shack. Auden said, half mad with delight, 'No! This is the one! Time me. I'm going to—'

Spencer shouted, '*What?*'

Auden said, 'Time me! Time! All right? Eight seconds, is it? Just watch this!'

'Seven! Seven! It's bloody *seven!*' Spencer shouted as another storage shed went up and filled the compound with thick white smoke, 'What am I doing?' He reached out for Auden and caught only smoke, 'What the hell am I doing arguing with you?' Spencer yelled into the smoke, '*Are you out of your goddamned mind?*'

Auden kicked down the door and yelled something.

Auden yelled, 'Got them!'

They were there, inside in the half blackness, glinting at him: the guns—all set up to go, the first with a phosphorous or fragmentation grenade to blow the door down, the other six with naked muzzles, one at the back with yet another grenade set on it, and behind, in rows, satchel charges to blow the whole place to pieces when the guns' work was finished. It looked like a death sentence in steel. Auden, delighted, said with triumph, 'Got you!'

Just like Christmas, he had exactly what he wanted.

He had an urge to sit down on the dirt floor amidst his prizes and, gurgling happily, have a little game with them.

*

At the phone, Feiffer said urgently, 'We have to go in and get them, Neal. They could be down—'

The Commander said, 'No. Nobody goes near the place until we find the sniper and his tunnels or until we find—'

Feiffer looked at O'Yee. O'Yee was up on the bonnet on one of the Dennis fire engines, scanning the area with field glasses and trying to see through the smoke.

Feiffer said, 'Neal, look—please . . .'

The Commander, like stone, said firmly, 'Harry, *no!*'

*

It was all wrong. It simply didn't look in real life the way it looked on the maps: it was all different, turned around, not flat, but undulating, and the green on his maps was not green at all, but grass and the contour lines were all—

Behind the farthest ambulance, Owlin craned his head to see

the cliffs on the other side of the burning factory. You couldn't see the cliffs. The factory was in the way. On a map, it was all flat and easy to read, but in reality, in the outside world, it was confusing and wrong and—

The world was not constructed properly. It should have been made the way the maps said it was: laid-out and readable and seen with a God-like eye, one dimensional and— Owlin said in annoyance, 'No! It shouldn't look like this at all. It's all wrong!'

He had his folded up map in his hand. He looked down at it quickly and touched at the cross he had made where the tunnel entrance was and found absolutely no correlation between that— the truth—and reality.

He saw something lying by a phone box with darkness all over its throat and neck and he realised with a start that it was a dead body.

He clenched his fist and looked down hard at his map to try again.

*

'*Where the goddamned, bloody hell is that tunnel?*' At the phone box, the Commander said, 'I have to clear the area. I don't know where the hell it is other than that it's probably underneath us and I don't know what the fuck is in it, but I have to clear the area!' He saw Feiffer wince as a series of explosions from the compound sent planks and wood splinters sailing and spinning up in a cascade of sparks, 'I'm sorry, Harry, but I—' The Commander ordered the Chief Fire Officer, 'Start to move everyone out! We're going to have to evacuate everyone along Beach Road and set up a defensive fire perimeter in case—' There was a giant roar and then a blast of hot air as one of the bigger shacks along the cliff edge towards the harbour must have ignited, 'Harry, if your people haven't come out of there by the time the main storage sheds go—' There was an overwhelming blast as one of the main storage sheds went. The Commander said urgently, 'We can't go in and get them!' He called out hard to the Chief Fire Officer, '*Start to move everyone back!'*

*

In the shed, Auden said, 'Heh, heh, heh...' It was too easy. He cut through the first burning fuse and let it fall to the earth floor with a chuckle. It was all too simple: the last ball in each of the Newton's Cradles was held back by nothing but a single piece of string and that was tied off with nothing more difficult than a single spluttering fuse. The fuse burned through the string, the string let the ball fall, the ball hit the next ball and then the next and then the last hit the upside down rifle right on the trigger. Too simple. The trigger guards of each of the rifles had been taken off to give a clear fall to each of the little balls and each of the little balls...

Auden cut through the next fuse with his penknife and went, 'Hey, heh, heh...' The fuses were all nice and long. He said, shaking with pleasure, 'Ha, ha, ha...' and cut through the next.

He looked at Spencer next to him, looking worried, and yawned. Auden said, 'Ho hum, too easy...' He cut another fuse, the one with the grenade set onto its muzzle, and took time out to stretch.

Auden, bored by the childish simplicity of his task, said languidly to Spencer, 'If you'd like something to do, old son, you can cut off some of the fuses on the satchel charges.' Auden cut another fuse. Bloody executive toys.

Soon-to-be Senior Inspector Phillip Auden, the saviour of the world, said happily, 'Hey, heh, heh...' He looked at Spencer's face and snapped, 'Oh, for Christ's sake, smile a little, will you?'

An explosion rocked the shed and Auden, drinking it all in, said, 'Ha!' He saw Spencer with the first of the satchel charges designed to blow the whole shooting match to pieces when it was done and Auden, all-knowing, said, 'Oh, the fuses on those will be a bit longer, so if you—'

Spencer held up one of the satchel charges and opened the flap.

It was empty.

189

The fuse was tied into the canvas bag attached to nothing and when it burned through...

Auden said, 'That's a bit odd.'

It would have burned through and ignited... Nothing. Auden said, 'I don't know, maybe he had another method of blowing the place up.' Auden cut through another fuse. He looked over at Spencer. Spencer was looking out anxiously through the open door at the glinting windows of the administraton building opposite. Auden said, 'Um, you don't think, do you, that...?'

Auden began rocking a little, like a mourner. Auden, with the last cut fuse in his hand fizzing away into nothingness, said in a strange, sad, strangled voice, 'Oh, no, Bill, they wouldn't do it to me again, would they?' Auden said, 'Not, not *again!*'

*

The Commander said, 'Harry—!'

Feiffer said, 'No!'

'You go with everyone else!'

'I can't!' He's here! I know he is!'

'Then tell me where the hell that bloody tunnel is!'

'I don't know where it is!' Feiffer, looking around, saw the fire engines and the ambulances starting to back up. There was nothing but grass and rocks and cliffs and the smoke pall from the burning factory. Feiffer said, 'I just don't bloodywell—know!!'

*

There was a bang and the centre window in the office block was gone and falling in glittering shards through the smoke. Auden said, 'Oh, no.' He looked at Spencer. Auden said, 'He worked for his father, didn't he. The second son?' None of them was a question. Auden said, 'He did, didn't he, and he had an office up there, didn't he, and all this was just a little too easy to find, wasn't it, and because it was such a simple set-up—just fireworks fuses and—' Auden said, 'We would have got The Fireworks Man to defuse it and he would have been standing in here looking up at that window as it broke and—and I've done it again, haven't I?' He was rooted to the spot, disappointed on unwrapping all his Christmas presents. They had been shoddy, bought at a five and dime and once you had played with them they just fell to pieces and—Auden said heartbroken, 'Aw, gee—'

There was a bang and Spencer shouted, PHIL! GET OUT OF HERE! IT'S A—'

It was a grenade.

For an awful moment, Spencer thought Auden was going to hold out his hands and catch it and put it in his pocket. He was in mid air and so was the grenade. Simultaneously, as the grenade hit the earth floor and buried itself fizzing, he connected with Auden and drove him hard into the corner of the shack and, protecting him, got his hands onto the back of the man's head and, in Auden's wandering sad mind, as a punishment for being naughty, shoved his nose deep into the dirt and held it there.

*

They had stopped. All the explosions had stopped and there was only the hissing of fires burning on bits and peices of destroyed shacks and on the roofs of the other empty buildings in the compound and inside the downed fence. White billowing smoke began dissipating back and forth with the slight wind in from the sea and Feiffer heard a siren a long way off from a ship and then there was nothing...

Silence.

Feiffer looked down at the grass under his feet. It was still, unmoving. Beneath him, the rocks and stratas of the earth ran in all directions and if there was a black, dark tunnel under there—

There was nothing but silence. All the engines of the fire brigade and the ambulances were still off.

It was growing dark. Long tentacles of blackness were there in the sky, stretching out from the sun and under the ground— It was becoming night and all the recognisable features of the land

191

were going and becoming nothing but lines and contours on a map.

It seemed like hours. It was only seconds.

The tunnel. Where the hell was the tunnel?

*

He heard it click. The grenade made a clicking sound. Under him, Auden said through the dirt, 'God—fzzipple—damn!' It felt like hours. It was only seconds.

Pressing harder, Spencer said over and over, 'No ... no ... no ...'

*

Owlin said again, 'There! I'm telling you, it's there! The old oak forest was there! The old roots are rotting and giving off marsh gas!' He had Feiffer by the shoulder and he was pulling him towards the edge of the grass. Owlin said, 'It's part of a natural granite tunnel! It's there. It's on my map! *There! The entrance to the tunnel is there!*'

Over the edge of the cliff, Feiffer saw it. It was ten feet away. It had been there all the time, a minor entrance, nothing: a hole in the side of the stone worn away by erosion. He saw the Commander look in his direction and start to come across. In the last failing light, Feiffer could see the blackness of the hole. It was big enough for one man. Feiffer ordered Owlin, 'See that man in the uniform with the megaphone? Tell him!' He saw the Commander point the bullhorn in his direction and draw a breath.

It was moving. The ground was moving. All the explosions in the fireworks factory had weakened something and the ground was moving under them. At the fire engines and ambulances men looked down at the ground as it shook and heaved under them.

It was moving. The earth was changing, subsiding—

The Commander, using his bullhorn, shouted, 'Out of here!

192

Pull back! It's going! Pull everyone out of here *now!*'

Feiffer yelled to the hesitating Owlin, 'Go to him! Tell him! Get the hell out of here!' and before either Owlin or the Commander could reply or react he was scrambling down the cliff face and, swivelling himself like a rock climber, slid into the black deep entrance of the tunnel and was gone.

*

Auden said, 'Damn it, it isn't going to go off!' He tried to get his head up and Spencer shoved it down again. The earth was rumbling and groaning against his ears. Auden said, 'This is another bloody humiliation! The dead bastard hasn't even got the bloody grace to finally bump me off! After everything he did to me while he was alive he didn't even have the goddamned fucking grace after he was dead to finally bump me off!' He got his head up, 'He didn't even have the—'

There was a click from the grenade.

Spencer said, 'It's going to go—!' He felt the earth move in readiness.

Auden said, 'Goddamn it, he—' and then there was the most brilliant flash he had ever seen in his life followed by a shattering, grinding blast that he thought killed him where he lay, and suddenly, as the concussion from the half buried grenade blew the earth floor and the supports under it to dust, the ground opened up to him, and he and Spencer, tumbling over and over like two Alices disappearing into the rabbit hole, fell down and down and down a long way into blackness and were, instantly, somewhere else.

15

The ground beneath his feet was shaking. An earthquake was coming. Beneath his feet O'Yee could feel the ground heaving and moving. All the cars and ambulances and fire tenders were going: above the roar of their engines he heard a series of sudden popping sounds as the earth subsided in giant footsteps and tore through the grass covering and devoured it. There was a brilliant flash that lit up the sky and the administration building had gone, then a series of deeper, throatier blasts as the single charges hidden away in its construction against rafters and structural walls exploded one by one and set the building to burning with a fierce yellow light. Below him, a little way down the cliff face, the tunnel entrance was changing, closing in on itself like a camera aperture. O'Yee yelled, 'Is that it? Is that the one?' The entire top of the cliff moved and began to give way.

All the lights of the vehicles were going. There was no one left. Bits and pieces of burning wood and plastic were falling down in parabolas from the burning building and setting more buildings on fire. There was another gigantic blast and the ground heaved again and sent a jet of white steam and foam out into the sea at the base of the cliffs and set the water boiling and foaming.

There was no one. Everyone was going. O'Yee had his gun out but there was nothing to do with it. Under him, the ground was moving, sliding. He pulled Owlin away to get to firm earth, but everything was moving inexorably. O'Yee shouted, 'There has to be another entrance! Where's the other entrance?' and a storage shack went up in a series of rapid fire explosions and drowned him out. O'Yee shouted, 'Think! Where's the other—'

Bits and pieces of burning paper from fireworks were falling

194

onto Owlin's hair and onto his shoulders. Owlin shouted, 'I don't know! There aren't any!' He was a log-roller: the ground under him span off to one side and he overbalanced, 'I don't know what's happening! I thought you got him! I saw him at the telephone! He was dead!' In the yellow light he tried to see O'Yee's face. The ground under him rocked as something deep within it changed and moved and exploded and he grabbed for O'Yee's coat and shouted, 'I want to go back! I can't take this! I want to go back to where I'm safe!'

Nothing to do. Nowhere to go. Under him, Feiffer was— O'Yee, hopping from one foot to the other and starting off and coming back again, said in desperation, 'That dead bugger was only trying to kill his own father! This bastard is trying to kill *everyone!*' The ground rocked and erupted under pressure like a great boil and then subsided again. O'Yee shouted uselessly, 'Find something! Find somewhere! Find me some way to get in!'

'How? There isn't anywhere!' Owlin said, 'I can't think! You're not leaving me time to think—!'

'There isn't any goddamned time to think! This is war!' He tried to grab for Owlin, but the man pulled away, 'All we have to do is stop him! There's nothing to it: no brainwork, nothing. Simple, like a war—all we have to do is find him and kill him!' He saw Owlin's face in the yellow glow, this thick glasses glinting, looking like a huge, dumb, un-understanding rabbit. O'Yee yelled above the detonations, 'Fine me somewhere! You're a scholar! Find me somewhere!' He tried to remember what The Fireworks Man had said. O'Yee yelled in sudden victory, 'The old air vents! Find me the old air vents!'

Owlin said, lost, 'I don't know. I don't know where I am in relation to— They'd all be covered up by grass! They'd be all—'

Nowhere to go. Nothing to do. Everyone had gone. O'Yee, hopping from one foot to the other, yelled at the top of his voice above the noise, *'Find me the old air vents before he decides to blow all the goddamned tunnels to bits!'*

*

195

They were sliding, falling, coasting. They were sliding on moving earth. There was a giant ramp of falling earth building up and making an enormous slide into the blackness and they were sliding down to its base, going over and over. Auden managed to get his head up to see the sky and the hole above him closed in as the sides collapsed and cascaded him with pebbles. He was hurt: he felt pebbles rip and tear at his clothes and lacerate his arms and spine and then he was rolling over and over onto soft dark soil and all the pain was being cushioned. Auden shouted, 'Bill!' There was nothing but blackness. He felt Spencer next to him, still falling over and over and he reached out and caught the man by the sleeve and almost wrenched his arm off. He called out into nothingness, '*Bill!*' and then Spencer seemed to go over the edge of an abyss and Auden was falling with him, still being cushioned by the soil, still falling away into nothingness.

Spencer called out, 'I've stopped!' He had his hand around something and was hanging on. It was a rock or a pebble—in the blackness it was impossible to see. Spencer shouted, 'I've got my penlight,' and then whatever it was he had hold of gave way and he was still falling. He got his finger onto the switch of the tiny flashlight and shot the beam up and over to the left, illuminating rock and shale and blackness. Spencer called out into nothing, 'Phil, are you—' He felt Auden crash over the top of him and then stop and he landed a little to one side of him in shale and stopped falling, gasping for breath.

Auden said, 'The light! Shine the light over here!' His face was in water. The water was coming along the stone floor of a tunnel and filling up. Auden shouted between gasps, 'Water! There's water coming in!' He saw the light waver and then stab out into the darkness and he was in a tunnel with a foot of water in it and there was a shadow at the end of it and Auden shouted, 'The light! Turn out the light!' It was him: The Bannin. Auden yelled, 'For Christ's sake turn out the light!'

It wasn't The Bannin. It was shadow. Auden said, 'It's—' and then a terrific blast somewhere behind him threw him hard

196

against a wall and the water came sluicing down behind him and spun him off onto the other wall. He was sliding again, all the ground giving away beneath him, the ramp breaking up and re-forming. There was another deep rumble and then a creaking sound as something gave way and then, cracking like a giant egg, a sharp report that sent a cascade of foaming water into his eyes and nostrils and swept him deeper into the maze.

Spencer had his torch held high above his body. He was lying full length like a surfer, being propelled along by a wave. All over his body he was hurting in pinpricks as the stones and shale on the floor cut through to him and scraped him full length. Spencer yelled out, 'They're behind us! The explosions are behind us!' and there was another deeper blast and a hail of biting, cutting seawater picked him up and drove him at a wall. His torch went under: he saw its light flicker for an instant and then turn grey then it came out again, strong and white. Spencer reached out for Auden and connected with nothing, then saw the man's feet being bumped and bounced along in front of him. The water was receding like waves in a bathtub, not deep, slowing. Spencer yelled, 'Phil, it isn't deep. Get up and—' and then there was a shock that swirled the water back again past him and he was talking under water with his mouth full of salt and the smell of the sea.

Auden yelled, 'The flashlight!' He saw for an instant something illuminated in the bobbing beam and he reached out for it, let his feet go past him in the surge, and then, at their full length, jerked hard and pulled and managed to get himself upright.

The smell in the tunnels was awful: dead things and gas. He saw bubbles foaming under the water near Spencer's face and he reached down to get him as Spencer brought his head out of the water streaming and the bubbles still kept going on and on. Auden said, 'Marsh gas! The place is full of—' and then, far away, there was a heavier, deep rumbling and the water foamed briefly and then became a cascade.

The Bannin was blowing up all the lower galleries. Auden shouted, 'There!' and wrenched Spencer's flashlight hand to the wall and saw the fissures forming in the granite and streaming water. Auden shouted, 'He's blowing it all up! We're below sea level!' He saw a gigantic fault line form like a sudden tear and he grabbed Spencer's wrist and pulled, 'Run! Run!' There was nowhere to run. The hole above them was closed, fallen in, or drowned. Auden shouted, 'Run!'

'Where? Where?'

There was only one place left. For a moment Auden caught sight of a hole in the roof of the tunnel, leading up into another gallery. Auden shouted, 'There! Up there!' The gas was bubbling in the water and rising to the surface and breaking. All the methane gas was going upwards. Auden shouted, 'Up there! To the next gallery! There's nowhere else!' He saw something move in the half light and he called out, 'It's him!' He had Spencer's wrist hard in his hand. Auden shouted, 'Up! We have to get *up!*'

*

It was all going like an old mineshaft. Behind him, Feiffer could hear the roof collapsing in the tunnel and driving the dust and debris down after him. His penlight was minute: it threw only a circle of yellowness on the earth in front of him. Through its rays he could see the dust rising and falling in anticipation as the roof groaned and moved above his head. His own running footsteps activated it. He looked up and the roof above him was creaking and moving: he saw it begin to go and ran hard towards the end of the tunnel. There was no end to the tunnel: it curved and then went deeper and he was running along a dark, stinking passage towards more darkness and stench. He stopped. He heard the roof behind him come down in a crash and then, deeper down, in the lower level, there was a rumbling and then a sharp, crashing explosion as a satchel charge went off.

Through the walls he could hear the sea boiling. All the walls were being weakened and holed and the sea at full tide was rushing in to fill the vacuum.

He heard a voice and then another crack and he shouted,

'Auden! I hear you!' and then behind him there was a brilliant flash of blue light as a pocket of marsh gas ignited and all the air seemed to go in an instant from his lungs and he was gasping and burning. He smelled sea water. Somewhere below him he heard it come crashing down a tunnel like storm torrents and the smell of fresh air and salt came up to him and filled his lungs with pure air.

Feiffer yelled, 'Auden! I hear you!' The roof above him groaned and he ran on, holding the torch and his gun out in front of him like a blind man's white stick. Under his feet the rocks were slimy and wet with the moisture. For an instant, on the wall, he saw an old electrical flex that had been fixed there for some long dead power connection and as the light and the water vapour got to it it fell to pieces in front of his eyes and seemed to fall to the ground as dust.

White, pumice-like, dry dust. It seemed to be coming from the roof in clouds. He smelled the methane gas. Desiccated. Everything was bone dry and desiccated, ready for destruction.

He heard another, deeper blast a long way off and then, in series, another and another, and then, at the extreme range of his light at a junction of two tunnels he saw, for an instant, Auden and Spencer.

Feiffer called out, 'Phil!' He saw a flash of light as Auden and Spencer moved their lantern and he thought—

What goddamned lantern?

Feiffer said, 'Christ!' a moment before The Bannin's light disappeared in a gigantic white flash and the bullet roared past his ear and tore off a chunk of rock and ignited all the marsh gas behind him in a brilliant sheet of blue flame.

All his air was gone. Feiffer, tripping on something, felt water at his elbows and then the flash was there again. He heard the bullet whine off a rock and tear a chunk of rock loose from the water and then, in a suddenly released stream, water was coming in and all the air was back.

Feiffer yelled, 'Auden! Spencer!' He saw two drowned looking figures in his torch light suddenly appear at the entrance to a smaller side tunnel and he went forward and dragged at them to

199

get them moving in the right direction.

Auden yelled with relief, 'Harry!' Feiffer saw Spencer looking drowned and breathless. He still had his issue penlight in his hand. Feiffer yelled. 'Move! Move!'

The Bannin at the end of the tunnel was gone. Feiffer could hear his boots ringing on the hard rock higher up as he ran. The two penlights together lit the tunnel for a distance of more than twenty feet and illuminated a rain of thick falling white dust and what looked like broken cobwebs.

Feiffer yelled, 'The whole place is bone dry and the water's making it fall to pieces!' He saw Auden looking at him dumbly in the light. The man's face was covered in scratches and lacerations. Feiffer shouted, 'Have you still got your gun?'

Auden said, 'Yes!'

'Bill?'

Spencer said, 'Yes!' He was bleeding through his wet coat, like a wounded hard hat diver. Spencer said, 'The place is full of marsh gas!'

He heard The Bannin running. There was a terrific explosion deep down in the catacombs and then the sound of roaring, rushing water. Feiffer shouted, 'Get after him!'

Spencer shouted, 'Harry, the place is full of marsh gas!'

'To hell with the goddamned marsh gas!' He heard the running sounds, magnified and echoing in all the tunnels. In the echo it sounded like an army. Feiffer yelled, 'The place is full of goddamned Japanese!' He saw Auden stare at him. Feiffer, pushing them both to start, shouted, 'For Christ's sake, don't you understand? He's running for the bloody *magazine!*'

*

On the surface O'Yee said, 'Where? Where the hell would the centre be? You're the bloody scholar! Where would the bloody redoubt be? The core of the place?' He jerked Owlin around to face the direction of the sea, 'There! That's where Harry went in'—he jerked him the other way—'And there, there's the other

200

sea front and there's the bloody point—now where the hell would the centre be? In the bloody middle or where? *Where?*' He saw Owlin in the glow of the fires shake his head and start to say something. O'Yee demanded, 'Would it be in the deepest part of the natural rock formation or what?'

Owlin said, 'Yes! Yes! It would be!'

'It would be *what?*'

'In the deepest part of the rock formation! Where the natural tunnel was deepest and—'

'*Which is where?*' He saw Owlin looked dazed. O'Yee said, 'Come on, you're the expert! Where the hell is the deepest part?'

'I don't know! Even if I found it how could you get down to it?'

The administration block was still burning. Bits and pieces of tar paper and fabric were still falling, alight, all over the compound. There was a series of rapid bangs as one of them must have gone straight through the open roof of a damaged storage shack and set off more fireworks. Owlin said, 'There! The deepest part is there under the hump on the grass!' It was hopeless. In the light he could barely see it and whatever was under it was at least fifty or sixty feet of solid rock. Owlin said, 'There! It has to be there! What good does that do for you?' He saw O'Yee pace out the distance and then look back in the direction where Feiffer's tunnel entrance had been. Owlin demanded, 'What do you think? That there's some sort of wheel with a central hub? Even if it was, the tunnel entrances radiating to it could be anywhere!' He saw O'Yee make for the cliff side to leeward along the imaginary line from the imaginary core of the imaginary hub and he shouted out, 'This is ridiculous! This isn't research—this is ridiculous!'

O'Yee was scrambling down the cliff face, grasping and yanking at rocks to get a hold.

Owlin shouted, 'Don't do that! That isn't the way to descend a cliff face!' He got over and grabbed O'Yee's hand and pulled him back up. Owlin said, 'No, that isn't the way! If you're looking for a tunnel entrance or a cave what you have to do is work out the structure of the rock strata and the—' He saw O'Yee's face with a look of contempt on it.

Owlin said with a snarl, 'I read a book about it! All right?' A hundred feet below him he saw the sea. It seemed in the sky-glow of the factory to be boiling.

Owlin said, 'All right! I'll find your goddamned second tunnel!' He saw a flash as something else in the factory suddenly ignited and then there was a heavy rumbling under his feet and below him, at the sea, a jet of boiling steam came out from the cliff base as the fiery blast hit the water and evaporated.

Owlin said, 'There! There's your evidence! It's there! Down there!' In the glow, the sea was phosphorescent. Owlin said, 'Right there! Where the sea's on fire! If you want a way in, *that's it!*'

*

In the maze of man-made tunnels leading off from the natural shaft all the wooden roof supports and braces were falling to bits in the beams of the flashlights. Thick strong beams of oak and juniper, they were disintegrating without reason and falling with the dust from the roof as splinters and shards of material no thicker than tissue paper. Mould was forming on them: in the absence of the methane gas the beams were going furry and white, then collapsing and floating down to the ground without weight. Behind them, in the lower levels, the water was rising: it came in great surges as the tide changed, pumped it in through holes and shattered rocks and seeped it through splitting fissures and faults. The smell of decay was overpowering. Spencer stopped, tried to clear his head, and almost fell over. He felt Feiffer grab him and propel him past a beam on the point of destruction, and then, as the beam fell in a curious absence of sound, he was around a corner and the smell of methane was gone and the air was fresh again.

Auden saw someone move. At the end of the tunnel, for an instant, he saw a shadow in Feiffer's flashlight beam and then the figure was gone. There were chambers at the end of the tunnel. Auden said, 'Harry! Ahead!' He heard a scuffling sound and then a click and he flattened himself against a wall and waited for the shot. It came, lighting up the methane in a sudden intense blue light, and Auden, getting his own giant gun up two-handed, let fly in the direction of the source. He heard the bullet whang off something hard, striking sparks, and then the blue sheet was there again, racing down the tunnel, burning all the methane pockets and he saw a figure.

Spencer said, 'I see him!' He got his own short barrelled gun up and it barked hard in the confined space and brought a shower of desiccated powder down. There were no sparks. The soft lead bullet ripped into a collapsing A frame support thirty feet ahead and tore it to pieces.

The Bannin was running again, moving. Feiffer heard his boots ringing on the floor. Spencer said, 'Harry! You said *Japanese*—how many of them are there? I thought there was just—' He saw a shadow and Auden's gun went off next to him and almost deafened him. The figure moved again: a shadow, and there was a brilliant flash and a ringing detonation as he fired back and went around a corner. By the corner there seemed to be chambers or rooms, all darkened. Auden saw at an acute angle something in one of the rooms and called out, 'Another one!' and got a single shot off that sparked and popped as it ignited pockets of methane near the roof.

The figure inside the chamber was either unreal or it had been killed or it was already dead.

They heard a click.

Feiffer yelled, 'There's a charge in there!' and as Auden let fly with another round to cover them, they ran past, flicking their torches into the room as they went by. Whatever was in there didn't shoot. For an instant Auden saw him in the periphery of a beam: a single figure sitting waiting with a rifle in his hands and he gave it two more shots as he went by and saw the figure fly to pieces as if it had been hit by a bomb. Auden said, 'I got him!' He felt his head start to swim and he slowed down, let everyone else go by, and decided to walk back in the darkness and ask the figure exactly where the bullet had gone.

Auden said, 'I just want actually to ask him if I got him, because the last time I was out in the range I was shooting really high and I thought that this character wouldn't mind if I check up whether—' He felt a grip of iron grab him by the collar and pull him forward and he said, 'Look, I don't think he'd mind. I mean, I've already killed him so I think he'd...' He was raving, his head full of methane gas. Auden said angrily, 'Look here, what the hell do you think you're doing pulling me around? Don't you know who I am? I'm Senior Inspector—'

Whatever it was inside the chamber went click and then there was a sort of soft fizzing sound and Auden said drunkenly, 'What the hell are you doing pulling me around?' He was being jerked by a total of four hands. He felt his knees give way and he was being dragged by the collar. His legs gave way. He felt his backbone turn to rubber and he was being—

The explosion from the chamber turned the tunnel bright white. Auden said, 'Now they're throwing depth charges at poor old Lew on his boat and they're—' He felt something acrid burn his lungs and he yelled, 'Phosphorous! It's a phosphorous genade! We have to get out of here!' but it was too late, he was already out into the next tunnel and Auden, somersaulting over in mid gasp and getting a face full of dust from the roof, shouted in protest, 'I'm all right! I'm all right! You can let me *go!*' He heard a series of deep thundering explosions a long way down in the galleries and then the roar of the sea and he yelled, wondering for a moment where he was, 'What's happening? I can hear the sea! What the hell's happening?'

He heard footsteps running.

Auden shouted, 'I shot him! He's dead! I can hear him running! How many of them are there!'

*

'There!' In the phosphorescence and the light from the burning factory, the sea was coming out from the sides of the cliffs like giant faucet flows, draining out in foaming cascades and falling back into the surf. Owlin said, 'There! Below the top fall—you can see the hole opening up! It's a tunnel!' The entire cliff face seemed to be going critical, becoming porous, springing giant leaks. Owlin shouted, 'It's coming in below sea level and filling up the galleries and then it's flowing out with the pressure!' The cascades were turning the darkness light with a fine white vapour. Owlin scrabbled for a hold on the cliff and got his hand to O'Yee's shoulder and pummelled him to get his attention, 'There! You can see the level of the flooded galleries and we can get in above there where the walls are collapsing with the pressure before the water rises!' He was no commando or policeman or rock climber: he was a researcher. Owlin said, 'You! You can get in!' The pressure holes were opening up all over the cliff at about the level of the roots of a good sized tree, an oak or a juniper or a— It wasn't possible that after all these years there could still be— He thought for a moment he saw the blackened roots of an ancient tree flow out with the sea.

Owlin said, 'There! There's a big hole opening up! There! At tree root level! There! We can get in there!'

*

Spencer yelled, 'It's on fire! The gallery is on fire!' He looked back and the entire tunnel behind him was bathed in a bright blue glow, banging and popping as the burning phosphorous ignited pockets and corners of gas and set the beams falling and burning. A long way off down the tunnel he heard a deep bang as an entire passage must have gone up. It was burning away from them, going deeper, looking for the heavier concentrations of gas. Spencer said, 'It's all right, it's—' and then the gas half way down his tunnel went up in a solid rolling ball of flame and the fires were moving towards them. The air was gone. He ran after Auden and Feiffer and turned a corner and he could smell the sea again. In Feiffer's flashlight beam there was a figure. It seemed to be standing watching him. Feiffer yelled, 'Look out!' and then there was a flash and a gunshot merged in with the sea and the roaring fires.

The figure was gone. It seemed to be leading them somewhere. Feiffer's flashlight went out and he flicked at it and it came back on. Feiffer shouted, 'Up! We have to get up to the next level!' Below him, literally under his feet, he felt and heard the vibration as tons of sea water came in through a suddenly collapsing gallery wall. The ground shook. Dust was falling down like white rain and getting in his nose and throat. It felt dry and old and then, suddenly, as the water vapour got to it, it was at once wet, then dry again, and then it had disappeared entirely.

The figure in the chamber. All the beams turning to powder. Flags disappearing. Feiffer said suddenly, 'Christ, I think I know what the hell's in here!' He came to what looked like stone steps cut in the end of the tunnel and he pushed Spencer ahead of him and yelled, 'Up! Up!' They were fifty feet below ground: they could have been fifty thousand. He heard the sea come crashing in in another gallery and then there was a series of explosions and the blue burning flame was behind him in the tunnel and he got up the stairs and saw it pass by.

Auden said, 'Footsteps! I can hear footsteps!' He saw something in a chamber and got his gun out to kill it. There was an instantaneous flash of white light and the chamber was gone. There was no smell of burning flesh. It was all the stink of powder and mould and old, wet wood. The explosion had seemed minute, muffled. He heard a hissing sound, a cracking, a groaning, and then the water came in and he followed Spencer and Feiffer quickly up higher on the stairs and got into the upper gallery and almost passed out.

The stench was awful. Spencer said between gasps, 'God Almighty!' He felt a gag reflex start in his throat and he thought he was going to be sick. He reached out and saw Feiffer with a handkerchief up to his face. Above the handkerchief his forehead and hair was white with rock dust. Spencer said, 'What the devil is it?' He knew. It was the latrines, the old, ancient, decaying excreta still swirling methane and nitrates. Spencer said, 'Harry, what the devil is it?'

They were in Feiffer's torch beam—great collapsed sections of the tunnel showing a strange changing colour in the yellow light. Staggering, Feiffer looked up. All the roof beams were perfect, preserved, bright and strong, as intact as they had been on the day they had been cut. He saw a chamber going off to one side and in the beam he saw the boxes of rifles and ammunition all pristine and oiled and mint. Feiffer said, 'It's here! They were all kept here! This entire area is a time lock!' He faltered and felt his head swirl with the gas. 'All this methane and the dryness has preserved everything intact.' He got the beam onto the holes in the gallery where the tons of still reacting muck were giving off their foul odour. One of The Fireworks Man's bombs must have blasted through somewhere near here and set off something and sucked all the air out in the implosion effect, and everything in here—' He could go on no longer. He saw a metal door at the far end of the gallery with white dust all over it and he shouted, 'There! He's gone in there! If there's anyone still alive in here, he's in there!' He knew what he would find. He saw Spencer stagger and Auden's eyes start to dilate in a mad drunkenness again and he got his arm around Spencer's shoulders and pushed him towards the steel door. He saw Auden get his gun out and he grabbed him too. There were pumice, talc-like marks all over the door, hand marks. The dust had come from the other galleries. He got his hand onto the handle of the steel door and from the room inside heard a crash as something hard and metal struck hard: a great re-inforced door slamming. The door came open easily and they were in the war room, moving towards the last steel door to the core of the arsenal.

There was a crash as Spencer slammed the door to the smashed latrines closed behind him and the air was warm and clear with the faintest breeze coming in from somewhere, tinged with the smell of salt water.

Feiffer said, 'There!' The beams from his and Spencer's flashlights were dying fast. He knew what he would find behind that door. Feiffer, cocking his gun, pulled at it and got it open with a single jerk.

The room behind was lit by lanterns. It was enormous. It was a cathedral, a place of reverence, and in it the last survivors of the Quartermasters' Section of the 38th Division of the Japanese Imperial All-Conquering Army in Hong Kong all awaited them.

All one hundred and three of them.

All dead.

All intact.

All preserved.

They were mummies.

Their faces, above the intact, tattered uniforms and the high polished cracked leather boots, were all covered in cobwebs.

16

It was Pompeii. They were all there: Tanino, Ozawa, Morishita, all dead for a very long time, dead the instant the bomb forty years ago had torn out all the air in the tunnels and burned their lungs away like paper, dead, twisted, uniformed, all their skins turned to leather by the dryness and the methane, their hands outstretched, clawed, their uniforms in tatters, their boots cracked and gleaming dully in the lantern light. Dozens of them, scores of them—they were everywhere: in mounds, in lines, in groups huddled together for protection in that awful millisecond, the hair all gone from their heads, their bloodless lips drawn back over yellowing animal teeth, all dead, all preserved, all there. Auden said, 'God Almighty, they're—' He saw something move in the light: a figure, a shadow and he yelled, 'Bill, look out!' as something behind a shadowy structure stepped out and turned the room into daylight with a muzzle flash. The bullet went past him and smashed itself into pulp on the steel door. Auden yelled, 'Look out—he's in here!' He saw Feiffer go for the ground with his snub nose revolver up and pointing at the flash and Auden, bringing his magnum up, got off a round that detonated like a cannon shell in the room and set everything vibrating.

There was a figure. It was standing up. Spencer said, 'There!' He saw something glint in the light. It was a rifle. Next to him, Auden's great gun went off again and the figure seemed to expand like a slow motion explosion then blow apart into dust. It was one of the corpses. Spencer yelled, 'No! They're already dead! He was all of them!' and the dust was falling down behind the shadows and spreading out towards him.

He had been all of them. Tanino, Ozawa, Morishita—The

Bannin had been all of them.

Spencer yelled, 'It isn't him! He's behind the other—' and for an instant he saw something with hair on its head—its face all blackened and burned by the exploding rifle—and let fly two quick shots that drew sparks off something metal and whined up to the roof. All the beams on the roof were wood. They shook, then changed, then collapsed. Spencer saw them coming down one by one as shards of wet black cardboard. Spencer yelled, 'There's moisture getting into here from the sea! They're all decaying!' He saw Feiffer on the ground behind a corpse and then a movement and Feiffer was shooting rapid fire at something on the back wall as it went towards a tunnel entrance.

There was something fizzing. Spencer rolled over and went on top of an outstretched claw hand that bit into his backbone. He rolled back and the dead, eyeless face was next to him. It was a Corporal: he saw the uniform and the insignia of rank. Spencer yelled, 'He's near the exit tunnel!' A bullet whined past him and he rolled again for cover. There was nowhere to go. All the uniforms were khaki and in his civilian clothes he stood out like a beacon. He saw Feiffer rolling over and over getting the cylinder of his gun open to get another load in and then he had the gun forward in front of him and was shooting out the lanterns. One went and spread flame onto one of the corpses and it began to burn, twisting as the dried out skin contracted and shrivelled with the heat.

It was a Sergeant. Auden heard a shout and then there was something dark moving towards the burning figure and shooting rapid fire. The bullets were ripping off the floor in front of him and ricochetting into the corpses. They were dancing with the blasts, moving, jumping, falling to pieces. Auden got a line on a far lantern and blew it to pieces and the flame from the spirit fell down the wall and set it on fire. He saw something move. He heard a fizzing sound. Something twisting and rolling came towards him and he moved to one side as the corpse, on fire, rolled over and over, making hissing sounds like a balloon. The firing from near the exit tunnel had stopped. Spencer got to his feet and

210

it started again and he dived behind something solid and black and got his hands to it to give him support. It was a sort of long steel ledge with heavy objects on it. In the darkness, he put his hand out and found they were round.

Auden yelled, 'Where is he? I can't see him! Which one of these bastards is he?' He saw something start to get up and he poured four shots into it and it jumped and blew to pieces. Dead men: he was killing dead men. Auden yelled, 'Harry, I can't—' and then another lantern went out with a gunshot and the flames were falling down the walls and running across the floor towards more of the dead. Auden yelled, 'Harry, which one is he—?' He saw a flash as something metal moved and then a light from a spark and he turned the gun on Spencer and was about to pull the trigger.

Spencer cried, 'They're naval shells! The things on the shelves! They're four inch naval shells—hundreds of them!' He saw a blast of sparks near his hand as yet another fuse set against the shells caught and went fizzing towards the main charges, 'He's got the whole place wired up to go!' He saw a flash and then a bullet actually struck one of the shells and ricochetted off the steel into the roof and brought down a shower of dust and stone. Spencer yelled, 'Phil! *I can't find the charges!*'

There was another lantern on the far side of the wall. The fires were falling down the rock and setting the rear section of the room alight a section at a time. The Bannin was somewhere near them. Feiffer drew an aim on another lantern, missed it, and then fired twice, and smashed the object to pieces. The fire came out in a solid ball and then fell down the wall in burning stalactites. He saw a shadow and then, for an instant, The Bannin. He was naked from the waist up, wearing a thousand stitches obi—God knew whose, another of the dead men's—and Feiffer shouted, 'You! You're—' and then there was a burst of rapid fire that ripped a corpse into powder ten feet from Feiffer's face and sent bits and pieces of shredded uniform and bone into the air like shrapnel.

At the ledges, scrabbling for cover, Auden said, 'Where? Where?' He saw the sparks and got his hand in to get the fuse, but it was deep between the shells and his hand was too big. Auden yelled, 'Push it over!' He strained on the shell, but it was too heavy. Auden shouted, 'Bill, you're thinner than I am! Get your hand in and get the fuse!' Feiffer cried, 'Bannin!' He saw the man's face, blackened, lacerated, going mask-like with the dust in the room. He saw him look at the flames on the wall. Feiffer yelled, 'Bannin! You're—' He saw the man grin with victory and he brought up his revolver and pumped round after round into his shadow until the gun clicked empty. He saw The Bannin start to advance and he rolled over and tried to get more ammunition from his soaking pocket and load it into the gun.

The Bannin was hissing, grinning. Feiffer shouted, '*Phil!*' and the giant gun went off from somewhere behind the shells and The Bannin was gone, Feiffer yelled, 'You got him!' an instant before, from somewhere totally different in the semi-darkened room, The Bannin got the rifle up and poured bullets against the steel door and the walls behind the shells. Feiffer yelled, 'Get behind the corpses! He's avoiding hitting some of the corpses!' So far he had hit three. They were three that didn't count: no longer people, for some reason, no longer worth taking into account.

Feiffer said, 'Christ Almighty!'

The corpses that were no longer corpses were the ones he had avenged: the people he had already been in Cuttlefish Lane and at the launch shooting and in the park. Feiffer saw a mummified creature lying grotesquely on the ground between him and the shells wearing high boots and what looked like silver badges of rank and half ran and half crawled to it and got behind it.

It was the real Major Takashima—he had been laid reverently on the ground and someone had tried to cut his fingernails and—his fingernails were all gone, fallen out a decade ago. Feiffer saw the man's tunic open: the old leather skin drawn back over an empty chest and stomach cavity. The obi was gone. The Bannin had left it at the phone box to draw them in. He was in the wrong place totally. All the rites had been done for the Major and this was his last battle The Bannin was fighting now. There was a single blast from the rifle and the bullet struck the corpse somewhere on the shoulder and lifted it up like an empty paper

212

sack and blew it to dust. Bits and pieces of white and yellowed bone shattered in Feiffer's face and he covered his eyes and felt the dead clothes and hands and bits and pieces of uniform covering him like a shroud. He rolled away, shooting, and the pieces were still falling in slow motion and the stench as the rotted hardened skin blew apart into gas almost overwhelmed him. There was a blue flash and then a sheet of flame from the far end of the room as a pocket of trapped methane gas caught and detonated in a popping sound and through the flames he saw The Bannin with the rifle in his hand, his mouth opening and shutting in some sort of warrior's war cry.

He was enjoying it. It was his final battle. The Bannin, seeing Spencer above the shells for an instant, turned the hose of his gun onto him and fired off a complete magazine that turned the storage area into a welder's room of yellow biting sparks. The shells were too thick to be penetrated by the bullets. For an instant Spencer thought the fuse was out, but in the sparks there was a brighter, insistent flame, and he tried to get his hand in to get it and ducked as a ricochetting bullet tore past his sleeve and almost took all his fingers off. Bits and pieces of the wall behind the flames seemed to be falling into fragments. The wooden roof beams were falling. Feiffer heard the sea rushing in under his feet in the lower galleries. The place was filling with moisture and everything was rotting, coming to pieces.

Feiffer saw the fuse burning and in its glow, Spencer bent over it like a worshipper at the shrine of some sort of fire god. The Bannin was gone. He was moving around in the darkness at the far end of the room and he was gone. All the lanterns at the far end had been shattered and the fire was spreading out across the room and setting the sleeves and hands of the dead on fire. There was a terrible crematorium stench starting and a glow from burning, dead skin. Spencer yelled, 'I can't get it!' and then Feiffer saw The Bannin in the far corner trying to get a bead on the man and fired a single shot that brought down a chunk of wood from the beams and missed The Bannin by an inch. He was moving around, at home, knowing where he was, enjoying himself, his face blackened and ruined by the exploding rifle in the park and the falling dust in the arsenal. For an instant Feiffer saw his eyes, wild with exultation and the effects of the methane, and he drew a steady line on his face and pulled the trigger.

The gun clicked empty.

The Bannin moved.

Feiffer yelled, 'Bill! He coming around to you!' and then Auden's big gun went off in the room and lit up all the naval shells with the flash. Feiffer got another load into his gun—his last—and lashed off a single shot at where The Bannin had been. He heard for an instant the laughing and then the sound of boots on concrete and he fired at the sound. Down below in the next gallery, the last of the satchel charges went off in a thundering roar and he heard the sound of the sea as it crashed in to fill the gap. The air in the arsenal was becoming moist and salty. The corpses were rotting, turning to jelly, deflating. He saw a grinning hairless head on the ground in front of him suddenly break lose from its neck vertebrates and it turned and seemed to look at him. It was a nightmare. The dead were all changing, burning, rotting away into nothingness. The water in the lower gallery seemed to be rushing in a torrent, going somewhere, coming up. There was a bursting sound as the pressure built up and then it came out in sudden hydrants on the floor and washed over the burning bodies and put them all out.

Auden yelled, 'Got it! You've got it!' The fuse came out in Spencer's hand, burning only inches from his knuckles. It had about four seconds left, three, maybe less. Spencer grabbed at it and said, 'I can't hold it!' At the end of the charge there were fragmentation grenades tied together like onions, all primed, set to a central charge of what looked like a cake of TNT. The fragmentation grenades, unlike bullets, would pierce the skin of the naval shells like razors, flying red hot and spinning into the central thick core of explosive and— Spencer grabbed for the fuse again and it burned him and he jerked his hand away. Spencer yelled, 'Phil, I can't—' and Auden was there with a strange look in his eyes, reaching for the fuse. Auden said wildly, 'Seven seconds, is it? Seven goddamned bloodyseconds, is it?' and then his eyes on Spencer, put his hand completely around the burning fuse and, holding it as it burned through to the bone, jerked it loose without the faintest expression of pain on his face. Auden said in triumph, 'Got you, you bastard!' He shouted out at something, at someone, in exultation, 'No bloody brains! That's me! No bloody promotion! No bloody brains! But by Christ, I'm not short on bloody *brawn!*' The fuse was out. He had it in his hand. He dropped it and tried to pick up his gun in the same hand, but it was a useless claw and he clenched it hard and gasped with the pain.

*

They were still in a natural tunnel. Coming from the other side of the headland, they were only about a hundred and fifty yards from the central core of the arsenal. Owlin said, 'Oak trees! Look!' In the light from O'Yee's flashlight he could see old blackened roots and bits and pieces of dead, fossilized leaves and branches hanging down. Owlin said, wrenching at O'Yee's shoulder, 'Look, that's what they did! *Look!*' The stink of methane was strong in the tunnel, coming up. Owlin shouted, 'Look! Look! *Look!*'

'*Shut up!*'

'Look! *Look!* That's what they did to my family! Look! They cut them! All of them! They cut all of them— They didn't leave even one!' Tugging at O'Yee's shoulder, hearing the gunfire, Owlin shrieked, half mad with the methane, 'I'm the last of the line and they didn't even leave me just one!' The dead remnants of the trees were everywhere. Once it had been part of a great, wonderful, growing forest. Wrenching at O'Yee as the man went quickly down the tunnel wih his gun out and ready, Owlin, his eyes wide and staring behind the thick glasses, yelled hysterically, 'Look! All I've ever been— Nothing! Nothing remains of the past! Nothing! Just nothing left!'

There was a second tunnel in the room, a second way out. The water was rising, putting out all the fires on the floor and swirling the bodies around as they broke up and separated. There were papers appearing, photographs, notebooks, floating around the raft corpses. The fuses on the shells were out. The water was coming up in sudden fountains, bubbling up from invisible pipes and flowering in the lantern light and then subsiding and washing across the floor. The bodies were all floating, bumping into each other, their parts becoming detached, turning into skeletons. In the necropolis Feiffer saw The Bannin making for the tunnel across the boiling water, his rifle still in his hand. He saw him turn and pull the trigger and then, looking down at he weapon, bring up a fresh magazine from somewhere and click it in quickly and expertly. The Bannin was naked from the waist up. Feiffer saw the thousand stitches obi around his waist suddenly turning another colour, all the writing and the wishes for success and victory written in ink suddenly starting to flow and melt and run. He saw The Bannin look down at it and make a grab for it before it decayed to nothingness and Feiffer fired a single, precious shot at him and missed. He saw The Bannin look up. With even the last remnants of the obi he was still invulnerable.

He saw The Bannin reach the tunnel exit and disappear into darkness.

He came to what looked like a rockfall. It was thin, only pebbles and a rotten beam down across the tunnel and O'Yee, pushing at it, got it to one side and got through. The stench in the tunnel was awful. He felt his eyeballs drying out in the gas and the powder. Behind him Owlin was raving about something to do with trees.

O'Yee heard a single shot, then a burst of rapid fire, then Auden's big gun going off, and then there was the thick smell of the sea and salt as something heavy gave way deep down and there was a roaring thundering sound as the sea broke through completely at the base of the cliff somewhere and came pouring in.

Owlin shrieked, 'More!' There were dead roots everywhere in the roof. Owlin shrieked, 'There were trees all over here! It was on my map, but I ever knew there were so many!'

O'Yee yelled, 'Harry!' He heard footsteps, running, boots on rock or cement and he flashed the beam of light as far as it could carry through the dust and yelled at the top of his voice, 'This way! There's a way out! *It's this way!*'

*

The Bannin was in the tunnel. At the shells, Spencer was down on his knees trying to get Auden's hand underwater to stop the burning. A body floated to him and he punched it to one side and the body turned over. The Bannin was out, running. His flag was burned and he had all the dead to avenge once he got out.

No more uniforms. This time he would kill anyone he saw. Feiffer yelled, 'Christopher! We're down here! He's in one of the tunnels!' He heard The Bannin running on dry stone and got up in the swirling water and slipped down again. Feiffer yelled, 'For Christ's sake, don't let him get out of here!' He heard O'Yee shout, 'Harry!' as if he hadn't heard and Feiffer, fighting the water to get upright, snapped open his gun and saw only a single live round left there. Feiffer yelled, 'He's in one of the tunnels! He could be coming your way!' He heard the footsteps, 'He's going up! He's got another way out! He's going up into the city!' He heard O'Yee yelling louder, 'Harry! Harry!' as he fought at some obstruction somewhere to get in through solid rock and, moving fast towards the tunnel, Feiffer shrieked at the top of his voice, '*For Christ's sake, don't let him get out!*'

*

The tunnel was collapsing. O'Yee yelled, 'Help me!' and a rotted oak beam, filled with moisture from the sea, fell down around him like soaked cardboard and felled him. His gun was gone. For an instant, O'Yee saw the roof move with a vibration and then glisten with moisture and then the rocks above him were creaking and groaning as, deep below or in the place where Feiffer was, something gave way. He heard footsteps. O'Yee yelled, 'Harry, he's coming this way!' His light was pointing up at the roof. He tried to reach it but it was too far away. Owlin was pushing past him from behind. He was stuck fast. He heard footsteps, boots on dry land. 'I can hear him coming!' The light flickered for a moment and he saw Owlin over the top of him, the glasses glinting. 'Stop him! Don't let him get past us!'

'*Those bastards cut down every tree my famly ever planted!*' Owlin was in a pocket of methane. His eyes were staring, his face shaking. 'They left me nothing! They turned me into something less than every member of my family who ever came before me!' He had O'Yee's gun in his hand. It was wavering as he ran. Owlin yelled into the deep blackness of the tunnel, 'You! Tree-cutter! If you're a shadow of forty years ago, *so am I!*'

*

He was at the entrance to the tunnel with his penlight held out in front of him. There was only one cartridge left. Feiffer, ducking his head to get in, flashed the dying beam ahead of him and saw only blackness. Maybe it was the wrong tunnel. He heard the running footsteps. They seemed to be everyhere, echoes, an army of ghosts running through a nightmare, coming closer, their eyes blazing. Feiffer called into the blackness, 'Christopher! Is it the right tunnel? Are you—'

He heard O'Yee's voice come back, 'Yes! There's a way out onto the cliffs!' There was a deep rumbling and then an explosion and from behind him Spencer's voice shouted, 'It's going! The water's coming in and putting out all the fires, but it's going!' He shouted in apology, 'Phil's almost out with the pain! I can't leave him!' There was a deep movement of the earth, 'The shells are safe!' Spencer yelled, 'All the bodies are breaking up! They're—'

'Christopher!' There was a confluence of two tunnels, both with beams filling up with water and starting to fall to pieces. The decay of decades—the pumice-like stone and the methane—was

218

free and swirling around. Feiffer yelled, 'Christopher, I've lost him! He's taken one of the tunnels and—'

'He's coming! I can hear him coming!'

'*Shoot him!* Bring him down! Shoot him! Kill him if you have to, but for Christ's sake, bring him down!' He saw a flash and then a shattering blast raced at him up the left hand tunnel and Feiffer yelled, 'He's to my left! Can you locate my voice? He's to my left!' He heard a voice say 'Yes!' and he shouted back, 'Who the hell is that? Owlin, is that you?' There was a hissing sound and then another and Feiffer yelled, 'Christopher, are you with him? I can hear Owlin!'

'He's got my gun! I can't move! I'm stuck here in the—'

'Owlin!' One bullet left. Feiffer, running, yelled, 'Owlin! That bastard can see in the dark! He lives down here! Do you hear what I said? *He can see in the dark!*'

'He cut down every one of my trees! Every one! He left me nothing!' The voice changed. Owlin yelled not at somewhere, but at some*one*, 'Every one! You left me *nothing!*'

He was there: The Bannin, his chest heaving, naked, his breath coming in short hard gasps. He was hissing. He was in the dark, looking at the glinting glasses and the man facing him and he smiled and made a chuckling sound in his throat. He reached down to touch his invulnerable obi and with the other hand, seeing in the dark, brought the muzzle of the rifle up to sweep Owlin away with contempt. The Bannin said in a whisper, 'Causes. Great causes and victories. Great...' He looked at Owlin in the dark and made a chuckling sound. He saw Owlin look up at something on the roof of the tunnel, something insignificant: a tree stump, some remnant from nothing more than a tree. The Bannin, ready to die for great glories, tensed in readiness.

There was nothing to a gun. He had once read a book on the subject and all it meant when you had thoroughly researched it was that it was nothing more than the simplest flint tipped weapon and that, like a spear, you only pointed it at someone and then you simply, unimportantly, without difficulty or thought—

Owlin, another man from below ground and from a long time ago, seeing clearly in the dark, raised the muzzle.

Great glories, victories—

The Bannin raised his rifle. Something in the faintest reflected light from the falling white dust glinted in his hand. It was the stock of his rifle, varnished wood, made, a long time ago, from what had once been a living tree.

Owlin looked up at the murdered ravaged stumps all around him. The ruins of his life were there and he stood beneath them. He saw the wooden stock glint, the stock of the last tree the last member of his family had planted, the last, single great tree left in the world, ruined, put to a shoddy, cheap use, not left to grow and blossom and inspire, but simply to—

The Bannin said in a whisper, '*Victory!*'

The revolver was pointing between the hissing man's eyes.

The Bannin said—

There were no words. Owlin closed his eyes and felt them full of tears.

All, all too late, All . . .

He wondered.

He wondered. He wondered what he might have been.

Like the Bannin, he would never know.

Owlin said softly, 'No . . .'

He said sadly, shaking his head, 'No.'

In the darkness, in all his adult life never having once wanted for its own sake to see a morning coming, out of a sudden, strange, unaccountable pity, Owlin pulled the trigger.

*

Into a clear blue sky . . .

At dawn they began bringing the remains of the bodies out one by one. Beneath the sheets on the stretchers, as Feiffer and O'Yee and Auden and Spencer watched with others, the shapes changed in the air and became different, ancient and timeless, and before they reached the line of ambulances waiting for them on the grass, like memory, without reason, decayed totally and were gone.